NORTH AMERICAN POPULAR MUSIC

Glenn Appell
Diablo Valley College

David Hemphill
San Francisco State University

Matt Vander Woude
York University

NELSON EDUCATION

NELSON / EDUCATION

North American Popular Music, First Canadian Edition

by Glenn Appell, David Hemphill, and Matt Vander Woude

Associate Vice President, Editorial Director:
Evelyn Veitch

Editor-in-Chief, Higher Education:
Anne Williams

Executive Editor:
Laura Macleod

Marketing Manager:
Amanda Henry

Managing Developmental Editor:
Alwynn Pinard

Photo Researcher/Permissions Coordinator:
Beth Yarzab

Senior Content Production Manager:
Imoinda Romain

Production Service:
Macmillan Publishing Solutions

Copy Editor:
Shirley Corriveau

Proofreader:
Dianne Fowlie

Indexer:
Dave Luljak

Production Coordinator:
Ferial Suleman

Design Director:
Ken Phipps

Managing Designer:
Franca Amore

Interior Design:
Pre-PressPMG

Cover Design:
Johanna Liburd

Cover Image:
Untitled X-Ray/Nick Veasey/ Getty Images

Compositor:
Macmillan Publishing Solutions

Printer:
Webcom

Library and Archives Canada Cataloguing in Publication

Appell, Glenn
    North American popular music / Glenn Appell, David Hemphill, Matt Vander Woude.—1st Canadian ed.

Includes bibliographical references and index.

ISBN 978-0-17-644126-5

    1. Popular music—North America—History and criticism—Textbooks. I. Hemphill, David, 1949– II. Vander Woude, Matthew, 1953– III. Title.

ML3476.A646 2009
781.64'097   C2008-906611-1

ISBN-13: 978-0-17-644126-5
ISBN-10: 0-17-644126-3

DEDICATION

In memory of Art Hall, my first guitar teacher.

CONTENTS

North American Popular Music, First Canadian Edition, is for general education courses in music, humanities, or in cultural studies. The text selectively incorporates the contributions by Canadian musicians into the general story of the continent's musical history and also provides critical perspectives on the key musical practices that combined to create the various streams of rock culture since the 1950s.

North American popular music continues to reinvent itself: its cultural mix is always in flux, and changing the mix is what makes our music unique. In a continuous evolution, the digital age of global communication invites the instantaneous exploration of new sounds and styles as music from around the world continues to influence—and be influenced by—popular music. Accordingly, the text also offers an opportunity for readers to critically reflect on the process of cultural *hybridity*—the blending of diverse cultural features to create new forms of expression.

Chapter 1 discusses how music can be analyzed for cultural meaning through studying the structural components of the sonic experience. Subsequent chapters of the book are organized around four separate but not mutually exclusive narrative histories. Section 1, Popular Music and the Music Industry, reviews the beginning of music publishing, the growth of Tin Pan Alley in New York City in the early twentieth century, and the musical practices which coalesced around the pop music industry until the beginning of this century. Section 2, The Blues Continuum, surveys the transformation of West African music into the blues and the attendant rock styles which emerged from this culture during the last half of the twentieth century. Section 3, Folk Ballad Legacies, traces the ballad tradition of the British Isles to the development of country music and follows this path through to the rise of the singer-songwriter in the mid-1960s. Section 4, Art Rock, Punk, Electronica and Hip Hop, discusses the streams of popular culture whose expressive gestures and artistic orientations are more closely aligned with Romantic and Post-Romantic aesthetic perspectives than they are with traditional folk music practices.

In recent years, the study of popular culture has gained prominence, with popular music providing a particularly powerful and visible dimension of popular culture. Popular music today has become one of the world's most pervasive forms of cultural expression and can also serve as one of the clearest identifying points of any culture. It is the authors' hope that this book will enable the reader to gain a deeper understanding of the cultural significance and musical richness of this music.

FEATURES

1. Timelines

Each historical section begins with a chronological timeline that calls out significant musical events within a larger historical context.

2. Listening Exercises, Historical Studies, and Discussion Questions

Each chapter concludes with a series of listening exercises and study questions that can be used for classroom discussions or individual review. To amplify the interdisciplinary nature of popular music history, the text provides a series of brief essays, observations, and questions that tie social and political issues to the historical narrative.

3. Key Terms and Glossary

Boldfaced key terms are presented throughout the book and are defined in an extensive glossary.

SUPPLEMENTARY MATERIAL

An Instructor's Manual written by Mickey Vallee of the University of Alberta contains a thorough chapter overview, additional examples, music, exercises, and suggested assignments and videos.

The website found at www.popmusic.nelson.com contains resources for students and instructors. Visit our site regularly to see what it has to offer. The Instructor's Manual is available to download from our password-protected portion of the site.

ACKNOWLEDGMENTS

I have many people to thank for the writing of this book. It was my good fortune to have at my disposal an exceedingly talented team of professionals at Nelson, and I would therefore like to express my gratitude to the following individuals for their generous assistance: Acquisitions Editor Laura Macleod, whose enthusiasm for the project swayed me to sign the contract and write the text; Developmental Editor Heather Parker, who offered many insightful suggestions during the initial stages of the project; Managing Developmental Editor Alwynn Pinard for her sense of humour and firm guidance; and Senior Content Production Manager Imoinda Romain, Project Manager Gunjan Chandola, and Copy Editor Shirley Corriveau for their painstaking work, timely assistance, and for making the book much better than it otherwise would have been.

To my colleagues in the music department at York University, I wish to extend my heartfelt thanks, namely to Michael Coghlan, who first encouraged me to take on a project of this nature, and to Catherine Robbin, who supported my successful application for a research grant. I am also grateful for the support I received from my friend and fellow musician, Alex Sinclair, who allowed me to tap into his deep and comprehensive understanding of Canada's folk traditions. Moreover, the work I received from my research assistant, Gena Meldazy, whose spirited involvement in Canada's punk culture caused me to reshape my fossilized understanding about that music, proved to be decisive in helping me to organize the final section of the book.

Some of my long-time personal friends unwittingly contributed to the project during our lengthy telephone discussions, long walks, long commutes, plates of food, and cups of coffee. I deeply appreciate the numerous conversations I have had with John Becker, Rob Bowman, Brian Cross, John Harris, Rob Lawrence, Michael Morse, Brent Orenstein, Howard Spring, and Bill Westcott, my teacher and mentor.

Most of all, I would like to acknowledge my wife, Leslie Wood, for her lifelong love of the arts, and to thank her for being so patient and supportive during the writing of this book; and my son, Joel, whose sophisticated interests in contemporary music have taught me that good music is not a baby boomer entitlement.

Thanks go also to the reviewers whose valuable feedback helped provide direction for the development of *North American Popular Music*. They are: Jacqueline Warwick, Dalhousie University; Alan Stanbridge, University of Toronto, Scarborough; and Norma Coates, University of Western Ontario.

Matt Vander Woude is an assistant professor of music at York University where he teaches Rock and Popular Music. He studied ethnomusicology at York University (M.F.A. 1986), specializing in performance practice analyses of popular music, jazz, and folk—particularly the music of Muddy Waters—and continues to conduct research into these areas. Since the mid-1980s, Matt has taught courses on popular music, music theory, and European classical music at the University of Guelph, the University of Waterloo, McMaster University, and at the Harris Institute for the Arts. He is also a guitarist who performs with a number of Toronto-area jazz, R&B, and rock ensembles.

Glenn Appell is a professional musician and educator who has been teaching at the college level for twenty years. He is currently the director of Jazz Studies at Diablo Valley College, teaching jazz and rock history, improvisation, jazz ensembles, and Latin jazz. He formerly directed the jazz program at Contra Costa College, and he taught at Solano College and Ohlone College. Glenn received his B.S. in Music Performance and Education from the City University of New York (CUNY) in 1980 and his interdisciplinary M.A. in Multicultural Music Education from San Francisco State University in 1998, where David Hemphill was his graduate advisor. Glenn has published on jazz education and music advocacy in urban schools.

Glenn has also maintained an active freelance career for over twenty-five years performing on trumpet, flugelhorn, harmonica, and Native American flute. He has toured and recorded with a variety of artists and performing groups including the San Francisco Mime Troupe, the Johnny Nocturne Band, Pete and Sheila Escovedo, Barbara Morrison, Clairdee, O. J. Ekemode, Charles Brown, Ruth Brown, John Santos, Junior Mance, David Bromberg, and Dr. Loco's Rockin' Jalapeño Band, as well as with songwriter Alex Call. In addition, Glenn has done extensive recording for documentary and feature films. He currently leads the Tutti Forza! Trumpet Quartet and the Just Say Jazz Sextet, whose primary focus is jazz education. This professional group has performed in over 150 schools, museums, and community centers in Northern California over the last fourteen years. Glenn also currently performs with the acclaimed ten-piece brass ensemble Brazzissimo.

David Hemphill is a university professor, multicultural researcher, university administrator, and musician. He is currently Associate Dean for Graduate Studies, Research, and Development in the College of Education at San Francisco State University, where he has been on the faculty for over twenty years. He also co-directs the Joint Doctoral Program on Leadership for Educational Equity with the University of California–Berkeley and two other California State University campuses, and he teaches graduate courses on critical and postmodern pedagogies; culture, cognition, and power issues in education; and education and globalization. Prior to coming to the university, David worked for ten years as a classroom teacher and program director in immigrant education programs in Oakland and San Francisco. He is the author of two language-teaching textbook series, an award-winning study of literacy and technology, and numerous articles and monographs. His most recent book, *Life at the Margins: Language, Literacy, and Technology in Everyday Life* (Columbia Teachers College Press), examines issues of language, literacy, culture, and technology. His textbook series include English That Works (Scott, Foresman) and *The Working Culture* (Prentice-Hall). He consults widely on issues of culture, language, and diversity in education.

David is also a trombonist and arranger. Since the 1970s, he has played professionally in funk, Latin, New Orleans jazz, swing, and R & B groups in the San Francisco Bay Area. He has shared the stage with R & B artists Jackie Wilson, Little Frankie Lee, and Jesse "Mister Soul" James; jazz artists Freddie Hubbard, George Duke, Gap Mangione, Barbara Morrison, Bill Bell, Clairdee, and Brenda Boykin; and Latin artists Sapo, Pete Escovedo, Karl Perazza, Ray Obiedo, and John Santos. He currently leads the horn section for East Bay Mudd, an eleven-piece R & B revival band.

CHAPTER 1

Close Listening and Popular Music Appreciation

Over the past fifty years, North American popular music has become a dominant force throughout the world. No corner of the globe has been left untouched by the scream of an electric guitar or the crunch of a funky backbeat. Popular music is also a primary embodiment of popular culture, a field that continues to grow in importance across multiple disciplines. This book therefore uses resources and techniques from different academic fields, such as musicology, anthropology and history to examine the broad implications of popular music and culture.

As we begin the study of popular music history, we must also examine how we listen to music, and we must develop a common musical vocabulary. Over hundreds of years, Western musicians and musicologists have evolved a language to analyze and describe music. Musicians in turn have added to these concepts, generating their own unique contributions to a language of music.

CULTURE AND MUSIC

Culture is a powerful process that is integral to what makes us human. According to researcher Sonia Nieto,

> Culture can be understood as the ever-changing values, traditions, social and
> political relationships, and world view shared by a group of people bound
> together by a combination of factors that can include a common history, lan-
> guage, social class and/or religion.[1]

Culture includes tangible elements such as music, food, clothing, holidays, and forms of artistic expression, as well as more subtle factors such as attitudes, communication styles, and thinking patterns. Culture is above all a system of meanings, which humans use to make sense of their lives, and it is constructed through symbol systems that are shared and transmitted over generations. One such system is language; another is music. Popular music is an especially powerful transmitter of cultural messages.

Culture constantly evolves in a fluid process. Further, there are no "pure" cultures; all cultures are blends, or hybrids. Music is a fascinating medium for

© CORBIS

Members of the early gangsta rap group NWA in 1990 (left to right, DJ Yella, MC Ren, Eazy-E, and Dr. Dre) standing in front of an abandoned convenience store.

understanding cultural **hybridity** and change, and jazz, rock, blues, salsa, reggae, hip hop, and country are all hybrids.

Popular music also often acts as a political medium, and it can influence our ideas or behaviours about right, wrong, who is powerful, and what is desirable. Music and other mass media often shape gender roles and cultural identities; alternatively, popular music and culture also serve to question the way things are. Throughout its history, popular music has functioned sometimes as a voice for change, sometimes as the voice of the status quo.

MUSIC IN A MULTICULTURAL SOCIETY

In multicultural societies like Canada and the United States, different cultural groups have access to different levels of power. A **dominant culture**, or one that is more powerful than other groups, stands at the centre of society. Cultures that are less dominant are called **subordinate cultures** because they lack access to power and resources. The history of popular music can help us see how subordinate cultures (African Americans, poor rural groups from "down east," or Mexican Americans, for example) have used music to create cultural strength, unity, and self-expression under conditions of domination. Although North American society has seen major social changes through the early twenty-first century, the dominant centre of our culture still reflects white, upper-middle-class, heterosexual male perspectives sometimes called **Eurocentrism**.

For many years the terms *culture* and *cultured* implied the appreciation of fine arts as defined Eurocentrically. People were cultured if they attended museums, the ballet, or the symphony; they were considered "culturally deprived" if they did not. In recent years, scholars in the arts, humanities, and social sciences have developed new perspectives in order to move beyond Eurocentric conceptions of culture. They have also begun to see that **popular culture**—the mass cultural forms of everyday life—are as important as the high culture of symphonies and art museums.

Questioning the presumed superiority of Eurocentric cultural forms is not easy, but in doing so scholars and artists have reexamined the Western **canon**—the body of cultural knowledge that is said to be important for an educated or cultured person to know. This questioning has engendered many changes. New York City's Lincoln Center, for example, one of the world's leading centres of fine arts, granted its jazz program full status in 1996. Jazz at Lincoln Center, directed by trumpeter Wynton Marsalis, now has the same status as the New York Philharmonic Orchestra and the Metropolitan Opera. This was a significant step toward reshaping the boundaries of art and culture in the United States.

Many of us have multiple cultural identities, viewing ourselves as part of more than one cultural group, and we often use music to express those identities. In some aspects of our lives (at work, for example), we might be part of the culture of the dominant centre, but in other parts of our lives we might be more outside the mainstream. Such circumstances make it particularly important to avoid stereotyping (overgeneralizing), which can have extremely destructive consequences. People can be stereotyped ("All white people from the rural South like country music"), and so can music ("All hip-hop is made by gangsters who disrespect women").

The challenge is to understand and respect our cultural diversity while avoiding narrow cultural definitions that create stereotypes, and it is a fine

Promotional photograph of one of the most popular Mexicano groups in the United States, Los Tigres Del Norte.

line to walk. For example, it would be absurd on the one hand to say that *Tejano conjunto* music is not a fundamental part of Chicano music and culture on the grounds that not all Chicanos identify with it, or on the other hand to say that *conjunto* music is a stereotype. It is a vital Chicano musical form that some—not all—Chicanos prefer. Similarly, while few people question that jazz originated primarily from African American culture, not all African Americans like or listen to jazz. Each cultural group includes numerous subcultures and unique individuals with different beliefs, values, styles, and musical tastes.

The cultures in our society are distinct, yet interconnected and interactive, and their boundaries and contents are flexible and fluid. Many people also find themselves in the cultural or transitional spaces between cultures where people do not belong fully to one culture or another, or may identify with multiple cultures. New immigrants, for example, often exist between cultures. **Borderlands** often generate cultural innovation. For example, many musicians affected by living in cultural borderlands have dramatically affected the history of all popular music. The history of North American popular music provides numerous examples of artistic creativity in the face of cultural displacement and adversity, and the use of music to cope with poverty or discrimination has motivated the development of the blues, jazz, country, *corridos* (Mexican ballads that provide historical narrative), folk music, and other styles.

The borderland experience has also fostered "crossing over" from one musical category to another, which in turn has ensured the commercial success of some songs. Musical **crossover** takes place when a song or musician associated with one style takes on the characteristics of another style and achieves popularity in two or more genres. Latin jazz percussionist and band leader Pete Escovedo reflected on the challenges and contradictions of crossing over to get radio airplay:

> I had an eight or nine year layoff where I did not record, so I had to get on the radio again and in the record stores. It was a way to get on the smooth jazz stations, and you have to get on those if you want to sell records. That's why I went with the cover songs [versions of other artists' popular songs]. I had to pick and choose what I wanted to play and I didn't want to lose my fan base. But this new one I'm going to put together, I'm going straight-ahead Latin jazz.[2]

© BETTMANN/CORBIS

Cowboy band leader Bob Wills and his vocalist and guitarist, Tommy Duncan, do a little impromptu cowboy swing at Bob's home in Hollywood, August 12, 1944.

HEARING VERSUS LISTENING

The pervasiveness of music in everyday life sometimes causes us to take it for granted. Just a little over one hundred years ago, music had to be heard live, because there was no sound recording. Today, people can hear recorded music virtually any time and anywhere in the world. Some of you probably have some music on as you read this book.

What is the difference between hearing and listening to music? *Hearing* music means that we are simply aware of its presence in our environment. When we enter a restaurant or store, recorded music is so pervasive that we often notice it only subliminally. On the other hand, most of us have also felt a familiar melody "jump out" at us from the soft haze of Muzak. Further reflection may reveal that this version lacks the vocals, drums, guitar, or other vibrant ingredients of the original. For a few moments our level of involvement has changed from hearing to listening.

Listening requires a greater level of attention than hearing does. To appreciate the range of musical styles presented in this book—to expand your awareness and understanding—you will need to develop the capacity to listen carefully. One often hears comments like "I hate country music!" or "I can't stand rap!" Everyone has certain preconceptions, but when we explore unfamiliar music, we must make a special effort to listen with an open mind. Although we are accustomed nowadays to channel surfing or jumping music tracks, we need to work against the tendency to turn off the unfamiliar. Listening with an open mind can lead us to appreciate unfamiliar styles.

EXPLORING MUSICAL TASTES

No one knows the true origins of music, but it has existed since the dawn of humanity and is deeply woven into the fabric of daily life in many cultures. Why do you listen to music—to relax, to worship, to party, to relive a memory, to dance, to express your identity, or just to feel good? Several factors affect our musical tastes. Our families' preferences affect us, and even though we may not embrace the music of our parents, we often have musical memories from childhood. Our cultures also affect our musical tastes, with music often serving as a fundamental source of identity and connection. Throughout history, music has played a central role in religion, so many people develop an affinity for music through spiritual practices. Where we live influences our musical preferences as well; despite globalization, significant musical differences remain among nations, cultures, and regions. Music often plays an important role in peer group interaction and identity—the music that our friends like can impact our tastes: admitting that we listen to music that our friends do not like can be difficult. Finally, our education also plays a part in developing our musical tastes, affecting our exposure to different musical styles.

To understand more about how you listen, think about your listening habits. How often do you listen to music for "music's sake," not simply as background for some other activity? Where do you listen to music—at home, at work, in the car, at parties, in the shower, at live concerts or night-clubs, in church, or somewhere else? The difference between experiencing a live performance and listening to recorded music cannot be overstated. Advancements in sound reproduction, notably the introduction of digital technologies in the 1980s, vastly improved the fidelity of recorded music, but hearing live music is still worth the effort. Recorded music cannot yet duplicate the visceral experience of being in the same time and space with the musicians who are creating music.

DEVELOPING A POPULAR MUSIC VOCABULARY

To discuss popular music, we need a common vocabulary. Here we introduce popular music terms that will be used throughout the book.

Rhythm

Rhythm refers to the arrangement of time in music. The term is derived from the Greek word meaning "to flow." Rhythm comprises four elements: beat (the underlying pulse of the rhythm), tempo (the speed of the beat), measure (a consistent grouping of beats in time), and metre (the way beats are grouped, or number of beats per measure). The **beat** has been a key feature of the rhythm of popular music over the past 100 years. Whether we call it the groove, the feel, or the energy, it is the element that makes us feel the music and move to it.

Most musicians trained in Western classical music—and most pop musicians—use Italian words such as *ritard, rubato, crescendo*, and *forte* to describe the details of musical performance. This tradition dates back to the seventeenth century, although other European languages have also been used to describe music since Beethoven's time. The fact that so many musicians still use these terms reflects the European influence on much of our musical language.

Tempo describes the speed of the beat in a piece of music. The tempo tells musicians how quickly or slowly to play a piece of music, often dramatically affecting its mood. In popular music, songs generally use strict tempos, or tempos that remain at one speed from beginning to end. This is because popular music is often played for dancing. However, shifting tempos within a composition can be used to create changes in mood. A common use of tempo change is to slow down at the end of a song—to *ritard*, which is a word of Italian origin. Another tempo-related Italian musical term is the word *rubato*, which signals that music is to be played in a relaxed, less strict rhythm.

Metre describes how beats are grouped and emphasized, and beats are divided into units of time called **measures.** Each measure of music in a composition generally contains the same number of beats throughout. While it is possible for a composition to change metre midway through a tune (for example, to go from a **waltz** to a march), few contemporary popular styles do this. The waltz is a style written in groupings of three beats, or three beats per measure. The formal term for this is simple **triple metre**, which is also called "three/four" (3/4) time. Triple-meter waltzes were quite popular at the end of the nineteenth century.

Most popular music of the past fifty years has been written in groups of four beats. The pattern, formally known as simple **quadruple metre**, is more often called "four/four" (4/4) time. Try counting and clapping the following pattern of four beats with an emphasis on the first beat of each group:

1 2 3 4 **1** 2 3 4 **1** 2 3 4

The **backbeat** is one of the most powerful four-beat rhythms of North American popular music. Created by emphasizing beats two and four, it is prevalent in almost every style, from New Orleans jazz to rock. The backbeat is also one of numerous popular music practices with African cultural roots. Listen to the difference as you count and clap from one to four with accents on beats two and four.

1 **2** 3 **4** 1 **2** 3 **4** 1 **2** 3 **4**

Syncopation describes rhythms that place the accent off the expected beat. Before the 1950s, the backbeat itself could have served as one of the easiest examples of a basic syncopation, but as popular music evolved into R & B and rock, the use of the backbeat has become so ubiquitous that we now expect its use. The creation of a rhythmic accent that occurs off the "expected" beat thus depends on the musical traditions the listener knows. A simpler definition of syncopation would be the placement of rhythmic emphasis on the weaker part of a beat. In contemporary music, syncopation is readily found in funk and Afro-Caribbean music, where rhythms are intentionally subdivided and accented in unexpected ways.

Melody

Another central ingredient of popular music is **melody**; for many people, the melody is the key to remembering a song. Melody can be defined as a succession of musical notes or pitches that seem to have a relation to one another and that express a musical thought. A melody can also be thought of as a song or tune. Melodies range from simple children's tunes to complex musical constructions, and every style of music contains endless melodic possibilities. Simple melodies are the first musical elements that most children learn; for many listeners, melody is the element that distinguishes one song from another.

The musical strength of a good melody is key to what makes a song popular, but what makes a melody work? Although no universal answer exists, we can say that culture influences how we interpret melody, and that we respond more positively to a culturally familiar melody than to an unfamiliar one. Moreover, melody does not exist in isolation; an exciting rhythm, for example, can interact powerfully with a simple arrangement of pitches and thereby turn it into a memorable experience. Another key to constructing a good melody is the way a composer uses melodic **intervals**—the distances in pitch between two notes. One component that can make a song memorable is what songwriters call the **hook**: a catchy melody, rhythm, or lyric that we cannot forget, even when we try. Hooks are often found in the chorus of a song, although they may appear anywhere, and some songs have two or more hooks.

Lyrics

Words or vocal sounds in musical compositions are called **lyrics**. For some listeners, the lyrics are the most important part of a song. We often derive our emotional connection to a popular song from the words, and lyrics and melody often go hand in hand, becoming intertwined in our memory. Lyrics can also be more than words. Popular songs are full of grunts, moans, nonsense words, and **sacred** sounds. Songs like "Tutti Frutti" by Little Richard use nonsense words as hooks, and the use of improvised nonsense syllables in vocal jazz improvisation is called *scat* singing. In Native American music, one often hears **vocables**, words with no definitive linguistic origin that are often considered sacred.

The art of lyric writing reflects the ability to use language rhythmically and poetically. Some songwriters compose both music and lyrics, but composers and lyricists working as a team have also produced much of our popular music. For example, songwriting teams such as Richard Rodgers and Oscar Hammerstein II, or George and Ira Gershwin, wrote many of Broadway's greatest shows. Similarly, the Motown era of the 1960s owed much to the songwriting team of Lamont Dozier and Brian and Eddie Holland. Rock in the late 1960s saw a shift in popular songwriting to singer-songwriters like Bob Dylan, who wrote music and lyrics and also performed their own songs.

Rap and hip-hop have pushed the envelope of popular song styles, often dropping the use of melody altogether and emphasizing the rhythm of the spoken lyric instead. While the popularity of these spoken-word styles has only recently come to commercial music, its roots lie in the tradition of the West African *griot* or tribal storyteller. The early history of rural blues in North America also contained many examples of story-songs performed in a half-sung, half-spoken style, and other echoes of the African spoken-word tradition occur in the work of R & B legend Louis Jordan from the 1940s.

The choice of whether to use English or another language can play a decisive role in a song's acceptance. Until recently, few songs in languages other than English had found commercial success. Because English is the language of the dominant culture in the United States, the choice by Latin music artists to perform in Spanish or in English, for example, has major commercial implications. Performing in English can lead to wider recognition and sales, but it can also alienate an artist's Spanish-speaking fan base. The work of the late Chicano superstar Selena was a case in point. Her first language was English, yet she chose to perform exclusively in Spanish. Only after she attained superstardom in the Chicano community did she choose to record in English, shortly before her tragic death. The early twenty-first century saw signs of increasing acceptance of bilingual songs in pop music, as popular Latino artists such as Jennifer Lopez, Marc Anthony, Christina Aguilera, and Shakira recorded bilingual hits. The first annual Latin Grammy awards ceremony in 2000 also marked a significant step forward in the commercial viability of Spanish-language musics.

Harmony

Another important musical concept is **harmony**. This term has three meanings in music: (1) two or more musical notes produced or sounded at the same time,

(2) the underlying chord structure of a song or piece of music, or (3) the study of the overall musical structure within a composition, genre, or style. For many of us, the first definition—two notes produced simultaneously—is the most familiar. Almost everyone can appreciate the beautiful sound of two well-matched human voices singing in simple, two-part harmony. Classical musicians use the terms **monophonic** to describe the sound of a single unaccompanied melody, and **homophonic** to describe the same melody performed with simple harmonic accompaniment. A **polyphonic** composition is one that contains a more complex harmonic structure than homophony, and in which different melodies and rhythms interlock. If you have ever sung a round like "Row, Row, Row Your Boat," you have sung polyphonic harmony. This is also known as **counterpoint**.

A second definition of *harmony* is the underlying chord structure of a song. A chord is a group of three or more notes sounded simultaneously or melodically. Almost all musics based on Western European music contain elements of harmony in this sense. There are of course exceptions; for example, some folk songs are monophonic—performed by solo voices or instruments with one melody and no harmony.

Although complex harmonic forms have developed in European classical music for over five hundred years, North American popular song styles have relied on somewhat simpler harmonies. The earliest influences on harmony in North American popular music were English parlour songs, church hymns, and folk music from the early nineteenth century. The birth of jazz a century later generated a much larger range of harmonic possibilities. In fact, some contemporary jazz compositions have surpassed the harmonic complexity of European classical music. Not everyone, however, finds these more complex forms appealing; as such, simple harmonic structures still largely dominate popular music in Canada and the United States.

Tone and Texture

The **sonority** of a particular piece of music, or its overall tonal texture, greatly affects the music's impact on the listener. Sonority results largely from the tone of the various musical sounds the listener hears. **Tone** has four main components: pitch (how high or low a given note sounds, measured as vibrations per second, or frequency), timbre (the unique quality of the sound produced by a specific instrument or voice, sometimes called **tone colour**), duration (how long a tone lasts), and dynamics (changes of volume within a piece). These components combine in complex ways to produce a variety of responses in listeners. New technologies continue to stretch the range of tonal possibilities through the production of electronic sounds that stretch our ideas of what is aesthetically acceptable.

Cultural background also partly determines which tones and related timbres will appeal to the listener. For example, traditional African musical aesthetics value the alteration of the timbre of an instrument or voice, while European aesthetics generally value "purity" of sound. A profound development in North American popular music was the broadening of its early European-derived musical aesthetics to encompass African and other aesthetics.

Texture is the overall timbre created by a variety of instruments or voices producing musical sounds in a performance. Texture is a direct result of **instrumentation**—the choice of instruments used in a performance. Musicians, for example, often say that they will "thicken" the texture of a composition by adding more instruments or voices. The resulting sonority and blending of any specific instrumentation can dramatically affect the listening experience.

Improvisation

Improvisation is the spontaneous creation of musical ideas—music that is composed "on the spot." Improvisation is found globally in many styles of music. It is a central component of North American popular music, and most styles of improvisation have African roots. Improvisation can occur in solo performance or in larger musical ensembles. When in an ensemble, it often takes the form of an improvised solo or melody spontaneously composed by a single musician based on the harmony implied by the chord structure of the song being played. Improvisation does not occur in a vacuum—it has to make sense in terms of the surrounding chord structure and musical style of the song being played. A complex blend of thought and emotion, improvisation serves as an important means of individual self-expression. It is the defining element of jazz but also occurs in many other styles, from rock and soul to gospel and country.

Form

Form refers to the organizational structure of a musical composition. The forms of North American popular music are not complex, and songwriters have generally relied on a few basic song forms. These popular song forms are in fact fairly simple, compared with many European classical forms. They often employ a form called *verse/chorus,* with melodic sections that repeat throughout the song. A **verse** is usually a lyric statement that tells a story; each verse of a song presents new information to the listener while following a similar melodic structure. A **chorus** is a new lyric and melodic statement, following the verse, that is often repeated periodically throughout the song. This use of repetition often causes the chorus to become the hook of a song. The origins of the verse/chorus form are found in the verse/refrain patterns in Anglo-Celtic **folk music**.

One prominent example of the verse/chorus form is the **32-bar form**, which dominated Broadway and **Tin Pan Alley** for the first half of the twentieth century. The form consists of an eight-measure verse (A) followed by a melodically identical eight-measure verse (A) containing new lyrics. An eight-measure chorus (B) occurs next, followed by a final eight-measure verse (A) that may contain new lyrics or a restatement of an earlier verse. This can also be described as an AABA structure. Note that the B structure here serves as what is called a **bridge** or *release*—a transitional passage that connects two musical passages of greater importance.

Other song forms are found in popular North American music. Much African American–influenced music often relies less on the use of the chorus and more on repeated melodic and rhythmic themes. These repeated, open-ended structures—sometimes called a **groove**, a **riff**, or a **vamp**—are often used in R & B, funk, hip-hop, rock, and jazz to form **groove-based tunes**. The blues is another pervasive form in North American popular music. With its strong African roots, the blues appears in almost every style and context. The traditional form of the blues blends the verse/chorus song form with the groove-based approach. The standard **12-bar blues** is written in three phrases of four measures each, and the form can be repeated many times without the use of a chorus.

The Rhythm Section

Over the past seventy-five years, popular music has come to rely on what is now a standard **rhythm section**—drum set, acoustic or electric bass, guitar, and piano or keyboard—to serve as a rhythmic anchor. There are many possible variations to this instrumentation that reflect changing cultural influences. For example, the use of Latin percussion (timbales, conga drums, **bongo, guiro, claves,** and cow bell) is common in salsa and Latin jazz, and the accordion is a defining component of *Tejano and conjunto* music. Rock musicians commonly use two or more guitars and sometimes no keyboard. The development of the rhythm section had strong African American roots; although the instruments did not originate in Africa, the way they now function reflects African rhythmic aesthetics. The emergence of jazz in the early twentieth century, notably the **swing** era, played a central role in the rhythm section's development.

The Drum Set

The **trap drum set** (drum set, trap set) was a uniquely North American invention that developed into a sophisticated set of interconnected percussion instruments. It originated around the turn of the twentieth century as drummers began to play more than one drum at a time. The drums used in assembling the trap set were originally part of the traditional marching band percussion section: bass drum, tom tom, snare drum, and cymbals. The use of a foot pedal connected to a mallet for the bass drum and the invention of the high hat (cymbal) enabled one drummer to play four instruments at once. The techniques used in trap set playing came initially from European classical percussion technique, and the music generally reflected **motor rhythm**, a constant beat played at a consistent tempo. Over time, African rhythmic influences became increasingly dominant in trap drumming.

Drumming traditions in American popular music are cultural hybrids. Marching band music, initially

MICHAEL OCHS ARCHIVES/GETTY IMAGES

Considered by many to be the true "King of Swing," bandleader and drumming legend Chick Webb poses behind an early trap set in the 1930s.

a European style, developed into jazz in New Orleans in the early twentieth century by taking on African influences. The evolution of trap set playing from marching band percussion furthered the blending, as African musical aesthetics gradually reshaped the use of European instruments and practices.

The Piano

The piano has played a central role in popular music since the early nineteenth century, when upright pianos were first widely sold. Long before the development of the rhythm section, the piano provided harmonic and rhythmic support for most popular music. The instrument's rhythmic possibilities emerged in the ragtime music that first developed at the end of the nineteenth century; **ragtime** was a highly rhythmic, percussive solo piano music that fed into the evolution of jazz and popular song. In the early twentieth century, the piano was used as the principal chord-making instrument in the early rhythm section, and piano styles in most popular genres evolved throughout the century. The invention of the electric piano and the keyboard synthesizer in the 1960s and 1970s further transformed the sound of the rhythm section. Ultimately, through electronic sampling technologies, the electronic keyboard developed the capacity to replicate the sound of almost any instrument.

The Guitar

The guitar is now the primary instrumental icon of North American popular music, but this was not always the case. At the turn of the twentieth century, the instru-

A Capitol records publicity photo from 1952 showing a giant Gibson electric guitar provocatively saddled by electric guitar and sound recording innovator Les Paul and his wife, vocalist Mary Ford.

ment played only a minimal role in the rhythm section, although its prominence in folk musics was already established. With the invention of the electric guitar in the 1930s, stylistic innovations began to take off, and with the birth of rock in the 1950s, the instrument took centre stage to transform the sound of the rhythm section. Today the guitar is the dominant voice in solo improvisation in popular music, and many styles use both piano and guitar in the rhythm section. Both instruments can work as the lead or melody instrument, and they share the role of keeping time as rhythm instruments by playing coordinated riffs or chords.

The Bass

The bass anchors the rhythm section. Early jazz and traditional concert band music often used the tuba for bass parts because it was louder than the unamplified string bass. An early rudimentary string bass consisted of a piece of catgut or wire connected to a washtub and a long bendable pole. Improvements in amplification technology caused the bass to become much more important during the twentieth century. The acoustic string bass and the electric bass guitar are now the most prevalent bass instruments in North American popular music. The role of the bass varies, depending on the style of music, but it often functions to emphasize the bass note or root of each chord, using these notes in a rhythmic way to build a groove. Many listeners feel the bass as much as hear it. The acoustic bass is the preferred instrument for acoustic styles such as straight-ahead jazz or folk music, while the electric bass guitar dominates rock, country, and R & B.

CHAPTER SUMMARY

- Culture can be defined as the changing pattern of human knowledge, belief, and behaviour learned and transmitted through generations. A culture is a meaning system. There are no "pure cultures"—all cultures are blends or hybrids. Culture can also act as a political medium.

- Many scholars now question the Eurocentric view that the fine arts of Western cultures set the standards for creative expression. Respect has grown for the importance of popular culture, including forms of popular culture such as popular music.

- When we examine music from a multicultural perspective, we must avoid creating stereotypes. Within each large cultural group are numerous subcultures and individuals with different beliefs, values, styles, and musical tastes.

- The concept of cultural borderlands helps explain the development of North American popular music. As we begin to understand the way cultures interact, we can see how hybrid styles and crossovers develop from those interactions.

- We all listen to music for different reasons. There is a difference between hearing and listening, in that listening requires focused attention. By practising open-minded listening, we open ourselves to a range of new musical experiences.

- Attending a live performance is still the best way to experience music. The physical presence of musicians playing live creates an energy that cannot yet be duplicated via recorded means.

- Music functions in society to embody a broad array of human experiences. Whether one is listening while working, driving, praying, or dancing, music plays a special role in our everyday lives.

- We need a vocabulary for understanding and discussing music, and the language we now use is a hybrid, based on classical European as well as contemporary popular sources. These include rhythm, melody, lyrics, harmony, tone and texture, improvisation, and form.

- The rhythm section is an important contribution of North American popular music that serves as the instrumental backbone of much popular music throughout the world. It generally consists of a drum set, piano, guitar, and bass.

LISTENING EXERCISES

1. **Music and Cultural Meaning**

   Listen to each of the following songs, which transmit differing cultural messages.

   - Hank Williams: "Your Cheatin' Heart" (sadness and loss)
   - Cypress Hill: "Insane in the Brain" (resistance and affirmation of identity)
   - Louis Jordan: "Saturday Night Fish Fry" (humour and community)

2. **Music and Hybidity**

   Listen to each of the following songs as examples of different kinds of hybrids.

   - Jimmie Rodgers: "Waiting for a Train" (a song by the "father" of country, blending the blues and southern mountain music)
   - Bill Haley: "Rock around the Clock" (early 1950s rock, blending R & B and western swing)

3. **"Crossover" Recordings**

   Listen to the following examples of songs that were crossover hits in different genres.

   - John Coltrane: "My Favorite Things" (a hit Broadway show tune, covered by a jazz innovator to produce his only pop crossover hit)
   - Bob Wills: "New San Antonio Rose" (a western swing hit of the 1930s that crossed over to the pop mainstream after being covered by crooner Bing Crosby)

- Sugar Hill Gang: "Rapper's Delight" (the first rap hit record for a major label, which crossed over to R & B and the mainstream market in 1979 to initiate the rise of hip-hop)

4. Musical Groove

Listen to James Brown's funk tune "Mother Popcorn" (1969). The tune focuses primarily on the beat . Brown was one of the inventors of funk, a highly syncopated style of pop music, and he was sampled extensively by hip-hop artists to create new grooves. Next, listen to the driving polka rhythm of *"Muchachos Alegres"* (1946) by Narciso Martinez, the "father" of *conjunto* music, an accordion-based hybrid style that emerged in Texas and northern Mexico in the 1930s. The *polka* is a European rhythm that became central to border music at the turn of the twentieth century. Finally, listen to "It's Mighty Dark to Travel" (1947) by bluegrass founder Bill Monroe. The song was one of the first definitive recordings of bluegrass music. Compare the different types of rhythmic drive in these three tunes.

5. Compound Metre

Listen to "(You Make Me Feel Like) A Natural Woman" (1967) performed by Aretha Franklin and written by Carole King. Can you hear the underlying three-beat pulse? Try counting and clapping this three-beat pattern, emphasizing the first beat of each three-beat group:

1 2 3 **1** 2 3 **1** 2 3

How common is triple metre in popular music today?

6. Simple Metre

Listen to ragtime composer Scott Joplin's "Maple Leaf Rag," written in 1899 . This classic song, which sold over a million copies as sheet music, is an example of 4/4 time—simple quadruple metre. Next listen to "I'm Your Hoochie Coochie Man" recorded in 1954 by blues legend Muddy Waters, the founder of the electric Chicago blues. The tune, also written in 4/4 time, uses the backbeat.

7. Syncopation

Listen again to James Brown's "Mother Popcorn." The tune's funk groove is layered with syncopation created by the interplay of the rhythm section, and it is further accented by the vocals and the horn section. Next, listen again to the salsa tune *"Plástico"* (1978) by Rubén Blades and Willie Colón. Latin music introduces a variety of syncopated elements into the basic groove, notably the clave—a syncopated two-measure rhythmic pattern that functions as the unifying rhythm of much Afro-Cuban music.

8. Musical Intervals

The opening phrase of "Maria" (1957) from the cast recording of the Broadway musical *West Side Story* by Leonard Bernstein demonstrates the dramatic power of intervals in songwriting. Focus on the first three notes of the melody sung to the word *Maria*. The first interval is called a *tritone*—an interval of three whole steps. This dissonant interval creates tension that is resolved as the melody climbs one half-step more to create the familiar interval of a perfect fifth. The melodies in several songs from *West Side Story* provide some of the finest examples of melodic construction in American musical theatre. Can you name other songs that make dramatic use of melodic contour to create excitement or tension?

9. The Hook

Listen to the classic 1960s soul tune "My Girl," performed by the Temptations. Many people recognize the tune before the first measure is even completed. Almost every section of the piece contains a powerful hook: in the lyrics, in the melody, or in the instrumental phrases. Next, listen to *"La Bamba"* (1958), a bilingual 1950s rock tune by Ritchie Valens. Where is the hook? Does the use of the Spanish language alter the effect of a melodic hook?

10. Vocal Techniques

Listen to "Tutti Frutti" (1954), written and recorded by Little Richard. Note how the rhythmic nonsense syllables—"a-wop-bop-a-loo-lop a-lop-bam-boo"—work as an attention-getting break used repeatedly throughout the song. Next, listen to Ella Fitzgerald scat singing on the jazz standard "How High the Moon" (1954). Do the scat syllables make her voice sound like a horn? Jazz singers frequently imitate horn players and vice versa. Finally, listen to the Native American a cappella vocal group Ulali singing the song "Mother" (1994). This is an example of the use of Native American vocables.

11. Narrative Lyrics

Listen to *"Folk Story"* performed by a contemporary *griot* named Wolof Gewel. Next, listen to the recording of "Saturday Night Fish Fry" (1947) by early R & B legend Louis Jordan. Finally, listen to the gangsta rap hit "Insane in the Brain" (1993) by Cypress Hill. What are the similarities and differences among the three songs?

12. *Bel Canto* and Timbre Variation

Listen to two examples of the song "Amazing Grace" performed by Clairdee. The first example is performed in a traditional European style; the second, in a jazzy gospel style. Which style do you prefer? The second example contains pitch and timbre alterations with slides between notes and guttural growls that have strong African roots. Some European aesthetic elements are also heard in the second example—much of the singing is performed with a clear, pure tone.

HISTORICAL STUDIES AND DISCUSSION QUESTIONS

1. **Eurocentrism and Musical Descriptions**

   Most musicians trained in Western classical music—and most pop musicians—use Italian words such as *ritard, rubato, crescendo,* and *forte* to describe the details of musical performance. This tradition dates back to the seventeenth century, although other European languages have also been used to describe music since Beethoven's time. The fact that so many musicians still use these terms reflects the European influence on much of our musical language. Does the use of these concepts influence how we think about music and how we interpret non-Western musics?

2. **Whose Aesthetics?**

   Cultural influences strongly affect our sense of musical aesthetics, and the concept of what is appealing changes from one culture to another. For example, traditional African musical aesthetics value the alteration of the timbre of an instrument or voice, while European Art Music aesthetics value "clarity" of sound. A profound development in North American popular music was the broadening of its early European-derived musical aesthetics to encompass African and other aesthetics. What does hybridity tell us about North American cultural identity, vis-à-vis, Africa and Europe?

STUDY QUESTIONS

1. What is culture?
2. Are there any "pure" cultures? What is hybridity?
3. What is cultural domination? Give some examples from North American popular music.
4. Why is it hard to describe particular cultures? What is the danger of stereotypes?
5. Why do we call the idea of "fine arts" a Eurocentric concept? Why are many scholars broadening this perspective to include popular culture?
6. What are cultural borderlands, and what does "crossing over" mean?
7. When, why, where, and how often do you listen to music?
8. How does cultural background influence listening experiences and musical preferences?

9. How have your experiences with live performances differed from your listening to recordings?

10. Why is rhythm an essential ingredient of popular music? What effect does the use of a backbeat produce in a song?

11. What are the musical components of melody?

12. How does a musical hook work? Name at least five songs with strong hooks.

13. What is the range of approaches to lyrics found in North American popular music?

14. How do European and African aesthetics of tone production differ?

15. What is improvisation, and what is its function in North American popular music?

16. How are the following song forms defined: 32-bar song, 12-bar blues, groove-based tune?

NOTES

1. Sonia Nieto, *Affirming Diversity: The Sociopolitical Context of Multicultural Education* (New York: Longman, 1992), 111.

2. Interview with the authors.

1605 Port Royal, Quebec, first permanent European settlement in North America
1607 First British community in America, Jamestown, settled
1640 *Bay Psalm Book* published, the first American collection of religious music ♪
1682 Philadelphia, largest colonial city, founded

1710 British Statutory Copyright Law governs publishing in British controlled colonies ♪
1716 Piano building begins in Quebec City ♪
1728 *The Beggar's Opera*, an early ballad opera, performed for the first time ♪
1745 "Yankee Doodle," a broadside ballad that became a revolutionary and popular song, is written ♪
1754–1763 French and Indian War
1776 Declaration of Independence and beginning of Revolutionary War
1778 William Billings writes "Chester," originally a hymn, which also becomes a revolutionary song in the American War of Independence ♪
1790 First American National Copyright Act passes, establishing early protection of intellectual property ♪

1800 Canadian music publishing begins ♪
1803 Louisiana Purchase annexes vast western lands from France
1808 *Moore's Irish Melodies*, an influential collection of parlour songs, is published ♪
1812 U.S. at war with Britain and Canada
1820s Birth of the American piano industries ♪
1825 First steam locomotive
1831 U.S. Copyright Act amended to include printed music: lyrics and melody only ♪
1837 Henry Russell writes "Woodman Spare That Tree," a classic parlour song ♪
1848 End of Mexican War; Southwest annexed by U.S.
1848 Stephen Foster writes "Oh! Susanna" ♪

1850s Proliferation of sheet music due to improvements in printing technology ♪
1857 Leon Scott invents Phonoautograph, the first mechanically reproduced sound ♪
1861–1865 Civil War
1863 Emancipation Proclamation
1865–1877 Reconstruction
1867 Canadian Confederation
1870s The Fisk Jubilee Singers introduce the U.S. and Europe to spirituals ♪
1877 Thomas Edison invents the first sound recording device ♪
1881 Tony Pastor, an early vaudeville entrepreneur, opens his most famous New York vaudeville theatre ♪
1881 First musical performance transmitted by telegraph wire ♪
1889 Aeolian Company builds the first player piano ♪
1893 Panic of 1893, a major economic recession
1897 The first player pianos become commercially available, broadening access to music reproduction ♪
1898 John Philip Sousa writes "Stars and Stripes Forever" ♪
1890s New York City becomes the centre of the music publishing industry, soon known as Tin Pan Alley ♪
1890s Imbedded popular songs in theatrical productions herald the beginning of cross-promotional advertising ♪
1892 Charles K. Harris publishes one of the first Tin Pan Alley hits, "After the Ball" ♪
1898 Spanish American War
1899 Scott Joplin's ragtime hit, "The Maple Leaf Rag," sells over a million copies ♪

1902 First Canadian recording by the Bellville Kilties Band ♪
1906 Canadian engineer Reginald Fessenden conducts first voice transmission from Boston to Scotland
1909 U.S. Copyright Law amended to include live and recorded performances of music ♪
1909 Emile Berliner opens Canada's first recording facility in Montreal ♪
1914–1918 World War I
1914 ASCAP formed to insure royalty payments to musicians and publishers
1920 U.S. Nineteenth Amendment gives women right to vote
1920 XWA (later CFCF), Montreal, gives first scheduled radio broadcast in North America ♪
1921 Canadian copyright legislation replaces British copyright law; includes protections for live and recorded music: lyrics and melody only ♪
1924 First use of electric microphone in recordings ♪
1924 Transcontinental railway radio CNRO (later CBC) begins broadcasting music ♪

1600	1700	1800	1850	1900

Popular Music and the Music Industry

1925 Berliner's Compo Company Ltd. issues first electrically recorded discs ♪

1925 CPRS (Canadian Performing Rights Society) is formed ♪

1925 CKAC becomes the first French Canadian radio station ♪

1927 *The Jazz Singer*, the first sound film, is released ♪

1927 First coast-to-coast radio broadcast in Canada ♪

1929 German engineer Fritz Pfleumer invents the Blattnerphone (or tape recorder) ♪

1929–1930s Great Depression; New Deal begins

1930s Thomas Dorsey pioneers new gospel music forms ♪

1941–1945 U.S. participates in World War II

1943 Richard Rodgers' *Oklahoma!* opens with first full integration of plot, music, and choreography ♪

1947 Gospel legend Mahalia Jackson records her biggest hit, "Move on Up a Little Higher" ♪

1948 Introduction of the 33 1⁄3 rpm LP recording ♪

1950–1953 Korean War

1954 The Crew Cuts (a.k.a. the Canadairs) cover The Chords'"Sh'Boom" (1954); Crew Cuts version sometimes cited (erroneously) as the first rock and roll recording ♪

1954 Brown vs. Board of Education, Topeka, Kansas: school segregation outlawed; Civil Rights movement begins

1954 Ampeg issues first U.S.-built tape recorders ♪

1960–1965 The Brill Building becomes the Tin Pan Alley of rock ♪

1962 Supreme Court bans school prayer; first black student enters University of Mississippi

1963 Civil rights march on Washington; John Kennedy assassinated

1963 Dutch electronics firm, Philips, issues the first cassette tape recorder ♪

1964 U.S. Congress passes Civil Rights bill

1964–1973 Vietnam War

1964 *Fiddler on the Roof*, the last of the fully developed musicals, opens ♪

1965 Eight-track tape recorder is introduced to Canada ♪

1965 Watts riots

1965 James Brown lays groundwork for funk with the groove-based "Papa's Got a Brand New Bag" ♪

1966 Motown is in its prime with hits by the Temptations and the Supremes ♪

1967 Urban riots in Detroit; "Summer of Love" in San Francisco

1968 Martin Luther King and Robert Kennedy assassinated

1969 "These Eyes," by The Guess Who, is the first Canadian release to reach Billboard Top 10 ♪

1970–1973 Philly soul smoothes out the sound of R & B, leads to disco ♪

1970–1971 Canadian content regulations are implemented ♪

1971 Blaxploitation films such as *Shaft* and *Superfly* become a venue for new R & B styles ♪

1974 Disco appears and begins a five-year run at the top of pop ♪

1974 Growth of Montreal's presence in international Disco scene ♪

1981 Creation of FACTOR (Foundation to Assist Canadian Talent on Record) ♪

1982 Introduction of digitally recorded compact discs ♪

1982 Michael Jackson's *Thriller* breaks the MTV colour barrier ♪

1984 MuchMusic begins broadcasting music videos in Toronto ♪

1986 French music video network, MusiquePlus, goes on air in Quebec ♪

1990s MP3 formats; file sharing introduced ♪

1990s High-tech "bubble" bursts

1990 French language content on Francophone radio in Quebec raised to 65 percent ♪

2002 Aboriginal Voices (FM 106.5), Canada's first First Nations radio station ♪

2003 "American Idol" TV show creates a new marketing format ♪

2008 Barack Obama elected first African-American U.S. President

1925	1930	1950	1960	1970	1980	1990	2000

CHAPTER 2

Musical Theatre, Parlour Songs, and Brass Bands

The first popular musical styles in North America—other than Native North American music—were of European origin. Influences of England, Ireland, Scotland, Italy, and other European cultures were gradually hybridized over three centuries with African, Latino, and other sources to form new musical traditions. This chapter discusses popular music of the seventeenth, eighteenth, and nineteenth centuries, which ranged from church music to patriotic tunes to parlour songs to brass bands.

Religious music was probably the earliest form of music that European settlers played in the New World. For example, colonists brought the Thanksgiving song "We Gather Together" from the Netherlands to New Amsterdam—now New York. By the mid-1600s, ministers in Massachusetts had published a collection of religious songs called the *Bay Psalm Book*. According to historian Wilfrid Mellers, "For worship in church the psalms were sung at rather fast tempi and in unison—so that God would have no difficulty in understanding the words."[1] People also sang psalms for entertainment at home, often in multipart harmony, following British musical practices. During the American Revolution, relatively little new popular music was written, because the Continental Congress banned theatrical activities. After the American War of Independence, however, development began in earnest as active music publishers sprang up in all major American cities. With the passage of the first National Copyright Act in 1790, hundreds of new songs were published.

When music publishing began in Canada in 1800, so too did the difficulties that would follow the industry into the twenty-first century. Foremost was the dependence of Canadian publishers for new music on their larger, well-capitalized British and American counterparts. The small population of the country's largest cities, along with high costs of printing, ensured that music publishing would remain a tertiary activity behind the more profitable pursuits of distributing foreign music and for selling musical instruments, particularly pianos. Although publishers boasted a catalogue of six hundred titles by home-grown and foreign composers in 1867, following the first Canadian copyright notice for "Canadian National Air" (1859), their efforts to build the Canadian market were continually stymied by the effects of technological change and by the realities of small market economics.

ENGLISH, IRISH, SCOTTISH, AND ITALIAN INFLUENCES

British composers wrote many of the most popular songs in North America in the late eighteenth century. They often intended for these songs to be used in London's pleasure gardens or in ballad and comic operas. **Pleasure gardens** were private parks featuring arbours, fruit trees, mineral springs, tea gardens, fireworks, and music. As gardens based on the British model arose in North America, composers often wrote love songs filled with rustic images. These later became the basis for parlour songs, a style that lasted for almost a century in England and abroad.

Other influential British styles included **broadside ballads** and ballad operas. Broadside ballads were witty, often ribald, topical verses that used everyday vocabulary. Usually sung to popular folk melodies, they were printed quickly and sold cheaply—"Yankee Doodle" is one famous example. A *ballad* is a song that usually tells a story, and **ballad opera** was a form of musical theatre that used spoken English dialogue and songs, in contrast to Italian opera. An early example of the new style, *The Beggar's Opera* (1728), featured a stage packed with criminals and street life rather than the kings and princes of grand opera. Ballad operas, such as *Rosina* by William Sheild, and *No Song, No Supper* by Stephen Storace (both British composers), were performed in Halifax in 1791. Often written to lampoon society, ballad operas were one precursor of the musical comedies of Gilbert and Sullivan which dominated North American musical theatre during the late nineteenth century.

The first theatre spectacle in the New World was produced in 1606 as a welcome celebration for Baron de Poutrincourt, Lieutenant Governor of Port Royal, Canada. The *Theatre de Neptune* was written by Marc Lescarbot and presented by a cast of settlers and local Aboriginal performers. The presentation, known as an *entrée royale* or *reception*, generally involved mimed scenes, some verse, and music. By 1810, it is estimated that approximately one hundred opera performances had taken place in Halifax, Quebec City, and Montreal.

The 1820s saw a growing interest in Italian **opera**. Although viewed as art music today, the genre originally appealed to a wide audience. When opera initially emerged in Italy in the sixteenth century, it opened new possibilities for dramatizing words set to music through introduction of characters and plot. An Italian style of singing called ***bel canto*** ("beautiful singing") accompanied opera; this style emphasized a clear understanding of vocal technique to produce a beautiful sound that was equally effective in the parlour or on the grand operatic stage. In 1825 Rossini's *Il Barbiere di Siviglia (The Barber of Seville)* was the first Italian opera produced in New York. Although greeted initially with enthusiasm, the genre was not well accepted until the introduction of English translations. Once an English version of Rossini's *La Cenerentola (Cinderella)* was performed in New York in 1832, it made its way to other North American cities (such as Montreal in 1841) where it stimulated demand for sheet music adaptations of this and other popular operas, including Mozart's *Magic Flute* and *Don Giovanni* and Verdi's *Rigoletto* and *Il Trovatore*. Spurred on by the growing popularity of opera, the late-nineteenth century witnessed the construction of dozens of 600–800 seat venues in communities throughout North America. Canada's first opera house, which was built in Quebec City in 1764, was followed in 1860 by the construction of two "Crystal Palaces": St. Patrick's Hall in Montreal, and Shaftsbury in Toronto. The growth in popularity of opera and sheet music coincided with the emergence of the North American piano industry. The first Canadian-made piano was built in 1816. Shortly thereafter, seventeen piano manufacturers existed in Quebec City, Montreal and Toronto, and numerous retail branches dotted the cities of Winnipeg, Saskatoon, Calgary and Vancouver. However, with the rise of recorded music and radio during the 1920s, the fortunes of Canada's piano industry of five thousand workers went into an irreversible decline, and eventually dragged down with it the under-sized market for sheet music.

OPERETTA

During the 1870s and 1880s, a European style of musical theatre called **operetta**, which blended plot, music, lyrics, dance, and an integrated story line, gained popularity in Canada and the United States. Based on European art music, the style was an important precursor to North American musical comedy. The first operettas, called *operas bouffes* (comic operas), were written in the 1850s by German composer Jacques Offenbach. British composers William Gilbert and Arthur Sullivan followed over the next two decades with a light and humorous style of operetta that became popular on both sides of the Atlantic and that works such as *H.M.S. Pinafore, The Pirates of Penzance*, and *The Mikado* exemplified. The first successful American composer of operetta was Irish immigrant Victor Herbert (1859–1924). He composed over forty operettas, blending the wit and syncopation of American popular song with European operetta to produce such works as *Babes in Toyland*. American and European operettas remained popular until the start of World War I, when a wave of patriotic fervour caused a backlash against works seen as "foreign."

MINSTRELSY

Minstrelsy emerged around 1830 and reached its height between 1850 and 1870 with variety show performances based on crude stereotypes of African Americans. For close to four decades, it was the most popular form of theatrical entertainment. In minstrelsy, white actors performed in **blackface**, a makeup style in which the face was darkened with burnt cork and exaggerated facial features such as large lips and big eyes were drawn. Black artists also performed in minstrelsy, and in the early twentieth century, black minstrel shows served to disseminate early blues. Minstrelsy was also one of the first examples of the appropriation and adaptation of African American music by whites, setting a pattern that would continue in North America for 170 years.

As early as 1769, what were then called "Negro songs" were being presented in blackface in New York theatrical productions, sometimes between the acts of plays or operas. The "father" of American minstrelsy was Thomas "Daddy" Rice, an actor from New York. Rice created a character called **Jim Crow**, a disabled black stable hand who moved with a shuffle. Although the songs sung by Rice belonged to folk traditions of Southern slaves, according to historian Eileen Southern, Rice changed the words in order to "disparage the black man and his life style."[2] During the same period, another minstrel character, Zip Coon, became popularized in a song whose melody resembled that of "Turkey in the Straw." **Zip Coon** was an African American "city slicker" who made imperfect attempts to imitate white city folk. These two contrasting characters—Jim Crow the country bumpkin and Zip Coon the city slicker—established the character foundations for the minstrel show, as well as stereotypes that lasted for over a century. Well into the 1950s, laws that enforced segregation in the South were still called "Jim Crow" laws, and the word *coon* persisted as a racist term.

Minstrel performances developed into full-length variety shows during the 1830s. The two most famous minstrel troupes, the Virginia Minstrels and the Christy Minstrels, began in the 1840s. The latter group performed on Broadway for ten years, formalizing the minstrel show genre. Cast members stood or sat in a semicircle around an "interlocutor" who dressed in formal attire and acted as MC. He bantered with two end men, "Mr. Bones," who rattled bones, and "Mr. Tambo," who played the tambourine. Shows opened with a chorus and grand processional, followed by jokes, dialogue, songs, sketches, and instrumental numbers. Because the performers spoke and sang in poor imitations of black English dialect, they were called **Ethiopian delineators.** Instrumentation consisted of many of the same instruments associated with plantation life: banjos, fiddles, tambourines, and bone castanets. Later minstrel shows incorporated wind band instrumentation as well as guitars and **mandolins**.

Debate about the origins of minstrel songs persists. Composers often claimed that their music was based on slave songs heard on plantations, and some did visit the South. However, by the time the music reached the stage, original elements had been changed, and clear influences of English, Irish, and Scottish folk songs could often be heard. For many white Americans at the time, minstrel music was linked to a sense of patriotism, and its popularity reflected an attempt to fashion a new American musical identity that rejected the sentimentality of British parlour songs. As historian Ken Emerson has observed, "A shared feeling of superiority to blacks was one of the few things that unified a nation of immigrants, many of them more recent arrivals than the African Americans they mocked."[3] Minstrel music may also have served as a vehicle to express nostalgia for an imagined "simpler" rural life amid early industrialization or to discuss "forbidden" topics like race, class, sex, money, and violence. America's greatest popular songwriter of the nineteenth century, Stephen Foster, wrote extensively for minstrelsy, including the popular tunes "Old Folks at Home," "Oh! Susanna," and "Camptown Races." Minstrelsy pervaded American popular music well into the twentieth century: *The Jazz Singer* (1927), the first motion picture with sound, featured popular entertainer Al Jolson performing in blackface.

PARLOUR SONG AND PATRIOTIC SONGS

Spurred by economic hardship and British political repression, Irish immigrants came to North America in large numbers beginning in the first decades of the seventeenth century. As historian Charles Hamm notes, "The Irish came early and often to America."[4] By the early nineteenth century, hundreds of thousands of Irish had settled in all parts of the North America, bringing with them a rich oral musical tradition and an appetite for newly minted songs by Thomas Arne, James Hewitt, and the Irish-born Thomas Moore. Following his visit to North America in 1803–04, Moore wrote "A Canadian Boat Song" (1805), the first popular song to reference Canada by name. Soon thereafter, the composer, whose songwriting style reveals a blend folk balladry and art song, published *Moore's Irish Melodies* in 1808, a collection of songs that sold an estimated 1,500,000 copies during the nineteenth century. Included in the folio are well-known pieces such as "'Tis the Last Rose of Summer" and "Oh, Believe Me, If All Those Endearing Young Charms." The vernacular nature of Irish music lent it directness and passion, and many of the songs were written in the first person, directly describing rich emotions from a personal point of view. Although Moore's collection predates the Tin Pan Alley era by approximately ninety years, his compositional techniques (shown below) became the template for writing popular songs for the next two hundred years.

Music
- One Octave Melodic Range
- 2-4 Bar Phrases
- Basic Harmony (I-IV-V)
- Simple Accompaniment
- Repetitive Forms
    8-Bar
    AABA (Da Capo Aria)
    ABAB (Verse/Chorus)
- Dance Music
    Current Metric/Rhythmic
    Patterns

Lyrics
- Romance Themes
- Alliteration
- Repetitive Rhyme Schemes
    Quatrain
    Couplet
- Symmetric Rhythms
- Personal Pronouns
- 1-2-3 Syllable Words

Scottish folk music also influenced North American popular music. Famed Scottish poet Robert Burns collaborated on the production of the *Scots Musical Museum*, a 1787 anthology of Scottish songs similar to *Moore's Irish Melodies*. The anthology included well-known works such as "Auld Lang Syne" and "Comin' Thro' the Rye," which later became popular as a gospel song. "The Blue Bell of Scotland," the most popular Scottish song of all time, was published in 1800.

Sentimental ballads called **parlour songs**, which spoke of life, home, hearth, and family, prevailed in nineteenth-century American popular music. "Home, Sweet Home" (1823), one of the most popular songs of the time,

This sheet music cover for a parlour song by Charles Henry emphasizes a nostalgic view of home and family typical of this mid-nineteenth-century genre.

exemplified the style with its familiar lyrics: "Be it ever so humble, there's no place like home." The sentimental appeal of the style was summarized by historian Denes Agay:

> These audiences it seems loved pathos, and craved tear-drenched sentimentality. They were deeply moved by "Lilly Dale," "Rosalie," "The Prairie Flower" and the entire sorority of young maidens who shared a curiously similar fate; they died young, and were resting in a flowery vale, in a "Fadeless Bow'r" under the mournful branches of the weeping willow or amidst other heart breaking or picturesque scenery.[5]

The demand for parlour songs grew apace with the piano industry, as the piano increasingly became an essential component of middle-class homes in the nineteenth century. Because recording technology was still only a fantasy and live performance was the only music available, parlour song sheet music fit the bill for performance on piano in the home.

One of the most dramatic events in U.S. history, the Civil War (1861–1865) aroused depths of feeling among Americans that remained long after its conclusion. The war also left a rich musical heritage, and as late as 1909 the bulk of an anthology of American patriotic songs called *Heartsongs* still centred on Civil War songs. "John Brown's Body," "When Johnny Comes Marching Home," and "Battle Hymn of the Republic" came from the North; "Dixie" and "Bonnie Blue Flag" from the South. Music played a key role in the war itself; as one Virginia soldier wrote, "We are on one side of the Rappahannock, the enemy on the other. Our boys will sing a Southern song, the Yankees will reply by singing the same tune to Yankee words." On another night before the Battle of Murfreesboro, a Northern band played "Yankee Doodle," a Southern band responded with a Southern tune, and then both bands played "Home, Sweet Home" together. The next day thousands were slaughtered in battle.

The famous Southern patriotic song "Dixie" was originally written for New York minstrel shows by Dan D. Emmett in 1859, but it soon became a Southern anthem. Another Southern song that stood the test of time was "Aura Lee." Written in 1861, it remained popular for over a century in several versions: first in its original form, then adapted as "Army Blue" (a traditional West Point song), and popularized again in 1956 with new words as "Love Me Tender" by Elvis Presley.

Patriotic songs were perhaps less abundant in Canada but certainly not less important. James P. Clarke (1807–1877), who emigrated from Scotland to Toronto in 1835, was an accomplished organist and choral director and wrote numerous patriotic songs, including "The Wild Stream Leaps," "The Maple Leaf," and "Songs of Canada." Clarke was also the first music director at the University of Toronto, and the first to earn its Bachelor of Music degree. The most widely known patriotic song in nineteenth century Canada was "The Maple Leaf For Ever" (1867). Penned by Alexandre Muir (1830–1906), a school principal, songwriter, and poet who lived in Newmarket, Ontario, "The Maple Leaf For Ever" was one of several songs written by the amateur musician to commemorate Canada's Confederation in 1867. Another famous patriotic song, "O Canada", first approved by Parliament of Canada in 1967 and later installed as the national anthem in 1980, was composed by Adolphe-Basile Routhier (lyrics) and Calixa Lavallee (music) in Quebec City in May 1880. Initially sung only in Quebec, "O Canada" eventually spread across Canada in a variety of English and French versions.

The legacy of patriotic songwriting continued through the twentieth century and into the present in one of the nation's greatest exemplars, Saint John, New Brunswick-born Stompin' Tom Connors (1936–). Inspired by his mother's singing of Wilf Carter (see Chapter 14) songs to him at an early age, Connors almost singlehandedly created from his own hard-lived experiences the largest and most identifiable collection of patriotic ballads about Canadian lives, places, and activities:

> Out of the two-hundred and fifty songs I've recorded, about one-hundred and fifty of them are about Canada. That's what songwriting is about for me: You write songs about what's going on in your country. I want to hear truck drivin' songs, songs about fishermen, about factory workers, about mine disasters, about cowboys, about places in Canada that people can identify with, and about the Canadian way of life."[6]

Some of Connors' better known songs include "Bud the Spud," "The Black Donnellys," "Sudbury Saturday Night," and the most frequently heard song in National Hockey League arenas, "The Hockey Song." Fiercely nationalistic, Connors strongly opposes the system which allows Canadian artists who live and conduct business in the United States to be nominated for Juno Awards in Canada; in 1978, he returned his six Junos in protest of the practice.

Stompin' Tom Connors energizing the crowd with his patriotic songs and stomping board at a Toronto Maple leafs hockey game in 2005.

CP/FRANK GUNN

Stephen Foster, the most popular U.S. songwriter of the nineteenth century, was also the first American composer to make a living as a composer of popular song.

PARLOUR SONG COMPOSERS

Henry Russell (1812–1900) was the first major North American composer of parlour songs, as well as the country's foremost popular songwriter prior to Stephen Foster. Historian Charles Hamm describes Russell as "an English-born Jew who studied music in Italy, moved to Canada and then the United States, and composed music in an Italian style with nostalgic, Irish-influenced lyrics."[7] Russell's best-known songs were "Woodman Spare That Tree" (1837) and "The Old Arm Chair" (1840). The simple and accessible melodies accompanied lyrics that covered common parlour song themes: home, parents, lost innocence, old friends, and nostalgia for youth.

In songs such as "Oh! Susanna," "Old Folks at Home" ("Way Down upon the Swanee River"), and "Camptown Races," composer Stephen Foster (1826–1864) developed a uniquely American style of songwriting that established a new tradition in popular song. The most important American popular song-writer of the nineteenth century, he composed over 200 songs in his lifetime, and his work retained sufficient appeal into the twenty-first century to win a 2005 Grammy for a traditional folk album. Minstrelsy, *bel canto*, Irish folk songs, and the musics of other immigrant communities all influenced Foster's songwriting style. Many of the composer's best songs included memorable hooks, and his position as America's greatest songwriter remained unchallenged until the birth of Tin Pan Alley in the late nineteenth century.

Foster's earliest successes came with rhythmic minstrel songs. He wrote twenty such tunes, most with lyrics that are offensive by contemporary standards. As his career progressed, Foster became concerned at the crude, racist nature of the songs. He had his name deleted from some and revised others to portray African Americans in a more sympathetic and humanistic light, which he then called **plantation songs.** He also eventually dropped the use of **Ethiopian dialect**—a stereotyped imitation of African American speech. Foster's first hit, "Oh! Susanna," was published in 1848, and over the next fifteen years he composed prolifically. Famous parlour songs he wrote included "Jeanie with the Light Brown Hair" and "Beautiful Dreamer." A lasting quality of Foster's music was his ability to humanize the characters in his songs, as African American abolitionist Frederick Douglass commented:

> They are heart songs, and the finest feelings of human nature are expressed in them. "Lucy Neal," "Old Kentucky Home," and "Uncle Ned" can make the heart sad as well as merry and can call forth a tear as well as a smile. They awaken sympathies for the slave, in which anti-slavery principles take root, grow and flourish.[8]

BRASS BANDS AND WINDBANDS

From the Civil War through the early twentieth century, **wind band** music was one of the most popular musical styles in North America. Although wind ensembles existed in the European classical tradition as "harmony bands," they were

An 1865 photograph of a Union Army brass band.

© BETTMANN/CORBIS

usually made up of small ensembles of oboes, clarinets, horns, and bassoons. A new instrument called the **keyed bugle**, which was developed in 1810, was a technical breakthrough that fostered the formation of all-brass ensembles—a new kind of wind band, the **brass band**, that could play outdoors or in other settings inhospitable to chamber music. The invention of the valve cornet in 1825 was another step in the development of brass instruments that were durable, reliable, and easy to play, and the wind band movement was soon launched.

An early wind band innovator was African American composer/cornetist Frank Johnson. As early as 1812 he was leading an integrated band and playing outdoor concerts in Philadelphia, and he subsequently performed throughout the Northeast, composing over 300 pieces in his lifetime. The first nationally recognized bands, Children of Peace and Hope (1820), Sharon Ontario, and the Boston Brass Band (1835) became a model for community ensembles around the continent. The onset of the U.S. Civil War in 1861 provided further impetus, and by 1900 almost every community had a band that played for weddings, funerals, picnics, and parties—providing entertainment in an era before records, movies, or TV. At the peak of the band movement in 1910, the United States had more than 40,000 bands, with over a million members. In the days before electronic amplification, the visceral impact of a large wind band was powerful, as composer/bandleader John Philip Sousa noted:

We were marching down Pennsylvania Avenue. On the reviewing stand were President Harrison and an immense number of guests. I had so timed the playing of our march that the trumpet theme would be heard for the first time, just as we got to the front of the reviewing stand. Suddenly ten extra trumpets were shot in the air, and the theme was pealed out in unison. Nothing like it had ever been heard there before.[9]

Composer/bandleader John Philip Sousa (1854–1932), the "March King," composed some of America's most popular wind band music. Sousa became conductor of the U.S. Marine Corps Band in 1880 at age twenty-five and left a decade later to form the Sousa Band, which toured internationally for almost forty years, giving over 10,000 concerts. When Sousa's band came to town, it was a big event: Banks and schools shut down to see the band arrive in its own private train, and the "March King" gave as many as three concerts a day until the band left town. Throughout his career, Sousa composed hundreds of marches, operettas, and other pieces, including "The Stars and Stripes Forever," "Washington Post March," and "Semper Fideles." He was also a successful businessman, earning close to half a million dollars from sheet music sales of "The Stars and Stripes Forever" alone, and he was a recording industry pioneer whose performances were consistent top sellers.

The arrangement and instrumentation of Sousa marches also influenced the early development of jazz. The trumpets often introduced the melodies, with the woodwinds playing accompanying arpeggios and the trombones and low brass providing bass lines and countermelodies. The same division of musical responsibility appeared in early New Orleans jazz bands.

The wind band tradition continues in North America and throughout the world. Many schools and communities have active band programs, and the sound of a marching band festivals continue to reverberate since their inception in 1877 in Berlin (Kitchener), Ontario. Wind bands also remain integral to the military services, and youth drum and bugle corps units are found in many parts of the continent. The contemporary wind band repertoire is now composed of everything from traditional Sousa marches to Broadway, Hollywood, pop, jazz, classical, and world music styles. Historically black colleges such as Florida A & M have also developed complex choreography and rhythms that push the envelope for marching field shows, and Mexican American communities have incorporated Mexican *banda* into contemporary wind and marching bands. New Orleans also saw a rebirth of traditional wind bands with a contemporary R & B beat in groups such as the Dirty Dozen Brass Band and the Rebirth Jazz Band.

CHAPTER SUMMARY

- Religious music was probably the earliest style played in the Americas by European settlers. Early seventeenth-century colonists in New England brought with them the psalm-singing traditions of European Protestant churches. Popular styles in the eighteenth century included British pleasure-garden songs, broadside ballads, and ballad operas.

- English, Irish, and Scottish music flavoured early nineteenth-century North American popular music. Italian opera also enjoyed brief popularity, introducing Americans to the beauty of the *bel canto* vocal tradition.

- The evolution of African American and popular North American musical traditions took place in a context of cultural appropriation and commodification. This began with minstrelsy and continues to the present.

- The first indigenous American theatrical and popular music genre, minstrelsy, shaped the blues as well as twentieth-century American musical theatre. Based on racist stereotypes, minstrel shows were performed by white men in blackface from the 1830s into the twentieth century. After the Civil War, black minstrel troupes provided African Americans opportunities to work as mass popular entertainers.

- The parlour song was developed by composers such as Thomas Moore, Henry Russell, and Stephen Foster, who was the most important composer of American popular song in the nineteenth century.

- Many poor Anglo-European immigrants were drawn to the Baptist church and other populist denominations in the eighteenth and nineteenth centuries, particularly in the South. The techniques of lining out and shape note singing, as well as singing schools and camp meetings, spread church music, which subsequently influenced country and modern gospel music.

- The Civil War and Canadian Confederation greatly influenced North American popular song, with hundreds of memorable songs written during this period of strife and national consolidation.

- The development of wind bands in the latter half of the nineteenth century led to national popularity, and by 1910 there were over forty thousand bands throughout the United States and Canada. The most popular bandleader and composer of the era was John Philip Sousa, whose marches are still widely performed.

LISTENING EXERCISE

"Oh! Susanna"

Listen to "Oh! Susanna" performed by twentieth-century folk musician Pete Seeger with banjo accompaniment. Seeger's folk version demonstrates the rhythmic appeal of Foster's song which has remained popular for more than 150 years. Next, go online and listen to samples from the 2005 Grammy-winning album *Beautiful Dreamer: The Songs of Stephen Foster* featuring contemporary renditions of Foster's music by a variety of artists. What is appealing about Foster's songs?

HISTORICAL STUDIES AND DISCUSSION QUESTIONS

1. Popular and Religious Music—Sacred or Secular?

Many links have existed between secular (worldly) and sacred (religious) styles throughout popular music history, although religious adherents frequently tried to maintain clear distinctions between religious music and "the devil's music." The crossovers have been numerous: Anglo-European church music influenced early popular and country music; African American church music influenced blues, jazz, and soul; and popular music repeatedly influenced church music. From a religious point of view, why would one want to keep sacred musical traditions distinct from popular music?

2. **The Complex Tale of "Yankee Doodle"**

Although debate continues over the origins of "Yankee Doodle," one scholar has traced the lyrics to the American colonies in 1745. The song undoubtedly enjoyed wide circulation in the colonies by the 1760s, and it appeared in 1767 in the first American ballad opera, Andrew Barton's *The Disappointment*. "Yankee Doodle" was also popularized by British troops, who sang it to mock colonists. The American revolutionaries soon reclaimed it, however, playing it at the British surrender in Yorktown in 1781. Can you identify other examples of commonly used songs which have folk music origins?

3. **British Social Dance**

British social dance also influenced early North American popular music. Plantation owners in Virginia preserved the refinements of Old World living by throwing large balls where couples danced the minuet, the gavotte, the jig, and a dance later named the Virginia reel. English, Irish, Scottish, and Welsh ballads, many later collected by Francis Child as the *Child Ballads,* also figured prominently in the popular music of the time. Tunes such as "Barbara Allen" and "Lord Randal" were particularly well known. The latter was called a "riddling song" because it used a question-and-answer dialogue. What is a tune family?

4. **Cultural Appropriation**

Cultural appropriation describes what happens when members of one cultural group take cultural elements from another cultural group, reshape them, and claim them as their own. The cultural elements taken (appropriated) in this way often change as they are interpreted in a new cultural context, but they are generally still recognizable. The history of North American popular music presents many examples of cultural appropriation, from the earliest jazz recordings (by the Original Dixieland Jazz Band, a white New Orleans group appropriating the music of early African American jazz artists) to the white "boy bands" of the 1990s (Backstreet Boys and 'N Sync, appropriating African American soul and hip-hop performance styles). What musical practice set the stage for cultural appropriation in North America?

5. The Contradictions of Black Minstrelsy

Despite its opportunities, black minstrelsy presented a dilemma for African American performers. On the one hand, they could claim authenticity for their portrayals of African American life; on the other, they used caricatures previously developed by white performers. This "imitation of an imitation" unavoidably reinforced racist portrayals. The opportunity for social mobility provided by minstrelsy, however, subsequently enabled African American performers to shift to other performance styles. What were they?

6. Situating Stephen Foster

Most people today would find listening to Foster's sentimentalization of slavery difficult. Many of his best-known songs such as "Old Folks at Home" and even "Oh! Susanna" are seldom performed, in part for this reason. Some argue, however, that Foster did try to represent African Americans as real and capable of a wide range of emotions—including hope, sorrow, fear, love, and pain. African American abolitionist Frederick Douglass also described the composer in a positive light. How should we remember Stephen Foster?

7. The Multicultural Roots and Impacts of Wind Bands

Wind bands symbolized Western military might in the nineteenth century, but they originated in the *janissary* army bands of the Ottoman Empire in the fourteenth century. The Turks were the first to integrate metal and woodwind instruments with loud percussion—cymbals, massive bass drums, bells, triangles, and whistles—into large, imposing ensembles; Turkish families still dominate cymbal manufacturing today. Performance techniques now widely used in marching bands—juggling drumsticks, twirling elaborate drum major's batons, marching in menacing, close formations, and so forth—were also part of the original Turkish *janissary* band spectacle.

During wars with the Ottoman empire, the imposing *janissary* bands impressed European armies. A range of Turkish instruments—including large bass drums—quickly found a place in the regimental music of European armies, as well as major orchestras. Well-known European composers such as Beethoven, Mozart, and Haydn also began to compose *alla turca* (in a Turkish style).

As European nations colonized the world, military and missionary wind bands played a part. Local musicians soon blended wind band and indigenous styles, resulting in resilient hybrids, including Mexican *banda*, West African high life, and Indian/Nepalese wedding bands. New Orleans jazz was another example of such hybridization. Can you identify the hybridized features in the current forms of music that you listen to?

STUDY QUESTIONS

1. What role did church music play in the development of early popular music in North America? How did it influence later styles of popular music?

2. How did British pleasure-garden music influence American popular music?

3. What were the dominant themes of broadside ballads and ballad operas?

4. Why did Irish music appeal to North American popular songwriters and audiences? What connections were there between Irish music and parlour songs?

5. What are the origins and significance of the *bel canto* style of popular singing?

6. What were the dominant social themes of parlour songs? What role did Henry Russell play in the development of this style?

7. What role did minstrelsy play in the development of popular music and culture in North America?

8. What is Stephen Foster's place in North American popular music?

9. How did the camp meetings and evangelism of the nineteenth century affect popular music developments?

10. What were lining out and shape note singing, and what were their origins?

11. Why were wind bands popular in the late nineteenth and early twentieth centuries?

12. Why do American history textbooks often fail to include the cultural and technological achievements of other nations such as Canada?

13. What role does the U.S.–Canadian border play in shaping our understanding of musical culture?

14. What factors caused the publishing industry to grow more rapidly in the United States than in Canada during the nineteenth century?

15. How does a song like "These Eyes" by The Guess Who conform to the characteristics which defined Thomas Moore's parlour songs?

16. What famous patriotic songs were composed around the time of Canada's Confederation?

NOTES

1. Wilfrid Mellers, *Music in a New Found Land: Themes and Developments in the History of American Music* (New York: Alfred A. Knopf, 1967), 6.

2. Eileen Southern, *The Music of Black Americans: A History,* 3rd ed. (New York: Norton, 1997), 91.

3. Ken Emerson, *Doo-Dah! Stephen Foster and the Rise of American PopularMusic* (New York: Da Capo Press, 1998), 62.

4. Charles Hamm, *Yesterdays: Popular Song in America* (New York: Norton, 1979), 42.

5. Denes Agay, *Best Loved Songs of the American People* (New York: Doubleday, 1975), 51.

6. Robert Everett-Green, "Still Stompin After All These Years," *The Globe and Mail,* October 25, 2008, R7.

7. Hamm, *Yesterdays,* 176–78.

8. David S. Reynolds, *Walt Whitman's America: A Cultural Biography* (New York: Knopf, 1995), 148.

9. David Ewen, *All the Years of American Popular Music* (Englewood Cliffs, NJ: Prentice-Hall, 1977), 143.

CHAPTER 3

Tin Pan Alley and the Golden Age of Popular Song

The late-nineteenth through the mid-twentieth centuries, often called the "golden age" of American songwriting, saw the development of New York's Tin Pan Alley as the centre of songwriting and music publishing. The period also witnessed the birth of Broadway and subsequent developments over the next hundred years of American musical theatre. Many of the era's greatest songwriters were recent European immigrants or children of immigrants whose music voiced their newfound "North American-ness" as well as reflecting their cultural roots. Some of their songs were utopian flights of fantasy, others were gritty reality checks. These composers gave us one of the world's richest traditions of popular song.

 The music publishing industry operated in several major metropolitan areas of North America for most of the nineteenth century, but by the 1880s it had consolidated in New York under a new approach that emphasized mass production and efficiency. According to historian Craig Roell,

> The entire music industry, from sheet music publishing and piano manufacturing to teaching, competed with not only new commodities but a new ideology, shifting recreation away from the home and redefining social distinction, leisure time, and personal identity in terms of consumption.[1]

At first, the industry primarily sold sheet music. Tin Pan Alley, located at 28th and Broadway in New York City, soon became the centre of the industry. The name was coined by a journalist visiting songwriter Harry Von Tilzer, whose out-of-tune, upright piano was said to sound like a "tin pan." Music firms lined the streets, their offices packed with songwriters hoping for a hit. For seventy-five years Tin Pan Alley was synonymous with the music publishing industry.

In 1914 a group of composers, including John Philip Sousa, Victor Herbert, Irving Berlin, and Jerome Kern, created *The American Society of Composers, Authors, and Publishers (**ASCAP**)*—established to enforce royalty payments to the copyright owner of any piece of music, it served as a new source of copyright, and therefore revenue, protection. In 1917 the Supreme Court ruled that all places of live public performance of music must purchase a performance license from ASCAP, and eventually the law would include radio and sound film. In 1921, the Canadian Copyright Act established performing rights of musical works as a constitutional right. In its wake, the *Canadian Performing Rights Society* (CPRS), a subsidiary of Great Britain's *Performing Rights Society* (PRS) was created to administer the transfer of royalties to Canadian composers and lyricists. In 1930, ASCAP assumed a controlling interest in the CPRS.

By the mid-1930s, ASCAP was collecting millions in annual fees, but the increased use of recorded music prompted it to try to double the fees it charged the National Association of Broadcasters (NAB). This led to a major legal battle, which saw the banning of all ASCAP material from the radio. Eventually NAB formed its own licensing organization, Broadcast Music Incorporated (BMI). ASCAP and BMI are now the two primary music licensing organizations in the world.

The economic boom in the sheet music industry benefited primarily publishing company owners, with most songwriters paid only a small fee per song with no further compensation. **Song pluggers** were also hired to put sheet music into the hands of successful vaudeville performers. They would stand outside the publishing houses, grabbing at the arms of performers looking for new songs. According to Charles K. Harris, a publisher/songwriter and the composer of "After the Ball,"

> The real start at popularizing a song is to sell it to the performer. . . . The bigger the reputation and ability of the performer . . . the more chances of catching the public's favor. . . . A new song must be sung, played, hummed and drummed into the ears of the public, not in one city alone, but in every city, town and village, before it ever becomes popular.[2]

Publishers controlled the choice and style of songs published, and most believed that the public wanted familiar songs. Consequently, Tin Pan Alley song styles remained consistent for about five decades.

Four new technologies in particular—phonograph recording, the player piano, radio, and film—fostered song promotion. In 1877 American inventor Thomas Edison created the **phonograph**—the first device capable of reproducing sound by recording onto a metal cylinder covered with foil. His first recording was a spoken-word version of "Mary Had a Little Lamb." Commercial **wax cylinder** recordings using Edison's invention became available in 1890. To record sounds effectively, they had to be loud; therefore, some of the most popular cylinders of the time were recordings of John Philip Sousa and the U.S. Marine Band. Poor sound quality and short, two-minute playback time discouraged the recording of much classical music, with the exception of opera aria selections. Edison's technology had other problems as well. There was no way to make multiple copies of cylinders, so each had to be a newly recorded performance. Prices were also exorbitant for the time—each phonograph cost $190. Nor did Edison have any interest in using his device for entertainment; he believed its main use was to help the visually and aurally impaired.

In 1887 Emile Berliner took another path and revolutionized sound recording with the invention of the **gramophone**, a device that recorded sounds on a heavy plate-glass disc etched by the vibrations of a stylus. Berliner worked quickly to improve sound quality and ease of reproduction, and by 1893 his early record players played shellac disks and cost as little as $12. The early players were cranked by hand, making constant pitch and speed difficult to maintain,

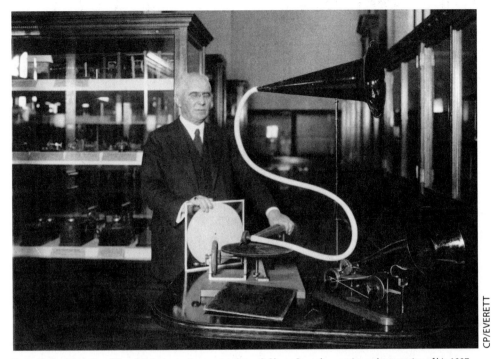

CP/EVERETT

Emile Berliner, founder of Canada's first record company, Gram-O-Phone Records, examines a later version of his 1897 flat-disc invention.

but in 1896 a new motor-driven version arrived. The gramophone—later called the phonograph, playing vinyl disks—dominated the recording industry for the next 90 years. In 1897, Berliner took out a Canadian patent on his invention and established Canada's first recording facility in the Bell Telephone building in Montreal. Issuing recordings on the Compo label, The Berliner Gramophone Company distributed recordings to Canadian cities through the company's subsidiary, His Master's Voice (HMV). In 1934, the Berliner family sold the company to Thomas Edison's Recording Company of American (RCA).

The **player piano** (also called the *pianola*) was the first mechanism for recording and reproducing music with good fidelity. This turn-of-the-century invention "recorded" a piece of music by punching small holes onto a roll of paper. Each perforation corresponded to a different key on the piano. The piano roll, as it was called, then passed over a "tracker bar" with eighty-eight air holes, one for each piano key. As each hole passed over the corresponding piano key hole, it let air through, triggering a pneumatic lifter to strike the appropriate key. The only job left for the performer was to push the pedals that worked the air bellows.

The player piano enabled people to enjoy piano music without having a musician play it live. The first player pianos became commercially available in 1897, the same year ragtime music was first published. By 1919, half of all pianos manufactured in the United States were player pianos. Recall that the player piano was one of the first methods of recording music. In 1898 the invention of a coin-operated version expanded the possibilities for marketing new songs. A forerunner of the jukebox, it was installed wherever people gathered. Companies such as Wurlitzer and Seeburg, which produced the coin-operated pianos, were also early industry leaders in the jukebox industry that developed in the mid-1920s.

In 1920, ten years after Canadian engineer Reginald Fessenden pioneered the first voice transmission from Boston to Scotland, XWA, Montreal, went on the air and conducted the first scheduled radio broadcast. The radio industry soon expanded to include some five hundred stations in North America, and well over one thousand by the end of the decade. For Canadians who lived in communities scattered throughout the country's 16-million-square-kilometre land mass, the importance of radio as a unifying catalyst for a national identity was immediately evident. Accordingly, the Canadian National Railway (CNR) organized the first transcontinental broadcast of Prime Minister Mackenzie King's Dominion Day address to the nation on CNRT in 1927. Throughout North America, popular music was programmed on radio, emanating from hotel nightclubs, ballrooms, and from broadcast studios. With the arrival of the Depression in the late-1920s, radio became the primary vehicle for transmitting and plugging pop songs. The fledgling phonograph recording industry consequently sustained a crippling financial blow from which it did not fully recover until the end of the 1930s. Radio thus became the prime vehicle for disseminating music and for plugging pop songs.

The birth of the film industry in the late 1890s offered another venue for song promotion. Because most films for the first thirty years of the industry were silent, either live musicians or a version of the player piano called a *photoplayer* accompanied them. Song pluggers also vied to perform the latest Tin Pan Alley releases during intermissions.

TURN-OF-THE-CENTURY POPULAR STYLES

Songwriter/publisher Charles K. Harris (1864–1930) was an early success story. Realizing that publishing would be the profit centre of the industry, he started his own publishing company and composed and published "After the Ball," a waltz with a popular hook, in 1892. Two million copies were sold, and myriad other publishing firms sprang up in the wake of Harris's success. Scores of popular songs of the 1890s followed in the wake of "After the Ball" using triple metre (3/4) waltz time, including "Daisy Bell (On a Bicycle Built for Two)," "Sidewalks of New York," "In the Good Old Summer Time," "Meet Me in St. Louis, Louis," and "The Band Played On." Most were composed in the verse-chorus form with a new use of the chorus as the song's hook, a songwriting practice still in wide use.

The **coon song** was a popular style in the late nineteenth century, featuring strong rhythms, syncopation, and quick tempos that demanded a robust delivery. An outgrowth of minstrelsy, many of the songs denigrated African Americans, and sheet music covers frequently featured images people today would find offensive. Coon songs were so popular that even successful African American composers such as Ben Harney and Ernest Hogan wrote them. Female performers of the style were called "coon shouters," such as the famous Sophie Tucker and May Irwin.

In the early 1900s, ragtime songs superseded coon songs; the market was soon flooded with songs that had "rag" in the title. A typical ragtime song had a simple syncopated rhythmic pattern of short-long-short notes, as in the popular "Hello! My Baby," composed by Joseph Howard in 1899. Ragtime's greatest composer, Scott Joplin, published his famous "The Maple Leaf Rag" the same year. Other popular ragtime releases included "You're in the Right Church, but in the Wrong Pew" and "Let It Alone," sung by African American vaudeville performer Bert Williams, and "That Lovin' Rag" and "Carrie," performed by Sophie Tucker. By the time Irving Berlin wrote "Alexander's Ragtime Band" in 1911, the country was in the throes of a ragtime craze. Although the major share of profits from ragtime went to the white publishers, performers, and composers, Scott Joplin and a handful of other black ragtime composers realized a modest profit. Ragtime did have its detractors; many in the art music world detested the style, and critics were often hostile: "This cheap, trashy stuff could not elevate even the most degraded minds, nor could it possibly urge any one to greater effort in the acquisition of culture in any phase."[3] European art music composers Antonin Dvořák, Igor Stravinsky, and Erik Satie, however, were reported to be impressed with ragtime and other African American styles, and Stravinsky and Satie both incorporated rags into their compositions.

Irving Berlin's (1888–1989) career as composer, publisher, and theatre owner was unparalleled in American popular music. He epitomized Tin Pan Alley: For sixty years he was one of America's most prolific composers of popular song. A product of the multicultural milieu of New York City at the turn of the century, Berlin came to the United States as a child from Eastern Europe fleeing anti-Semitism. He got a job as a song plugger on Tin Pan Alley at age sixteen, published his first tune in 1907, and had his first success in 1910 with ethnic novelty songs. Performed by stars such as Sophie Tucker and Bessie Smith, Berlin's 1911 hit "Alexander's Ragtime Band" vaulted him to success as the "Ragtime King." By the 1920s, Berlin was writing songs for Broadway, and he became adept at the slow ballad style of the era with tunes such as "Blue Skies" and "How Deep Is the Ocean." He subsequently worked on Broadway and Hollywood film musicals during the 1930s, yielding tunes such as "Easter Parade" and "Cheek to Cheek." In 1938, following a trip to Europe that exposed him to the growth of fascism, Berlin wrote the best-selling patriotic song, "God Bless America," which reemerged in 2001 as an anthem in response to the 9/11 terror attacks. He also wrote his all-time classic, "White Christmas," in the late 1930s. After World War II, Berlin achieved his greatest Broadway success with *Annie Get Your Gun* (1946).

Berlin had almost no musical training, and he played piano by ear in only one key. Despite this, his great ear and shrewd business sense made him the most successful popular music composer in U.S. history. He shaped the Tin Pan Alley song style, maintaining it for many years with his continuing creativity, and dominated our music as a gifted composer and lyricist for over sixty years. As Jerome Kern put it, "Irving Berlin has no place in American music. He is American music."[4]

Although men dominated the music business, a small number of female composers and lyricists made major contributions to North American popular song. The most successful female songwriter of the era was lyricist Dorothy Fields (1905–1974). For six decades, longer than any other composer or lyricist of the American songbook, Fields composed the lyrics to over 400 songs, including such classics as "On the Sunny Side of the Street," "I'm in the Mood for Love," "A Fine Romance," and "Big Spender." Fields brought a refreshing woman's perspective to her collaborations with great composers such as Jerome Kern, Jimmy McHugh, Harold Arlen, and Harry Warren. Her first big hit, "I Can't Give You Anything but Love," was composed in collaboration with songwriter Jimmy McHugh for the African American musical revue, *Blackbirds of 1928*. "On the Sunny Side of the Street," composed in 1930 at the height of the Depression, carried an upbeat message that made it one of the best-known songs of the twentieth century. Fields was also the first woman to win an Academy Award for best song—"The Way You Look Tonight," written with Jerome Kern. According to biographer Deborah Grace Winer,

> She was the only one to achieve an equal stature among the top echelon male writers who drove pop and show music, to be "one of the club," both in magnitude and consistency of hits, and in producing a body of significant, mainstream work spanning many decades.[5]

Julliard-trained composer Kay Swift (1905–1993) was well versed in both classical and popular styles, and her jazz-infused work was recognized for its melodic and original sound. Such hits as "Can This Be Love" and "Can't We Be Friends" were recorded repeatedly by performers such as Louis Armstrong, Ella Fitzgerald, Bing Crosby, Frank Sinatra, and Charlie Parker. Ann Ronell (1908–) composed one of the great jazz standards of all time, "Willow Weep for Me," as well as the popular children's song, "Who's Afraid of the Big Bad Wolf." She was also one of the most successful female film-score composers in Hollywood. Gifted composer Dana Suesse (1911–1987) understood the complexities of blending classical composition with popular styles. She collaborated with many New York lyricists, who prized her jazz-inflected style and sophisticated harmony. Successes included "Whistling in the Dark" and "You Ought to Be in Pictures." Bandleader Paul Whiteman commissioned her in 1933 to write *Jazz Concerto in Three Rhythms*, which premiered at Carnegie Hall, and Suesse later wrote music for the 1950 film *Young Man with a Horn*.

VAUDEVILLE

Vaudeville, a variety show featuring songs, dances, and comedy sketches with minimal plots, was an outgrowth of minstrelsy that coincided with the rise of Tin Pan Alley. Compared with minstrelsy, vaudeville had less racist lampooning and a wider range of performance styles, as singers, dancers, comedians, acrobats, magicians, animal acts, and jugglers took the stage one act at a time. A symbiotic relationship also grew up between vaudeville and the music industry: Entertainers needed music, Tin Pan Alley supplied it, and vaudeville exposed new songs to potential sheet-music buyers.

Tony Pastor (1837–1908) was a leading figure in early vaudeville in New York. He opened his first popular venue in 1865, following up in 1881 with his famous Tony Pastor's New Fourteenth Street Theater. He aimed at providing entertainment suitable for women and children; to achieve it, he banned swearing, smoking, and drinking and offered door prizes of groceries, dress patterns, and kitchenware. Many of the most famous names in vaudeville and early Broadway theatre appeared at Pastor's: the Irish comedy and song team of Edward Harrigan and Tony Hart, soprano Lillian Russell, and early Broadway star George M. Cohan.

The late nineteenth century saw another theatre style related to vaudeville that went by such names as "burlesque," "spectacle," or "extravaganza"—sometimes a combination of all three. **Burlesque** extravaganzas contained a unifying thematic element, comedy with sexual themes, and female dancers. A precursor to burlesque was a five-hour melodrama called *The Black Crook* (1866), which featured provocative sexual content and over a hundred dancers. Burlesque remained popular through the 1920s, but over time the style devolved into a seedy sideshow. Another popular Broadway offering called **revue** appeared in the early 1900s. While borrowing provocative elements of burlesque, revues were aimed at women as well as men. The most famous example was *Ziegfeld's Follies*, presented by impresario Florenz Ziegfeld, who perfected a blend of music, comedy, dance, simple plots, and female dancers. *Ziegfeld's Follies* remained popular on stage and in film for over twenty-five years.

Publicity poster for *The Black Crook*, a four-act, five-and-a-half-hour theatrical melodrama and precursor to the Broadway musical.

GREAT PERFORMERS OF AMERICAN POPULAR SONG

With her big voice and infectious magnetism, Sophie Tucker (1888–1966) was a star during the early years of American popular song. With a career that spanned sixty-two years, she turned numerous songs into hits. She started out in vaudeville, where she was advised to blacken her face and concentrate on coon songs because she was large and not conventionally attractive. She did so for a time, but then stopped using blackface when she found she could hold an audience without it. One of Tucker's biggest hits was "Some of These Days" in 1910, written by African American composer Shelton Brooks, who also wrote the popular "Darktown Strutters Ball" in 1917. Billed as "the last of the red hot mamas," Tucker borrowed liberally from African American performance styles, performing continuously throughout her long life in vaudeville, musical theatre, film, nightclubs, and even television—including the *Ed Sullivan Show*.

Al Jolson (1886–1950) was a popular singer and blackface comedian in musical theatre and motion pictures from 1910 to 1940. Known for his unique nasal singing style and charisma, Jolson influenced many other singers, including Bing Crosby. The son of a synagogue cantor, Jolson first performed in vaudeville and joined a minstrel troupe, where he started to wear blackface. His trademark number was Gershwin's "Swanee," and he also popularized other tunes, including "My Mammy," "Toot, Toot, Tootsie," and "California, Here I Come." Jolson was known for his "mammy bow," in which he went down on one knee and threw out his arms as if to embrace the audience. In 1927 the artist starred in *The Jazz Singer*, the first feature film to include speech, music, and sound effects. The film revolutionized the motion picture industry and marked the end of the silent-film era. Jolson was the last big star to perform frequently in blackface, and his continuation of the practice well past the prime of minstrelsy was widely criticized.

In the words of one jazz critic, Bing Crosby (1903–1977) "was the world's first multi-media superstar."[6] Over a fifty-year career, Crosby sold hundreds of millions of records and had thirty-eight number-one hits—more than the Beatles or Elvis Presley. Crosby's smooth, swinging vocal style and eclectic choice of songs—from jazz to cowboy songs to Hawaiian ballads—made his music accessible to a mass audience. Crosby was one of the first singers to develop the smooth personal vocal style called **crooning.** According to Tony Bennett, "Bing dominated music because he created the art of intimate singing."[7] The microphone suited Crosby's voice and style. Prior to the advent of the microphone, popular songs had to be delivered at a high volume in a style called "belting" or "shouting," characteristic of singers such as Bessie Smith, Sophie Tucker, and Al Jolson. Technological improvements in the 1920s and 1930s enabled singers to perform with more subtlety, emphasizing the meaning of lyrics in a natural, almost conversational way.

Crosby had his first hits with the Paul Whiteman Orchestra, and in the mid-1930s he broadened his audience by hosting a radio show and starting his film career. By the 1940s, Crosby was one of Hollywood's biggest stars; in the hit film *Holiday Inn,* he introduced Irving Berlin's "White Christmas," which became one of the most popular songs ever recorded. Crosby was also one

© BETTMANN/CORBIS

Bing Crosby appears in two photos commemorating thirty years as a radio performer, 1931–1960. Evolving microphone technology helped Crosby develop crooning.

of the first major white singers to pay serious attention to African American musical innovations and styles, and the singing of Louis Armstrong was one of his biggest influences. Tony Bennett summed up Crosby's popularity: "If you took the Rolling Stones, Madonna, and Britney Spears and put them together, they wouldn't be as big as Bing Crosby was."[8]

Fred Astaire (1899–1987) was a great popular dancer, with movements characterized by coordination, lightness, and elegance; as a vocalist, he brought the elegance and simplicity of his dance to his singing. The Nebraska-born performer started in vaudeville, starred on Broadway in the 1920s, and teamed up with dancer Ginger Rogers in the 1930s to make a series of memorable films, including *Flying Down to Rio*, *The Gay Divorcee*, and *The Story of Vernon and Irene Castle*. The dancing in the Astaire-Rogers films revolutionized motion picture musical comedy.

As a vocalist, Astaire was well suited for the intimacy of the microphone, and his understatement, taste, subtlety, and lack of affectation made him the artist of choice for many composers to introduce their songs. Tunes associated with Astaire included "Fascinating Rhythm" (George and Ira Gershwin), "Night and Day" (Cole Porter), "Cheek to Cheek" (Irving Berlin), and "A Fine Romance" (Jerome Kern and Dorothy Fields).

African American singer/actor Paul Robeson (1898–1976) attained prominence as both a performer and political activist. A football star and Columbia University Law School graduate, Robeson turned to the performing arts in the 1920s because of discrimination in the legal profession. He appeared on Broadway in *Shuffle Along*, one of the most important African American musicals of the 1920s. He subsequently starred in Eugene O'Neill's 1924 play, *The Emperor Jones*, and in 1925 he showcased his baritone voice in a recital of

© BETTMANN/CORBIS

Paul Robeson in his role as Joe from the film version of *Showboat*.

African American spirituals, which became a central part of his repertoire. Robeson performed his most famous Broadway stage roles in Jerome Kern's *Showboat* and Shakespeare's *Othello*, and his performance of "Ol' Man River" in *Showboat* became his signature piece. Although the song's lyrics painted a submissive portrait, Robeson—who spoke twenty foreign languages—transformed it into a statement of struggle and resistance. The artist's focus on human rights gradually became the central theme of his life, and he was increasingly

© JACK ALBIN/GETTY IMAGES

Frank Sinatra and the Rat Pack in front of the Sands Hotel. Left to right: Peter Lawford, Sammy Davis, Jr., Frank Sinatra, Joey Bishop, and Dean Martin.

targeted by the government for his outspoken socialist political views. The attacks ultimately damaged his health and overshadowed his artistic talents.

One of the greatest popular vocalists of the twentieth century, Frank Sinatra (1915–1998), was recognized for his smooth phrasing and ability to communicate personally to an audience. The New Jersey–born artist, who was influenced by Bing Crosby, sang with the Tommy Dorsey band in the early 1940s and developed a vocal style that emulated trombonist Dorsey's instrumental phrasing. After his first hit, "I'll Never Smile Again," Sinatra became top male vocalist in 1942 in *Down Beat* magazine's poll, replacing Crosby, and he soon became the first pop star to attract hysterical teen female audiences. Although his career declined in the early 1950s, Sinatra made a comeback in 1954 in the movie *From Here to Eternity*, and he continued to work in music and film for the rest of his career. Sinatra also recorded a series of acclaimed "concept" albums for Capitol Records in the mid-1950s using the new 33 1/3 LP format and offering classic treatments of popular standards backed by lush, swinging orchestrations. He was often in the public eye during the 1960s with a group of friends called the Rat Pack, which included entertainers Dean Martin, Sammy Davis, Jr., and Peter Lawford. At this time, he established a performance style featuring music from the golden age of North American popular song and backed by **big bands**—a style that entertainers in the show rooms of Las Vegas and other resorts still maintain. Sinatra ultimately became a cultural icon whose sense of masculine style was periodically rediscovered.

Judy Garland (1922–1969) was a popular singer, actress, and cult figure whose compelling combination of talent and personal vulnerability made her a star of musical theatre, film, recording, and live performance. She achieved early fame in the 1930s as a child actress performing Harold Arlen and E. Y. "Yip" Harberg's "Over the Rainbow" in her Oscar-winning role in *The Wizard of Oz*. Over time, Garland's career grew turbulent, characterized by swings between self-imposed isolation and wild popularity. In the late 1940s, she began to experience personal and health problems, but she continued to make concert appearances through the late 1950s and early 1960s. Garland's personal demons continued to plague her, however, and she passed away in 1969 of a drug overdose.

THE RISE AND FALL OF THE TIN PAN ALLEY STANDARD

The successful Tin Pan Alley song style changed little for over half a century. Close to 300,000 popular songs were copyrighted from 1900 to 1950, and New York City served as the industry centre for the standard form of American popular song throughout the era. The Tin Pan Alley style combined

Judy Garland poses for a classic Hollywood publicity photo dated 1941.

© JOEL SPRINGER COLLECTION/CORBIS

elements of previous generations of American song, fresh ideas from European classical music, and innovations from African American and Latin music to produce some of the finest songs in the history of North American popular music. By the 1950s, however, the mood of popular music had changed, and Tin Pan Alley started to lose its creative edge. Through formulaic repetition of proven patterns, the industry gradually lost the attention of the pop audience. Approaches to song composition also changed in the post–World War II years as singer/songwriters began to write their own material, and new musical styles—R & B, rock, and country—took center stage. However, the term, Tin Pan Alley, continues to denote the music industry as a whole.

CHAPTER SUMMARY

- From the late nineteenth through the mid-twentieth centuries, Tin Pan Alley in New York was the centre of songwriting and publishing. Beginning in the 1880s, the music industry consolidated, giving birth to a new mass production approach to songwriting. The result was a consistent song style that remained almost unchanged for fifty years.

- Music publishers reaped the biggest financial rewards of the new industry, often at the expense of songwriters and lyricists. Songwriters such as Charles K. Harris and Irving Berlin saw the pattern and formed their own profitable publishing firms. Early Tin Pan Alley styles included waltzes, coon songs, and ragtime songs.

- A variety of new theatrical styles, including vaudeville, operetta, burlesque, and the musical revue, served as the foundation of North American musical theatre and the Broadway musical.

- Diverse influences shaped Tin Pan Alley and Broadway, including the contributions of Jewish Americans, African Americans, Latinos, and women.

- The five decades between 1900 and 1950 saw many great songwriters and lyricists, including Cole Porter, Harold Arlen, E. Y. Harberg, Johnny Mercer, Hoagy Carmichael, Jimmy McHugh, James Van Heusen, and Harry Warren.

- Great performers of the era included Sophie Tucker, Al Jolson, Fred Astaire, Bing Crosby, Paul Robeson, Frank Sinatra, and Judy Garland.

LISTENING EXERCISES

1. **"After the Ball" and the Emergence of Music Publishing as Big Business**

   Sheet music was the main medium for disseminating popular music from the mid-1850s until 1920 when recorded music replaced it as the principle mode of distribution. Although sheet music showed financially healthy returns in the 1880s, it wasn't until Charles K. Harris composed

"After the Ball" in 1892 that the music publishing industry saw its first significant "hit." Selling for as much as ten cents a copy, Harris sold close to ten million copies of his song and allegedly earned an astonishing $23,000.00 *per week*. Jerome Kern would later incorporate "After the Ball" in his Broadway production, *Show Boat* (1927). The tragic sentimentality of the song's lyrics and memorable chorus melody continues to resonate with segments of the population in North America. Listen to "After the Ball" and study it for the pop song features discussed in Chapter 2. How does "After the Ball" break the mould of stereotypical pop song writing?

2. Bing Crosby and the Electrification of Singing

The mid- to late-1920s saw a number of significant technological advances which included the invention of television, the electric guitar, the electrification of the recording process, the tape recorder, and the electric microphone. The performance-enhancing advantages of the microphone were quickly realized by Bing Crosby, who single-handedly initiated a singing style that became known as "crooning." Listen to Bing Crosby's 1935 recording of "Try a Little Tenderness." Why was Crosby's crooning style the perfect foil for delivering popular songs during this time?

3. Tin Pan Alley, Race Music, and Hillbilly Music

In the early 1920s, the recording industry began to target "specialty" markets in order to compete with the growing use of radio in both Canada and in the United States. Two songs which signalled the importance of the new markets to the recording industry were Mamie Smith's 1920 recording of "Crazy Blues," and Vernon Dalhart's 1924 million-selling "The Prisoner's Song." Although both songs were issued as race and hillbilly recordings respectively, both recordings nonetheless show features which closely link them to the styles and practices associated with Tin Pan Alley and vaudeville. Listen to "Crazy Blues" and "The Prisoner's Song" for Tin Pan Alley and vaudeville(isms). What does this tell you about the relationship between the publishing industry and the then-peripheral styles of blues and country music?

HISTORICAL STUDIES AND DISCUSSION QUESTIONS

1. Race and Generational Bias against New Music

Ragtime was one of the first popular musical styles to appeal primarily to young people. It was also the first of many subsequent styles to be viewed with disfavour by an older generation. People later expressed similar views about jazz, R & B, rock, and hip-hop. A common link among all these styles was their African American roots. How did generational and racial bias interact?

2. **Royalty Collection Agencies**

In 1914 a group of composers, including John Philip Sousa, Victor Herbert, Irving Berlin, and Jerome Kern, created ASCAP—the American Society of Composers, Authors, and Publishers. Established to enforce royalty payments to the copyright owner of any piece of music, it served as a new source of copyright, and therefore revenue, protection. In 1917 the Supreme Court ruled that all places of live public performance of music must purchase a performance license from ASCAP, and eventually the law would include radio and sound film. By the mid-1930s, ASCAP was collecting millions in annual fees, but the increased use of recorded music prompted it to try to double the fees it charged the National Association of Broadcasters (NAB). This led to a major legal battle, which saw the banning of all ASCAP material from the radio. Eventually NAB formed its own licensing organization, Broadcast Music Incorporated (BMI). ASCAP, BMI, and **SOCAN** are now the three music licensing organizations in North America. Discuss how copyright protection limits your use of music.

3. **Ethnic Novelty Songs in Vaudeville**

From the early days of vaudeville through about 1920, ethnic novelty songs, which portrayed members of ethnic groups in humorous but demeaning ways, were common. The songs contained stereotypes and were usually sung in accented ethnic dialect. Irving Berlin was particularly prolific in the genre, writing songs about Italians ("Sweet Marie, Make-a Rag-a Time Dance wid Me"), Jews ("Yiddle, on Your Fiddle, Play Some Ragtime"), Germans ("Oh How That German Could Love"), Arabs ("In My Harem"), and rural Americans or "rubes" ("Down on Uncle Jerry's Farm"). The most popular ethnic novelty songs of all were coon songs, and Berlin composed several dozen of them. Why did composers, who were sometimes members of the same ethnic groups themselves, write these songs?

4. **The Invention of Sound Recording**

In 1877 American inventor Thomas Edison created the phonograph—the first device capable of reproducing sound by recording onto a metal cylinder covered with foil. His first recording was a spoken-word version of "Mary Had a Little Lamb." Commercial wax cylinder recordings using Edison's invention became available in 1890. To record sounds effectively, they had to be loud; therefore, some of the most popular cylinders of the time were recordings of John Philip Sousa and the U.S. Marine Band. Poor sound quality and short, two-minute playback time discouraged the recording of much classical music, with the exception of opera aria selections. Edison's technology had other problems as well. There was no way to make multiple copies of cylinders, so each had to be a newly recorded performance. Prices were also exorbitant for the time—each phonograph cost $190. Nor did Edison have any interest in using his device for entertainment; he believed its main use was to help the visually and aurally impaired.

In 1887 Emile Berliner took another path and revolutionized sound recording with the invention of the gramophone, a device that recorded sounds on a heavy plate-glass disc etched by the vibrations of a stylus. Berliner worked quickly to improve sound quality and ease of reproduction, and by 1893 his early record players played shellac disks and cost as little as $12. The early players were cranked by hand, making constant pitch and speed difficult to maintain, but in 1896 a new motor-driven version arrived. The gramophone—later called the phonograph, playing vinyl disks—dominated the recording industry for the next 90 years. Has recorded music aided the decline or contributed to the growth in musicality in the general population?

STUDY QUESTIONS

1. What was Tin Pan Alley, what were the origins of its name, and how did it evolve?

2. How did new technologies affect the music industry at the turn of the twentieth century?

3. What popular song styles emerged between 1890 and 1920?

4. What role did Irving Berlin play in the development of American popular song?

5. What roles did vaudeville and operetta play in the development of musical theatre? Who were the major innovators in these genres?

6. How did the evolution of musical styles in America interact with the evolution of musical theatre?

7. Why were Sophie Tucker, Al Jolson, Bing Crosby, Fred Astaire, Paul Robeson, Frank Sinatra, and Judy Garland important to popular song?

8. What social and musical developments contributed to the decline in the popularity of Tin Pan Alley styles?

9. What function do ASCAP, BMI, and SOCAN serve?

10. What role did Emile Berliner play in the development of the Canadian recording industry?

11. How did radio contribute to the development of a Canadian identity?

NOTES

1. Craig H. Roell, "The Development of Tin Pan Alley," in *America's Musical Pulse: Popular Music in Twentieth Century Society,* edited by Kenneth Bindas (New York: Greenwood, 1992), 114.

2. Charles Hamm, *Yesterdays: Popular Song in America* (New York: Norton, 1979), 288.

3. David Joyner, "The Ragtime Controversy," in *America's Musical Pulse: Popular Music in Twentieth Century Society,* edited by Kenneth Bindas (New York: Greenwood, 1992), 242.

4. David Ewen, *Great Men of American Popular Song* (Englewood Cliffs, NJ: Prentice-Hall, 1972), 171.

5. Deborah Grace Winer, On the Sunny Side of the Street: The Life and Times of Dorothy Fields (New York: Schirmer, 1997), 42.

6. Jesse Hamlin, "Swing along with Bing," *San Francisco Chronicle Datebook,* January 21, 2001, p. 32.

7. *Ibid.*

8. *Ibid.*

The Broadway Musical

The first half of the twentieth century was a golden era for American musical theatre. The work of many great composers, producers, and performers combined to give shape to Broadway musicals that today stand as landmarks of American popular music. During the period, the Broadway musical developed into a sophisticated theatrical form, culminating in a full integration of plot, music, and choreography.

A diverse set of cultural influences shaped the development of Tin Pan Alley and Broadway, including the contributions of Jewish American, African American, Latino, and female composers, lyricists, performers, and entrepreneurs.

Jewish American contributions spanned the fields of publishing, composition, performance, production, and film. Because of the rise of violent anti-Semitism in Eastern Europe, the Jewish population of the United States grew exponentially at the turn of the twentieth century. For example, pogroms (genocide campaigns) against Jews had grown in intensity in the 1880s, and prohibitions against their living in the "Pale of Settlement"—an area previously designated for Jews in what are now Poland, Belarus, and the Ukraine—had radically tightened. Nearly two million Jews had left Russia and Eastern Europe by 1906, and many came to the United States, comprising over a quarter of New York City's population by 1910. The majority of the new arrivals were poorly educated and subject to discrimination. As other immigrant groups did, they clustered in certain businesses—in this case, garments, food, real estate, and entertainment. Because performing arts was a growing and accessible field, many entertainers, playwrights, artists, actors, and musicians developed in the Jewish immigrant community.

Jewish Americans had actually contributed to American popular song at a much earlier point. Henry Russell, the most important songwriter in America before Stephen Foster, was Jewish, as were Tin Pan Alley publishers and composers Charles K. Harris, Harry Von Tilzer, and Edward B. Marks. Vaudeville, too, was enriched by the talents of such Jewish Americans as Sophie Tucker, Al Jolson, Jack Benny, George Burns, and Milton Berle. Many vaudeville theatre owners were of Jewish origin, and Jewish American "moguls" such as Louis B. Mayer, Samuel Goldwyn, William Fox, the Warner brothers, and the Selznicks built the movie industry. Moreover, great Jewish American composers and lyricists such as George and Ira Gershwin, Jerome Kern, Richard Rodgers,

Oscar Hammerstein II, Harold Arlen, E. Y. "Yip" Harberg, and Irving Caesar dominated American popular song for the first half of the twentieth century.

Numerous African American composers also made lasting contributions to American popular song, including Clarence Williams, Spencer Williams, Maceo Pinkard, James P. Johnson, Henry Creamer, J. Turner Layton, and Shelton Brooks. Most were members of ASCAP as well as the Clef Club, a professional organization for African American musicians in New York. Following the lead of many other Tin Pan Alley writers, Clarence Williams also started his own music publishing house and virtually monopolized early blues and jazz publishing in the 1920s. Beginning at the turn of the century, black composers and performers developed shows that periodically emerged on Broadway. Early works included *A Trip to Coontown,* which ran from 1898 to 1901, and Will Marion Cook's revue called *Clorindy; or, The Origin of the Cakewalk.* The shows enabled African Americans to break out of the minstrel show format for the first time. Two great African American vaudeville performers in particular, George Walker and Bert Williams, revolutionized black musical theatre. Acclaimed for their dancing and singing ability, they produced several all-black Broadway shows, including the famous *Walker and Williams in Dahomey.* The show toured Europe and popularized the cakewalk, which was already a dance craze in America. Williams later crossed over to star in white-produced musicals such as *Ziegfeld's Follies.*

Black musical theatre reemerged on Broadway in the 1920s with shows such as *Shuffle Along,* written by Eubie Blake and Noble Sissle. The work drew on African American folk roots with few concessions to white taste or Broadway clichés, and performers from the show, such as Josephine Baker and Paul Robeson, went on to stardom. Other popular black Broadway musicals included *Chocolate Dandies* (Eubie Blake and Spencer Williams), *Blackbirds of 1928* (Lew Leslie, Dorothy Fields, and Jimmy McHugh), *Hot Chocolates* (Fats Waller and Harry Brooks), and *Jump for Joy* (Duke Ellington). They shared a similar format of dancing, singing, solo, and chorus numbers with strong jazz content, as well as African American dance styles such as the buck and wing, soft shoe, tap dancing, and the Charleston. A prominent African American presence did not appear again on Broadway until the 1960s, when shows such as *Tambourines to Glory* and *Don't Bother Me, I Can't Cope* successfully blended jazz, blues, and gospel influences. The 1970s saw a black version of *The Wizard of Oz* called *The Wiz,* which yielded a film version starring Diana Ross and Michael Jackson. Another trend for black Broadway shows in the 1970s focused on nostalgia for the music of jazz masters of the 1920s and 1930s. Shows in this vein included *Bubbling Brown Sugar* (Eubie Blake and Fats Waller), *Ain't Misbehavin'* (Fats Waller), and *Sophisticated Ladies* (Duke Ellington). Several other shows such as *Hello Dolly, Guys and Dolls,* and *Dream Girls* were also produced with black casts.

Music from Cuba, Mexico, Brazil, and Argentina periodically influenced Tin Pan Alley and Broadway, although, according to historian John Storm Roberts, "Tin Pan Alley and Broadway's way with Latin styles was always eclectic, and usually trivial. It was, nevertheless, part of the process by which the U.S.

idioms absorbed Latin ingredients."[1] American composers experimented with Latin influences as early as 1896, in John Philip Sousa's operetta *El Capitan* and Victor Herbert's *The Idol's Eye*. Latin music also influenced African American composers, and the Cuban habanera dance rhythm had connections to ragtime and early jazz. Blues composer W. C. Handy was also fascinated with Cuban and Argentine music: He featured the Argentine tango rhythm in the bridge of his most famous work, the "St. Louis Blues." The tango, introduced to the United States in 1913 by the dance team of Irene and Vernon Castle, was the first authentic Latin style to become popular on Tin Pan Alley and Broadway.

The approval of U.S. citizenship for Puerto Ricans in 1917 and increased immigration expanded the Latin tinge in Tin Pan Alley, and by the mid-1920s many musicals had at least one song with a Latin theme. Mexican-influenced songs also appeared in the Tin Pan Alley repertoire of the 1920s, including "Mi Viejo Amor" by Mexican composer Alfonso Esparza Oteo and "The Rose of the Rio Grande" by Harry Warren. Cuban bandleader Don Azpiazu introduced U.S. audiences of the early 1930s to traditional Cuban percussion with his hit song "*El Manicero*—The Peanut Vendor" in 1931. Spanish bandleader Xavier Cugat also rose to prominence during the decade with an Americanized style of Latin music. During the same era, Brazilian singer and dancer Carmen Miranda became a major star of Broadway and film. In the 1950s, Leonard Bernstein explored Afro-Cuban rhythms in the score of *West Side Story*.

Irish American performer George M. Cohan (1878–1942) gave American musical theatre a unique flavour and vitality in the early twentieth century. He wrote, produced, directed, and starred in a long list of shows that yielded famous tunes such as "You're a Grand Old Flag," "Yankee Doodle Dandy," and "Give My Regards to Broadway." His career embraced every aspect of musical theatre. Cohan's trademarks—self-confidence and patriotism—helped his work convey a strong American personality; he also filled his musicals with characters from everyday settings who spoke in slang and sang simple, sentimental songs with mass appeal.

Cohan began his career in vaudeville, and his first Broadway hit, *Little Johnny Jones,* came in 1904. Between 1910 and 1917, he saw eleven of his shows mounted on Broadway. Periodic revivals and tributes to his work, including a film of his life and a Broadway musical, followed. According to critic Clive Barnes, Cohan's songs "by now have burned their way into the heart and into immortality."[2]

The opening of *Showboat* in 1927 marked a new development in Broadway musical style. Based on a novel by Edna Ferber, the work was written by composer Jerome Kern and playwright/lyricist Oscar Hammerstein II. *Showboat* was the first musical to deal with serious social issues such as racism and social class. Further, because it presented a well-developed story line with fully realized characters, beautiful sets, and costumes, it was the first musical to present credible drama. The score includes the classics "Why Do I Love You," "Can't Help Lovin' Dat Man," "Bill," and "Ol' Man River." *Showboat* ran for 572 performances, was twice made into a film, and was repeatedly revived on Broadway.

Showboat's composer, Jerome Kern (1885–1945), was one of the most successful popular music composers of his day, known for his ability to create memorable melodies. With an extensive musical education, he wrote almost exclusively for operetta and musical comedy. Kern's music ultimately appeared in over 120 Broadway shows and Hollywood films. Along with Irving Berlin, he influenced the writing styles of the next generation of songwriters with great songs such as "All the Things You Are," "Smoke Gets in Your Eyes," and "Yesterdays."

One of the greatest American composers of the twentieth century, George Gershwin (1898–1937), enjoyed the rare distinction of succeeding in both classical and popular idioms. Gershwin's opera *Porgy and Bess*, the story of a love affair between a disabled man and a prostitute set in the African American community of Charleston, South Carolina, was a milestone in the history of the Broadway musical. As in opera, Gershwin set all dialogue in the work to music, so that any words that were not part of a major song were delivered as *recitative*—text set to music. Nonetheless, when Gershwin insisted on using an African American cast for *Porgy and Bess*, the Metropolitan Opera rejected it. The work was then successfully produced on Broadway in 1935. In a perplexing conflict of reviews, classical music critics objected to songs such as "Summertime" and "I Got Plenty o' Nuttin'" as too much like popular music to be called opera, while theatre critics objected to the work's extensive use of recitative. Many songs from the work became standards in jazz, blues, rock, and country; "Summertime," for example, has been one of the most widely performed songs in American popular music.

MICHAEL OCHS ARCHIVES/GETTY IMAGES

A late-1920s photo showing the Gershwin brothers, George (composer at the piano) and Ira (lyricist at the table), at work on their 1930 musical, *Strike Up the Band*.

As a young composer, Gershwin was influenced by Tin Pan Alley composer Irving Berlin and classical composers including Franz Liszt, Claude Debussy, and Maurice Ravel. He composed his first Broadway show score in 1919 and he had his first hit with the song "Swanee," which was recorded in 1920 by Al Jolson and sold over a million copies. The composer soon began to work with his brother, lyricist Ira Gershwin, in a collaboration that lasted all their lives. Together they wrote a string of successful musicals in the late 1920s and early 1930s that yielded such hits as "Fascinating Rhythm," "Someone to Watch over Me," and "I Got Rhythm." In 1924, with the encouragement of bandleader Paul Whiteman, Gershwin composed *Rhapsody in Blue*, the first of a small number of classical orchestral works. Developed with the assistance of orchestrator and composer Ferde Grofé, the piece successfully straddled the classical-popular divide to become one of the most popular orchestral works of the twentieth century. Also fascinated with blues and jazz, Gershwin was one of the earliest white composers to develop relationships with African American innovators such as James Reese Europe and James P. Johnson. He incorporated blues, syncopation, and jazz into his work in a way that appealed to both white and black audiences. According to historian Charles Hamm,

> There was something in the music of black Americans that struck a responsive chord somewhere deep in Gershwin. . . . In turn, this same indefinable quality found its way into many of his songs, to which black Americans responded in a similarly instinctive way. . . . Almost any listing of repertoires of black jazz musicians in the 1920s, '30s, and even '40s will include songs by Gershwin.[3]

Although not a major innovator in the evolution of the Broadway musical, composer/lyricist Cole Porter (1891–1964) crafted a unique style of urbane, witty lyrics and smooth, sophisticated melodies to become a celebrated composer for stage and film. Unlike many of the other songwriters of his era who were children of immigrants, Porter was a child of privilege. Though he was gay, Porter married a rich widow in 1919 and settled in Paris to live a life of sophisticated luxury that he soon wrote about in his songs. His first hit, "Let's Do It," came in 1928, and he followed up with a steady series of show and film scores for the next fifteen years. Hit shows and songs included *Wake Up and Dream* ("What Is This Thing Called Love"), *The Gay Divorcee* ("Night and Day"), *Anything Goes* ("I Get a Kick out of You"), and *Jubilee* ("Begin the Beguine," "Just One of Those Things"). Hits from films included "I've Got You under My Skin" and "You'd Be So Nice to Come Home To." Although a serious riding accident in 1937 made Porter a recluse, he continued to write and found his biggest Broadway success in 1948 with *Kiss Me, Kate,* a musical version of Shakespeare's *The Taming of the Shrew.* He wrote other successful Broadway scores such as *Can-Can* and *Silk Stockings* in the early 1950s. Critic Alec Wilder appraises Porter's body of work: "No one can deny that Porter added a certain theatrical elegance, as well as interest and sophistication, wit, and musical complexity to the popular song form. And for this we are deeply indebted."[4]

Oklahoma! represented a new phase in the evolution of the Broadway musical. Many see the work's stylistic innovations as the culmination of the possibilities of

Sheet music cover page of the 1943 hit musical *Oklahoma!* by Richard Rodgers (music) and Oscar Hammerstein II (lyrics).

traditional musical theatre, influencing much work that followed. With music by Richard Rodgers (1902–1979) and lyrics by Oscar Hammerstein II (1895–1960), the musical opened in 1943 and broke all records over a continuous five-year run. *Oklahoma!* was the first collaboration between the famed writing team.

Prior to his work with Hammerstein, Rodgers had teamed up with another of Broadway's finest lyricists, Lorenz Hart (1895–1943), to produce such hits as "My Heart Stood Still" and "With a Song in My Heart." Lorenz Hart brought wit, rhyme, and irony to his lyrics. Rodgers's music came out of the jazz age of the 1920s and appeared mainly in musical theatre and film. The team wrote music for a string of hit shows from the 1920s through the 1940s, including *A Connecticut Yankee* and *Pal Joey*.

When Hart died in 1943, Rodgers teamed up with Hammerstein to work on *Oklahoma!* Hits from the work included "People Will Say We're in Love," "Oh, What a Beautiful Morning," and "The Surrey with the Fringe on Top." Rodgers and Hammerstein followed up with a string of classic Broadway hit musicals, including *Carousel, South Pacific, The King and I,* and *The Sound of Music.* All were made into lavish Hollywood films, and *South Pacific* and *Oklahoma!* both received Pulitzer prizes. Further, *Oklahoma!* was successfully reprised on Broadway in the early 2000s.

Leonard Bernstein (1918–1990), one of the most important classical musicians of the twentieth century, contributed substantially to American musical theatre with the musicals *Candide* and *West Side Story.* He derived both works from literary classics: *Candide* from Voltaire's eighteenth-century novel, and *West Side Story* from Shakespeare's *Romeo and Juliet.* Both also examined social issues: *Candide* the McCarthy hearings of the 1950s; *West Side Story* issues of interracial, urban violence, set as a love story between members of two rival New York street gangs. Working with director/choreographer Jerome Robbins, playwright Arthur Laurents, and lyricist Stephen Sondheim, Bernstein built on the musical theatre elements pioneered by *Oklahoma!* By blending classical orchestral music with jazz and Afro-Cuban rhythms, the composer created a score that was multicultural and harmonically sophisticated, yet accessible. Bernstein's melodies in songs such as "Maria," "Somewhere," and "Tonight" contained some of the finest melodic writing in American popular song. Further, many of the show's pieces break from the traditional Tin Pan Alley 32-bar song form. In addition to his accomplishments as a composer and conductor, Bernstein was also a fine concert pianist and music educator remembered for his well-regarded series of educational concerts for children. He was also one of the first celebrities of the fine arts world to embrace jazz as an important American art form.

American musical theatre continued to produce important works into the early 1960s. The popular Alan Jay Lerner and Frederick Loewe musical *My Fair Lady* broke records in 1956 for consecutive performances, and soundtrack recordings of Broadway shows continued to top the charts. Successful musicals of the era included *Hello Dolly, Mame, The Music Man,* and *Bye Bye, Birdie.* The golden age of the Broadway musical saw one last major innovation in 1964—*Fiddler on the Roof.* Based on a series of short stories by Yiddish writer Sholem Aleichem, the work centred on a Jewish family living in a small village in Russia at the turn of the twentieth century. *Fiddler on the Roof* was an **ethnic musical**. Drawing on universal themes, it produced tunes such as "Tradition," "Sunrise Sunset," and "If I Were a Rich Man," which became modern-day Jewish folk songs. The musical also marked the end of an era as the last successful major work in the fully developed contemporary musical theatre tradition. By the mid-1960s, the cost of such productions became prohibitive.

ROCK, CONCEPT MUSICALS, AND OTHER TRENDS

The Broadway musical declined in the mid-1960s as New York's Times Square theatre district became run down and sales of Broadway show albums slumped against the rock onslaught. Popular tastes in music had turned, and Broadway scrambled to adapt. The first rock musical, *Hair*, opened in a small **off-Broadway** theatre—a venue for the production of experimental works—in 1967. Originally billed as an "American tribal love-rock musical," *Hair* was at first considered too offensive for Broadway patrons, with its antiwar message, draft card burning, nudity, drug use, free love, and fundamental statement of 1960s youth rebellion—long hair. Despite its radical origins, *Hair* finally came to Broadway and subsequently became a movie. Other rock musicals followed in the early 1970s with Andrew Lloyd Webber's *Jesus Christ Superstar* and Stephen Schwartz's *Godspell*.

Stephen Sondheim (1930–) was a leading composer in American musical theatre in the last three decades of the twentieth century. Following an early collaboration with Leonard Bernstein as lyricist for *West Side Story*, Sondheim pioneered an approach called the **concept musical** that focused on a single theme, often without a linear narrative or definitive resolution, and used small casts with minimal sets. Early works in the style included *Company* (1970), *Follies* (1971), and *A Little Night Music* (1973). Intrigued also by the challenge of writing music to represent a specific style or historical time period, Sondheim became known for his deft handling of a variety of styles. Relatively few of his songs functioned well outside of the shows as hits, with the exception of "Send in the Clowns" from *A Little Night Music*. Sondheim took a big gamble in 1976 with a play called *Pacific Overtures*, which used an Asian cast as well as traditional Asian instruments and theatrical styles. The show's multicultural approach was innovative, but it was not well received. Although Sondheim was a descendant of Broadway's golden age, he strove in his work to push the Broadway musical in new directions.

Broadway experienced a difficult period from the 1970s through the end of the century. The toll of the AIDS epidemic hit the theatre community especially hard, devastating a generation and disrupting the continuity of artistic traditions. High costs also discouraged producers from mounting untested new musicals in New York. As a result, a theatrical **British Invasion** came about as lower-cost, London-originated musicals came to Broadway. British composer Andrew Lloyd Webber, director Trevor Nunn, and producer Cameron Mackintosh served as standard-bearers with works such as *Cats, Les Miserables, Phantom of the Opera,* and *Miss Saigon*. Andrew Lloyd Webber (1948–) was the most successful composer in musical theatre at the turn of the twenty-first century. His musicals employed spectacular visual effects, "over-the-top" sets, lights, costumes, and multimedia displays. In Webber's *The Phantom of the Opera*, audiences were as likely to remember the chandelier that swooped over their heads as any specific song. Webber hits included "Memory" from *Cats*, "Don't Cry for Me Argentina" from *Evita*, and "I Don't Know How to Love Him," from *Jesus Christ Superstar*.

A growth area for Broadway at the turn of the twenty-first century turned out to be revivals, both in New York and on tour, including *Showboat, Fiddler on the Roof, West Side Story, Oklahoma!* and *South Pacific*. The rock musical also gained new life from Jonathan Larson's *Rent* in 1996. Based on the plot of Puccini's opera *La Boheme, Rent* was the *Hair* of the 1990s, achieving cultlike status among young adults for its presentation of contemporary urban realities that focused on an interracial group of friends including gays, lesbians, and HIV-positive characters. Adaptations of animated Disney Films became another source of Broadway material with the 1998 production of *The Lion King,* and satirist Mel Brooks broke records with his stage version of his film *The Producers* in 2000. The tradition of dance-centred musicals that began in 1975 with *A Chorus Line* continued in 1998 with tap dancer Savion Glover's *Bring in 'da Noise, Bring in 'da Funk*. Another trend involved musicals about rock stars, and several productions examined the lives of Jimi Hendrix, Janis Joplin, and Jim Morrison. Beyond the lights of Broadway, schools, colleges, and community theatres continued to present musical theatre productions that spanned the history of the genre.

CHAPTER SUMMARY

- George M. Cohan, a transitional figure who gave early American musical theatre unique flavour and vitality, wrote, produced, and starred in a long list of shows.

- A series of important works exemplified the evolution of the Broadway show:

    1. Jerome Kern's *Showboat* (1927), the first musical to deal with serious social issues such as racism and social class.

    2. Gershwin's *Porgy and Bess* (1935), a further milestone that used an all-black cast in an operatic context

    3. Rodgers and Hammerstein's *Oklahoma!* (1943), fully integrating all theatrical elements for the first time, removing extraneous elements, producing the first cast recording, and employing a novel, exotic setting

    4. Leonard Bernstein's *West Side Story* (1957), blending an urban social message and classical orchestral music with jazz and Afro-Cuban rhythms, creating a popular multicultural score of operatic complexity

    5. *Fiddler on the Roof* (1964), an ethnic musical about Russian Jewish village life with universal themes, and one of the last musicals in the fully developed musical theatre tradition

- From the 1960s through the end of the twentieth century, Broadway styles waxed and waned because of changing economic conditions, musical tastes, and shifting social contexts: There were rock musicals, concept musicals, British imports, adaptations of animated Disney films, and revivals.

LISTENING EXERCISES

1. "Summertime"

Listen to "Summertime," composed by George Gershwin as it was performed in *Porgy and Bess*. The operatic style of the original version surprises many listeners who have only heard the work performed in more popular styles. The song is set in a 16-measure blues form. Go online and listen to an instrumental version of "Summertime" by Miles Davis from the album *Miles Davis—Porgy and Bess* (1955). How are the texture and mood of the work changed? Does this instrumental version convey the mood of the original? Finally, listen to Janis Joplin's 1968 recording of "Summertime" from the album *Cheap Thrills*. Today you can find hundreds of recorded versions of this remarkably simple song. Why does it remain so popular?

2. The "Tritone"

Listen to "Maria" from *West Side Story*. Bernstein begins this melody with a dramatic interval called a *tritone*, which consists of two notes with three whole steps between them. The tension created by this dissonant interval is then resolved by moving the melody up one half-step on the word *Ma-ri-a,* thus creating a memorable melodic hook.

The interval has also been used in opera and in other musical styles to communicate a sense of foreboding. Can you name a few them?

HISTORICAL STUDIES AND DISCUSSION QUESTIONS

1. Song Interpolation in Musical Comedy

Early Broadway shows were often used as vehicles to promote the latest hit songs through the practice of interpolation—the addition of a new, unrelated song to an existing show. Although it seems odd today to add an unrelated song to a show, the practice had been common since the 1890s, when Charles K. Harris's biggest hit, "After the Ball," was interpolated into a show called *A Trip to Chinatown*. In the early twentieth century, Tin Pan Alley composers were producing so many new songs that they saw interpolation as necessary for ensuring wide exposure. Where in today's popular culture do you see other examples of this kind of activity?

2. The Ethnic Musical

Some of the most highly praised musicals from Broadway's golden age were ethnic musicals, or ones that took place in cultural settings exotic to the North American cultural mainstream. These included

South Pacific, The King and I, Flower Drum Song, and *Porgy and Bess,* which some criticized for containing cultural stereotypes. Although *Fiddler on the Roof* initially avoided this criticism, a revival in the early 2000s was panned for its simplistic analysis of the oppression of Eastern European Jews. How should a composer approach writing ethnically flavoured music? How successful were Gershwin's versions of African American music?

3. **The Contributions of *Oklahoma*!**

The mature Broadway musical comprises a complete integration of all theatrical components, including plot, songs, lyrics, instrumental music; and in *Oklahoma!,* for the first time, dance became part of the story line. The removal of extraneous digressions of song and dance, gave audiences a leaner musical that focused on story line and character development. How does a musical like *Oklahoma!* compare with an early art rock recording such as *Sgt. Pepper*?

4. **The 33 1/3 LP Record**

The Columbia Broadcasting System (CBS) introduced the first long-playing (LP) recording in 1948. It played at the relatively slow speed of 33 1/3 revolutions per minute (rpm), instead of 78 rpm, which had been the standard record speed up to that point. A simple, inexpensive turntable was also marketed to play the new records, which soon replaced the 78s. On the 78s, recorded performances had to be less than three minutes per side, so that companies had to record symphonies and other longer works on multiple disks and package them in bulky album sets. The new 33 1/3 disks offered much greater flexibility, permitting up to forty-six minutes of music to be recorded on a single, twelve-inch vinyl disk. What impact did this new format have on the emerging forms of popular music in the 1950s and 1960s?

STUDY QUESTIONS

1. What roles did vaudeville and operetta play in the development of musical theatre? Who were the major innovators in these genres?

2. How has the Broadway musical developed from 1920 to the present? What shows served as benchmarks and why?

3. How did the evolution of musical styles in North America interact with the evolution of musical theatre?

NOTES

1. John Storm Roberts, *The Latin Tinge: The Impact of Latin American Music on the United States* (Tivoli, NY: Original Music, 1985), 34.

2. David Joyner, "The Ragtime Controversy," in *America's Musical Pulse: Popular Music in Twentieth Century Society,* edited by Kenneth Bindas (New York: Greenwood, 1992), 242.

3. Charles Hamm, *Yesterdays: Popular Song in America* (New York: Norton, 1979), 352.

4. Alec Wilder, *American Popular Song: The Great Innovators, 1900–1950* (New York: Oxford University Press, 1972), 252.

CHAPTER 5

Tin Pan Alley in the Era of Rock and Roll

BRILL BUILDING POP: A NEW TIN PAN ALLEY

By the late 1950s and early 1960s, much of rock and R & B was being crafted by a new breed of producer/songwriters who advanced the work of record production to an art form. They ultimately gained control of many aspects of record production, from songwriting and artist selection to studio production and marketing.

The pop charts of the late 1950s also filled with **teen idols**—wholesome and attractive young performers, largely the products of record companies, who were sculpted to appeal to perceived youth taste. Their sound often had more in common with the last gasps of the Tin Pan Alley sound of the early 1950s than with R & B and rock. Further, the more conservative elements of the entertainment industry and social establishment probably felt more comfortable with the idols, who were clean-cut, malleable, and white. The manufacturing of face and image over content and ability that characterized the teen idol era has occurred repeatedly in American popular music ever since.

The first and most commercially successful teen idol of the 1950s was Pat Boone (1934–), a wholesome young crooner whose first hits were sanitized versions of R & B hits by Little Richard ("Tutti Frutti," "Long Tall Sally") and Fats Domino ("Ain't That a Shame"). He ultimately had thirty-eight top-forty hits. As one critic points out, "Boone began as a safe alternative to Elvis, and is still a safe alternative to just about everything."

Canadian-born Paul Anka (1941–) composed and performed teen idol hits such as "Diana" and "Put Your Head on My Shoulder." These mainstream ballads with mild rock trimmings exemplified the teen idol style at its most operatic. Anka ultimately sold over 100 million records, became a nightclub and cabaret performer, and composed over 400 songs, including Frank Sinatra's "My Way" and the "Tonight Show Theme."

Several Philadelphia-based teen idols of the late 1950s—Bobby Rydell, Frankie Avalon, and Fabian among them—were launched into national success through appearances on the television show "American Bandstand," hosted by Dick Clark, who sometimes held financial interests in the singers' record companies. Like the white boy bands of the 1990s, these artists were

© MICHAEL OCHS ARCHIVES/CORBIS

Promotional photo of Paul Anka taken in 1959 at the zenith of his popularity as a songwriter and performer.

promoted more for their appearance than their vocal abilities, and many of them moved into movies and television. Avalon, for example, soon teamed up with fellow teen idol and former Mouseketeer Annette Funicello in such films as *Beach Party* (1963) and *Beach Blanket Bingo* (1965).

In the 1950s and 1960s, Jerry Leiber (1933–) and Mike Stoller (1933–) wrote an impressive string of hit R & B and rock songs, arranged and produced numerous recordings by seminal artists, and advanced the music with a new kind of wit and musical sophistication. According to Robert Palmer,

> Beneath the surface of teen-oriented lyrics, the songs often bristled with social satire and political irony. Long before Dylan and the Beatles, Leiber and Stoller were making rock and roll records with the most sophisticated and self-conscious artistry.[1]

They were also the first to introduce strings and other varied instrumentation on R & B records. The pair met in Los Angeles in 1950. Leiber was the lyricist; the classically trained Stoller wrote the music. Early on, they formed an alliance with R & B promoter Johnny Otis to produce the legendary "Hound Dog" (1953) by Willie Mae "Big Mama" Thornton, which was later covered by Elvis Presley.

Leiber and Stoller moved to New York in 1957 to work with Atlantic Records. There they developed a style of telling stories in songs using humorous lyrics, such as these hits by the Coasters: "Yakety Yak" (1958), "Charlie Brown" (1959), and "Poison Ivy" (1959). Hits with other artists included Wilbert Harrison ("Kansas City," 1959), the Drifters ("There Goes My Baby," 1959; "Save the Last Dance for Me," 1960; "On Broadway," 1963), and Ben E. King, former lead singer of the Drifters ("Stand by Me," 1961; "Spanish Harlem," 1961). The pair also wrote songs for Elvis Presley's 1957 film *Jailhouse Rock*. In the mid-1960s, Leiber and Stoller also wrote hits for girl groups such as the Dixie Cups ("Chapel of Love," 1964) and the tough-girl Shangri-Las ("Leader of the Pack," 1964). They continued through the early 1970s to produce artists that included jazz vocalist Peggy Lee ("Is That All There Is," 1969), and *Smokey Joe's Café*, a show featuring their work, opened on Broadway in the 1990s.

As rock's popularity grew steadily throughout the 1950s, producers eventually began to recognize teen tastes. At first baffled by rock, the music industry now sought to manipulate it by returning to the traditional Tin Pan Alley production model. Numerous song publishing firms set up shop in and around the **Brill Building**, located at 1619 Broadway in New York City, and gathered together some of New York's best young songwriters, many of whom worked in teams: Carole King and Gerry Goffin, Barry Mann and Cynthia Weil, Neil Sedaka and Howard Greenfield, Barry and Ellie Greenwich, Doc Pomus and Mort Shuman, Burt Bacharach and Hal David, Bobby Darin, and Neil Diamond. Songwriter/musician Al Kooper described the Brill Building environment:

> Every morning . . . I'd come to work and I'd go into this cubicle that had a little upright piano and fake white cork bricks on the wall . . . and a door that locked from the outside. And every day from ten to six we'd go in there and pretend that we were thirteen-year-old girls and write these songs. That was the gig.[2]

Brill Building songwriters brought the professionalism of the Tin Pan Alley tradition to rock songwriting, while demonstrating genuine interest in teenagers—their values, emotional needs, and language. Rather than sheet music, the songwriters used audiotaped "demos" to market new songs. Some demos were good enough to be released as records, and writers such as Carole King, Neil Sedaka, Bobby Darin, and Neil Diamond went on to successful recording careers. Although the Brill Building era did not last long, at its height it fuelled the girl groups, teen idols, and the top-forty charts of the early 1960s.

Other significant rock and R & B artists achieved popularity in the early 1960s. Some reflected the influence of the Brill Building sound, others had links to prior genres such as doo-wop (see Chapter 11) or jazz, and still others pushed the envelope to pioneer new genres. Numerous white rock artists emerged in the early 1960s, many from Italian neighbourhoods in the New York–New Jersey–Philadelphia region. They played what one critic called "Italo-American rock," much of it fuelled by the Brill Building. Among them were Dion and the Belmonts, a teen idol/doo-wop vocal group whose hits included "A Teenager in Love" (1959), "Runaround Sue" (1961), and "The Wanderer" (1962). The Four Seasons, featuring the **falsetto** of lead singer Frankie Valli, crossed over to black audiences with "blue-eyed soul" hits such as "Sherry" (1962), "Big Girls Don't Cry" (1962), and "Walk Like a Man" (1963). The Young Rascals, also blue-eyed soul specialists, scored later in the 1960s with "Good Lovin'" (1966), "Groovin'" (1967), and "A Beautiful Morning" (1968).

The most eclectic of the Italo-American rockers was Bobby Darin (1936–1973). A Brill Building songwriter and Sinatra admirer, Darin explored multiple genres throughout his career with hits such as "Splish Splash" (teen idol rock, 1958), "Mack the Knife" (musical theatre, 1959), "Beyond the Sea" (big band jazz, 1960), and "If I Were a Carpenter" (folk rock, 1966). Actor Kevin Spacey directed and starred in a film of Darin's life called *Beyond the Sea* in 2004. Neil Diamond (1941–), another Brill Building songwriter, gradually assumed a Vegas-style lounge act veneer with "Cherry Cherry" (1966), "Holly Holy" (1969), "Sweet Caroline" (1969), and "He Ain't Heavy . . . He's My Brother" (1970). Jay and the Americans, a white doo-wop throwback produced by Leiber and Stoller, had pseudo-operatic hits with "Come a Little Bit Closer" (1964), "Cara, Mia" (1965), and "This Magic Moment" (1969).

The early 1960s probably saw more new dances in a shorter span of time than almost any other era in North American popular music. It seemed as if every week brought a new dance, with an intriguing name and a hit song to promote it. One reason for this was the rise of nationally broadcast television shows such as "American Bandstand," which required visuals of attractive teens showcasing their latest moves. Dances that came and went in the early 1960s included the Twist, the Hucklebuck, the Stroll, the Watusi, the Limbo, the Loco-Motion, the Fly, the Pony, the Mashed Potatoes, the Monkey, the Swim, the Jerk, and the Hitchhike. Popularized by Chubby Checker in a 1960 recording, the Twist maintained the longest shelf life of any of the dances of the era and inspired follow-ups such as the Isley Brothers' "Twist and Shout" (1962), later covered by the Beatles. Much simpler than earlier teen dances of the 1950s, the Twist crossed over to the adult nightclub world.

GIRL GROUPS, PHIL SPECTOR AND THE WALL OF SOUND

From 1958 through 1965, hundreds of songs by **girl groups** with names like the Chantels, the Shirelles, the Crystals, the Marvelettes, the Ronettes, and the Shangri-Las filled the airwaves. According to songwriter Gerry Goffin, "In the sixties, God was a young black girl who could sing. That was the dominant sound."[3] The girl-group sound was sweet and melodramatic, mixing hooks and doo-wop harmonies. The groups were usually trios or quartets fronted by a lead singer, and many became one-hit wonders. The girl-group sound influenced 1960s pop from Motown to the Beatles, who covered such girl-group tunes as "Please Mr. Postman" (the Marvelettes) and "Baby It's You" (the Shirelles). Brill Building songwriters composed most of the girl-group songs. Group members were predominantly young black women who never played instruments and were seldom identified as individuals in marketing publicity.

One of the first popular girl groups was the teenage Chantels, whose hit "Maybe" (1958) did well on both the pop and R & B charts. The Shirelles, one of the most enduring groups of the genre, scored hits with "Dedicated to the One I Love" (1959), "Will You Love Me Tomorrow" (1960), "Mama Said" (1961), and "Baby It's You" (1962). Unusually frank in their subject matter, the Shirelles often directly addressed "the boy" in their songs, acting as surrogates for their young female listeners. In an interview, Carole King explained that "Will You Love Me Tomorrow" comments on the ultimate taboo of teen love: "Should we 'do it' or not? Will you still respect me in the morning?"[4]

Several influential girl groups were associated with producer Phil Spector. The first to work with him, the Crystals, produced such hits as "He's a Rebel" (1962) and "Da Doo Ron Ron" (1963). Spector's classic mid-1960s girl group was the Ronettes, whose towering black beehive hairdos and dark eye makeup made them the first group to have a public relations identity and a major male audience because of their smoldering, "bad-girl" sexuality. Their major hits included "Be My Baby" (1963) and "Baby I Love

You" (1963). The Shangri-Las were one of the last girl groups. The group's producer injected innovative touches, such as the sounds of crashing waves and revving motorcycles into songs about dead bikers, teenage runaways, and doomed love affairs, into their songs. According to researcher Patricia Juliana Smith, the Shangri-Las

> specialized in . . . spoken bits of conversation between group members interpolated into the song itself—against a backdrop of gothic terror displaced onto a contemporary urban, working-class setting with an ample dose of soap opera sensationalism.[5]

Memorable Shangri-la hits included "Leader of the Pack" (1964) and "I Can Never Go Home Anymore" (1965).

Phil Spector (1940–), probably the most influential producer in the history of rock, became best known for his **wall of sound** production technique. He achieved this without stereo or multitrack recording by packing the studio with musicians, running prior recordings through the studio **sound system** to fill out the sound, and using echo chambers. Spector also used some of the best songwriters of the day, as well as the best L.A. studio musicians, whom he called his "wrecking crew." He brought sophistication and complexity to record production, scoring hits from 1962 through 1966 for the Crystals, Darlene Love, the Ronettes, and the Righteous Brothers.

The Bronx-born Spector came to Los Angeles as a teenager, where he produced his first hit, "To Know Him Is to Love Him" (1958), at age eighteen. He then moved back to New York to work as an understudy for Leiber and Stoller, and there he coauthored Ben E. King's solo debut, "Spanish Harlem" (1960), as well as other hits. During the early 1960s, back in Los Angeles, he fully realized his "wall of sound" with a series of girl-group hits including the Crystals' "He's a Rebel" (1962) and "Then He Kissed Me" (1963) and the Ronettes' "Be My Baby" (1963) and "Baby I Love You" (1964). Spector's career reached its high point with the release of the blue-eyed soul-flavoured Righteous Brothers' tune "You've Lost That Lovin' Feelin'," which reached number one in 1964. He followed with "Unchained Melody" (1965) and "Ebb Tide" (1966), also by the duo.

Spector's self-inflicted downfall came in 1966 when his production of "River Deep, Mountain High" by Ike and Tina Turner, a costly and monumental pop symphony, fared only moderately well on the charts. Chagrined by what he perceived as a failure, Spector became a recluse, emerging only occasionally to work with artists such as John Lennon ("Instant Karma"), the Beatles (*Let It Be*), George Harrison (*All Things Must Pass*), and Leonard

The Ronettes (left to right): Estelle Bennet, Ronnie Bennet, and Nedra Talley in the early 1960s.

MICHAEL OCHS ARCHIVES/GETTY IMAGES

Cohen (*Death of a Ladies' Man*). Critic Mary Elizabeth Williams summarizes Spector's contributions:

> He was the man who gave the "American Bandstand" generation a darker and more sexual edge, the prodigy who inspired everyone from the Beach Boys to the Rolling Stones to Bruce Springsteen. He was the first punk, the visionary who fused the pathos of jazz with the vitality of rock 'n' roll.[6]

SURF MUSIC

A West Coast phenomenon of the early 1960s, **surf music** enjoyed two incarnations: instrumental and vocal. Although surfing had been introduced to California from Hawaii at the turn of the twentieth century, not until 1959 did the sport receive national attention thanks to the movie *Gidget,* the tale of a girl in love with two surfers. Naïve and mythic, surf music romanticized a white male teen culture of hot rods, surfing, and "honeys." It featured twangy, trebly guitars, Chuck Berry–style guitar licks, falsetto male vocal harmonies, throbbing tom toms, and topical lyrics of car and surf culture. For a brief time in the early 1960s, according to historian Timothy White,

> At Capitol, Dot, Liberty, Decca, Columbia, Tower, RCA, Warner Brothers, Mercury, and dozens of smaller labels there was a feeding frenzy afoot for anything that smelled of sea air, surf wax, and West Coast fuel exhaust.[7]

Surf music helped create the myth of the good life in Southern California and fuelled the fantasies of young listeners at great distances, reaching as far as Europe and Japan. The genre lasted briefly as a national craze until the British Invasion hit in 1964.

Instrumental surf music first became popular around 1960, when artists such as the Ventures, the Surfaris, the Chantays, and Dick Dale and His Del-Tones broke out. Flavoured by reverb-drenched guitar and rolling instrumentals designed to sound like crashing waves, the music was harmonically simple, while exploring new sonic territories. Except for the Ventures, who had a long run of popularity in Japan to sustain them, most instrumental surf artists were one-hit—or "no-hit"—wonders. Yet instrumental surf music showed its staying power with tunes such as the Ventures' "Walk—Don't Run," the Surfaris' "Wipeout," and Dick Dale and His Del-Tones' "Miserlou." Further, surf rock's influence appeared later in the music of Blondie, the Go-Go's, and U-2's lead guitarist, the Edge. The style made a splash again when Dick Dale's tune "Miserlou" was used on the soundtrack of *Pulp Fiction* (1994).

The originator of the surf guitar style, Dick Dale (1937–) was the fieriest, most technically gifted musician the genre produced. Once called the "father of heavy metal," Dale worked closely with the California-based Fender company to push the limits of electric amplification technology. He helped develop new equipment to produce thick, clearly defined tones at high volumes, and he pioneered the use of portable reverb effects, creating a signature sonic texture. An avid surfer, Dale sought ways to mimic the surging sounds of the ocean on his guitar. The exciting instrumental sound performed at surfer "stomps" in beachfront auditoriums by Dick Dale and His Del-Tones built a fan base, who helped Dale's "Let's Go Trippin'" (1961) and "Miserlou" (1962) become hits.

The Ventures were the most prominent exponents of an early 1960s instrumental guitar ensemble style often lumped with surf music. Unlike Dale, the Ventures created no startling new sound; they consolidated what other musicians had done before them, producing a clean, rhythmic, lyrical sound. The Seattle-based group had hits with "Walk—Don't Run" (1960), "Slaughter on Tenth Avenue" (1964), and "Hawaii Five-O" (1969).

Two groups wrote the history of vocal surf music: Jan and Dean and the Beach Boys. Although Jan and Dean achieved mass popularity first, the Beach Boys, propelled by the songwriting/producing genius of Brian Wilson, eclipsed them over time.

Jan Berry (1941–) and Dean Torrence (1940–) charted thirteen top-thirty singles and sold over ten million records worldwide from the late 1950s to the mid-1960s. Initially a doo-wop act, Jan and Dean became surf music converts after sharing the same bill with the nascent Beach Boys in 1962. With the writing assistance of Beach Boy Brian Wilson, they scored a number-one hit with "Surf City" (1963), followed by "Dead Man's Curve" (1964) and "Little Old Lady from Pasadena" (1964). Although not rock innovators, Jan and Dean did host the influential concert film *The T.A.M.I. Show* in 1964, which showcased James Brown, the Rolling Stones, Marvin Gaye, the Beach Boys, the Supremes, and the Miracles. Jan Berry also influenced Brian Wilson, introducing him to L.A. studio musicians and production techniques.

The essence of sixties surf music, the Beach Boys defined the California myth of surfers, hot rods, sun, beaches, and girls. Led by songwriter/producer Brian Wilson (1942–), the group wrote their own material at a time when most rock artists sang tunes provided by professional songwriters. By the mid-1960s, Wilson's increasingly sophisticated productions employed a wide range of instrumentation, styles, and sound effects rivalled only by the Beatles and their producer, George Martin. The Beach Boys were also the only American rock group who challenged the popularity of the Beatles. Made up of three brothers and a neighbourhood friend, the group originated in a coastal suburb of Los Angeles, spurred by Wilson's fascination with the jazz-inflected harmonies of such white 1950s vocal groups as the Four Freshmen. Wilson also admired Phil Spector's "wall of sound" production techniques, and often cited Spector as the single "most important influence" in his creative life.

Early Beach Boys hits included "Surfin' Safari" (1962)—virtually a remake of Chuck Berry's "Sweet Little Sixteen"—"Surfin' U.S.A." (1963)," "Fun, Fun, Fun" (1964), and "I Get Around" (1964). The group went on tour in 1964, recording the first live rock album to top the charts. After suffering a nervous breakdown, Brian Wilson quit touring and went back to the studio to produce the acclaimed "California Girls" (1965), which showcased elaborate production techniques, and the *Pet Sounds* album, which was said to influence the Beatles' *Sgt. Pepper*. Dismayed by the album's lack of commercial success, Brian returned to the studio and worked obsessively for six more months to

MICHAEL OCHS ARCHIVES/GETTY IMAGES

The Beach Boys from the cover of the single "Surfin' USA" (left to right): Brian Wilson, Mike Love, Dennis Wilson, Carl Wilson, and David Marks (Al Jardine had temporarily left the group).

produce "Good Vibrations" (1966), widely regarded as his crowning achievement. As he continued work on the next album, *SMILE*, Wilson's mental state declined, his drug use accelerated, and he ultimately destroyed many of the album's tracks. The Beach Boys—minus Wilson—continued to tour, eventually becoming reduced to the oldies circuit. Wilson made a comeback with a Grammy-winning reconstruction of *SMILE* in 2004.

CHAPTER SUMMARY

- The early 1960s brought an impressive scope of innovation in rock and soul music. Multiple-overlapping, new genres emerged in the decade.
- The 1960s began with the rise of a new breed of record producers/songwriters who made record production into an art form. In Los Angeles, the team of Mike Leiber and Jerry Stoller, along with "wall of sound" producer Phil Spector, played prominent roles in the new production style. In New York's Brill Building, rock, pop, and soul songwriters such as Carole King and Gerry Goffin, Barry Mann and Cynthia Weil, Neil Sedaka and Howard Greenfield, Bobby Darin, and Neil Diamond ushered in a brief new era of contemporary popular songwriting in the tradition of Tin Pan Alley.

- The early 1960s also saw the rise of the girl groups, including the Chantels, Shirelles, Crystals, Marvelettes, and Ronettes. The sweet and melodramatic girl-group sound mixed hooks and doo-wop harmonies. The groups were usually trios or quartets fronted by a lead singer, and many were one-hit wonders.

- Early 1960s white rock artists included the Four Seasons, Dion and the Belmonts, Paul Anka, and Neil Diamond. A plethora of new dance styles also appeared, including the Twist, Huckbuck, Stroll, Watusi, Limbo, Loco-Motion, Fly, Pony, Mashed Potatoes, Monkey, Swim, Jerk, and Hitchhike.

- Guitarist Dick Dale led the emergence of surf music, which was brought into the national spotlight by the Beach Boys, with their close harmonies and mythic California images of cars, girls, and surf.

LISTENING EXERCISE

Pop Music and Youth Markets

Listen to "Will You Love Me Tomorrow," performed by the Shirelles and composed by Carole King and Gerry Goffin. In a recent interview, Carole King explained that this classic girl-group record from 1960 comments on the ultimate taboo of teen love: "If we make love tonight will you respect me in the morning?" The lyrics also reflect the genius of Brill Building songwriters, who managed to capture essential elements of the teen experience in the early 1960s. How does the apparent young age of the performers affect the believability of the message?

HISTORICAL STUDIES AND DISCUSSION QUESTIONS

1. Girl Groups and Gender Roles

Created at a time when the nuclear family and marriage served as the paradigm of normalcy for girls and women, girl-group songs documented the sexual mores of the early 1960s. Lyrics of many of the songs focused on "the boy" as a fantasy object. Many feminist scholars now view girl-group music as a way of documenting changes in female consciousness and social conditions at a time when gender roles and relations were beginning to shift. Can you identify when those key changes were reflected in popular music?

2. The Arabic Roots of Surf Guitar

Dick Dale was born as Richard Monsour to a Lebanese father and Polish mother. Attracted to the hypnotic, minor-key Middle-Eastern melodies of his father's homeland—as well as Eastern European scales—he incorporated them into his guitar playing. Dale was among the first in any genre of popular music to use these cultural sources.

Dale also picked single notes on his guitar in a rapid staccato fashion, particularly on songs such as the Greek-origin "Miserlou," in a style he had heard an uncle use on the *oud* (an Arabic ancestor of the guitar). Can you think of any recent examples of North American popular music which incorporate Middle Eastern music?

STUDY QUESTIONS

1. Why were the 1960s a prolific era in the history of American popular music? What social, political, and commercial issues served as catalysts for the explosion of musical styles?

2. Discuss the contributions of the L.A.-based producer/songwriters and the New York–based Brill Building songwriters to early 1960s pop music. Who were important figures in this movement toward professionalism in rock and roll and R & B?

3. Who were the girl groups of the 1960s, and what was their significance?

4. What was surf music? Who were some of its major artists? What was its cultural significance?

NOTES

1. Robert Palmer, *Rock and Roll: An Unruly History* (New York: Harmony Books, 1995), 33.

2. Ibid., 35.

3. *Ibid.*

4. "Episode 2: In the Groove," in *Rock and Roll*, video recording, produced by David Espar and Hugh Thomson (South Burlington, VT: WGBH, 1995).

5. Patricia Juliana Smith, "Ask Any Girl," in *Reading Rock and Roll: Authenticity, Appropriation, and Aesthetics,* edited by Anthony DeCurtis, Kevin Dettmar, and William Richey (New York: Columbia University Press, 1999), 110.

6. Mary Elizabeth Williams, "Brilliant Careers: Top of the Pops: How Phil Spector Invented Teen Lust and Torment," http://www.salon.com/bc/1998/11/cov_10bc.html, accessed May 8, 2005.

7. Timothy White, *The Nearest Faraway Place: Brian Wilson, the Beach Boys, and the Southern California Experience* (New York: Holt, 1994), 194.

CHAPTER 6

Tin Pan Alley and the Singer-Songwriter

Over the latter half of the twentieth century, singers who wrote and performed their own songs—singer-songwriters—became prominent in North American popular music (see Chapters 18 and 19). The phenomenon ran counter to the Tin Pan Alley practices that prevailed during the first half of the century, when professional songwriters provided the material for performers. Tin Pan Alley had started to lose its grip by the early 1950s, and by the 1960s Bob Dylan was spearheading a more introspective, autobiographical, and political song style.

As one of the great Brill Building songwriters, Carole King (1942–) had already established her reputation in rock history with such 1960s hits as "Will You Still Love Me Tomorrow" and "Loco-Motion" before she started a solo career. King's album *Tapestry* (1971) went platinum, producing the hits "So Far Away" and "It's Too Late." Two other artists also had hits with songs from the album: James Taylor with "You've Got a Friend" and Aretha Franklin with "(You Make Me Feel Like) A Natural Woman."

Sonny and Cher were a middle-of-the-road pop duo with modest folk-rock roots. Sonny Bono (1935–1998) was an apprentice to producer Phil Spector when he met the teenage, big-voiced Cher (Cherilyn Sarkisian, 1946–). The pair signed with Atlantic records and had a series of hits from 1965 to 1967 that included the Dylan-penned "All I Really Want to Do," "I Got You Babe," and "The Beat Goes On." They starred in a hit television show in the early 1970s, and Cher later pursued a solo career which produced sporadic dance pop hits.

Another L.A. group, the Mamas and the Papas, plied the folk-rock genre, a blend of folk and rock music with folk-style vocals backed by guitars and drums. The vocal quartet featured lustrous vocal harmonies backed up by some of the finest studio musicians in Los Angeles. Their first album, *If You Can Believe Your Eyes and Ears* (1966), topped the American charts in a rare challenge to the Beatles with hits such as "California Dreamin'" and "Monday, Monday." Bandleader John Phillips also co-produced the Monterey Pop Festival and wrote "San Francisco (Be Sure to Wear Some Flowers in Your Hair)," the song that drew thousands of young Americans to San Francisco in the 1967 "Summer of Love."

Simon and Garfunkel (Paul Simon, 1941–) (Art Garfunkel, 1941–) became one of the most successful folk-rock acts of the mid-1960s with an appealing, close-harmony vocal style influenced by the Everly Brothers, along with intellectual, socially conscious lyrics. The duo recorded their first album, *Wednesday Morning, 3 A.M.* (1964), in an acoustic 1960s folk style but saw little success. Without the duo's knowledge, their producer, who also produced Dylan, later remixed one of the album's cuts, "The Sound of Silence," adding electric guitar, bass, and drums to produce a major folk-rock hit. Simon and Garfunkel's subsequent albums, *Sounds of Silence* and *Parsley, Sage, Rosemary, and Thyme* (1966), followed the new folk-rock style and fared much better. The artists next recorded the successful soundtrack to the 1968 movie *The Graduate*, featuring their hit song "Mrs. Robinson," followed by *Bookends* (1968) and their fourth and final album, *Bridge over Troubled Water* (1970). Although the Grammy-winning record brought them huge success, the duo parted ways.

Paul Simon continued with a successful solo career, crafting songs that exploited a wide variety of musical styles. He drew extensively from African and Latin American sources, and he stood at the forefront of the blending of world music and pop. His popular *Graceland* album (1986), recorded in South Africa, featured the vocal group Ladysmith Black Mambazo. While doing the album, Simon made a controversial move by breaking an international boycott against travel to South Africa. His explanation that his interests were musical and not political did not persuade those who viewed his work with world musicians as a form of cultural **appropriation**. Major hits for Simon as a solo act included "Mother and Child Reunion" (1972), "Me and Julio Down by the School Yard" (1972), "Loves Me Like a Rock" (1973), "Still Crazy after All These Years" (1975), and "Graceland" (1986).

James Taylor (1948–) furthered the singer-songwriter tradition with introspective songs that blended folk, rock, jazz, acoustic guitar, and an understated tenor voice. Throughout his career, Taylor balanced standards such as Stephen Foster's "Oh! Susannah" and Carole King's "You've Got a Friend" with his own material. The artist's *Sweet Baby James* (1970) album produced hits with the title song as well as "Fire and Rain" and "Country Road."

British pianist/vocalist Elton John (1947–) shared a gift for melody and a charismatic stage presence that made him one of the biggest singer-songwriter stars in rock. Billy Joel describes John's musical approach as follows:

> Elton brought back fantastic piano-based rock. Elton knows what his instrument is capable of. The piano is a percussion instrument like a drum. . . . You bang and strike a piano. . . . Elton knows exactly how to do that—he always had that rhythmic, very African, syncopated style that comes from being well versed in gospel and good old R & B.[1]

In live performance, John became known for his outrageous stage antics and wild costumes. He was also one of the earliest rock performers to acknowledge his bisexuality openly. John released his first album, which contained the hit "Your Song," in 1970. He followed this with a succession of early-1970s hits including "Rocket Man," "Goodbye Yellow Brick Road," and "Don't Let the Sun Go Down on Me." John also collaborated on the Grammy-winning music for the 1994 Disney film *The Lion King*.

RECENT SINGER-SONGWRITERS

Bruce Springsteen's (1949–) plain-spoken style and high-energy live shows made him one of the biggest stars of rock in the 1980s. Given his repertoire of songs about the lives of real people, many viewed Springsteen as the working-class voice of rock. The artist's post-9/11 album, *The Rising* (2002), was also viewed as one of the strongest pop music statements on the event. According to Jackson Browne,

> In many ways Bruce Springsteen is the embodiment of rock and roll. Combining strains of Appalachian music, rockabilly, blues and R & B, his work epitomizes rock's deepest values: desire, the need for freedom and the search to find yourself.[2]

Springsteen first rose to prominence in the 1970s, and he scored a hit with "Born to Run" in 1975. Springsteen's landmark album, *Born in the USA* (1984), catapulted him permanently into the national spotlight. By the 1990s, Springsteen had scaled back his sound to the point where his album *The Ghost of Tom Joad* (1995) won a Grammy for Best Contemporary Folk Album.

Beginning in the 1980s, a new generation of female singer-songwriters with a primarily acoustic, folk-based flavour attained national prominence. Suzanne Vega (1959–) and Tracy Chapman (1964–) surprised the music business in the late 1980s with the success of their "uncommercial" releases. Vega's quiet folk-pop sound and literate lyrics laid the groundwork for what became the trademark sound of Lilith Fair, an annual musical tour featuring a new generation of female pop artists. Vega first scored with "Luka" (1987), a song about an abused child. Chapman succeeded with her Grammy-winning folk-style debut album, *Tracy Chapman* (1988), which yielded "Fast Car."

k.d. lang (1961–) and Melissa Etheridge (1961–) became heroes to gay and lesbian communities when they both publicly came out in the early 1990s. The Canadian-born Lang established herself as a country-pop star with a smooth voice and a campy approach to country fare in two Grammy-winning albums: *Shadowland* (1988) and *Absolute Torch and Twang* (1989). Etheridge's earthier approach succeeded with the hit album *Yes I Am*, which featured the Grammy-winning song "Come to my Window" (1994). Annie Lennox (1954–) first came to light in the 1980s as the stylish, crew-cut lead singer of the British **synth-pop** group the Eurythmics. In the 1990s she embarked on a solo career that produced the well-received *Diva* (1992) and *Bare* (2003).

Sarah McLachlan (1968–), like Joni Mitchell, is known for her confessional ballads, such as "Angel," "Building a Mystery," "Adia," and "Possession." She has sold over 40 million albums worldwide, and her best-selling album to date, *Surfacing*, won eight Juno Awards and three Grammy Awards. McLachlan moved to Vancouver, British Columbia from Halifax in 1988, and recorded her first album, *Touch*, and then her subsequent breakthrough release, *Solace*, in 1991. Following the success from *Fumbling Towards Ecstasy* in 1997, McLachlan launched the highly popular *Lilith Fair* tour. The tour brought together two million people over its three-year history and raised more than $7 million for

CP / TORONTO SUN / THOMAS AOYAGI

Sarah McLachlan making a televised appearance at the Toronto MuchMusic studio in 1997.

charities. It was the most successful all-female music festival in history, one of the biggest music festivals of the 1990s.

Virtuoso pianist Tori Amos's (1963–) intimate style exemplified the dominant theme that attracted many fans to the great female singer-songwriters of the era. She wrote about issues facing young women—including her own rape—in the song "Me and a Gun" from her debut album, *Little Earthquakes* (1992). In *Boys for Pele* (1996), she further challenged pop conventions by blending multiple styles and song structures. Recent releases have included *The Beekeeper* (2005) and *American Doll Posse* (2007).

Ani DiFranco (1970–) became a thorn in the side of the music industry when she refused to sign with a major label and instead founded her own, amassing sales of over two million. Her well-regarded albums included *Out of Range* (1994), *Not a Pretty Girl* (1995), and *So Much Shouting, So Much Laughter* (2002). DiFranco built a following with a series of successful releases in the 1990s featuring an eclectic punk-funk-folk style.

SOFT ROCK

Soft rock—also referred to as *lite rock, mellow rock,* or *adult contemporary*—was a smooth, melodic style popular from the 1960s through the 1980s that met the casual listener's need for a pleasant, undemanding listening experience. The soft-rock sound typically consisted of slow-tempo, melodic songs with vocal harmonies performed over simple rhythmic grooves.

The L.A.-based songwriting team of Burt Bacharach (1928–) and Hal David (1921–) retained a bit of the flavour of Tin Pan Alley while scoring a series of definitive soft-rock hits in the 1960s with songs performed by Dionne Warwick (1940–), including "Walk on By," "Do You Know the Way to San Jose," and "This Girl's in Love with You." Warwick's soulful yet sparse vocal style endowed Bacharach's deceptively simple melodies with an appealing presence.

The Tijuana Brass was an instrumental soft-rock group led by trumpeter and future record-industry mogul Herb Alpert (1935–). The band scored a string of hits, including "The Lonely Bull" (1962) and "A Taste of Honey" (1965), with an Americanized pop mariachi sound that blended two trumpets playing Spanish-inflected melodies in a smooth, Bacharach style over a soft-rock rhythm section. The group's success led to the formation of A & M records, which went on to become the country's largest independent record label.

The Grammy-winning Carpenters, the sibling duo of Karen (1950–1983) and Richard (1946–) Carpenter, dominated soft rock in the 1970s. Karen's compelling alto voice and Richard's lush arrangements maintained the duo's place at the top of the charts until Karen's death from anorexia in 1983. According to critic Sue Cummings, "Karen may have been revered in her musicians' world as a great naïve genius, but her voice sounded worldly to an eight-year-old. . . . She was like a knowledgeable big sister intoning the esoteric mysteries of romance."[3] Hits included Bacharach's "Close to You" (1970) and "We've Only Just Begun" (1970), the Oscar-winning "For All We Know" (1971), "Rainy Days and Mondays" (1971), and "Superstar" (1971). Although scorned by rock purists, the Carpenters' wholesome, polished sound struck an appealing chord with many listeners. Karen Carpenter's work was reevaluated in a positive light in later years by such artists as Madonna, k.d. lang, Chrissie Hynde, and Sheryl Crow.

First formed in 1967 as part of the second wave of British Invasion bands, Fleetwood Mac was a perennially popular group that performed in a melodic pop-rock style, with a clean, accessible sound which typified the nascent internationalism of the idiom. Inspired by the Beatles and the Beach Boys Beatles, the group hit its stride in the mid-1970s with the success of a self-titled album that yielded "Landslide" (1975), later covered by the Dixie Chicks in 2002. Turmoil and multiple permutations in romantic relationships among group members served as the source of material for the group's next record, the Grammy-winning *Rumours* (1977), which yielded "Go Your Own Way," "Dreams," and "Don't Stop."

CHAPTER SUMMARY

- The singer-songwriter tradition that began in the 1970s went in multiple stylistic directions. The 1980s and 1990s welcomed a new generation of powerful female voices to the tradition.

- The 1970s saw the soft-rock sounds of the Carpenters and others, who were heavily influenced by the late-1960s work of Burt Bacharach and Dionne Warwick. Fleetwood Mac subsequently perfected an appealing blend of country, pop, rock, and blues to become one of the most popular bands of the late 1970s.

LISTENING EXERCISES

1. Creative Tourism and World Music

The 1965 Beatles release of "Norwegian Wood," which includes George Harrison's Ravi Shankar-inspired sitar playing, represented the leading edge of a growing interest in non-Western music. Though many Western pop musicians followed Harrison into this creative arena, few attained the commercial success that Paul Simon achieved with his 1986 release of *Graceland. Graceland* features an eclectic mixture of musical styles, including the vocal group Ladysmith Black Mambazo, the Ghanaian master drummer Okerema Asante, and American influences featuring *zydeco* and *cajunto*. While the album drew worldwide attention to the music of South Africa, Simon faced numerous accusations that he misappropriated and exploited the music and musicians for personal gain. While there is perhaps a grain of truth to this claim, Simon's effort, however, under-lines the perils that await any artist who crosses culturally demar-cated boundaries of race, class and ethnicity to create a new musical hybrid. Listen to *Graceland,* and to similar releases by artists like Ry Cooder and John McLaughlin, and discuss the pros and cons of this kind of creative activity.

2. Sexism and the Music Industry

Since its arrival in the 1950s, rock and roll has been overwhelmingly dominated by male musicians, male industry functionaries, and a male press corps. Not surprisingly, sexism – defined as the systematic dis-crimination and degradation of women – found its way into almost all quarters of the culture. The institutionalization of sexist values built up almost insurmountable obstacles to females who wished to become involved in any phase of the music business. Paradoxically, the industry that renders women as absent or insignificant, is also the same industry that invites the full participation female fans because the success of many (male) bands depend upon their appeal to this cohort. The arrival of the Folk Revival in the 1960s, however, saw a growing number of female singer-songwriters, such as Joni Mitchell, Buffy Sainte-Marie, Laura Nero, Carole King, and Carly Simon, who rightfully staked out claims to practise and make a living from their art. While Mitchell's confessional songwriting style influenced scores of male and female artists, the radi-calized feminist perspective did not fully emerge until the arrival of Patti Smith in the 1970s. Listen to Joni Mitchell's *Blue* (1971), Patti Smith's *Horses* (1975), and Tori Amos' *The Beekeeper* (2004) and examine the lyrical content and performance style of each album as a barometer of the expanding expressive range which celebrates a uniquely female perspective.

HISTORICAL STUDIES AND DISCUSSION QUESTION

Artistic Growth versus Commercial Success

Some popular music performers have experimented and grown artistically, only to disappoint their original fans. Such was the case with Joni Mitchell and Neil Young. Beginning in the 1960s, as many singer-songwriters grew unwilling to accept the demands of commercial conformity, they evolved in new directions, often leaving fans to wonder what had happened to the "old" versions of their favourite artists. In one particularly perplexing challenge to artistic growth, Neil Young was sued by his own record label for recording "unrepresentative albums"—in other words, for "not sounding like Neil Young." Have you ever attended a concert where your favourite performer has disappointed you by neglecting your favourite song or by performing in an unfamiliar new style? On the other hand, how will musicians grow as artists if they do not receive support in their experiments with the new and unfamiliar? Is artistic autonomy possible to achieve in the commercial environment of popular music?

STUDY QUESTIONS

1. How did the evolution of rock in the early 1970s draw on the music of the 1960s? What were the major styles and bands to emerge in this era? Which styles and artists had the longest-lasting impact on rock?

2. How did the singer-songwriter tradition evolve over three decades from its inception in the 1970s? Discuss dominant figures and their musical contributions.

3. Who were the central artists of soft rock? Why was the style so popular in the 1970s? Is there an equivalent music style today?

4. Is Canada's robust singer-songwriter culture a significant attribute of the country's cultural identity?

NOTES

1. Billy Joel, "Elton John," *Rolling Stone,* April 15, 2004, 140.
2. Jackson Browne, "Bruce Springsteen," *Rolling Stone,* April 15, 2004, 102.
3. Sue Cummings, "Karen Carpenter," in *Trouble Girls: The Rolling Stone Book of Women in Rock,* edited by Barbara O'Dair (New York: Random House, 1997), 241.

CHAPTER 7

Gospel Sounds and Popular Music

SACRED ROOTS: SPIRITUALS AND EARLY GOSPEL MUSIC

The earliest Christian religious music developed by African Americans in the eighteenth and nineteenth centuries took the form of **spirituals** (see Chapter 10), which were used to construct community, provide hope for a better life, offer metaphors of liberation, and preserve African cultural memory. Their development resulted from an exchange of musical styles between whites and blacks. Originally relying on Protestant hymns by English composers, the African American church began to develop its own music by publishing its first hymnal in 1801. Further significant innovation took place at **camp meetings**, which formed a part of the Second Awakening revival movement of the early nineteenth century. Outside the confines of a formal church setting, traditional African melodic concepts blended easily with the simple hymn melodies to energize and transform the music. In the 1870s, the Fisk Jubilee Singers, a group from all black Fisk University in Nashville, first introduced spirituals to the world. They began touring the country in 1871, presenting concerts devoted exclusively to African American religious music. These concerts provided one of the first opportunities for mainstream audiences to hear serious African American music, as opposed to minstrel songs.

The latter part of the nineteenth century witnessed the development of a new style called **gospel**. While spirituals were born in rural camp meetings, gospel evolved in urban settings. Early gospel songwriters blended spirituals with popular Tin Pan Alley styles and instrumentation. This new genre began to take off in the early twentieth century, particularly in the churches of holiness, sanctified, and Pentecostal sects. Many of these groups employed African traditions as well as contemporary popular music styles and instruments, though at first mainstream African American denominations disapproved of the energy and rhythmic abandon of the new style.

The first important gospel hymn writer, Philadelphian Charles Tindley (1851–1933), published a popular collection of his music in 1916, and in 1921 the largest black church denomination embraced the style by publishing a song collection called *Gospel Pearls*. Chicago became the centre for the development of the genre in the 1920s, and much of that development came from pianist/composer Thomas A. Dorsey (1899–1993), the "father of gospel music." Born in Georgia to a religious family, Dorsey took a detour at a young age to work with some of the greatest blues artists of the era, including singer "Ma" Rainey. Known as "Georgia Tom" in the blues world, he teamed with Chicago blues great Tampa Red to produce such earthy blues hits as "It's Tight Like That" (1928). Dorsey also began to write gospel songs while he was still an active blues pianist and writer. As he put it, "If I could get into the gospel songs the feeling and the pathos and the moans and the blues, that [would get] me over."[1] During the Depression, Dorsey moved into the gospel field exclusively and began to innovate rapidly, bringing to bear his experience from the pop music world. He organized the first female vocal gospel quartet in history, established the world's first gospel choruses in Atlanta and Chicago, set up a national gospel choral organization, and formed his own gospel music publishing house. Ultimately Dorsey composed close to a thousand gospel songs, including the beloved "Precious Lord, Take My Hand" (translated into over fifty languages) and "There'll Be Peace in the Valley."

By the end of the 1930s, gospel was an established commercial genre, with professional gospel performers touring the church-concert circuit. Gospel was also presented in for-profit venues, and Thomas Dorsey pioneered gospel competitions, calling them "battles of song" and charging an admission fee. The competitions manifested the African American musical tradition of the **cutting contest**, in which musicians competed to best one another, and the events became important in the gospel world. Independent record companies also recognized gospel as a profitable commodity, and many of the same labels that marketed race records also kept major rosters of gospel artists. In 1938 "Sister" Rosetta Tharp (1921–1973) took gospel into a **secular** setting for the first time: She performed with bandleader Cab Calloway in a show at the Cotton Club in New York, accompanying herself on guitar. The legendary "Spirituals to Swing" concert at Carnegie Hall, a retrospective of African American musical heritage, also featured gospel that year.

By the mid-twentieth century, three distinct categories of gospel performance had arisen: soloists, gospel quartets, and gospel choruses. Important soloists included Mahalia Jackson, Clara Ward, Alex Bradford, Shirley Caesar, and James Cleveland. Several of these performers also led their own vocal ensembles, and Caesar and Cleveland were ordained pastors. Gospel vocal styles, including vocal turns and embellishments called **melismas**, influenced soul, R & B, and eventually most U.S. pop vocal styles.

MICHAEL OCHS ARCHIVES/GETTY IMAGES

Legendary gospel singer Mahalia Jackson.

Mahalia Jackson (1911–1972) was probably more responsible than any other performer for bringing gospel to the attention of mainstream audiences. Jackson began recording regularly in 1946, and she had her best-known hit, "Move on up a Little Higher," in 1947. She toured extensively in the United States and abroad and had her own weekly network radio show beginning in 1954. Other appearances included the *Ed Sullivan Show*, the Newport Jazz Festival, and the 1961 inauguration of President John Kennedy. In her most moving performance, Jackson sang just before Martin Luther King, Jr., delivered his famous "I Have a Dream Speech" at the civil rights march on Washington in 1963. Jazz critic Marshall Stearns once described audience reaction to a 1959 Jackson performance:

> Gentle old ladies on all sides start to "flip" like popcorn over a hot stove. Directly in front, an angular woman springs to her feet, raises her arms rigidly on high, and dances down the aisle shouting, "Sweet Jesus!" A white-clad nurse, one of thirty in attendance, does her best to quiet her. This is religious possession, as old as Africa itself.[2]

Dubbed the "crown prince of gospel," James Cleveland (1931–1991) was a hallmark vocal performer and one of the most gifted composers of his generation, influencing many artists, including Billy Preston and Aretha Franklin. Starting off as a gospel quartet member, he founded the first of several groups in 1959 and became a leading gospel figure in the 1960s. Major recordings included *The Love of God* and *Peace, Be Still*. Cleveland also became an ordained minister and founded an influential church in Los Angeles.

Gospel vocal quartets also influenced North American popular music heavily, and many artists in the soul and R & B world got their start in such groups. The style shaped 1950s doo-wop (see Chapter 10), the subsequent R & B vocal group stylings of groups such as the Temptations, the O'Jays, and Boyz II Men, as well as the white boy bands of the 1990s such as 'N Sync. The quartets, which were usually male, sang a cappella with barbershop harmony, and they added percussive effects by snapping their fingers and slapping their thighs in the African American tradition of **patting juba**. The quartets generally fell into two distinct styles: "sweet" gospel—characterized by close harmony, precise attacks and releases, and understated rhythm—and "hard" gospel, characterized by emotive singing, preaching delivery, physical gestures, and strong rhythms. Major sweet gospel groups included the Dixie Hummingbirds, the Soul Stirrers, and the Swan Silvertones. Well-known hard gospel groups included the Blind Boys of Alabama, the Five Blind Boys of Mississippi, and the Mighty Clouds of Joy. Popular R & B or soul figures with roots in gospel quartets included Sam Cooke (the Soul Stirrers), Johnnie Taylor (the Soul Stirrers), Bobby Womack (the Womack Brothers), Lou Rawls (the Pilgrim Travelers), Wilson Pickett (the Violinaires), and the Isley Brothers.

An influential gospel keyboard accompaniment style rooted in ragtime, barrelhouse, and Protestant hymns became established in the middle part of the twentieth century, further adding to the characteristic gospel sound. By the 1960s, the keyboard style was fully developed and had begun to permeate American popular music. The approach featured heavy **chords** played at the centre of the keyboard, rolling bass and punctuated riffs in the upper register.

Gospel pianists also improvised in a call and response format, filling open spaces in songs or sermons. Major gospel keyboard stylists included Arizona Dranes, Clara Ward, James Cleveland, Jessy Dixon, and Alex Bradford. The "queen of soul," Aretha Franklin, was also a fine gospel pianist, frequently accompanying herself in gospel and soul performances.

Skillful gospel keyboardists frequently integrated both piano and organ. The Hammond B-3 organ, first introduced to gospel in 1939, brought percussive effects and reverberating crescendos into the church. R & B and jazz performers eventually adopted the organ after its introduction through gospel music. Important gospel organ innovators included Alfred Bolden and Billy Preston, who also worked with the Beatles and had his own pop recordings in the 1970s.

By the 1960s, gospel had become big business; major artists filled large venues, performance fees rose exponentially, and hits such as "O Happy Day" (1969), recorded by Edwin Hawkins with a gospel chorus, and the funky gospel/soul tune "I'll Take You There" (1972) by the Staples Singers received major airplay. Musical changes accelerated in the 1990s as younger performers began to explore blending secular genres with gospel. Artists such as the Winans, Take 6, and Kirk Franklin explored pop-gospel boundaries and created fusions of gospel with R & B, hip-hop, and jazz. Traditionalists such as Shirley Caesar, however, remained dedicated to the core of gospel tradition. Both types of artists sought to carry on the legacy of Thomas A. Dorsey, who was himself the first pop-gospel crossover artist.

By the late 1950s, black and white pop music had become resegregated for the most part, and the rock and roll package tours that formerly featured many black artists had become primarily white. Nonetheless, important black artists continued to cross over, bringing the sounds of black gospel and vocal group music into the rock mainstream and laying the basis for soul music.

Sam Cooke (1931–1964), one of the most popular and influential black singers of the late 1950s, successfully blended gospel and pop. With his clear, sensual tenor voice, Cooke pioneered what would later be called soul music. He was also one of the first black artists to write his own songs and control his recording career by establishing a record label and music publishing company. Cooke's vocal influence would appear in the work of artists as diverse as Otis Redding, Rod Stewart, and Al Green. The son of a Chicago minister, Cooke began his career in black gospel music; by 1950 he was lead singer of the Soul Stirrers, one of the most influential gospel quartets of the era. In 1956 he crossed over to secular music and scored hits with "You Send Me," "Chain Gang," "Twistin' the Night Away," "Cupid," and "Having a Party." According to critic Robert Palmer, "Sam Cooke was drop-dead, supper-club cool at watering holes like the Copa; for r&r/r&b gigs . . . the jacket,

MICHAEL OCHS ARCHIVES/GETTY IMAGES

Smooth and soulful crooner Sam Cooke.

tie, and cuff links came off and the sexy soul man took charge."[3] Cooke launched his own record label and music publishing house in 1961, but his promising career was brought to a premature end by gunfire in 1964.

One of the premier black vocalists of the late 1950s and early 1960s, Jackie Wilson (1934–1984) effortlessly combined the raw style of James Brown with the polished, gospel-pop of Sam Cooke. Later emulated by Michael Jackson, his stage moves were legendary, and his ringing vocal style ranged from up-tempo rock to ballads. As Robert Palmer put it, "Jackie Wilson squeezed every drop of emotion out of his ballads and punctuated his up-tempo vocal gymnastics with faultless splits, spins, and knee-drops."[4] After his discovery in 1951 by Johnny Otis, the Detroit native joined the Dominoes. He went solo in 1956 to score hits such as "Lonely Teardrops" (1958), "Baby Workout" (1963), and "(Your Love Keeps Lifting Me) Higher and Higher" (1966). Wilson's career was eventually eclipsed by soul music in the 1960s.

Vocalist/keyboardist Ray Charles (1930–2004) brought together the energy of black gospel music, the secular lyrics of the blues and country, and the sophistication of big band jazz in a hybrid that became enormously popular with both black and white audiences in the late 1950s and early 1960s. Charles's throaty, gospel-based vocal style influenced virtually all of the soul singers of the 1960s, as well as many English rockers, including Mick Jagger, Eric Burdon, and Joe Cocker. Charles introduced the electric piano to the rock and jazz world with his first major pop hit, "What'd I Say" (1959), a tune that embodied the classic call and response of the African American church. The song was later covered by Elvis Presley, Jerry Lee Lewis, and Bobby Darin. Charles was also the first black artist to score hits in the country field, and he was well regarded in the jazz world.

MICHAEL OCHS ARCHIVES/GETTY IMAGES

Ray Charles performing with the Raylettes, backed by his big band in the 1966 movie *Blues for Lovers*.

Charles started his career in the early 1950s as a crooner in the blues style of Nat "King" Cole and Charles Brown, but he began infusing secular songs with gospel sounds in the mid-1950s with tunes such as "I Got a Woman" (1955) and "Hallelujah, I Love Her So." He followed "What'd I Say" with a Tin Pan Alley ballad ("Georgia on My Mind"), as well as up-tempo R & B hits ("Hit the Road Jack" and "Unchain My Heart"). In the early 1960s, he formed his own record and music-publishing companies and released a series of crossover country ballad smashes that included "I Can't Stop Loving You" and "Your Cheatin' Heart." Charles continued to record throughout the rest of the twentieth century, retaining control over most of his music, and he was the subject of the Oscar-winning 2004 film *Ray*.

SOUL MUSIC

When rock was developing in the 1950s, the term R & B seemed sufficient to describe the new blues-based music being produced by black and white artists. Rock, however, had started to differentiate from R & B by the end of the decade, so that by the early 1960s most black-oriented music had come to be known as **soul music**. The soul sound was a hybrid of gospel styles and secular music, as vocalist Cissy Houston recalled,

> You started to hear gospel in black popular music in the mid-fifties because that's what was going on in black life. Everybody was getting crazy that R & B was making it big, crossing over for whites and all. But gospel stations were just as exciting to listen to. Gospel was making folks jump in a big, big way.[5]

From the late 1950s through the early 1960s, artists increasingly used gospel vocal styles as a source of excitement and intense emotion. By the mid-1960s, the soul style became fully realized, with musical arrangements consciously constructed to complement the sound.

While Ray Charles, Sam Cooke, and Jackie Wilson had laid the groundwork of soul in the late 1950s, other important black artists also contributed to the style's early development. Ben E. King (1938–), formerly the lead singer of the Drifters, made R & B sophisticated and accessible to mainstream pop audiences with his smooth baritone voice and clear enunciation. King's hits, "Spanish Harlem" (1961), "Stand by Me" (1961), and "Don't Play That Song (You Lied)" (1962), were forerunners of the Motown sound.

Admired for her gritty, precise, and penetrating voice, Dinah Washington (1924–1963) felt equally at home in R & B, jazz, and pop, and she influenced many subsequent R & B and jazz artists, including Nancy Wilson and Esther Phillips. Although already a major R & B star in the late 1940s and 1950s, Washington crossed over to the pop charts with "What a Diff'rence a Day Makes" (1959), "Baby (You've Got What It Takes)" (1960), and "This Bitter Earth" (1960).

Ike (1931–2007) and Tina Turner (1939–) first came on the R & B and pop scene in the late 1950s. Prior to forming the Ike and Tina Turner Revue, Turner was an influential artist and producer on the Memphis R & B scene who had led the backup band on the original rock classic, "Rocket 88" (1951). The Turners, who had one of the most potent live R & B acts before a publicized breakup in the mid-1970s, generated the hits "A Fool in Love" (1960) and "River Deep—Mountain High" (1966). After some restyling in response to pop trends of the late 1960s, they had crossover hits with covers of the Beatles' "Come Together" (1970), Sly Stone's "I Want to Take You Higher" (1970), and Creedence Clearwater's "Proud Mary" (1971). When Tina Turner split from her increasingly abusive husband, she recast herself as a mainstream rocker in the 1980s with hits such as "What's Love Got to Do with It" (1984) and "Private Dancer" (1985). A film, also called *What's Love Got to Do with It* (1999), was later made of Tina Turner's life.

The Impressions and leader/songwriter Curtis Mayfield (1942–1999) exemplified the rich late doo-wop/early soul scene of Chicago in the 1960s. The Impressions launched the careers of soul legend Jerry Butler as well as Curtis Mayfield. Sweet harmonies, Mayfield's guitar, occasional Latin rhythms, and the evolving use of civil rights themes marked the Impressions' style. Hits included "For Your Precious Love" (1958), "Gypsy Woman" (1961), "Keep on Pushing" (1964), "Amen" (1964), and "People Get Ready" (1965). After Mayfield left the group in the early 1970s, he scored again with the soundtrack to the blaxploitation film *Superfly* (1972) and other well-received projects.

Tina Turner "steppin' out" sometime in the 1980s.

© NEAL PRESTON/CORBIS

Two artists stood out in the development of soul: James Brown and Aretha Franklin. Though they came from different backgrounds and produced divergent sounds, both embodied the essence of the music.

James Brown (1928–2006) was like a cat with at least nine lives. Despite repeated brushes with the law, the "Hardest Working Man in Show Business" excelled for most of his seven decades as a performer, dancer, composer, bandleader, businessman, and musical visionary. Critic Robert Palmer describes Brown in performance:

> His band locks into a chopping rhythm riff and Brown strides purposefully from the wings. . . . His head jerks to the beat, his hips shimmy, and suddenly he's snaking across the stage on one foot, his other leg windmilling along with his long, limber arms, he does a split, erupts into a pirouette, whirls like a dervish, and ends up at the microphone just in time to shriek "bayba-a-a-ay."[6]

The artist embodied the soul explosion, and then pioneered funk—an entire new style—almost single-handedly. Brown continued to tour into the 2000s

© FRANK DRIGGS COLLECTION/GETTY IMAGES

The godfather of soul, James Brown, in 1968.

with his twenty-piece funk band of two drummers, two bassists, three guitarists, several horn players, and numerous singers and dancers. Having learned gospel while imprisoned as a youth, the Georgia-born artist formed a band called the Famous Flames after his release. Brown's first hit, "Please, Please, Please" (1956), remained a signature tune throughout his career. He followed up with "Think" (1960) and "Night Train" (1962). With a tightly rehearsed and choreographed show polished to perfection, he played to sellout audiences in African American communities across the country in the early 1960s, and his 1963 recording *Live at the Apollo* firmly established him as a major artist.

Brown made music history with the release of the seminal "Papa's Got a Brand New Bag" in 1965. Here, Brown threw away traditional song structure to focus on the groove—the entire song was an extended vamp, with few chord changes and little melody. The song also featured a new guitar sound made by choking the guitar neck and strumming percussively to produce a sound Brown called "chank." A highly syncopated and percussive bass grounded the tune with a powerful pulse, and the drums locked in tightly with the bass. Brown realized that he had found something powerful:

> I had discovered that my strength was not in the horns, it was in the rhythm. I was hearing everything, even the guitars, like they were drums. . . . Later on they said it was the beginning of funk. I just thought of it as where my music was going.[7]

Brown followed up with "Cold Sweat" (1967). According to Atlantic Records producer Jerry Wexler, "'Cold Sweat' deeply affected the musicians I knew. It just freaked them out. For a time, no one could get a handle on what to do next."[8] By 1968 Brown had shifted to civil rights themes with "Say It Loud I'm Black and I'm Proud," and he was credited with helping quell riots after the assassination of Martin Luther King, Jr. He continued to make cutting-edge dance music into the 1970s with a funky rhythm section that included bassist Bootsie Collins: "Mother Popcorn" (1969), "Get Up (I Feel Like Being a) Sex Machine" (1970), "Super Bad" (1971), and "The Payback" (1974). Along the way he shifted record labels in a deal that gave him creative control and allowed him to bring his past catalogue of recordings to the new label.

Despite recurring legal problems, Brown continued to tour and record into the 2000s, periodically surfacing in films, hip-hop samples, and other facets of popular culture. He pioneered two major musical genres—soul and funk—and his single-minded artistic vision and riveting performance style made him a legend. Brown's accomplishments as an American popular music innovator placed him alongside giants such as Louis Armstrong, Duke Ellington, and the Beatles in pop music history.

Aretha Franklin (1942–) was the most exciting and influential female soul singer of the 1960s. Her gospel roots ran deep: While still a teenager, she began her performing career touring with the gospel troupe of her father, the Reverend C. L. Franklin. According to Franklin, "The best, the greatest gospel singers passed through our house in Detroit. Sometimes they stayed with us. James Cleveland lived with us for a time, and it was James who taught me to play the piano by ear."[9] Vocalists Mahalia Jackson and Clara Ward were also frequent visitors, and they served as mentors to the young Franklin.

When Franklin signed with Columbia Records in 1960, the label toned down her powerful voice, banished her soulful gospel piano playing, and cast her as a jazzy, Tin Pan Alley–style vocalist. It was not a good match: After nine albums, all Columbia had to show was a minor Franklin hit with the Al Jolson standard, "Rock-A-Bye Your Baby with a Dixie Melody." The young vocalist became confused and depressed, but once Columbia released her in 1966, Atlantic Records immediately signed her. Within a year, Franklin had become the most successful singer in the nation. Her 1967 recordings "I Never Loved a Man (the Way I Love You)" and "Do Right Woman—Do Right Man" were immediate hits, and the album that contained them, *Lady Soul,* also produced the soul classics "Dr. Feelgood" and "Respect." Franklin's version of "Respect," written by Otis Redding, made the tune a feminist anthem and turned the girl-group sound on its head with strong vocals and a powerful female gospel trio for backup. Saxophonist King Curtis described how Franklin made songs her own: "When Aretha records a tune she kills a copyright. Because once she's worked out the way to do it. . . . it's damn sure you're not going to be able to improve on how she's done it, her way."[10] Franklin also recorded "(You Make Me Feel Like) A Natural Woman," "Chain of Fools," and "Think" in the same period. Producer Jerry Wexler describes her musicianship:

> I needed Aretha to finish "Do Right"—in a hurry. . . . She came to the studio . . . and made a miracle. She overdubbed two discrete keyboard parts, first playing piano, then organ; she and her sisters hemstitched the seamless background harmonies; and when she added her glorious lead vocal, the result was perfection.[11]

Ultimately, Franklin scored ten major hits in an eighteen-month span between early 1967 and late 1968, as well as a steady stream of hits for the next five years. She was probably the first soul artist to conceive of her albums as whole, thematically unified pieces of work, and they were huge sellers. Her choice of material could also be interesting and eclectic, encompassing originals and gospel, blues, pop, and rock covers of the Beatles ("Eleanor Rigby"), the Band ("The Weight"), Simon and Garfunkel ("Bridge over Troubled Water"), Stephen Stills ("Love the One You're With"), Elton John ("Border Song"), Sam Cooke ("You Send Me"), and Ben E. King ("Spanish Harlem"). Franklin's commercial and artistic success continued

An early publicity shot of the queen of soul, Aretha Franklin.

© BETTMANN/CORBIS

into the early 1970s, when she produced two of her most respected and earthiest albums: *Live at Fillmore West,* which expanded her popularity with a young white audience and reflected Fillmore impresario Bill Graham's philosophy of blending styles in the acts he booked, and *Amazing Grace,* a double album, recorded with James Cleveland and the Southern California Community Choir, that reconnected her to her gospel roots.

During her years of preeminence, 1967–1970, Aretha Franklin found more success than virtually any other black pop artist had. She achieved phenomenal record sales, critical praise, and massive support from both black and white audiences. Having completed the transition from gospel to soul, Franklin symbolized the essence of the new genre. According to producer Jerry Wexler,

> "Genius" is the word. Clearly Aretha was continuing what Ray Charles had begun—the secularization of gospel, turning church rhythms, church patterns, and especially church feelings into personalized love songs.[12]

MOTOWN

Motown in its mid-1960s musical heyday knew no peers in African American popular music: It was the most successful record label and publishing house in the history of soul. At a time when most independent record labels had died out, Motown marketed a mass-produced pop sound that was drenched in black tradition, and Motown hits of the 1960s revolutionized American popular music. Much of the label's success came about because of the company's founder, Berry Gordy, Jr. A former boxer and record-store owner, he synthesized the musical lessons of the previous decade, taking ideas from the Brill Building, independent labels, doo-wop stylists, and girl groups. For more than a decade, Gordy and his talented artists, songwriters, **arrangers**, and musicians embodied the company's slogan: "The Sound of Young America." According to vocalist/songwriter Smokey Robinson,

> Berry wanted to make crossover music. Crossover at that time meant that white people would buy your records. Berry's concept in starting Motown was to make music with a funky beat and great stories that would crossover, that would *not* be blues. And that's what we did.[13]

Gordy started his musical career in the 1950s as a songwriter in Detroit looking to capitalize on the developing R & B scene. Early hits that he produced included Marv Johnson's "You've Got What It Takes" (1960) and Barrett

Strong's classic "Money (That's What I Want)" (1960). These successes enabled Gordy to form the Tamla label in 1960, and he immediately scored a hit with "Shop Around" written by Smokey Robinson, who was then a member of the Miracles vocal group. Gordy brought him into the company's management, and Robinson proved to be a superb songwriter responsible for an impressive range of Motown hits over the years. Singer-songwriter Bob Dylan once described Robinson as "one of America's greatest poets."[14]

Gordy's studio, literally a converted bungalow, teemed with aspiring artists, including Marvin Gaye, Mary Wells, and the Marvelettes. Gordy expanded his stable of writer-producers by forming the prolific team of Lamont Dozier and Brian and Eddie Holland. Starting with "Heat Wave" (1963) by Martha and the Vandellas, the team systematized Gordy's production techniques and amassed eighteen top-twenty hits in three years. The signature sound of Holland-Dozier-Holland—and Motown—reached its pinnacle in hits such as the Four Tops' "Reach Out, I'll Be There" (1966) and the Supremes' "You Can't Hurry Love" (1966). Motown's sound also owed much to the label's house band, the Funk Brothers, which featured bassist James Jamerson. According to historian Robert Palmer,

> Everyone at Motown . . . agreed that James Jamerson . . . was the band's real linchpin, its most consistently creative player. The other musicians might be given specific figures to play; Jamerson, given a chord sheet for the song and perhaps a run-through with voice and piano, created his own parts, and in the process became the most influential bassist of the 60s.[15]

Motown was not just about the sound—it was also about Gordy's goal of breaking into the mainstream market. To do this, he admitted that he adopted an assembly-line approach: "I worked on the Ford assembly line, and I thought, 'Why can't we do that with the creative process?' You know, the writing, the producing, the artist development."[16] He turned Motown into a "finishing school" with classes in choreography, music theory, and social graces. He fostered competition among the producers and songwriters as well, much as had been done in the Brill Building, pressuring writers to produce the next hit for the Temptations or the Supremes. Rifts appeared in the Motown family near the end of the 1960s as producers and artists jumped ship over monetary and creative disputes. Major artists such as Marvin Gaye and Stevie Wonder also negotiated new contracts that gave them artistic control, and Motown moved its headquarters from Detroit to Los Angeles. The old Motown system dissolved, acts drifted away, and Gordy sold his company to MCA in 1988. Jerry Wexler of Atlantic Records sums up Gordy's accomplishments:

> Berry Gordy and Motown found something that we [at Atlantic Records] didn't or couldn't do. . . . He went with his version of black music directly to the white teenage buyer. Motown has left its impact on people in a way that no other music has done.[17]

Throughout its heyday, Motown was blessed with a talented roster of artists. Although Berry Gordy dictated the direction of the sound, and the producers and the house band provided material and instrumental backup, the individual vocalists ultimately conveyed the Motown image, producing an impressive array of hits during the 1960s.

Marvin Gaye (1939–1984) served as one of soul music's most charismatic and enigmatic figures, as well as one of its most important stylists. With a career spanning the history of R & B, from 1950s doo-wop to 1980s dance music, Gaye embodied the Motown sound with some of the most enduring hits of the 1960s and then broadened the boundaries of soul in the 1970s with an intensely personal and political form of expression. The gospel-trained artist scored hits throughout the 1960s such as "Pride and Joy" (1963)," "How Sweet It Is to Be Loved by You" (1965), "Ain't That Peculiar" (1965), and "I Heard It through the Grapevine" (1968). He also joined vocalist Tammi Terrell for such hits as "Ain't No Mountain High Enough" (1967) and "Ain't Nothing Like the Real Thing" (1968). Gaye demanded and received an unprecedented level of artistic control for his 1971 *What's Going On* album—a bold musical experiment filled with social commentary and prophetic language. The best-selling album Motown had ever released, it compared favourably with the Beatles' *Sgt. Pepper,* yielding hits such as "What's Going On," "Mercy, Mercy Me (The Ecology)," and "Inner City Blues (Make Me Wanna Holler)." Gaye subsequently cut loose with a sensual masterpiece, *Let's Get It On* (1973), and later followed the same vein with "Got to Give It Up" (1977) and "Sexual Healing" (1982).

Motown's most successful female group, the Supremes, scored ten major hits between 1964 and 1967, briefly rivalling the Beatles. With their sophisticated though sometimes formulaic sound, they embodied Berry Gordy's dream of crossover success. Early hits included "Where Did Our Love Go?" (1964), "Baby Love" (1964), "Stop! In the Name of Love" (1965), and "I Hear a Symphony" (1965). They toured Europe in 1965 and achieved Gordy's goal of performing in top U.S. nightclubs such as New York's Copa Cabana. As the group's lead singer, Diana Ross (1944–), started to receive top billing, the hits kept coming: "You Keep Me Hangin' On" (1966), "Love Child" (1968), and "Someday We'll Be Together" (1969). When Ross left the Supremes in 1970 to pursue a solo career, Gordy shifted focus to promote her as a multimedia star. Ross had several hit songs ("Ain't No Mountain High Enough," 1970; "Touch Me in the Morning," 1973; "Do You Know Where You're Going To," 1975), acted in three films, and performed on Broadway. Ross's star began to fade in the late 1980s, however, and as critic Diane Cardwell puts it,

> Today she is something of a camp artifact, an icon of fabulous bitchiness and Vegas glitz rather than the serious recording artist and vibrant performer she once was. . . . It is a universal irony of icons: to freeze in the very image they create.[18]

The Temptations were Motown's most popular and longest-lasting male vocal group. The quintet featured two lead singers and precise onstage dance routines. Despite personnel changes, they maintained a consistent sound, and they were one of few Motown acts to remain viable into the 1970s. The group originally came together in the late 1950s, signing with Berry Gordy in 1960.

MICHAEL OCHS ARCHIVES/GETTY IMAGES

A classic record publicity photo of Smokey Robinson (third from left) and the Miracles from the mid-1960s.

In 1964 they achieved the first in a series of thirty-seven top-ten hits with "The Way You Do the Things You Do," followed up with "My Girl" (1965), "Get Ready" (1966), and "Ain't Too Proud to Beg" (1966). Around 1967 producer Norman Whitfield took over the Temptations and began to experiment with Sly Stone–style funk flavourings and socially conscious lyrics to produce hits such as "Cloud Nine" (1969), "Ball of Confusion" (1970), and "Papa Was a Rolling Stone" (1972), while still producing a sweet vocal sound in tunes such as "Just My Imagination" (1971). According to critics Joe McEwen and Jim Miller, "The Temptations quite simply stood as the finest vocal group in Sixties soul: they could outdress, outdance and outsing any competition in sight."[19]

MEMPHIS AND MUSCLE SHOALS

Soul music produced in the South, sometimes called the **southern groove,** differed from the Motown sound: It was hard-edged, more gospel-based, and less arranged. It also appealed more often to black than to white audiences. Historian Charlie Gillett describes the making of the southern groove:

> Session men . . . instead of playing written arrangements which represented a producer's concept, evolved their own **"head arrangements,"** jam session "grooves" which were gradually rationalized to accommodate verse structures of songs.[20]

The development of the sound involved a web of relationships among Atlantic Records in New York, Stax Records in Memphis, and a pair of studios in Muscle Shoals, Alabama. Atlantic had the marketing muscle and many of the most popular artists under contract, while Stax and Muscle Shoals had the studio musicians to produce the musical texture. Great performances by artists such as Otis Redding, Wilson Pickett, Solomon Burke, Aretha Franklin, Joe Tex, Carla Thomas, Sam and Dave, Percy Sledge, and Booker T and the MGs were produced through the set of shifting alliances. The studio musicians who crafted the black-oriented southern groove were a racially mixed group; the band at Stax in Memphis was fully integrated, while the groups in Muscle Shoals were almost all white.

Atlantic Records, founded in New York in 1947, was one of the original independent labels of the 1950s that give birth to R & B. It was also the most successful of the independents, surviving multiple takeover attempts by major record labels and expanding throughout the 1960s. Led by Ahmet Ertegun and Jerry Wexler, Atlantic employed a hands-on approach with great R & B artists of the 1950s such as Ruth Brown, Big Joe Turner, the Coasters, Clyde McPhatter, and Ray Charles. In the 1960s, the label shifted to southern soul, bringing out classic work by Otis Redding, Wilson Pickett, Sam and Dave, Aretha Franklin, and Solomon Burke, as well as groundbreaking rock records by Buffalo Springfield, Led Zeppelin, and Crosby, Stills, and Nash.

The southern soul sound coalesced for Atlantic in the mid-1960s with singer Wilson Pickett (1941–), a hard gospel shouter, whom the label recorded backed by the band at Stax Records in Memphis. According to producer Jerry Wexler,

> I called Jim Stewart in Memphis and said, "Would you let me bring an artist down there, cut him in the studio with your band?" He said, sure. So I took Wilson down there, and opened up that southern thing for us.[21]

White-owned but black-oriented, Stax Records began operating in 1959, out of an old theatre building in the African American section of Memphis. A record shop in the front of the theatre was used to test new records. According to the label's owner, Jim Stewart,

> Now what we were doing was called the Stax sound or the Memphis sound. It wasn't Chicago, and it wasn't New York, and it sure wasn't Detroit. It was a southern sound, a below-the-Bible-Belt sound. It was righteous and nasty.[22]

The label's early hits by Rufus and Carla Thomas—"'Cause I Love You" (1960) and "Gee Whiz" (1961) by Carla Thomas—piqued Atlantic's interest in developing a national distribution agreement with the label. By 1965 Stax had produced a series of hits (distributed on ATCO, Atlantic's second label) by Otis Redding, one of the greatest southern soul singers. The Stax rhythm section (Booker T and the MGs) sounded to Wexler like just the right fit for Pickett. When the artist walked into the Stax studio, he immediately sat down with guitarist Steve Cropper to produce "In the Midnight Hour" (1965), one of the biggest soul hits of all time. As Cropper recalled,

> Somebody came up and says, "Hey, write a tune for Wilson." . . . I grabbed the only album of his I could find . . . and at the end of each fade-out he'd say,

"Yeah, wait for the midnight hour, baby." . . . I thought that would be a heck of an idea for a tune, and when he came in I presented it to him, and he said . . . "I've got this little rhythm thing I've been working on for a good while." There was really nothing to it.[23]

The classic Stax sound dated from that session. Eddie Floyd's "Knock on Wood" (1966) and Sam and Dave's "Hold on I'm Coming" (1966) and "Soul Man" (1967) all had a similar feeling to "In the Midnight Hour."

Although the Atlantic–Stax sound collaboration succeeded, business disagreements cut it short, and Atlantic looked further south to Alabama for the gritty, soulful southern flavour. Stax continued to produce hits for several more years, as well as a successful live concert film called *Wattstax* (1972). Major Stax artists included Carla and Rufus Thomas, Booker T and the MGs, the Bar-Kays, the Staples Singers, Albert King, Little Milton, Johnnie Taylor, the Dramatics, the Emotions, and Isaac Hayes. The Stax sound was resurrected in 1980 in the film *The Blues Brothers,* which featured tunes by Stax artists and members of the original Stax rhythm section.

Atlantic's search for an alternative to Stax led in 1965 to a small studio near Muscle Shoals, Alabama, called Fame Records, which had already scored soul hits with vocalist Joe Tex ("Hold What You've Got," "One Monkey Don't Stop No Show"). Almost all the Muscle Shoals musicians were white, producing a consistent sound hard to distinguish from the Memphis Stax sound. According to Charlie Gillett,

On slow numbers, Muscle Shoals arrangements tended to be more "churchy," with piano or organ conjuring images of heads bowed in humble dedication. . . . On fast ones, [producer] Rick Hall's trademark was to have a particular riff on guitar repeated throughout a song.[24]

Early in 1966, Wexler took Wilson Pickett to record in Muscle Shoals, producing "Land of 1000 Dances," "Mustang Sally," and "Funky Broadway." Another Muscle Shoals artist, vocalist Percy Sledge, had a hit around the same time with "When a Man Loves a Woman." Wexler also brought the newly signed Aretha Franklin to Muscle Shoals in 1967 for her first Atlantic recording session, producing Franklin's breakout hits—"I Never Loved a Man (the Way I Loved You)" and "Do Right Woman—Do Right Man." Wexler later transported key members of the Muscle Shoals band to New York to record on other Franklin records such as "Respect," "(You Make Me Feel Like) A Natural Woman," and "Chain of Fools."

The black–white musical collaborations that produced southern soul continued through 1968, until the assassination of Martin Luther King, Jr., in Memphis. Although soul and R & B were already changing because of James Brown and Sly Stone's funk innovations, King's murder pushed soul toward a more rigorously black sound and message. As Muscle Shoals producer Rick Hall recalls

Pickett was here in Muscle Shoals when Dr. King was shot in Memphis. The whole mood and atmosphere in the studio suddenly changed, and in fact we called off the session, out of respect to Dr. King. . . . But there was a change from that night on.[25]

MICHAEL OCHS ARCHIVES/GETTY IMAGES

Soul legend Otis Redding.

The two studios in the Muscle Shoals area shifted to backing up white country and rock artists for the next decade, including the Osmonds, Paul Anka, Jerry Reed, Alabama, Joe Cocker, Leon Russell, Paul Simon, Rod Stewart, and Bob Seger.

Otis Redding (1941–1967) was the greatest of the 1960s southern soul men. He broadened the appeal of soul to white audiences with a raw, spontaneous style that sharply contrasted with Motown. According to Robert Palmer,

> He combined a pleading vulnerability (mostly on ballads) with an aggressively rhythmic, highly improvisational up-tempo style, interpolating "got-ta-gotta-gottas" and "nah-nah-nahs" so freely that his creations frequently eclipsed the song's original melody and lyrics.[26]

Redding wrote or cowrote most of his own songs, and some became hits for other artists (such as "Respect" for Aretha Franklin and "Sweet Soul Music" for Arthur Conley). When Redding brought soul music to new crossover heights at the 1967 Monterey Pop Festival, he did so by sticking to his roots: Macon, Georgia, by way of Memphis. His early work reflected Little Richard, but by the time of his first Stax hit ("These Arms of Mine," 1963), Redding's style had fully formed. He toured regularly, usually backed by one of Stax's two bands, Booker T and the MGs or the Bar-Kays, and became popular in Europe. In 1965 he broke through in the United States with "I've Been Loving You Too Long (to Stop Now)" and "Respect," followed up in the next two years with "I Can't Turn You Loose," "Try a Little Tenderness," and a cover of the Rolling Stones' "Satisfaction." Appearing as the only soul act at the Monterey Pop Festival in 1967, Redding drew legions of new white fans with his incendiary stage performance. Sadly, he passed away in 1967 at age twenty-six in a plane crash, and the posthumous release of his chart-topping "(Sittin' on) The Dock of the Bay" gave further evidence of his talent.

R & B FROM THE 1970S TO THE MILLENNIUM

Although R & B went through several name changes between 1970 and 2000, it continued to serve as the bedrock for much of American popular music. Just as R & B had been the source of rock in the 1950s, it provided the basis for the new funk, disco, and hip-hop styles of the 1970s and 1980s. R & B also inspired the new dance pop genre and, through disco, the evolution of electronica. If the television show *American Idol* was any gauge, classic R & B had become the "default" style of American popular music by the early 2000s.

In the 1970s, R & B saw the decline of soul and the rise of two styles—funk, a hard-core, black-oriented, groove-based dance music, and a smoother, heavily produced crossover soul style that ultimately fed into disco. Black-themed films with R & B soundtracks also became a Hollywood staple. Much of 1970s R & B was dominated by the genius of Stevie Wonder, who integrated Motown, jazz, funk, and Tin Pan Alley influences to form a distinctive amalgam that influenced generations of R & B artists.

Al Green (1946–) was the first great soul singer of the 1970s and the last southern soul man. Green blended elements of gospel with the influences of Sam Cooke and Otis Redding. Critic Robert Christgau describes the artist's signature vocal work: "Soft-edged, almost indolent phrasing, full of audacious slurs, with his startling falsetto adding an intensity that was suffering soul and sweet pop at the same time."[27] Tight and quietly funky, the rhythm section that backed Green featured shuffle-style drums that counterpointed with simple, melodic horn and string lines. When the artist reached the peak of his popularity in the mid-1970s, personal excesses caused him to return to his gospel roots. Hits included "Tired of Being Alone" (1971), "Let's Stay Together" (1972), and "Call Me" (1973).

One of the most influential and acclaimed musicians of the early 1970s, Stevie Wonder (1950–) remained an integral part of American popular music for over four decades:

> His skills at writing sinuous melodies and gently uplifting harmonies, and his cheerful yet determined eclecticism—from funk to ballads, bossa nova to quasi-show tunes—have made Mr. Wonder a one-man Tin Pan Alley through two decades of rock.[28]

Wonder, who came up through the Motown system, became best known for his classic albums of the early 1970s: *Music of My Mind*, *Talking Book*, *Innervisions*, *Fulfillingness' First Finale*, and *Songs in the Key of Life*. Hits from the period included

R & B legend Stevie Wonder in the early 1970s.

MICHAEL OCHS ARCHIVES/GETTY IMAGES

"Superwoman" (1972), "Superstition" (1972), "You Are the Sunshine of My Life" (1973), and "Living for the City" (1973). Wonder ushered in an era in which R & B albums became cohesive artistic statements. He also pioneered the use of synthesizers in R & B and introduced the funky sound of the clavinet, an electronic keyboard with a distinctive organlike tone. The artist's vocal approach, with its shifting timbres and melismatic swoops and dives, influenced a generation of R & B singers, including Brian McKnight, D'Angelo, R. Kelly, and Usher. Wonder earned seventeen Grammys as well as an Oscar, and his record sales ranked alongside those of the Beatles and Elvis Presley.

A smooth style called **Philadelphia soul** also flavoured early 1970s R & B. The style was orchestrated with strings and horns; supported by a relaxed, steady groove; flavoured by the innovative textures of the marimba, vibes, or sitarlike electric guitar; and fronted by gospel-tinged vocals. As critic Jim Miller notes, Philly soul owed much to the work of a team of key producer/songwriters:

> Architects of a new style in dance music, Top 40 hitmakers of a proven caliber, creative artists in a cutthroat field—[Kenny] Gamble, [Leon] Huff, and Thom Bell are to the Seventies what Holland-Dozier-Holland and Smokey Robinson were to the Sixties: the preeminent soul producers of the decade.[29]

Also like Motown, the Philly soul groove came from a veteran group of studio musicians, in this case called MFSB (Mother Father Sister Brother). The streamlined pulse of MFSB in tunes such as "Love Train" (O'Jays, 1973), "TSOP (The Sound of Philadelphia)" (MFSB, 1974), and "Bad Luck" (Harold Melvin and the Blue Notes, 1975) shaped the subsequent disco style of the 1970s. Major artists of the Philly soul era included the Stylistics, the O'Jays, the Spinners, Harold Melvin and the Blue Notes, and the last group's lead vocalist, Teddy Pendergrass.

Seventies R & B featured prominently in the blaxploitation movies of the early part of the decade. With funky soundtracks, stylish clothes, and flashy cars, the black-themed action films capitalized on a mass public fascination with African American style. The first such film, *Sweet Sweetback's Baadasss Song* (1970), directed by Melvin Van Peebles, set the standard for the new genre. The most influential blaxploitation films were *Shaft* (1971) and *Superfly* (1972). *Shaft*, the story of a black private eye in Harlem, featured an Oscar- and Grammy-winning soundtrack by Isaac Hayes. *Superfly*, a film about drug dealing, was distinguished by Curtis Mayfield's powerful soundtrack. Blaxploitation soundtracks proliferated, influencing the sound of R & B. According to critic Nelson George,

> Longer, more orchestrated, more introspective—some black albums had the continuity and cohesion of soundtracks even when they weren't. Latin percussion . . . suddenly became rhythmic requirements, adding a new layer of polyrhythmic fire to the grooves. Minor chords, frowned on during the soul years, began appearing.[30]

The film *Jackie Brown* (1997) served as director Quentin Tarantino's homage to blaxploitation films.

FUNK

Funk, a dance-tempo R & B style that emphasized complex, syncopated, rhythmic interplay, developed out of R & B in the early 1970s. Originating from an African American slang term for "stink," funk was the rawest, most African form of R & B up to that time.

Funk was not confined to the classic verse/chorus song structure; using the same concept that rappers would soon employ, funk artists took what had been the break or extended jam section of an R & B tune and stretched it into an entire song. True to its African roots, funk also allowed for more freedom and improvisation once the groove was established. Though seldom at the top of the charts, funk ultimately shaped disco, **jazz-rock fusion**, and hip-hop. The tunes most often cited as the origins of funk are James Brown's "Papa's Got a Brand New Bag" (1965) and Sly Stone's "Thank You (Falettin Me Be Mice Elf Agin)" (1970). James Brown took the key step of placing rhythmic emphasis "on the one" (the downbeat), turning R & B's traditional emphasis on the backbeat on its head. Brown's bassist from the early 1970s, Bootsy Collins, continued the rhythmic style in George Clinton's groups. Sly Stone's band furthered the development of funk by adding a rock-influenced **fuzz-tone** guitar, slap-style bass, chant-style choral vocals, and the synthesized drum machine. Major funk acts of the 1970s included Kool and the Gang; Earth, Wind, and Fire; the Ohio Players; Rufus and Chaka Khan; and the Commodores.

The most commercially successful funk band of the mid-1970s, Earth, Wind, and Fire incorporated jazz, soul, gospel, pop, rock, and African music. The group could harmonize like a Motown quartet, work a groove like James Brown, and improvise like a jazz fusion group. Major hits included "Reasons" (1975), "Shining Star" (1975), "Got to Get You into My Life" (1978), and "September" (1979). Earth, Wind, and Fire was one of the most popular bands in the world during the late 1970s. According to historian Ricky Vincent

> Earth, Wind, and Fire . . . [wore] brightly colored skin-tight suits, platform shoes, ridiculous lapels, streamers, bellbottoms, and thousands of sequins. . . . Wall-to-wall splash, sprints, slides, screams, sweat, and soul, Earth, Wind, and Fire was a soul christening.[31]

George Clinton (1941–) was a visionary, theatrically inclined artist who took funk to a new level in the early 1980s. With two large funk aggregations, Parliament and Funkadelic, Clinton delivered freewheeling performances that disseminated an eclectic mythology of space-age cartoon images about motherships, star wars, and atomic dogs—all driven by a band clad in silver jumpsuits, diapers, and rainbow wigs. Critic Arthur Kempton described the visual impact of Clinton's shows:

> A "mothership" . . . descend[ed] thunderously from the eaves of cavernous public spaces. . . . Clinton, the ringmaster who wore long "fright" wigs, tall boots, and outlandish sci-fi raiment, would make his entrances riding in a "polyester pimpmobile." . . . A half-decade before MTV, Clinton had conceived of aural videos.[32]

Clinton had more lasting influence on subsequent developments in black music—hip-hop in particular—than did any other musician of his era. He introduced the electronic "clap" sound, synthesizer-bass (bass track played by a keyboard), and elaborately layered horn and vocal lines. Major hits included "Tear the Roof off the Sucker (Give up the Funk)" (1976), "One Nation under a Groove" (1978), and "Atomic Dog" (1983).

DISCO

In the 1970s, a new genre of popular dance music began to evolve out of R & B. Initially taking the form of disco, it subsequently morphed into dance pop and electronica in the 1980s and 1990s. **Disco** was a formulaic, R & B-based commercial sound accompanied by a hedonistic party scene that cut a wide swath through top-forty music. The discotheque, a stylish dance club with flashy decor and recorded dance music, originated in France in the early 1960s, where club owners hired **DJs** to save money on live bands. As the trend spread to the United States, it was first adopted in the gay, black, and Latino communities of New York and other major cities. Rooted in funk and R & B, disco music featured rhythm tracks with nonstop bass lines and repetitive drumming varying so little that DJs could spin records continuously without breaking the groove. As critic Nelson George observes, "At least the Philly disco records sounded like they were made by humans. Soon, Eurodisco invaded America. . . . It was a music with a metronomelike beat . . . almost inflectionless vocals, and metallic sexuality."[33]

Disco first hit the airwaves in 1974 with two soundalike tunes—"Rock the Boat" by the Hues Corporation and "Rock Your Baby" by George McCrae. Another popular disco group, KC and the Sunshine Band, also scored with "Get Down Tonight" and "(Shake, Shake, Shake) Shake Your Booty." "The Hustle" (1975) by Van McCoy, accompanied by a dance of the same name, provided another influential disco hit. Barry White (1944–2003) crafted a sexy, soulful sound by blending lush orchestration, funky grooves, and his own half-sung, half-spoken baritone delivery. White and his group, the Love Unlimited Orchestra, scored a string of early 1970s hits with "Can't Get Enough of Your Love, Baby," "Never Gonna Give You Up," and "Love's Theme." Donna Summer (1948–) was the reigning diva of the disco era. Her first hit, "Love to Love You Baby" (1975), was a seventeen-minute ode to lovemaking. She followed up with the Grammy-winning "Last Dance" (1978) and "Hot Stuff" (1979). Vocalist Gloria Gaynor (1949–) contributed the Grammy-winning "I Will Survive" (1975), one of the last anthems of the disco era.

The disco era reached its zenith with the release of the film *Saturday Night Fever* (1977). The movie, which starred actor John Travolta as a disco king, produced the most successful soundtrack album of all time. It featured music by numerous R & B artists, as well as a string of new songs by British pop veterans the Bee Gees including "Stayin' Alive," "Night Fever," and "How Deep Is Your Love." Disco went into decline by the late 1970s, but the Village

People—a theatrical, gay, disco vocal group—scored two major hits to close out the era with "Macho Man" (1978) and "YMCA" (1979).

Outside of New York, Montreal was considered to be the second most important disco market on the continent. Disco's popularity in Montreal, and indeed throughout Quebec, was nurtured within a web of record companies and disc jockeys, who by the end of the 1970s had become important remixers of dance music for the global market. Further, the scene afforded Canadian artists Patsy Gallant, Claudja Barry, and Lisa Dalbello to build successful careers in the receptive environments of Quebec's discotheques and MusiquePlus, the French language music television station, began in 1986. Montreal's continuing role as a leader of electronically-oriented dance music remains a significant legacy of the city's disco culture.

QUIET STORM, DIVAS, AND DRUM MACHINES

While R & B spun off new genres in the 1980s such as hip-hop, it also maintained a core style that emphasized melody. Much of the R & B of the decade received airplay on radio stations that broadcast in formats variously called "urban contemporary," "retro nuevo," or "quiet storm." A far cry from the gritty soul of the 1960s, 1980s R & B showcased a new generation of vocalists

Promotional portrait of 1970s Canadian disco star Patsy Gallant.

who aimed at crossing over with a smooth, upscale sound. The sound also drove away some in the hip-hop generation, as Public Enemy's Chuck D proclaimed in a rap tune: "When the quiet storm comes on I fall asleep."[34] The advent of hip-hop, however, also revitalized up-tempo, dance-oriented R & B to generate the beat-happy, rap-infused New Jack Swing style, so that throughout the decade, sampling and synthesizers ruled.

Major female vocalists in the 1980s included the ultimate R & B diva Whitney Houston, the jazz-inflected Anita Baker, and the smoothly sensual Sade. Whitney Houston (1963–) had a powerful voice and vocal technique that dominated the charts from 1985 to the mid-1990s. Trained as a gospel singer, Houston's best-selling debut album in 1985 produced multiple hits: "You Give Good Love," "Saving All My Love for You," and "The Greatest Love of All." After another successful album in 1987, Houston turned her talents to soundtrack albums for films in which she appeared, such as *The Bodyguard* (1992) and

Waiting to Exhale (1995). Produced by Victoria, BC–born David Foster, the artist's recording of the Dolly Parton–penned "I Will Always Love You" for *The Bodyguard* was the one of the biggest-selling singles in pop music history. According to critic Gerri Hirshey,

> Whitney had the genes, the pipes, the looks, the connections and the iron will that have since sustained her through countless trials-by-tabloid. . . . The truth is, any time she chooses, Whitney Houston can sing the bejesus out of the Yellow Pages. It is the mark—and prerogative—of the true diva to do exactly as she pleases.[35]

Important male R & B vocalists of the decade included the smooth cross-over crooner/songwriter Lionel Richie, soulful ballad virtuoso Luther Vandross, and other smooth soul men such as Jeffrey Osborne, Peabo Bryson, and Frankie Beverly and his band Maze. Lionel Richie (1949–) got his first break with the funky Commodores, but once he developed his songwriting in the late 1970s, he detoured from funk to smooth crossover ballads. In critic Nelson George's account, "Richie's voice, oozing with country melancholy, projected lyrics as sentimental and courtly as roses on the first date. . . . Richie's early funk voice was just a facade. He wanted to be Kenny Rogers."[36] Hits included "Endless Love" (1981), "Truly" (1982), and "All Night Long" (1983). Luther Vandross (1951–2005) was one of the most gifted vocalists of his era, as well as a successful producer. Major hits included "Bad Boy/Having a Party" (1982), Burt Bacharach's "A House Is Not a Home" (1982), "Here and Now" (1989), and "Endless Love" (1994).

By the late 1980s, R & B producers began to integrate a more street-oriented feel into R & B vocal music to create a style called **New Jack Swing**. Pioneered by producer Teddy Riley and Prince alumni Jimmy Jam and Terry Lewis, the male-dominated sound employed snippets of **rap**, synthesized drum and bass lines, and multipart doo-wop harmony. As historian Rickey Vincent observes, "The 'New Jack Swing' sound mixed hip-hop beats with soulful melodies to bring bite-sized portions of funk for a new generation to digest."[37] Major New Jack artists included Bobby Brown, Keith Sweat, Bell Biv Devoe, Tony Toni Tone, and Boyz II Men. Boyz II Men, who called their group vocal harmony style "hip-hop doo-wop," released their first album Cooleyhighharmony (1991) to yield hits such as "Motownphilly" and "It's So Hard to Say Goodbye to Yesterday." Recognizing that their greatest appeal lay in their lush four-part harmonies, the group abandoned up-tempo New Jack Swing in favour of ballads, subsequently scoring with "End of the Road" (1992) and "I'll Make Love to You" (1994). The New Jack style went on to influence dance pop of the 1990s and early 2000s.

URBAN/CONTEMPORARY AND NEO-SOUL

R & B displayed several substyles in the 1990s, and while the urban/contemporary sound was still common, a new, street-flavoured vocal approach called hip-hop soul appeared. A fresh crop of R & B divas also hit the airwaves, and doo-wop–styled close harmony returned in some female and male vocal groups. The next generation of soulful male ballad crooners, some sweetly emotive, others down and dirty, also entered the scene. In addition, a new sound that prized rootsy, soulful authenticity called neo-soul emerged.

The R & B diva pipeline seemed inexhaustible in the 1990s, with sounds ranging from the smooth flavour of Toni Braxton to the hip-hop street sass of Mary J. Blige. Other young divas such as Aaliyah, Beyoncé, and Canadian singers, Keisha Chante and Deborah Cox, struck a stylistic middle ground. The designer-attired queen of hip-hop soul, Mary J. Blige (1971–), evoked a blend of sophistication and street. Blige began her career as the protégé of producer Sean "Puffy" Combs with the debut album *What's the 411?* (1992), and her powerful mix of modern R & B and edgy hip-hop impressed listeners. Often compared favourably to Chaka Khan or Aretha Franklin, Blige brought new textures and flavours to R & B. As critic Gerri Hirshey observes, "Having lived the kind of gritty urban life Mariah Carey would hire rappers to describe, Blige turned inward, began writing her own material, and re-emerged as a smart, sad-eyed survivor."[38] Major hits included "Real Love" (1992), a cover of Chaka Khan's "Sweet Thing" (1993), and "Not Gon' Cry" (1996).

The 1990s also saw the rise of several female R & B vocal groups who packed vocal power, gospel harmonies, and sexy, in-your-face delivery, including En Vogue, SWV, TLC, and Destiny's Child. One of the most popular female R & B groups of the late 1990s and early 2000s, Destiny's Child produced major hits with "Say My Name" (2000), "Survivor" (2001), and "Soldier" (2004). Lead singer/songwriter Beyoncé Knowles also went solo to score with *Dangerously in Love* (2003).

© REUTERS/CORBIS

Destiny's Child perform at the thirtieth anniversary of the *Soul Train* television show in 2001 (left to right): Kelly Rowland, Beyoncé Knowles, and Michelle Williams.

Not to be outdone by female vocal groups, Blackstreet carried the torch for male vocal group harmony. Founded by New Jack Swing pioneer Teddy Riley, the group merged soulful vocal harmonies with catchy, bass-heavy, hip-hop beats, and they incorporated appearances by hip-hop artists as well. Major hits included "Before I Let You Go" (1994) and "No Diggity" (1996).

A raft of new male crooners—many flavoured by hip-hop—gained prominence in the 1990s and early 2000s. These vocalists, including Babyface, R. Kelly, and Usher, recast the soulful, romantic male R & B voice. R. Kelly remained popular throughout the decade with multiplatinum releases such as the carnally flavored "Bump 'n' Grind," "You Remind Me of Somethin'" (1995), and the Grammy-winning "I Believe I Can Fly" (1996) from the film *Space Jam*. Usher started out in R & B in the late 1990s as a teen pop star, but he moved to the sultry adult side with his third album, *8701*, in 2001. In 2004 he released *Confessions*, which contained the chart-topping hit single, "Yeah!"

A new R & B substyle called **neo-soul** emerged in the late 1990s in the work of artists who consciously paid homage to the "old-school" soul of the 1960s and 1970s. Neo-soul had a sweet, retro tone as well as a social conscience, and many of the style's artists also wrote and performed their own material, resuscitating the singer-songwriter tradition in R & B. The work of Lauryn Hill, first with the Fugees and later on her own in 1998, greatly influenced the neo-soul scene, as did the appearance of Erykah Badu in 1997. Other female neo-soul artists included Macy Gray, Jill Scott, India. Arie, and Alicia Keys. Male artists in the style included D'Angelo, Maxwell, and Raphael Saadiq. The Fugees, comprised of rappers Pras and Wyclef Jean and vocalist Lauryn Hill (1975–), blended rap, soul, reggae, and R & B in their Grammy-winning 1996 album *The Score*, which included new arrangements of Roberta Flack's "Killing Me Softly with His Song" and Bob Marley's "No Woman No Cry." Hill followed in 1998 with her smash solo album, *The Miseducation of Lauryn Hill.* Alicia Keys (1981–) debuted with the Grammy-winning album *Songs in A Minor*, which produced "Fallin'" (2001), to follow in 2003 with *The Diary of Alicia Keys*, which yielded "You Don't Know My Name" and "I Ain't Got You."

CHAPTER SUMMARY

- African American gospel music came into its own in the mid-twentieth century, establishing a unique, indigenous American genre and spinning off numerous artists who contributed important innovations to R & B, soul, and rock.

- R & B began to evolve into soul, featuring such artists as Ray Charles, Sam Cooke, Jackie Wilson, Ben E. King, Dinah Washington, Ike and Tina Turner, and Curtis Mayfield and the Impressions.

- Soul came into full flower in the mid-1960s, embodied by artists such as James Brown and Aretha Franklin. Motown produced a northern version of soul with such artists as the Supremes, the Temptations, Smokey Robinson, and Marvin Gaye. A grittier style of southern soul emanated from Atlantic, Stax, and Muscle Shoals to flavour the work of artists such as Wilson Pickett and Otis Redding.

- Seventies R & B was flavoured in part by funk, in part by the 1970s soul of Stevie Wonder and Al Green, and in part by the smooth grooves of Philadelphia ("Philly") soul.

- The disco era dominated the popular music of the mid-1970s. Artists such as Donna Summer, Barry White, and the Bee Gees became household names as the era climaxed with the film *Saturday Night Fever* in 1977.

- The R & B of the 1980s and 1990s was dominated by the smooth urban contemporary sound, New Jack Swing, neo-soul, and multiple generations of divas and vocal groups.

LISTENING EXERCISES

1. The Gospel Sound

Listen to Mahalia Jackson's recording of "Nobody Knows the Trouble I've Seen" (1963). How does Jackson's powerful and passionate delivery interact with the lyrics of this gospel standard? Notice Jackson's use of vocal turns and embellishments, known as melismas, which have become standard in pop music today. What contemporary vocalists can you identify who make frequent use of this essential element of gospel vocal styles? How is modern gospel music different from traditional spirituals?

2. Sacred Continuations in Secular Practices

Listen to Aretha Franklin's recording of "(You Make Me Feel Like) A Natural Woman," composed by Brill Building songwriters Carole King and Gerry Goffin. Does Franklin's background in gospel music show in her performance? What is the metre of the song? How does her vocal performance on the bridge affect the emotional energy and drive of the arrangement? Is Franklin's performance style appropriate to the message of the lyrics?

3. The Motown Sound

Listen to "My Girl" (1965), composed by Smokey Robinson and performed by the Temptations. Recorded during the studio's most successful period, this classic example of the Motown sound was one of the most well-crafted songs of the era. Good pop songs require memorable musical hooks, and "My Girl" has an impressive variety of them. Although recorded over forty years ago, most listeners still instantly recognize the song. What makes "My Girl" the quintessential Motown recording?

4. The Godfather of Funk

Listen to an excerpt from James Brown's funk classic "Mother Popcorn" (1969). Is there a melody? What is the song about? How would you describe the groove? Listen carefully for each instrument in the rhythm section. How do the parts overlap? Brown's shouts and shrieks on this recording are legendary. Can you identify other music funk characteristics in this recording?

HISTORICAL STUDIES AND DISCUSSION QUESTIONS

1. The Cultural Borderland between R & B and Gospel

Despite the common origins of R & B and gospel music in African and African American musical cultures, the two are separate genres. From the first emergence of the blues, many Christians—black and white—called the blues "the devil's music." Leaving gospel for secular music, as well as integrating secular music into gospel performances, was controversial. Many artists who crossed over to the secular side—including Little Richard, Al Green, and Solomon Burke—subsequently returned to gospel.

The work of contemporary artists CeCe Winans and Kirk Franklin offered interesting case studies of pop-gospel boundaries. Winans created controversy in the early 1990s by collaborating with brother BeBe on a pop-influenced album called *Different Lifestyles,* which topped the R & B charts and scored two number-one hits. In subsequent years, however, she began working her way back to a more traditional gospel sound. Kirk Franklin burst onto the gospel and R & B scene in 1996 with a controversial gold album called *Whatcha Lookin' 4,* which incorporated hip-hop elements for the first time. In subsequent work, however, he more closely aligned himself with core gospel traditions by collaborating with gospel icon Shirley Caesar. What do these experiences tell us about the complexities of making art in cultural borderlands?

2. Racial Politics and the Production of Soul Music

Northern soul music was dominated by Motown, a black-owned firm with black performers, black producers, and mostly black musicians. Although the label served as a pioneering example of black capitalism, its goal ("The Sound of Young America") was to avoid the blues and aim for the white market. Motown's Berry Gordy also played on his black identity when marketing his artists to black radio stations. When Motown hit it big, however, Gordy stopped using black booking agencies and shifted to white industry giants such as the William Morris agency.

Much grittier than Motown, southern soul targeted the black market. Yet the white-owned Atlantic and Stax labels dominated the style. The artists were black, the producers were black and white, the musicians in Memphis were black and white, and the musicians in Alabama were all white. What do these examples tell us about the complex interplay of race, economic power, appropriation, and identity in American culture and music?

STUDY QUESTIONS

1. What were the origins and development of African American gospel music? What are some examples of its influences on R & B and rock?

2. Discuss the evolution of soul music. What were the principal styles that emerged? What were Motown's accomplishments, and who were some major artists?

3. What was the Southern groove? How was it produced, and who were some of its major artists?

4. What is funk? What were its musical origins? What role did funk play in 1970s music and in subsequent genres?

5. Why was Stevie Wonder considered one of the greatest artists of the 1970s? What contributions to the development of R & B did he make?

6. What were the key features of the disco era? Who were the biggest stars, and what led to the era's demise?

NOTES

1. Eileen Southern, *The Music of Black Americans: A History,* 3rd ed. (New York: Norton, 1997), 460–61.

2. Clarence Boyer, *How Sweet the Sound: The Golden Age of Gospel* (Washington, DC: Elliot & Clark, 1995), 189.

3. Gerri Hirshey, *Nowhere to Run: The Story of Soul Music* (New York: Times Books, 1984), 26.

4. Robert Palmer, Rock and Roll: *An Unruly History* (New York: Harmony Books, 1995, 33.

5. Hirshey, *Nowhere to Run,* 26.

6. Robert Palmer, "James Brown," in *Rolling Stone Illustrated History of Rock and Roll,* edited by Jim Miller (New York: Random House, 1980), 136.

7. James Brown and Bruce Tucker, *James Brown: The Godfather of Soul* (New York: Thunder's Mouth Press, 1997), 158.

8. Palmer, *Rock and Roll,* 245.

9. Hirshey, *Nowhere to Run,* 231.

10. Charlie Gillett, *Making Tracks: Atlantic Records and the Growth of a Multi-Billion Dollar Industry* (New York: Dutton, 1974), 211.

11. Jerry Wexler with David Ritz, "The Queen of Soul," in *Rock and Roll Is Here to Stay: An Anthology,* edited by William McKeen (New York: Norton, 2000), 510.

12. *Ibid.,* 506.

13. Hirshey, *Nowhere to Run,* 133.

14. *Ibid.,* 137.

15. Palmer, *Rock and Roll,* 87–88.

16. *Ibid.,* 86.

17. *Ibid.,* 89.

18. Diane Cardwell, "Diana Ross," in *Trouble Girls: The Rolling Stone Book of Women in Rock,* edited by Barbara O'Dair (New York: Random House, 1997), 122.

19. Joe McEwen and Jim Miller, "Motown," in *Rolling Stone Illustrated History of Rock and Roll,* edited by Jim Miller (New York: Random House, 1980), 243.

20. Gillett, *Making Tracks,* 172.

21. *Ibid.,* 185.

22. Hershey, *Nowhere to Run,* 294.

23. Gillett, *Making Tracks,* 194.

24. *Ibid.,* 201.

25. Palmer, *Rock and Roll,* 96.

26. *Ibid.,* 93.

27. Robert Christgau, "Al Green," in *Rolling Stone Illustrated History of Rock and Roll,* edited by Jim Miller (New York: Random House/Rolling Stone Press, 1980), 361.

28. "Past Honorees: Stevie Wonder," The Kennedy Center Honors, 1999, http://www
    .kennedy-center.org/programs/specialevents/honors/history/honoree/wonder.html,
    accessed May 12, 2005.

29. Jim Miller, "The Sound of Philadelphia," in *Rolling Stone Illustrated History of Rock and Roll*,
    edited by Jim Miller (New York: Random House/Rolling Stone Press, 1980), 373.

30. Nelson George, *The Death of Rhythm and Blues* (New York: Penguin Books, 1998), 124.

31. Rickey Vincent, *Funk: The Music, the People, and the Rhythm of the One* (New York: St. Martin's,
    1996), 187–88.

32. Arthur Kempton, Boogaloo: The Quintessence of American Popular Music (New York:
    Pantheon, 2003), 402.

33. George, *Death of Rhythm and Blues*, 154.

34. Alan Light, "Rap and Soul: From the Eighties Onward," in *Rolling Stone Illustrated History of
    Rock and Roll*, 3rd ed., edited by Anthony DeCurtis and James Henke (New York: Random
    House, 1992), 684.

35. Gerri Hirshey, *We Gotta Get Out of This Place: The True, Tough Story of* Women *in Rock* (New
    York: Atlantic Monthly Press, 2001), 149–50.

36. Nelson George, *Buppies, B-Boys, BAPs and BoHos: Notes on Post-Soul Black Culture* (Cambridge,
    MA: Da Capo Press, 2001), 201.

37. Vincent, *Funk,* 305.

38. Hirshey, *We Gotta Get Out of This Place*, 175.

CHAPTER 8

Tin Pan Alley in the Era of Music Television

The growth of dance and rock-oriented pop gained momentum from MTV (Music Television) and MuchMusic, a late-1970s brainchild of the new cable television industry. When cable was first established, many of its networks focused on single themes such as movies, news, or weather—and, in this case, music. Founded in 1981 by Warner Communications and American Express, MTV at first consisted of three-minute video clips of musical groups signed to Warner. Programming mimicked radio formats, with **VJs** (video DJs) introducing the latest releases. A new record-marketing process was thus established; hit songs would now also require hit videos. In August 1984, MuchMusic, the Canadian competitor to MTV, began broadcasting videos under the same content regulations which dictated programming for Canadian radio broadcasters. As a one-time subsidiary of CHUM Ltd., now owned by CTV-Globe Media, MuchMusic and the Quebec affiliate, MusiquePlus (1986), contributed greatly to the development and to the eventual world recognition of such Canadian talents as Bryan Adams and Celine Dion.

Musician, photographer, and social activist Bryan Adams (1959–), was born in Kingston, Ontario, and spent most of his young-adult life honing his musical skills while living in Vancouver, BC. In 1978, at the age of eighteen, Adams was signed to A & M Records in Toronto and has since released fourteen albums. During the early 1980s, Adams co-authored a number of songs with Jim Vallance for the Vancouver-based band Prism before striking out on his own. Adams' second album, *You Want It, You Got It*, contained the FM radio hit "Lonely Nights"; but it was not until his third album, *Cuts Like A Knife* (1983), that he broke through with four hits in 1983, most notably with the title track. *Reckless* was released in November 1984, and reached number one on the *Billboard* album chart and gave rise to six hit singles, including "Run To You," "Summer of '69" and Adams' first number-one single, "Heaven." Buoyed by extensive video play on both MuchMusic and MTV, the recordings by both Adams and Bruce Springsteen defined the hard rock style which dominated mainstream popular music during the mid-1980s. One of Adams' most successful albums, *Waking Up the Neighbours* (1991) featured the single "(Everything I Do) I Do It For You" and made record-breaking sales of 3 million copies in the United States.

For its first few years, MTV was an all-white medium; the network's editorial policy stated that it was a rock network whose market was white suburban youth. Ultimately, however, the dance pop sound of the early 1980s—led by

© NEAL PRESTON/CORBIS

Guitarist, singer-songwriter Bryan Adams in concert in 1998.

Michael Jackson's *Thriller* (1982)—broke through MTV's colour barrier. As the self-proclaimed "King of Pop," Michael Jackson (1958–) was one of the most successful performers in North American pop music history, as well as one of its most perplexing personalities. Jackson began his career as a child singing lead for the successful family vocal act, the Jackson 5, scoring hits that included "I Want You Back," "ABC," and "I'll Be There." The entire Jackson family received a congressional citation for "contributions to American youth" in 1972. When Michael Jackson released his first major solo album, *Off the Wall* (1979), he achieved a record-setting four top-ten hits: "Don't Stop Till You Get Enough," "Rock with You," "Off the Wall," and "She's Out of My Life." His next album, *Thriller* (1982), sold more copies than any other record in pop music history, over 50 million copies worldwide. A collaboration with legendary producer Quincy Jones, the album yielded an unprecedented seven top-ten singles, including "Thriller," "Billie Jean," and "Beat It," which featured a blazing guitar solo by metalist Eddie Van Halen. The album's music was flavoured by Jackson's signature vocals, funky synthesized bass lines, interwoven keyboard and guitar parts, and well-arranged, R & B–style horns. Producer L. A. Reid describes the sound of another song from that album, "Billie Jean":

> Everything in that song was catchy and every instrument was playing a different hook. You could separate it into twelve different musical pieces and I think you'd have twelve different hits. Every day I look for that kind of song.[1]

Through the rest of the 1980s, Jackson's support for social causes and continuing musical success enhanced his reputation. During the 1990s, however, the artist's star began to tarnish. Charges of inappropriate behaviour, coupled with

The Jackson 5 in an early seventies publicity shot. (Michael is seated, right.)

his own increasingly surreal appearance, incurred negative media attention, and mixed reviews of his music cast shadows on his career.

Michael Jackson's sister, Janet Jackson (1966–), followed her brother in the 1980s to her own pop stardom. Though she did not have the musical talents of her brother, Janet produced a string of hit records that relied on New Jack Swing and dance-oriented videos. A decade later, dance pop divas such as Britney Spears and Christina Aguilera would replicate the artist's formula. Jackson followed her successful breakout album, *Control* (1986), with the popular *Rhythm Nation 1814* (1989). Her work in the 1990s and early 2000s featured material with increasingly sexual overtones.

The work of Prince (1958–) played a central role in the advancement of dance pop. Widely recognized as one of the most talented musicians of his generation, he demonstrated his versatility by singing and playing all the instruments on many of his records. Beginning in the late 1970s, Prince recorded more than twenty albums with a unique blend of funk, rock, and R & B. He also followed a tortuous path mapped by a lengthy battle with the record industry as well as his own quirks. Prince emerged from Minneapolis, Minnesota, releasing a series of albums that displayed a penchant for erotic songwriting, most apparent on his third album, *Dirty Mind* (1980). Interest in the artist's work grew steadily, fostered by the release of *Controversy* (1981) and *1999* (1982). When the hit single and video of "Little

© CORBIS

Prince "embraces" his guitar in this 1981 performance.

© CORBIS

Madonna in one of her many guises (1986).

Red Corvette" (1983) provided the artist's MTV breakthrough, he joined Michael Jackson to become one of the first African American artists to achieve significant airplay on MTV. Next, Prince's Grammy- and Oscar-winning autobiographical film, *Purple Rain*, yielded hits with "When Doves Cry," "Let's Go Crazy," and "Purple Rain." The artist's career entered a strange period of decline in 1993 when he changed his name to an unpronounceable symbol as part of a multiyear battle with his record label. The end of the dispute at the turn of the millennium, however, saw the reinvigoration of his career.

Madonna (Madonna Louise Ciccone, 1958–) transformed her image and style with a skill and frequency that kept her at the forefront of popular culture for over two decades. With entertainment industry acumen, a feminist image of self-determination, multiple "personalities," and the ability to stir controversy, Madonna became an enduring pop music icon. Raised in Michigan, the artist made her first forays into pop music at the end of the disco era in New York and scored her first record deal in 1982. Madonna's timing was perfect for achieving extensive MTV exposure, and she stirred early controversy with an interracial love scene in a video. With modest vocal skills but great production values, the artist carefully synchronized her music with her evolving looks, which included a Marilyn Monroe-esque "Material Girl," a prim Evita Perón, and a provocative haute couture dominatrix. Madonna scored a string of dance pop hits beginning with *Madonna* (1983), followed by the controversial *Like a Virgin* (1984), which yielded the hit title song as well as "Material Girl." New controversy sprang from the release of "Papa Don't Preach" (1990), which encouraged single women to keep their babies, and "Like a Prayer" (1990), which the Vatican censured. When Madonna set up her own production company in 1992, she cemented her position as one of the most successful business women in pop music history. In 1995 she played the lead role in the film version of Andrew Lloyd Webber's Broadway musical *Evita*.

Céline Dion (1968–) emerged as a teen star in the French-speaking world after her manager and future husband René Angélil mortgaged his home to finance her first record. Her music has been influenced by a range of musical styles, and is renowned for her technically skilled and powerful vocals. By the end of the 1990s, Céline Dion had sold more than hundred million albums worldwide, and had won numerous industry awards, including a 1997 Grammy Award (Best Album of the Year) for her David Foster-produced *Falling Into You*. In early 2002 Dion had initiated a three-year, six-hundred-show contract to appear five nights a week in an entertainment extravaganza *(A New Day) at Ceasar's Palace, Las Vegas*. The show was a combination of dance, music, and visual effects. Dion made her debut into the Anglophone market with *Unison* (1990). Singles from the album included "(If There Was) Any Other Way," "The Last to Know," "Unison," "Where does My Heart Beat Now," the single which became her first single to chart on the U.S. *Billboard* Hot 100. Her real international breakthrough came when she sang on Disney's animated film *Beauty and the Beast* (1991). Dion kept to her French roots and continued to release many Francophone recordings between each English record. These included *Dion chante Pamondon* (1991); *A l'Olympia* (1994); and *D'eux* (1995), which would go on to become the best-selling French album of all time.

Grammy-winning pop superstar Mariah Carey (1970–) burst onto the scene in the early 1990s with a five-octave range and a soulful voice to power the sales of over 140 million records. Carey's music was a mix of pop ballads

CP/ROBERT GALBRAITH

Superstar Céline Dion honouring hockey legend Maurice "Rocket" Richard at the Montreal Forum in 1998.

and up-tempo dance pop rooted in soul and gospel music with a touch of funk. Hits included "Emotions" (1991), "Hero" (1993), "Fantasy" (1995), and a collaboration with Boyz II Men, "One Sweet Day" (1995). Former Mouseketeers Britney Spears (1981–) and Christina Aguilera (1980–) emerged on the dance pop scene as major teen stars in the late 1990s. Both singers initially portrayed a contradictory appeal of innocence and sexuality that drew public attention, and they were marketed in a fashion similar to the marketing of the teen idols of the 1950s. While Aguilera's vocal power matched her celebrity status, Spear's singing ability was viewed more skeptically by some. Spears scored her biggest hit with "Baby One More Time" (1999); Aguilera did so with "Genie in a Bottle" (1999).

BOY BANDS

In the mid-1990s, a new wave of young white male vocal groups called boy bands hit the dance pop market. Among the best known were New Kids on the Block, the Backstreet Boys, 'N Sync, and 98 Degrees, all of whom were carefully moulded by producers to appeal to young female audiences as the teen idols of the late 1950s had done. The boy bands produced sterile renderings of soul, contemporary doo-wop, and New Jack Swing, specializing in dance pop, ballads, and hip-hop choreography.

The first white boy band, New Kids on the Block, enjoyed a string of hits in the late 1980s, topped by "Hangin' Tough." The Back Street Boys and 'N Sync followed up as the genre's most successful acts of the 1990s. Both groups emerged from Orlando, Florida, and used close connections to the Disney Corporation to implement successful marketing strategies. By the early 2000s, the boy band phase had drawn to a close, with only 'N Sync lead singer, Justin Timberlake, able to transition to a solo career.

CHAPTER SUMMARY

- The development of music television in 1981 changed the way music was disseminated and promoted. This coincided with the emergence of a new generation of dance pop music exemplified by superstars such as Michael Jackson, Madonna, Prince, Bryan Adams, and Celine Dion.

LISTENING EXERCISE

Video Analysis

Music videos, along with the introduction of compact discs, helped rescue a declining music industry in the early 1980s. The first twenty-four hour, nonstop commercial cable channel, MTV, was founded in 1981 on the same formatting principles that drove the Windsor, Ontario, radio station CKLN (The Big 8) to the top of the commercial radio industry during the 1960s. By 1991, MTV had 28 million subscribers and became the central gatekeeper for launching the careers of new artists. The two artists who reaped great benefits from MTV exposure were Michael Jackson and Madonna. Analyze Michael Jackson's "Thriller" and Madonna's "Like a Virgin" and discuss the following questions. Do the videos follow a narrative (time-sequenced) structure, or do the present a non-linear sample of images? Are the settings realistic or fantastical? Are the videos constructed around the performances of the songs, or are the songs secondary to the filmic experience. What kinds of themes are presented and how are the issues addressed? How does the music you are hearing relate to the video, i.e., do the video edits coincide with changes in the structure of the song?

HISTORICAL STUDIES AND DISCUSSION QUESTIONS

1. **James Brown and Tina Turner—Dance Pop Role Models**

   When Michael and Janet Jackson, Prince, and Madonna set the tone for contemporary dance pop performance, they owed a debt to their predecessors, James Brown and Tina Turner, who themselves had built on decades of black performance traditions. Brown and Turner were two of the most dynamic performers in the history of popular music, and their onstage acrobatics were emulated by many, but mastered by few.

   Tina Turner set the female benchmark for high-energy pop singing and dancing, and although many contemporary dance pop stars such as Janet Jackson and Britney Spears rely on prerecorded vocal tracks to sing and dance simultaneously, Turner had no need of such support. And while Prince and Michael Jackson amazed fans with their intricate dance steps and choreography, most of it had been done before by James Brown. Brown was the master of high-energy live performance and one of the greatest dancers in pop music history. Channelling the prior collective history of African American stage performance of such legendary performers as Bill "Bojangles" Robinson, Cab Calloway, and Louis Jordan, Brown laid the groundwork for most great R & B dancers who followed in his footsteps. When did white performers begin to adopt the dance styles of black entertainers?

2. **Madonna—Role Model or Sex Object?**

   Building on the women's movement of the early 1970s, women in pop music in the 1980s contributed to new, independent female role models in Western popular culture. Few female figures in popular culture became more visible in this realm than Madonna. Madonna further complicated matters with allusions to lesbianism, bisexuality, and sadomasochism.

Some feel she is a model of feminist independence, some say she is a sex object who plays to sexist stereotypes, and others have the opinion she is a bit of both. What is your opinion and, based on Madonna's works, why do you feel that way?

3. Boy Bands, Cultural Appropriation, and Race

In an interesting twist of race and power, the white boy-band phenomenon of the 1990s was actually initiated in the late 1980s by Maurice Starr, an African American producer. Starr had been a force behind the successful early-1980s African American vocal group, New Edition; following the demise of that group, Starr sought to replicate and even surpass their success with a group of young white vocalists. He did this with New Kids on the Block, and the white boy-band phenomenon was born. Ultimately, the greatest profits from the boy bands still went to white producers and artists—particularly the Orlando, Florida-based teen pop mastermind Lou Pearlman, who managed 'N Sync, the Backstreet Boys, and O-Town. But in a complex racial role reversal, it is a black producer who invented the first white boy-bands. What does Starr's decision to produce a white boy band say about race and North American popular music? Is this the first instance of "strategic" planning in popular music?

STUDY QUESTIONS

1. How did MTV and MuchMusic affect the marketing and distribution of music?

2. How did Michael Jackson become one of the biggest stars in pop music history? What musical elements pushed Jackson to the top, and what was his role in breaking MTV's colour barrier?

3. What role did Madonna play in the evolving image of women in popular culture? How did she maintain her star status for more than twenty years?

4. What impact did MuchMusic and MusiquePlus have on popular culture in Canada?

NOTE

1. *Rolling Stone Magazine*, April 15, 2004, 124.

1603 Mathieu de Costa, a free man, is the first person of African descent to set foot on Canadian soil
1607 First British community in North America, Jamestown, settled
1619 First African slaves brought to America
1682 Philadelphia, largest colonial city, founded

1700s American colonies expand
1700s Instruments such as the banjo develop, demonstrating African retentions in a new hybrid form ♪
1700s Slave "musicianers" provide music for social functions, reflecting African *griot* traditions and setting the stage for itinerant bluesmen ♪
1700s African Americans perform in military bands and other groups, taking on European influences to blend with African retentions ♪
1707 Isaac Watts's first hymnal published, influencing African American religious and secular music ♪
1775 *Quebec Gazette* reports musicians of African descent performing in Canada ♪
1776 Declaration of Independence and beginning of Revolutionary War
1789 U.S. Constitution ratified
1794 African Methodist Episcopal (AME) church founded, establishing an important centre of community activity

1800s African slaves participate in camp meetings; begin to adapt European religious music, producing spirituals ♪
1800s African American work-, social-, and religious music develop ♪
1801 AME church publishes *Richard Allen Hymnal*, first African American hymnal ♪
1803 Louisiana Purchase annexes vast western lands from France
1812 War with Britain
1821 Liberia founded in Africa
1821 African Grove Theater founded in New York, the nation's first black theatre ♪
1830s Minstrelsy emerges, establishing a pattern that would influence the blues and American popular theatre ♪
1831 Nat Turner slave revolt in Virginia
1833 Abolition Act ends slavery in Canada
1839–1860 Underground Railroad operates to help escaped slaves reach the North
1849 Stephen Foster publishes "Oh! Susanna" ♪
1861–1865 Civil War and Emancipation Proclamation
1863 Emancipation Proclamation
1865–1877 Reconstruction
1865 After emancipation, new styles develop: gospel, blues, and jazz ♪
1867 *Slave Songs of the United States*, the first collection of African American spirituals, is published ♪
1870–1900 African Americans migrate to Northern U.S. cities
1870 Georgia Minstrels, a black minstrel group, tours Europe ♪
1877 Thomas Edison invents first sound recording device

1902–1903 First written reports of the blues: Charles Peabody and W. C. Handy ♪
1914–1918 World War I
1914 W. C. Handy's "St. Louis Blues" is published and becomes first blues hit ♪
1917 Large African American migration to North is underway
1919–1933 Prohibition
1920 Mamie Smith's "Crazy Blues," the first blues record ♪
1923 Bessie Smith's "Downhearted Blues" sells 750,000 copies ♪
1926 Blind Lemon Jefferson makes "Black Snake Moan," the first rural blues recording ♪
1927 The great Mississippi River flood
1929–1930s Great Depression; New Deal begins

1930s Bluebird Records in Chicago promotes urban blues and creates first record studio "house sound" ♪
1930 First electric guitar marketed by Dobro company ♪
1933 Wurlitzer manufactures first jukeboxes ♪
1936 Gibson markets first Les Paul electric guitar ♪
1936 Robert Johnson records seminal "Cross Road Blues" ♪
1938 First "Spirituals to Swing" concert in New York ♪

| 1600 | 1700 | 1800 | 1900 | 1930 |

The Blues Continuum

1940s African Americans continue migrating to Northern industrial cities

1941–1945 U.S. participates in World War II

1941 Muddy Waters, architect of electric blues, first recorded by Alan Lomax ♪

1945 Louis Jordan scores major R & B and pop hits ♪

1946 DJ Alan Freed first uses the term *rock and roll* on the air ♪

1947 Chess Records founded in Chicago; Atlantic Records founded in New York ♪

1947 T-Bone Walker releases "Call it Stormy Monday" ♪

1948 *Billboard* magazine initiates R & B chart, ceases use of "race records" category ♪

1948 WDIA in Memphis, first all-black station, goes on the air ♪

1948 Columbia introduces 33 ⅓ rpm LP album format ♪

1948 Wynonie Harris and Roy Brown record "Good Rockin' Tonight" ♪

1949 RCA introduces the 45 rpm single record format ♪

1949 *Billboard* establishes separate pop, country, and R & B charts ♪

1950–1953 Korean War

1950 "Your Hit Parade" radio show moves to TV ♪

1950s 12-bar blues becomes a standard form in early rock ♪

1951 "Rocket 88"—the "first rock and roll record"—is released ♪

1952 DJ Alan Freed hosts first rock and roll show in Cleveland ♪

1953 Bill Haley's "Crazy, Man, Crazy" is the first white rock hit ♪

1954 School segregation outlawed; civil rights movement begins

1954 Big Joe Turner records "Shake, Rattle, and Roll" ♪

1955 Elvis Presley, Little Richard, Bo Diddley, and Chuck Berry first make the pop charts ♪

1955 The film *Blackboard Jungle* is released

1956 Soviet Union invades Hungary; Cold War is in full swing

1956 Elvis Presley breaks out with major hits and TV appearances ♪

1957 Dick Clark's "American Bandstand" premieres on national TV ♪

1958 First U.S. satellite launched

1958 Elvis is drafted into the Army

1958 Ronnie Hawkins begins performing in Toronto ♪

1959 Cuban Revolution; Alaska and Hawaii become states

1959 Plane crash kills Buddy Holly, Ritchie Valens, Big Bopper ♪

1960 Congress begins payola hearings ♪

1963 Civil rights march on Washington; John Kennedy assassinated

1964–1973 Vietnam War

1964 British Rhythm and Blues Revival bands (Rolling Stones, Yardbirds, Animals) and American counterparts (Paul Butterfield, Charlie Musselwhite) spark wider interest in urban blues culture ♪

1964 Newport Folk Festival "discovers" blues artists ♪

1968 Martin Luther King and Robert Kennedy assassinated

1969 B. B. King and Muddy Waters cross over to a mainstream audience and perform at Fillmore East ♪

1970 Led Zeppelin and Black Sabbath pave the way for heavy metal ♪

1968–1969 "Prime Minister of the Blues" Dutch Mason and Toronto-based Downchild Blues Band record first albums: respectively, *Live at the Candlelight* and *Bootleg* ♪

1973 Led Zeppelin breaks box-office touring records: stadium rock is born ♪

1976 Holger Peterson founds Stoney Plain Records in Stoney Plain, Alberta ♪

1980 *Blues Brothers* movie released ♪

1983 Metallica blends metal with punk on *Kill 'em All* ♪

1985 Toronto Blues Society is created to promote the growth of blues culture in Canada ♪

1986 Robert Cray releases *Strong Persuader* ♪

1989 Bonnie Raitt wins Grammy for *Nick of Time* ♪

1997 Canadian blues recording label Electro-Fi Records is founded ♪

1997 First Maple Blues Awards ceremony honours top Canadian blues performers ♪

2001 Creation of Northern Blues record label ♪

2008 Barack Obama elected first African-American U.S. President ♪

| 1940 | 1950 | 1960 | 1970 | 1980 | 1990 | 2000 |

CHAPTER 9

African Origins, Slavery, and Slave Culture

AFRICANS AND COLONIAL CANADA

The first black person to set foot in Canada was Mathieu de Costa, a free man who travelled with explorer Samuel de Champlain and arrived in Nova Scotia sometime between 1603 and 1608. Shortly thereafter, groups of black people began to arrive in communities along Canada's east coast. The first group came as free persons who were serving in the French Army and Navy; the second group arrived when white American Loyalists brought with them their African American slaves during the War of Independence; and the third were the Trelawney Maroons, a collectivity of independent rebels who moved from Jamaica to Nova Scotia in 1796. The next major migration occurred between 1813 and 1815 when refugees from the War of 1812 fled the United States to settle in North Preston, East Preston, and Africville. With the slavery Abolition Act of 1833, and spurred on by the Underground Railroad from the late-1820s until the American Civil War began in 1861, there grew in Southern Ontario a sizable population of 30,000 black Canadians who lived in communities stretching along the north shores of Lake Erie and Lake Ontario.

Though post-slavery Canada did not witness the institutionalized brutalities of the Southern U.S. in the decades following the Emancipation Proclamation, Canadian black communities were nonetheless forced to endure a gauntlet of racist policies which arched the period dating the earliest black settlements through to the urban communities of the latter half of the twentieth century. For example, the Charter of the City of St. John, New Brunswick, was amended in 1785 specifically to exclude blacks from practising a trade, selling goods, fishing in the harbour, or becoming freemen; these provisions stood until 1870. In 1792, due to the unkept promises of the British government and the discrimination from the white colonists, 1,192 African American men, women and children left Nova Scotia and were relocated to West Africa in what is now Sierra Leone. In the early-1900s, an unofficial policy that restricted blacks from immigrating to Canada was formalized by Prime Minister Sir Wilfrid Laurier in 1911. More recent examples include Africville, a small black village in Nova Scotia which was demolished in the 1960s to facilitate the urban expansion of Halifax; and discrimination made it difficult until the mid-1940s for black musicians to perform in Toronto in any but local halls catering exclusively to black audiences.

The earliest documented instance of a black musician in Canada is a notice in the *Quebec Gazette* of 30 November 1775 for a runaway slaved named Locanes. Through the nineteenth century, music in black communities was centred in the church, and though few hymns and spirituals have survived the passage of time, African musical retentions have been observed in current practices of older Black Pentecostal churches in the Windsor area.

AFRICAN ROOTS

African and African American musics have contributed fundamentally to world popular music, profoundly impacting styles as diverse as the blues, jazz, rock, R & B, Latin, and country music. Given the history of slavery and racism in the U.S. and in Canada, the influence of African musical retentions is particularly significant. Examining these African origins is challenging because they were **vernacular music**, which means they existed as folk or traditional music played in communities as a part of everyday life. As producer and historian Chris Strachwitz notes, "Vernacular traditions are on the one hand neglected or even discarded, while on the other exploited and devoured by the dominant mass culture."[1] Because fewer resources have been dedicated to the study of vernacular music than of European classical music, less concrete historical information on the former exists. Moreover, there was no sound recording before 1900. Finally, flawed presentations of African American culture by eighteenth- and nineteenth-century historians have compounded the problem. Nonetheless, the last five decades have seen dramatic growth in research in rich musical heritage of the African **diaspora**.

A HOLISTIC APPROACH TO LIFE

The African approach to life was holistic, with few distinctions between religion and everyday life. Music played a major function in the daily lives of Africans, as historian Eileen Southern explains: "For almost every activity in the life of the individual or the community there was an appropriate music; it was an integral part of life from the hour of birth to beyond the grave."[2] Music embodied life events ranging from the mundane to the spiritual. It was used for ceremonial functions such as the installation of kings, agricultural rites, religious ceremonies, rites of passage, preparations for war, hunting expeditions, and recreation. The integration of African music into everyday life helps explain how it survived and evolved even under the oppressive conditions of slavery.

One European explorer, Thomas Edward Bowdich, described a West African festival in 1817:

> The king, his tributaries, and captains, were resplendent in the distance, surrounded by attendants of every description. . . . More than a hundred bands burst at once on our arrival, [all playing] the peculiar airs of the several chiefs;

the horns flourished their defiances [fanfare melodies], with the beating of innumerable drums and metal instruments, and then yielded for a while to the soft breathings of their long flutes, which were truly harmonious; and a pleasing instrument like a bagpipe without a drone, was happily blended.[3]

The music of West Africa from the seventeenth through the nineteenth centuries was a highly evolved art form, according to musicologist and composer Gunther Schuller:

> It is a misconception that African musical forms are "primitive." African music is replete with highly "civilized" concepts. . . . Some observers have confused their very complexity with formlessness. . . . Nothing could be further from the truth.[4]

Held in high regard, West African musicians often served as honoured members of a tribal king's household. Every village had master musicians, the most important of whom was the *griot*, serving as storyteller, tribal historian, and entertainer. Although of low social caste, *griots* were of paramount importance, admired as performers and valued as oral historians. The performance style of modern *griots* is a half-sung, half-spoken delivery, often accompanied by the *kora* (twenty-one-string lute) or a drum.

© LINDSAY HEBBERD/CORBIS

African musician Vieux Diop plays the twenty-one-stringed *kora*, one of the traditional instruments of Aftican *griots*.

AFRICAN MUSICAL AESTHETICS

The aesthetics of African music profoundly affected American popular music, from the passionate guttural exclamations of James Brown to the shrieking, wailing guitar of Jimi Hendrix. One important feature of African musical aesthetics is what African American composer Olly Wilson called a heterogeneous [consisting of many different, contrasting elements] sound ideal: "A mosaic created by the interaction between lead voice, chorus, rattle, metallic gong, hand clapping, various wind or string instruments, and drums, which exist in greater or lesser degrees of complexity in all African ensemble music."[5] A good example of this in North American music is the collective improvisation of a traditional New Orleans jazz band, where each instrument has its own discrete musical voice, yet the ensemble plays together in a unified way.

Another important attribute of African music is call and response—a musical statement by a singer or instrumentalist followed by a response from other vocalists or instruments. Sometimes the response repeats the call; other times, the response completes the musical idea stated in the call. Although call and response is found in the music of many cultures, the African version of the technique flavours the blues, jazz, ragtime, gospel, and R & B.

African vocal performance styles also have several unique characteristics. One involves guttural effects such as screams, moans, and shouts. Another is lyric improvisation, by which vocalists change lyrics to achieve desired effects. Other vocal features include shifts between singing and speaking modes, falsetto singing, and vocal *rhythmization*—using vocal sounds for rhythmic purposes. Vocal rhythmization is used in jazz scat singing, gospel, rock, and soul. African American vocal styles also employ metaphors and figures of speech with hidden meanings. Such "musical codes" enabled African American music to serve as a means of communication during slavery. Finally, influential African vocal features include "bending" notes (microtonal inflections) and using **blue notes** (the flatted third, fifth, and seventh of a major scale).

African rhythmic features such as syncopation, rhythmic improvisation, the groove, and swing have also shaped popular music. As we have seen, syncopation unexpectedly accents the weak rather than strong pulses in a measure, and rhythmic improvisation allows for spontaneous rhythmic variations. The groove is built by playing several highly rhythmic parts simultaneously, creating a momentary feeling of resolution when multiple parts arrive on the same beat. When the complex rhythmic parts of a rap, funk, jazz, hip-hop, or gospel tune "lock in," as James Brown would say, "the groove is here." Swing is another African-derived rhythmic feature of American popular music. Here, the term does not refer to the style of music popularized in the 1930s but to the triplet-based rhythmic feel often encountered in jazz, blues, and R & B. The rhythmic pulse of swing creates a lilting feeling of forward momentum; it is easy to feel but difficult to notate (write down).

African melodic features also influenced American popular music through the use of the minor **pentatonic scale** (five-note scale) and the **blues scale**. While the minor pentatonic scale occurs in music around the globe, African versions of the scale were a primary source for American popular music. In the key of C, the notes of this scale would be C, Eb, F, G, Bb, and C. Much African American folk music prior to the twentieth century featured pentatonic melodies, and gospel, blues, rock, and R & B still do. The blues scale is an African American creation closely related to the minor pentatonic scale. It uses six notes, including the flatted third, fifth, and seventh, to reach an octave and it is called a hexatonic (six-tone) scale. This, too, is used in gospel, blues, jazz, rock, and R & B. In the key of C, the blues scale would be C, Eb, F, Gb, G, Bb, and C.

African music also uses microtones in ambiguous modes. A **microtone** is a note that falls between two notes on the Western chromatic twelve-note scale. You can visualize this by imagining a note that falls between two adjacent keys on the piano. The flatted third of the blues is sometimes described as a microtone that actually falls between the major third and the flatted third of a major scale. Ambiguous mode means that one cannot tell if a tune is written in a major or a minor key. In most Western classical music, the distinction between major and minor modes is quite clear, but in African American music this is not always the case.

AFRICAN INSTRUMENTS

Ethnomusicologists, scholars who study music in sociocultural contexts, classify traditional instruments of African music into four principal groups: membranophones (drums), idiophones (other percussion), aerophones (wind instruments), and chordophones (stringed instruments). **Membranophones,** which came in every shape and size, were made from animal skins stretched over hollowed logs and played with fingers, palms, or crooked sticks. The drum is a sacred instrument in many cultures, and it is probably the earliest musical instrument other than the human voice. African drums provided a powerful form of communication, often audible over great distances, and people used them to communicate with the spirit realm and to create trances. Slave owners in much of the South forbade drumming, fearing its political and religious effects.

Idiophones were instruments such as bells, gongs, shakers, rattles, thumb pianos, and xylophones that were made of materials that had their own unique sound, such as wood, ceramics, or metal. **Aerophones** appeared less in African music, though people played horns and trumpets made of elephant tusks and animal horns. Most numerous were small flutes, some of which were connected to progressively longer flutes to form panpipes. African Americans called panpipes "quills," because the instrument was sometimes made of porcupine quills in Africa. The flutelike instruments were made from reeds or other local materials in the rural South.

Chordophones included fiddles, harps, lyres, lutes, and zithers. Lutes and fiddles were made of gourds covered by animal skins cut open for the sound to resonate, with long sticks for the neck and wood or bone for the bridge. Strings were made of horse or cow hair, and instruments had varying numbers of strings. Fiddles were played by plucking the strings or using bows. European travellers in Africa compared the sound of harplike instruments they encountered to the banjo, which was an African American hybrid.

AFRICAN AMERICAN MUSIC DURING SLAVERY

Two key factors influenced the retention and development of African musical traditions in the Americas: the cultures of the slave owners and the cultures of the African slaves. Spanish, French, and Portuguese colonists who settled in New Orleans, the Caribbean, and Central or South America were relatively tolerant of African culture, allowing slaves to maintain their musical traditions. In New Orleans, for example, slaves and free Africans were allowed to gather every Sunday in **Congo Square** to drum and dance, and the practice continued until the late nineteenth century. Slaves in Cuba under Spanish rule were sometimes allowed to buy their own freedom, and music flourished in this environment, retaining many African elements. African musical influences also abounded in Brazil, which had the largest population of people of African descent in the Western Hemisphere.

Congo Square in New Orleans was one of the few places in the United States where African music and dance traditions were permitted during much of the nineteenth century.

Slaves in French, Spanish, and Portuguese Catholic colonies also continued to practise African religious traditions by embedding them in the rituals of Roman Catholicism. This process produced the hybrid religions of *Santeria* and *Abakuá* in Cuba, *Voudou* in Haiti, and *Candomblé* and *Macumba* in Brazil. Adherents of the religions used music and drumming as a central focus of their spiritual practice. In contrast, British and American slave owners in North America often believed it was their duty to convert slaves from their traditional belief systems to Protestant Christianity by eliminating vestiges of African culture. Further, when concern grew in the nineteenth century over slave rebellions, most plantation owners forbade drums, in order to prevent their use for communication or religion. Slaves were instead encouraged to perform church music, **work songs**, and European popular music to entertain slave owners. Although Christianity was not a choice at first for Africans, many embraced the religion and found solace. In doing so, they also transformed existing worship styles to create spirituals, gospel, and the blues.

African slaves were resilient and creative within the confines of their captivity, and although families were intentionally broken up and those of similar language background separated, slavery could not eliminate the African integration of music and daily life. Drums may have been forbidden, but syncopated rhythms could still be stomped, tapped, and clapped; anything in the environment that could make a sound was turned into an instrument. The body became a rhythm instrument through clapping, foot tapping, and patting juba (body drumming—striking the knees, shoulders, or other body parts with the hands to produce a rhythmic sound). Later incarnated as hambone or hand jive, patting juba served as the source of rock and R & B rhythms generations later.

The two most commonly played slave instruments were the banjo and the fiddle. An African American invention, the banjo was based on African stringed instruments; banjolike instruments made of gourds with necks and various

© CORBIS

Nineteenth-century drawing of freed slaves playing music for Union troops during the Civil War.

numbers of strings first appeared in the United States in the late seventeenth century. The European violin, similar to several African stringed instruments, was particularly popular among African Americans prior to the Civil War, and slaves who learned to fiddle were often highly respected. In later years, African American musicians contributed to the development of the string band and jug band, now more commonly associated with white musicians of Appalachia.

African slaves who played music professionally were called **musicianers**. They sometimes received special privileges and occasionally could buy their freedom, but for the most part they remained as valuable property used to entertain whites. Slaves also sometimes played in European-style marching bands or fife and drum corps, and such music became a part of southern black folk culture. The music also fed into the street parade styles of New Orleans in the late nineteenth century.

Not all African Americans were enslaved, and free blacks were often musically active in the North. New York City, for example, saw the founding of the African Grove Theater, the nation's first black theatre, in 1821. It offered tragedies, operas, and musicals. Free African Americans also played in brass bands, dance bands, and orchestras. Historian Eileen Southern cites the example of Frank Johnson, a famous nineteenth-century African American cornetist and bandleader in Philadelphia:

> During his short career he accumulated an amazing number of "firsts" as a black musician: first to win wide acclaim in the nation and England; first to publish sheet music; first to develop a school of black musicians; first to give formal band concerts; first to tour widely in the nation; and first to appear in integrated concerts with white musicians.[6]

MUSICAL STYLES DURING SLAVERY

The absence of instruments encouraged singing among slaves in work as well as worship. **Field hollers** were an early example, usually sung or chanted by individual workers in rhythm with their work. Hollers subsequently evolved into group work songs, which often included **call and response**: A lead singer acting as foreman sang a lyric to direct the work, then workers answered and performed the required task. The rhythm of the singing helped coordinate loading barges, driving mules, or laying railroad ties. Field hollers and work songs contributed greatly to the development of African American music. In them one can hear African melodic inflection, microtones, and pentatonic melodies.

The development of spirituals resulted from an exchange of musical styles between the races in the eighteenth and nineteenth centuries when many African Americans converted to Christianity. Spirituals offered biblical stories as metaphors for liberation, offered hope for a better life, and helped preserve African cultural memory. For over two centuries, the hymns of English composer Isaac Watts (1674–1748) were particularly popular among African Americans, and these hymns served as the improvisational basis for the development of spirituals. Because most people, white and black, could not read music or text, hymns were often learned through the Scottish custom called lining out. In **lining out**, leaders sang one line at a time to the congregation, who repeated the newly learned material in a call and response format. The African American church also developed its own liturgy and music with the establishment of the first African Methodist Episcopal (AME) church in Philadelphia in 1794. The church's minister, Richard Allen, subsequently published the first hymnal of the African American church in 1801.

Innovation in the development of early spirituals also took place at camp meetings, which stemmed from the Second Awakening, an evangelical movement of the early nineteenth century. The revivals were large, multiday, outdoor religious celebrations attended by both blacks and whites, where worship went on day and night. Blacks at the events spent hours singing, praying, and participating in the **ring shout**—a shuffling circular dance of chanting and hand clapping that often transported participants into an ecstatic trance. Refrains from hymns provided the starting point for improvisation, and spontaneous songs were composed with frequent affirmations such as "Hallelujah" and "Amen." At the camp meetings, outside the confines and restrictions of the formal church setting, African musical practices blended with simple hymn melodies to generate new hybrids. The songs that developed were called camp-meeting hymns or spiritual songs, and the first collection of this music, *Slave Songs of the United States,* was published in 1867.

CHAPTER SUMMARY

• African music and culture of the seventeenth through the nineteenth centuries greatly influenced North American music, despite the oppressive conditions of slavery. The accuracy of our knowledge of African music prior to the age of sound recording is hampered by the lack of written records, but recent research and interest in vernacular music has improved our understanding.

- Music played a central role in African life and was incorporated into festivals, agricultural rites, religious ceremonies, preparations for war, hunting expeditions, recreation, and rites of passage.

- African culture held musicians in high regard. *Griots,* or tribal storytellers, served as historians and entertainers with the important task of maintaining and transmitting history through poetry and song.

- African music employs a complex system of aesthetics that differs from that of European classical music. Historically, many key African musical elements were retained and further developed in American popular music.

- There are four principal groups of instruments in West Africa: membranophones (drums), idiophones (percussion instruments), aerophones (wind instruments), and chordophones (stringed instruments).

- Several African instruments took on hybrid forms in North America: the banjo, the flute, and the quills (panpipes made of reeds).

- European slave owners had different standards of conduct for slaves. The Spanish, French, and Portuguese permitted them to keep their drums, play African music, and maintain African religions; the British and Americans banished drums and most African traditions, although work songs and field hollers were allowed, and many slaves were required to attend church, leading to the development of spirituals, blues, and gospel.

- The end of slavery in 1865 in the United States saw increased personal freedom for African Americans, resulting in new musical developments such as gospel, blues, and jazz.

LISTENING EXERCISES

1. African Retentions in the Blues

Listen to "Folk Story" (1986), recorded by *griot* Wolof Gewel. This is an example of modern *griot* performing in the narrative song style. How do the music and rhythm of the instrument and the voice interact? Next, listen to the alternating phrases of Henry Ratcliff's blues lament entitled "Louisiana," juxtaposed with the work song of a Senegalese field worker. What similarities do you hear between these two musicians?

2. African Retentions in Funk

Listen to James Brown's "Mother Popcorn." How does Brown's use of syncopation work to create a unified groove? How does this song exemplify the heterogeneous sound ideal? What other African retentions are evident?

3. "Classic" Blues Characteristics

Listen to the 1928 recording of Bessie Smith singing "Empty Bed Blues." This recording includes most of the African musical aesthetics we have examined, including metaphors, call and response, blues inflections, blues scales, swing, syncopation, and improvisation. Smith also employs the classic form of the 12-bar blues. What role does the trombone play in relationship to the singing?

HISTORICAL STUDIES AND DISCUSSION QUESTIONS

1. Music as Coded Resistance

African American music served as a means of communication during slavery, when hymns and songs were used to promote escape to the North. Music was also vital to the operations of the Underground Railroad, an organization that helped fugitive slaves escape to freedom. How are the aspirations of escaping slaves affirmed in the spiritual "Follow the Drinkin' Gourd"?

2. Linguistic Retentions

The word *juke* is probably an African retention meaning "evil, disorderly, or wicked." In American English, *juke* has multiple meanings: to *juke* is to dance; a *juke box* is a mechanized record player found in a nightclub or restaurant; and a *juke joint* is a rudimentary nightclub or bar, usually located in an old building outside of town. Juke joints were generally open on weekends, providing entertainment for African Americans in the rural South. During Prohibition (1919–1933), jukes freely sold moonshine and provided a place for gambling, music, and dancing. Jukes were important performance venues for rural blues, and by the end of the twentieth century their ambience was commodified by the "House of Blues" nightclub chain. What other West African expressions can you identify in North American linguistic culture?

STUDY QUESTIONS

1. When did slavery end in Canada?
2. Why did African musical retentions persist despite oppressive conditions of slavery?
3. What roles did music play in African cultures during the seventeenth through nineteenth centuries?
4. What is the African heterogeneous sound ideal?
5. What are some features of African musical aesthetics?

6. What are the principal instrument groups in traditional African music?

7. What American musical instruments are of African origin?

8. What was the function of musicianers and what instruments did they play?

9. What were camp meetings and how did they influence musical innovation?

10. Why did African American slaves embrace a religion in which they were at first forced to participate?

11. What effect did Emancipation have on African American music and culture?

NOTES

1. Interview with the authors.

2. Eileen Southern, *The Music of Black Americans: A History,* 3rd ed. (New York: Norton, 1997), 5.

3. *Ibid.,* 5–7.

4. Gunther Schuller, *Early Jazz: Its Roots and Musical Development* (New York: Oxford University Press, 1968), 26–27.

5. Olly Wilson, "The Heterogeneous Sound Ideal in African-American Music," in *New Perspectives on Music: Essays in Honor of Eileen Southern,* ed. R. Wright and S. Floyd (Warren, MI: Harmonie Peak Press, 1992), 330.

6. Southern, *Music of Black Americans,* 107.

CHAPTER 10

Emancipation, Blues Origins, and History

THE EMANCIPATION AND THE BEGINNING OF A NEW MUSIC

Slavery was abolished in Canada in 1833, and later in the United States at the conclusion of the Civil War in 1865. With the end of the Civil War and the demise of slavery, the South was in turmoil. Although most newly freed slaves were as impoverished as before, the change in their level of personal freedom was revolutionary. They could now travel, seek work, and make personal choices. This newfound freedom contributed to advances in music, including the development of gospel music, the blues, and jazz. Gospel music expanded on spirituals to integrate popular influences and up-tempo rhythms, the blues reflected new social realities in the black population by reflecting complex emotional needs, and jazz represented a new interpretation of the African tradition of collective improvisation. The new genres, all rooted in African music, also marked the beginning of a new African American popular culture of performance that would have an enduring impact on North American music.

BLACK MINSTRELS

Minstrelsy provided a contradictory venue for early mass exposure of African American artists. Black minstrel troupes performed as early as the 1840s, and solo black performers of "Ethiopian music" were found even earlier. "Signor Cornmeali" (Mr. Cornmeal) performed as a street vendor in New Orleans, influencing "Daddy" Rice, who added a skit called "Cornmeal" to his routine. Dancer William Henry Lane ("Master Juba") was one of the first African Americans to tour and perform with white minstrel groups, and his work reflected traditional African American performance styles.

The end of slavery in 1865 broadened choices for African American performers, and many more black minstrel troupes formed. The Georgia Minstrels were the most famous of these; with a large cast and thirteen-piece brass band, they successfully toured Europe in 1870. The troupes served as a major source of employment for African American entertainers well into the twentieth

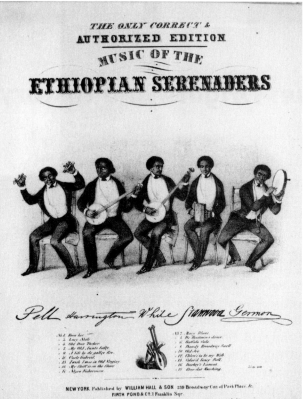

Sheet music cover for minstrel music of the Ethiopian Serenaders, dated 1847. Notice the formal attire of the participants, the stereotyped images, and the classic minstrel show instrumentation of banjos, tambourines, and bone rattles.

century, and many great artists—including W. C. Handy, Bessie Smith, Ma Rainey, T-Bone Walker, Louis Jordan, and Rufus Thomas—started out in minstrelsy. According to bandleader/composer W. C. Handy, "The minstrel show at that time was one of the greatest outlets for talented musicians and artists. All of the best talent of that generation came down the same drain. . . . The minstrel show got them all."[1] James Bland was the most important African American composer of minstrel music, with such tunes as "Carry Me Back to Old Virginny," "In the Evening by the Moonlight," and "Dem Golden Slippers" to his credit.

ORIGINS OF THE BLUES

In his book, *Father of the Blues*, W. C. Handy related a legendary story about his "discovery" of the blues. In 1903, while stranded at a railroad station in Tutwiller, Mississippi, Handy lay down uncomfortably to take a nap. Some time during the evening, an African American man in tattered clothes sat beside him and started to play the guitar. Handy awoke to the sound of the guitar being played with a knife pressed against the strings, creating a slurred, moaning sound. In Handy's words, "It was the weirdest music I ever heard." The man sang, "Goin' where the Southern cross the Dog," repeating the line three times in a call and response style with the guitar. When Handy asked him what the words meant, the singer explained that south of the station the tracks of the Southern Railroad crossed those of the Yazoo and Mississippi Valley Railroad—also known as the "Yellow Dog." He was singing about his destination.[2] What Handy described was an early example of the blues. He had heard work songs and field hollers before, but never anything quite like this. The guitar playing was intricate, with complex rhythmic patterns and melodic responses to the singing. The experience made a lasting impression, and Handy went on to publish some of the earliest blues music.

For some, the blues is a specific musical style; for others, it is an emotion evoked by music with blueslike features; for still others, it is a form of social commentary:[3]

> The Blues always impressed me as being very sad, sadder than the Spirituals, because their sadness is not softened with tears, but hardened with laughter, the absurd, incongruous laughter of a sadness without even a god to appeal to. (Langston Hughes)

© KEAN COLLECTION/GETTY IMAGES

I've got a disposition and a way of my own
When my man starts kicking I let him find another home
I get full of good liquor, walk the streets all night
Go home and put my man out if he don't act right
Wild women don't worry, Wild women don't have them blues.[4] (Ida Cox)

Musical roots of the blues lay in the music of itinerant black musicians called **songsters**, and in the field hollers and work songs of slaves. Songsters played instruments and sang an eclectic and multicultural repertoire with European and African sources that included comic songs, social songs, ballads, minstrel songs, and eventually the blues. In the late nineteenth century, the blues-like qualities associated with field hollers began to appear in the Delta region of Mississippi, although early blues star Ma Rainey also spoke of hearing music called the blues while travelling with a tent show in Missouri in 1902, and pianist/composer Jelly Roll Morton told of hearing songs called the blues in New Orleans in 1905. Similar stories placed the blues in regions throughout the South. Mississippi blues legend Son House also gave his take on the roots of the blues:

> People wonder a lot about where the blues come from. Well, when I was coming up, people did more singing in the fields than they did anywhere else. . . . They'd make it sound good, too. You could hear them half-a-mile off, they'd be singing so loud. . . . You'd hear them talking and one would say, "You know ol' so and so can really sing the blues!"[5]

In northwestern Mississippi, the Mississippi and Arkansas Rivers intersect to form a triangle called the Mississippi Delta. This was one of the poorest areas in the United States at the turn of the twentieth century. Land was farmed by poor African American sharecroppers who rented land, seed, and tools from white landowners and worked with little chance of coming out ahead. The region's hot climate, backbreaking work, and unending cycle of debt formed the context of the **Delta or rural blues**. Songsters in the region started to merge field hollers with simple guitar chords and lyrics describing hardships and hopes. The chords they used were probably influenced by the harmonic structure of church hymns, and earthy themes of love and lust also found a home in the music's AAB lyric structure. Many legendary blues performers were born or grew up in the Delta, including Charley Patton, Son House, Robert Johnson, Muddy Waters, John Lee Hooker, Howlin' Wolf, and B. B. King.

MARKETING THE BLUES AND BLUES SOUND RECORDING

The earliest blues songs were transmitted orally by songsters performing throughout the South, but it was a handful of music promoters who saw the style's appeal and brought it to a wider audience. The most prominent blues entrepreneur was W. C. Handy (1873–1958), a formally trained musician from a middle-class background who was working as trumpeter/bandleader for Mahara's Minstrels in the Delta. Because sound recording was still in its infancy, the main market for music lay in sheet music publishing. Handy published his first blues, the "Memphis Blues," in 1912, and he followed up with "St. Louis Blues," one of the most enduring songs of the twentieth century, in 1914. The song was not a pure 12-bar blues: Its first and second verses used the 12-bar form, while the third verse was a tango, a popular rhythm recently arrived from Argentina.

Just before 1900, the recording industry in the United States began, and it grew steadily during the first twenty years of the new century. Although early sound quality was poor, the novelty of the invention and continuing drops in price encouraged consumers to give recorded music a chance. White artists dominated the early recording industry, with opera and wind band music the most popular styles recorded. Nonetheless, the industry included a few African American artists. Some of inventor Thomas Edison's best-selling recordings of the late nineteenth century featured a former slave, George Washington Johnson, performing "The Laughing Song" and "The Whistling Coon." Bert Williams, one of the last great African American minstrel performers, also recorded a variety of vaudeville and minstrel songs between 1900 and 1920, and recordings of African American bandleader James Reese Europe's influential syncopated wind band music were released in 1914.

The first blues record, Mamie Smith's "Crazy Blues," did not appear until 1920. When the tune sold 75,000 copies in its first month, the era of recorded blues had begun, established as a new category called "race records." Most African American pop vocal recordings, regardless of style, were subsequently classed as race records until 1948 when the category was renamed "rhythm and blues" by *Billboard* magazine. Black artists who followed up on Smith's recording success were primarily vaudeville (variety show) performers. Many of them toured throughout the country with shows produced by the white-owned Theater Owners Booking Association (**TOBA**—many performers swore it stood for "tough on black asses"). Early blues legends Ma Rainey, Bessie Smith, and others worked the TOBA circuit. Conditions for performers varied widely; headliners fared well, others did not. Touring schedules were nightmarish; artists faced low salaries, poor working conditions, and segregation; and they often travelled in fear of racial harassment. Nevertheless, according to historian Daphne Duval Harrison,

> Black communities across the country benefited economically and culturally when a train uncoupled the show car at the local railroad siding. The traditional parade that followed not only brought folks to the show, it brought business to the little shops, cafes, and "joints" as people crowded in to mingle with the show people. And high spirits remained for weeks after the train was gone.[6]

CLASSIC BLUES

By 1921, records were challenging sheet music in the marketplace. Race records had also unlocked a vast new African American market, so that record companies pushed to record anything with "blues" in the title. For the next few years female blues artists such as Ma Rainey, Bessie Smith, Ida Cox, Alberta Hunter, and Ethel Waters dominated the market with an early style now called **classic blues**. It had a sophisticated and distinctively urban flavour, with accompaniments by early jazz masters such as trumpeter Louis Armstrong and pianist Earl "Fatha" Hines.

Gertrude "Ma" Rainey (1886–1939) was often called the Mother of the Blues. The Georgia-born Rainey was a powerful and exciting singer, and although her vocal range was only one octave, the soulful qualities of her contralto voice made up for it. According to Thomas Dorsey, Rainey's musical director (and later a major gospel music innovator),

> She was a natural born artist . . . didn't need no school didn't go to no school; didn't take no music didn't need no music. . . . Ma had the real thing she just issued out there. It had everything in it needed, just like somebody issue a plate of food out say everything's on the plate . . . take it or leave it.[7]

With a gold lamé headband, sequins, plumes, and a necklace of $20 gold pieces, Rainey burst out of a giant cardboard gramophone in her stage show. Funny and charismatic, she performed songs of alienation, infidelity, revenge, and lost love. One of the biggest stars on the TOBA circuit, she became the first African American pop star, with numerous recordings. Rainey was also a successful businesswoman, like several other female blues stars of the period.

Bessie Smith (1894–1937), known as the "Empress of the Blues," began her career in a minstrel troupe and debuted with the hit "Down Hearted Blues" in 1923. She made 160 recordings and sold almost ten million records.

PHOTO BY FRANK DRIGGS COLLECTION/GETTY IMAGES

Ma Rainey with her Georgia Jazz Band, including blues and gospel innovator Thomas Dorsey at the piano. Notice the jazz band instrumentation and primitive drum set in the foreground.

Attracting black and white audiences, Smith was a superstar in the 1920s, and she appeared in one film, *The St. Louis Blues,* as well as a Broadway show. At the height of her career, she travelled in her own private railroad car, supporting an entourage of 40 musicians, dancers, singers, and comedians. Smith's repertoire was eclectic, encompassing show tunes and Tin Pan Alley songs such as Irving Berlin's "Alexander's Ragtime Band" as well as the blues. Her expressive style and phrasing influenced musicians of many styles, including jazz, gospel, and R & B. Smith's blues "emanated from the violence and complexities of the urban experience and its effects on black women."[8]

The end of the 1920s saw the decline of the classic blues. The Depression played a part in the shift, as did the development of sound films and the demise of vaudeville, tent shows, and TOBA performances. Female classic blues singers continued to perform, however, and artists such as Ethel Waters and Alberta Hunter influenced the development of an evolving jazz vocal style.

By 1925 the record industry began to pay attention to Delta or rural blues. The industry sought out new artists throughout the South and recorded them in makeshift studios set up in hotel rooms or store fronts. The trips yielded recordings of a range of rural blues artists, including Charley Patton, Son House, Huddie Ledbetter ("Leadbelly"), and Robert Johnson. Record producer Frank Walker described how he worked with rural blues performers:

> We recorded in a little hotel in Atlanta, and we used to put singers up and pay a dollar a day for food and a place to sleep in another little hotel. . . . You couldn't bring songs to them because they couldn't learn them. Their repertoire would consist of eight or ten things that they did well, and that was all they knew. So when you picked out the three or four that were best in a man's so-called repertoire you were through with that man as an artist. That was all. . . . They went back home. They had made a phonograph record and that was the next best thing to being the president of the United States in their mind.[9]

Unfortunately, the record industry's narrow commercial conception of the blues limited the recorded repertoires of many of the rural songsters. The record companies also created the myth of the solo itinerant blues singer singing his "lonesome, tragic tale." Many early rural blues performers actually performed in ensembles and played a variety of musical styles, but record companies recorded them solo and playing only one style, because it simplified production and marketing.

RURAL BLUES

Texas-born Blind Lemon Jefferson (1897–1930) made one of the first successful rural blues recordings, "Black Snake Moan," in 1926. He was a virtuoso guitarist and songster fluent in a range of styles. Jefferson's high-pitched singing had a direct urgency, and his skilled guitar work encompassed multiple influences. Jefferson spent much of his life as an itinerant musician in the South and the Midwest, and he made over 100 recordings that impacted rural blues styles.

Charley Patton (1887–1934) is often referred to as the "Father of the Delta Blues." Born of mixed African and Native American heritage, he grew up on Dockery's plantation in Mississippi, a location rich in blues mythology. The plantation played a central role during the early development of the blues, with numerous accounts of musicians travelling to Dockery's to learn the blues from Patton. Like many rural blues songsters, he knew a wide variety of styles in addition to the blues, and his intense singing was accompanied by slide guitar in a call and response. The slide guitar style, developed from the one-string instrument known as the Diddley Bow, was incorporated into rural blues and country music in the late 1920s, and Patton was an early innovator of the technique. Also known as "bottleneck," the style was played with the guitar tuned to an open chord, which allowed the musician to change chords by sliding a hard object over the strings. Patton used the blunt edge of a knife or the neck of a glass bottle to slide across the strings, creating haunting instrumental responses to his voice. Patton performed at parties, social gatherings, and **juke joints**.

One of Charley Patton's best-known disciples was Son House (1902–1988), a pivotal figure in the evolution of rural blues. He learned the blues from Patton and went on to influence such greats as Robert Johnson and Muddy Waters, but he was

This "autographed" photo from the 1920s is the only known image of Blind Lemon Jefferson and originally appeared in a Paramount record catalogue. Jefferson, the first commercially successful rural blues recording artist, died mysteriously on a Chicago doorstep in a snowstorm at the age of 33 in winter 1930.

conflicted about being a blues musician. As a part-time preacher, he personified the split between church music and secular music. Despite the common origins of the blues and gospel music, the two styles became separate genres, and many Christians, black and white, called the blues "the devil's music." Although the two styles shared many musical features, their lyrical content differed greatly. Son House played and sang with the rhythmic intensity of a rural preacher delivering a sermon, but an inner conflict between the blues and his religion made him shut down his blues career several times. He was rediscovered in 1941 by researcher Alan Lomax, who was recording rural blues artists for the Library of Congress.

Robert Johnson (1911–1938) was the most famous of the rural blues artists, with a rich lore surrounding his name. He was said to have sold his soul to the devil in exchange for his prodigious musical talents at a lonely crossroads somewhere in the Delta. With provocative song titles such as "Hellhound on My Trail," "Me and the Devil Blues," "Cross Road Blues," Johnson built the myth of the blues artist as a romantic and dangerous loner on the move. The Mississippi-born Johnson was influenced by Son House, performed in juke joints, and practised an itinerant lifestyle that led to an early death by poisoning at 27. Only months after Johnson's death, producer John Hammond came south looking for him to perform in New York at Carnegie Hall in the legendary "From Spirituals to Swing" concert, a program that traced the history of African American music. As a singer and guitarist, Johnson added much to the vocabulary of the blues. The intensity of his acoustic guitar style foretold the amplified sound of Chicago blues and the impending emergence of the electric guitar as a major voice. Johnson's entire output consisted of twenty-nine songs recorded between 1936 and 1937, and only one of his tunes, "Terraplane Blues," became a minor hit, selling fewer than 4,000 copies. By contrast, the 1990 release of *Robert Johnson: The Complete Recordings* sold over 600,000 copies in six months. Johnson's songs were repeatedly covered by a wide variety of artists, including Eric Clapton and Cream, Johnny Winter, the Rolling Stones, the Allman Brothers, Bonnie Raitt, and the Red Hot Chili Peppers. In the words of guitarist Eric Clapton,

> Robert Johnson to me is the most important blues musician who ever lived. . . . I have never found anything more deeply soulful than Robert Johnson. His music remains the most powerful cry that I think you can find in the human voice.[10]

URBAN BLUES

Lured by good-paying jobs, large numbers of African Americans migrated to the North in the first two decades of the twentieth century. By the 1930s, sizable black populations lived in many major Northern cities, and the newcomers demanded down-home music from entertainers. As African American culture became urbanized, the blues followed suit. One of the first urban blues tunes, "How Long How Long Blues," was recorded in 1928 by pianist Leroy Carr. The song had an introspective flavour, with lyrics that pondered the distance travelled from the rural South to the urban North. It presaged the development of the urban blues of the 1930s. The urban blues was characterized by the coordinated use of guitar, piano, and sometimes a full rhythm section in an ensemble setting, playing a consistent, often up-tempo rhythm. Chicago played a central role in the development of the urban blues style, with artists such as Tampa Red, Memphis Minnie, and Big Bill Broonzy setting the tone in the 1930s. According to Francis Davis, "The blues scene in Chicago revolved around Tampa Red, whose apartment over a pawnshop was . . . a 'madhouse' of old musicians."[11] Tampa Red's 1928 hit, "It's Tight Like That," had a lighter feel than either the classic or rural blues, anticipating much of the music recorded in Chicago for the next decade.

Bluebird Records was the best-known Chicago blues label in the 1930s. It was also the first label to develop a consistent "house sound"—the Bluebird beat—an approach later used by Chess Records, Blue Note, Motown, and others. Bluebird records were light and happy, with little of the soul-searching of the rural blues. They had a regular, danceable beat driven by a combination of guitar, piano, and bass, eliminating the unpredictable rhythmic variations and contrasting timbres characteristic of the rural blues. Leading Bluebird artists included Tampa Red, Big Bill Broonzy, and Memphis Minnie.

Prominent on the Chicago blues scene of the 1930s, vocalist/guitarist Memphis Minnie (1897–1973) was an early innovator on the electric guitar. Her career transcended and combined two blues stereotypes—the female classic blues singer and the male itinerant rural blues singer. The Louisiana-born artist made her recording debut in 1929 with "When the Levee Breaks," a song recalling the catastrophe of the great Mississippi River flood of 1927. This major disaster extended through much of the Midwest and left thousands of African Americans stranded. Minnie's powerful singing and guitar work embodied the transition from rural to urban blues. She was also a beautiful woman who modelled her stage presence on classic blues stars of the 1920s. Poet Langston Hughes sums up the urban blues experience in a description of a Memphis Minnie performance he attended in 1943:

> Memphis Minnie sits on top of the icebox at the 230 Club in Chicago and beats out blues on an electric guitar. . . . She grabs the microphone and yells, "Hey now!" . . . Then, through the smoke and racket of the noisy Chicago bar float Louisiana bayous, muddy old swamps, Mississippi dust and sun, cotton fields, lonesome roads, train whistles in the night.[12]

The blues continued to evolve throughout the 1930s and 1940s, influencing jazz and other popular music styles. The emergence of radio and the electric guitar, as well as the onset of World War II, shaped this evolution. The invention of radio hastened the development of African American music by making it freely available on a wide basis for the first time. Although the first experimental sound radio broadcasts were made around 1906, several decades passed before commercial radio developed. By the 1930s, radio featured live performances, recordings, and a wide range of cultural programming. By the late 1940s, blues and gospel programs were being broadcast to wide audiences throughout the South. One of the most famous blues outlets was KFFA in Helena, Arkansas, which covered the Delta region. The station's most popular blues show was "King Biscuit Time," sponsored by a local grocer. It was broadcast live daily at noon and made stars of the artists whose music it showcased. WDIA in Memphis, which called itself "America's only 50,000 watt Negro radio station," served a large African American market throughout the South with blues and gospel programming that made Memphis a magnet for people migrating north. Blues artist Howlin' Wolf also got his start broadcasting on the radio in Memphis in 1948 with an electric blues band, and a year later bluesman B. B. King started out as a Memphis DJ.

The development of the electric guitar was central to the evolution of the blues, R & B, and rock. Until the 1930s, the acoustic guitar was used in rural blues and country music as a rhythm instrument, although some rural blues artists developed it as a solo voice. In jazz, banjos rather than guitars were used in rhythm sections throughout much of the 1920s, but by the 1930s jazz bands were switching to guitar. Although it fit well into the sound of swing, the guitar was often too soft to be heard, so musicians and inventors began to experiment with amplification. The **Dobro** company commercially manufactured the first electric guitar in 1930, followed a year later by Rickenbacker. In 1936 Gibson contributed its own model, further legitimizing the new instrument.

The advent of World War II also influenced stylistic developments in the blues. Many African Americans moved from the South to other parts of the country to take jobs in defence industries; these jobs had become available because of an executive order issued by Franklin Roosevelt in 1941 in response to strong African American labour union pressure. Migrants took the most direct routes from their homes to the new jobs: People from the Southeast went to New York, those from the Deep South went to Chicago and Detroit, and those from the Midwest and Southwest often ended up on the West Coast. New regional blues styles developed as a result.

ELECTRIC URBAN BLUES

A key architect of the electric blues was Chicago-based vocalist/guitarist Muddy Waters (1915–1983), and his work heavily influenced artists such as the Rolling Stones, Eric Clapton, Bonnie Raitt, and B. B. King. The **electric blues**, which began in the 1940s, used amplified, sometimes distorted instrumental sounds of the guitar and harmonica in an ensemble setting. Differing electric styles developed in Chicago, Memphis, and Texas. The Mississippi-born Waters grew up on a cotton plantation learning blues guitar and vocal styles from Delta blues masters Charley Patton, Son House, and Robert Johnson. When folklorist Alan Lomax came through town in 1941 looking for undiscovered blues artists to record, he helped Waters make his first recording. Waters headed for Chicago in 1943, where he found work in a paper factory and started playing music. He soon realized that there was a new style of amplified blues being played in the town: "I started playing amplified guitar when I came to Chicago. Everybody else was playing them and I had to get something to go with that too."[13]

At first, Waters's down-home Delta blues sound was too raw for club owners, who were looking for the smoother, jazzier sound of popular artists such as Louis Jordan, Charles Brown, or Nat "King" Cole. Waters started to record for Chess Records in 1947, beginning a string of hits that included "I Can't Be Satisfied" and "I Feel Like Going Home." His greatest accomplishment was the development of an electric blues band sound. Working from the old Delta blues, the Waters band had a raucous and powerful sound flavoured by the **distortion** of amplified instruments. Willie Dixon's fine songwriting ("Just Make Love to Me" and "I'm Your Hoochie Coochie Man"), the band's brawling amplified sound, and Waters's vocals combined to produce the classic Chicago-style electric blues. After Waters, the sound of electrical

© TERRY CRYER/CORBIS

Muddy Waters, the architect of the Chicago blues.

distortion and overloaded amplifiers became a staple of rock and blues, from Jimi Hendrix to heavy metal to grunge. In the words of B. B. King,

> Muddy might have been the most magnificent of all the bluesmen to come out of Mississippi. . . . Muddy became a father figure to generations of musicians, black and white. . . . No one had Muddy's authority. He was the boss of Chicago and the reason some call Chicago the sure-enough home of the blues.[14]

Anyone who has enjoyed the music of B. B. King, Buddy Guy, Chuck Berry, Robert Cray, Eric Clapton, Stevie Ray Vaughan, Johnny Winter, or Albert King has heard echoes of guitarist/vocalist T-Bone Walker (1910–1975). As one of the first electric bluesmen, Walker forged the connection between the older acoustic blues and the new electric sound, successfully blending the Delta and Texas blues traditions. Raised in Dallas, Texas, as a boy Walker led bluesman Blind Lemon Jefferson around the streets of Dallas:

> Blind Lemon I remember well. Though I was only a kid, he had me to lead him around. He kept the guitar strapped on his chest, a tin cup on the neck. . . . Lemon sang things he wrote himself about life—good times and bad. Mostly bad, I guess. Everybody knew what he was singing about. There's nothing new in the blues. It's everything that's going on.[15]

Walker soon performed with travelling shows, and his flashy stage moves—including doing the splits and picking up a table with his teeth—were perfected

MICHAEL OCHS ARCHIVES/GETTY IMAGES

Guitarist/vocalist T-Bone Walker during the 1940s in a legendary performance pose. His stage style predated the guitar heroics of such artists as Chuck Berry and Jimi Hendrix.

at an early age. As he developed on the guitar, he became friends with jazz guitar legend Charlie Christian, also a Texan. By 1934 Walker was fronting his own group, and in 1936 he moved to Los Angeles, where he was so popular by the end of the decade that he worked in the most fashionable white clubs on Sunset Strip. Walker mastered the new sound of the electric guitar in the early 1940s, and from 1945 through 1947 he recorded over fifty tunes, including such classics as "T-Bone Shuffle" and "Call It Stormy Monday." He toured frequently in package shows with other artists, but nobody wanted to follow Walker; his stage act was so spectacular that he always closed the shows.

Vocalist/guitarist B. B. King (1925–) has become the best-known bluesman in the world, with a simple melodic style that blended gospel, jazz, and Delta blues. He has influenced generations of blues and rock guitarists—including Buddy Guy, Eric Clapton, Mike Bloomfield, the Butterfield Blues Band, Bonnie Raitt, Robert Cray, Keb' Mo', and Stevie Ray Vaughan. The Grammy-winning artist's career spanned more than four decades, over fifty albums, and numerous awards. As a performer, King patterned himself after vocalist/saxophonist Louis Jordan, while his guitar style used bends, **vibrato**, and jazzy runs influenced by T-Bone Walker. According to King,

> I've never really been accepted by the blues purists because they say I use too many clichés. I could never be a real jazz musician because I don't improvise well enough. . . . So I'm kind of in-between. I don't sing gospel well enough to be considered a gospel singer.[16]

King hailed from the Mississippi Delta, and his first musical influence was gospel. But he soon found that he could triple his day wages by playing the blues on street corners, and he headed for Memphis in 1946. King described his first impression of the city:

> It was like a fantasy come true. . . . Beale Street was famous, of course, because of W. C. Handy, Father of the Blues, and his composition "Beale Street Blues.". . . I knew Handy was black and that he stayed in Memphis and was known the world over. . . . His stature gave the blues pride. . . . Walking down Beale, I saw white people shopping the same street as blacks. That was new for me.[17]

Memphis was also developing as a recording centre in the late 1940s. Sam Phillips started his Sun Records studio there in 1950,

© BETTMANN/CORBIS

B. B. King publicity photo for BluesWay Records from the late 1960s.

recorded numerous blues greats, and pressed Elvis Presley's first recordings. Other influential blues and R & B artists to record in Memphis included Howlin' Wolf, Ike Turner, Bobby "Blue" Bland, and Rufus Thomas. King was hired to play on blues radio shows and was soon promoted to DJ, calling himself "Beale Street Blues Boy," later shortened to "B. B." His first hit was "Three O'Clock Blues" in 1952, and though he toured the R & B circuit throughout the 1950s and early 1960s, he could not cross over to mainstream acceptance the way so many other R & B artists had in the fifties rock era. Around 1965 the final barriers to blues popularity began to fall when white America first heard the music of Son House and other Delta blues artists at the Newport Folk Festival. King capitalized on the new interest with the 1966 release of his signature hit, "The Thrill Is Gone," and he built on it to record and tour extensively before mainstream audiences. He ultimately became the face of the blues for mainstream America.

FROM RACE MUSIC TO R & B

Although no one can say exactly when rock was born or who recorded the first rock song, historians agree that R & B was rock's closest musical relative. R & B developed as a result of several factors, as critic Nelson George argues,

> The term originated in the 1940s as a description of a synthesis of black musical genres—gospel, big-band swing, blues—that, along with new technology, specifically the popularization of the electric bass, produced a propulsive, spirited brand of popular music. A decade later it would be called rock & roll to camouflage its black roots, and subsequently soul, disco, rap, and other offspring would rise from these roots.[18]

Recall that, beginning in 1920, producers called popular music recordings by African Americans *race records,* and the term remained in use until the late 1940s. *Billboard* magazine had just begun to chart the sale of race music in 1946 when record labels became uncomfortable with the term and started to use coded alternatives such as "ebony" or "sepia." In 1949 *Billboard* without comment redesignated the category as *rhythm and blues,* using a term coined by a young writer, Jerry Wexler (later an Atlantic Records producer).

Early rhythm and blues (R & B) was a hybrid that mainly served as dance music for the African American community. As R & B pioneer Louis Jordan said, "I wanted to play music on stage that made people forget what they did that day."[19] By the end of World War II, the swing era of the 1930s and 1940s had peaked; however, although the new bebop style was moving jazz away from its dance-based roots, some swing band elements lived on in R & B. An aggressive rhythmic style known as **jump blues**, which began in the 1930s with Count Basie's Kansas City–based, riff-style big band, served as the prototype for postwar R & B. The format was ideal for smaller postwar bands that featured simple, blues-based tunes, explosive improvised solos, and the spontaneity lacking in many swing bands of the time. According to historian Charlie Gillett,

> At a time when the contemporary white big bands of Glenn Miller, Les Brown, and the Dorsey Brothers . . . were tending to impose arrangements on their musicians, the black bands had opened up and let their musicians run free. The

sound of a sax solo breaking loose from a series of driving riffs is one of the most exciting experiences of this century's music.[20]

Known to many as "the father of rhythm and blues," alto saxophonist, singer, and band leader Louis Jordan (1908–1975) had a string of hits in the late 1940s that made him the first artist to chart in all three popular music categories simultaneously. According to historian Arnold Shaw,

> Jordan is the pivotal figure in the rise of R & B . . . because his fantastic success on disk, on the radio, in personal appearances, and on the screen fired the imagination of black artists and independent record producers. He demonstrated that, not only was there a market for black-oriented material and black-styled music, but it was a big market, white as well as black."[21]

Jordan's **boogie-woogie**-based jump blues and performance style directly influenced both white and black artists, including Bill Haley, Chuck Berry, B. B. King, and James Brown. He was also the unrecognized "grandfather" of rap, owing to his satirical, spoken-word commentaries on social topics that were set to a jump-swing groove. In addition, Jordan and his band, the Tympany Five, were one of the first acts to dress in wild costumes and perform elaborate, tightly rehearsed shows. This outrageous visual style enabled the artist to produce some of the first *soundies,* late-1940s film equivalents of music videos that people viewed through visual arcade jukeboxes.

The Arkansas-born Jordan began his career with the Rabbitfoot Minstrels, where he developed versatile entertainment skills. In the late 1930s, he joined

© BETTMANN/CORBIS

Influential R & B legend Louis Jordan at a recording session in 1954.

the Chick Webb Orchestra, which also featured singer Ella Fitzgerald. As one of Webb's vocalists, Jordan started performing the novelty songs that became central to his repertoire. A **novelty song** is a humorous song, often with a non-sense theme, sometimes employing special sound effects. Shortly thereafter, Jordan moved to start his own band, and by the late 1940s he was a household name. His success partly stemmed from his association with Decca Records, one of the first major labels to dispense with the race record category, which promoted Jordan's recordings to both black and white audiences. The artist's string of hits included "Five Guys Named Moe" (1942); "G.I. Jive" (1943); "Caldonia" (1945); his roots-of-rap classic, "Beware" (1945); and "Saturday Night Fish Fry" (1947). By the early 1950s, his musical style was influencing R & B and early rock artists throughout the country. Although his music was central to the formation of rock, Jordan never crossed over to the new genre, and by the late 1950s he had disappeared from the limelight.

SHOUTERS, CRIERS, AND HONKERS

Historians often group early R & B performers into three categories: shouters, criers, or honkers. **Shouters** came out of the riff-based big band tradition, in which a jump-style band was fronted by high-energy, blues-based vocals that were very nearly shouted. Famous R & B shouters included Wynonie Harris, Big Joe Turner, Jimmy Witherspoon, Ruth Brown, Little Esther Phillips, and Willie Mae "Big Mama" Thornton. Although only a few shouters crossed over to rock, they did influence rock vocal styles. Ruth Brown's (1928–2006) sophisticated blues style scored hits with "Teardrops from My Eyes" (1951) and "Oh What a Dream" (1954). Big Joe Turner's (1911–1985) major hit "Shake, Rattle, and Roll" (1954) was covered with great success by Bill Haley and Elvis Presley. Although not a crossover success, Wynonie Harris (1915–1969) had an R & B hit with his 1948 recording of "Good Rockin' Tonight," later covered by Elvis Presley. Some historians identify "Good Rockin' Tonight" as the first rock and roll song. Despite their appeal, most R & B shouters were considered too adult in style, their lyrics too sexual, for the ears of white teenage rock fans.

With close connections to black gospel music (see Chapter 7), the R & B **crier** tradition, which projected the image of one overcome by emotion, also greatly affected rock vocal styles. The crier tradition influenced a host of blues, R & B, and rock singers, including Elvis Presley, Little Richard, Jackie Wilson, James Brown, and B. B. King. Singer/songwriter Roy Brown (1925–1981) was a consummate blues crier. He composed and recorded the first version of "Good Rockin' Tonight" (1948), covered by Harris later that year, and released other crier-style tunes such as "Hard Luck Blues" (1950) and "Big Town" (1951). Other R & B criers included Amos Milburn and Little Willie John.

The sound of the **honker**, or a performer playing a screaming, honking tenor saxophone, provided another essential ingredient of R & B and early rock. According to historian Charlie Gillett,

During the first period of rock 'n' roll, 1954 to 1956, its most distinctive "trademark" was a break two-thirds of the way through the record, in which a saxophone player produced a sound that was liable to tear the paper off the walls, a fast screech that emphasized almost every beat for several bars.[22]

The honking R & B sax style was embodied in the work of players such as Earl Bostic, Bill Doggett, Sam "the Man" Taylor, Big Jay McNeely, and King Curtis. Particularly prolific, Curtis recorded with the Drifters and many other R & B artists. Throughout much of the 1950s, one could hear the sound of a blazing sax solo on almost every rock record.

The West Coast played a major role in the evolution of R & B, according to R & B pioneer Johnny Otis,

> Now R & B started here in LA. Roy Milton was here, Joe Liggins was here, T-Bone Walker was here, Charles Brown was here, I was here, and others, too. By '48 or '49 it was set—we had an art form, though we didn't know it then.[23]

Industrial growth during World War II drew over two million African Americans to California from Texas, Arkansas, Oklahoma, and Louisiana, and the wartime social climate encouraged desegregation of public places. One important West Coast stylistic innovation was a new style of ballad-oriented, smooth blues singing associated with Nat "King" Cole and Charles Brown. Another was the heightened prominence of the electric guitar, pioneered by T-Bone Walker. He was the first R & B performer to use the sustained tone made possible by electric amplification to play the guitar like a horn. He was also the first to make the guitar a central theatrical focus of his act—playing behind his back, over his head, with his teeth, and between his legs—well before Chuck Berry's duck walk of the 1950s or Jimi Hendrix's psychedelic antics of the 1960s.

Band leaders Johnny Otis (1921–) and Roy Milton (1907–1983) made major contributions to the L.A. R & B scene. While most early innovators of R & B were African American, Otis was a white Greek American who identified strongly with the African American community. In the 1950s, he led one of R & B's most successful acts, the Rhythm and Blues Caravan. Otis described the sound that he and others were developing:

> It surely wasn't a big band; it wasn't swing, it wasn't country blues. It was what was to become known as rhythm and blues, a hybrid form that became an art form in itself. It was the foundation of rock 'n' roll.[24]

Otis had his first hit with "Harlem Nocturne"(1946), and he made the shift to rock in the 1950s with such hits as "Willie and the Hand Jive" (1958). In addition to performing, he found success as a writer and producer who discovered and promoted major R & B artists including Jackie Wilson and Little Esther Phillips.

Roy Milton and the Solid Senders had one of the biggest R & B hits of the 1940s called "R.M. Blues." The million-selling jump blues was one of the first tunes to use a rock backbeat, and Milton's innovative drumming became central to the development of rock drum patterns. Other influential West Coast R & B artists included Ruth Brown, Ivory Joe Hunter, and Lowell Fulson. Charles Brown influenced Ivory Joe Hunter's early work, and Hunter later became one of the earliest black artists to cross over to the country charts.

Nat "King" Cole (1917–1965) was already an accomplished jazz pianist when he introduced his smooth vocal style in the mid-1940s. Although many West Coast nightclubs were beginning to integrate, upscale Hollywood clubs generally remained segregated because they had no interest in blues and R & B. Because the patrons of such clubs wanted to converse over a quiet musical background, Cole played lounge-style piano backed by smooth, warm vocals. A black singer who crooned like Bing Crosby was a novelty, and Cole's subdued baritone voice became an immediate hit. Ultimately, Cole's style stood so far removed from African American performance traditions that white audiences often found him more popular than black audiences did. His hits included "Straighten Up and Fly Right" (1944), "Get Your Kicks on Route Sixty Six" (1945), "The Christmas Song" (1947), "Mona Lisa" (1950), and "Unforgettable" (1952). The last song was posthumously rerecorded in 1991 as a duet by Cole's daughter Natalie.

Although Nat "King" Cole was never a blues singer, his vocal style significantly influenced the smooth, bluesy, ballad style of singer/songwriter/pianist Charles Brown (1922–1999). Brown in turn influenced a generation of R & B artists with his own emotion-laden, crooning blues style. According to vocalist/guitarist Bonnie Raitt,

> Charles was the master of the blues ballad. In the evolution from blues and jazz in the 30s and 40s to modern R & B and pop, Charles Brown's importance simply can't be overstated. . . . He introduced the nuances of great pop and jazz singing into the world of R & B. And you will hear his legacy in everyone from Ray Charles to Sam Cooke, to Marvin Gaye, to Babyface, to D'Angelo.[25]

The Texas-born Brown began his musical career in Los Angeles as pianist with Johnny Moore's Three Blazers, a group that fashioned its sound on Nat "King" Cole's trio. Brown's own melancholy, smooth blues sound flavoured his first hit, "Driftin' Blues" (1946), which sold a million copies and knocked Louis Jordan out of first place. The lyrics to the song struck a raw nerve with soldiers, sailors, and migrant workers throughout the country who had been cut adrift by war:

> I'm driftin' and driftin' like a ship out on the sea
> I ain't got nobody in this world to care for me.[26]

After Brown left the Blazers to record under his own name, he scored numerous hits throughout the 1940s. His holiday blues classic "Merry Christmas Baby" (1948) was covered by artists as diverse as Elvis Presley, Otis Redding, Lou Rawls, and Bruce Springsteen.

VOCAL GROUP ORIGINS

We can trace the roots of the R & B vocal group tradition back to two legendary African American vocal groups—the Mills Brothers and the Ink Spots. The father of the original Mills Brothers, a barber in Ohio, belonged to a black barbershop quartet; the brothers first sang in front of their father's barbershop and in African American church choirs. The Mills Brothers' first hit, "Tiger Rag" (1931), was the first vocal-group recording to sell over a million copies. They generally started songs in a sweet ballad style, picking up the tempo in the second verse. They also developed a repertoire of vocal imitations of musical instruments that became a trademark. Other hits included "Paper Doll" (1942) and "Glow-Worm" (1952).

The Ink Spots began their career in the early 1930s singing fast jump tunes. Later in the decade they switched to a ballad style often interspersed with spoken dialogue. The group's main hits included "If I Didn't Care" (1939), "Java Jive" (1940), and "I'll Never Smile Again" (1940). The work of both the Mills Brothers and the Ink Spots was characterized by clear standard English diction and songs with unprovocative, neutral content, which enabled them to cross over to white audiences.

EARLY DOO-WOP

Primarily an urban African American phenomenon, doo-wop was usually performed by young men and featured group harmony with traditional choir arrangements (tenor, baritone, bass), often with an added falsetto (high voice). Increasing numbers of gospel artists (see Chapter 7) entered the record market in the 1940s, and gospel harmony fed the new doo-wop vocal style. The use of nonsense syllables on background parts was also standard, evolving from "doo-wahs" and "doo-wops" to more-complex articulations. Singers could start a doo-wop group with no instrumental accompaniment, and rehearsals could take place anywhere, anytime—in attics, in garages, or on street corners.

Doo-wop groups often took the colourful names of songbirds or cars: the Orioles, the Ravens, the Penguins, and the Flamingos, as well as the Impalas, the Fleetwoods, and the El Dorados. Popular early doo-wop groups included the Ravens, who scored hits with "Write Me a Letter" (1948) and "Rock Me All Night Long" (1952); the Orioles, a Baltimore group, who made the charts with "It's Too Soon to Know" (1949) and "Crying in the Chapel" (1953); and the Dominoes, who found success with the controversial "Sixty Minute Man" (1951), whose lyrics boasted of sexual prowess and provoked the ire of white conservatives. Two lead singers from the Dominoes, Clyde McPhatter and Jackie Wilson, went on to successful solo careers.

After leaving the Dominoes, McPhatter formed the Drifters. When McPhatter left to become a soloist, he was replaced by Ben E. King, who led the Drifters through a series of hits, including "There Goes My Baby" (1959), "This Magic Moment" (1960), and "Save the Last Dance for Me" (1960). Hank Ballard and the Midnighters scored with "Work with Me Annie" (1954), "Sexy Ways" (1954), and "Annie Had a Baby" (1954). The three songs together told a sad story of pleading, gratification, and the laws of cause and effect—three of doo-wop's central themes. There were numerous doo-wop "one-hit wonders," including the Chords, whose megahit was "Sh-Boom" (1954), and the Penguins, who produced "Earth Angel" (1955). The Crew Cuts, a white doo-wop group, released covers of black doo-wop hits which often charted higher than the originals.

Doo-wop entered its golden age in the late 1950s, as groups began to integrate advanced choreography and white doo-wop acts started to record original material. Frankie Lymon and the Teenagers, who later influenced Michael Jackson and other Motown artists, scored one of the biggest doo-wop hits of all time with "Why Do Fools Fall in Love?" in 1956. The Coasters and the Platters gained particular prominence in the late 1950s. The Coasters, who featured novelty songs with spoken words, had hits with "Yakety Yak" (1958), "Charlie Brown" (1959), and "Poison Ivy" (1959). The Platters, sometimes called "the new Ink Spots," were the first black doo-wop group to reach number one on the pop charts with "The Great Pretender" (1955). Other hits included "Only You" (1955) and "Smoke Gets in Your Eyes" (1958).

While most doo-wop groups were male, some successful female and mixed-gender vocal groups gained popularity. The most prominent all-female group, the Chantels, charted with "He's Gone" (1957), "Maybe" (1958), and "Every Night (I Pray)" (1958). Many white vocal groups of the late 1950s were Italian American. Dion and the Belmonts, the most popular of the groups, had a

MICHAEL OCHS ARCHIVES/GETTY IMAGES

The Coasters (left to right): Cornel Gunther, Will "Dub" Jones, B Guy, Carl Gardner, and guitarist Adolphi Jacob.

million-seller with "Teenager in Love" (1959). The Four Lovers, after changing their name to the Four Seasons, became stars in the early 1960s with hits such as "Sherry" (1962) and "Walk Like a Man" (1962). Although the doo-wop era ended by 1960, it paved the way for the girl-group and Motown vocal ensemble sounds of the 1960s.

INDEPENDENT LABELS AND BLACK-ORIENTED STATIONS

In the 1940s, small, regionally based record labels began distributing the new sound of R & B. Although a few major R & B artists, such as Louis Jordan and Nat "King" Cole, recorded for large record companies, most others recorded on the new independent labels. One reason for this was a shift in how music was licensed and published in the era. The major labels, associated with ASCAP, geared their product for the mass white audience. BMI, on the other hand, was aggressively signing R & B and country songwriters. The new record labels also set their sights on the underserved, marginal markets. The independent labels were central to the development of R & B and early rock for two decades.

New radio stations—some with powerful transmitters that provided national coverage—also expanded the reach of R & B in the late 1940s. Located mainly in the South and West, the stations began to program for the African American market for the first time, simultaneously giving greater voice to the new sounds of R & B. The financial logic was clear, according to Nelson George:

> The sales staff of Memphis's powerful 50,000-watt WDIA weren't shy about the fact that they reached 1,237,686 Negroes (10 percent of all black Americans) and that Negroes constituted 40 percent of the Memphis market.[27]

In addition to R & B, the stations often also played blues, gospel, and jazz. Whites owned almost all the black-oriented stations, and their sound was defined by the personalities of their DJs, who were both white and black. Many black and white listeners—including a young Elvis Presley—received their early musical schooling from the R & B stations.

CHAPTER SUMMARY

- The blues is a core element of popular music. Almost all styles of popular music, including jazz, gospel, rock, R & B, and country, reflect its influence.

- The evolution of African American and popular American musical traditions took place in a context of cultural appropriation and commodification. This began with minstrelsy and continues to the present.

- The first indigenous American theatrical and popular music genre, minstrelsy, shaped the blues as well as twentieth-century American musical theatre. Based on racist stereotypes, minstrel shows were performed by white men in blackface from the 1830s into the twentieth century. After the Civil War, black minstrel troupes provided African Americans opportunities to work as mass popular entertainers.

- The blues includes many characteristics, including the 12-bar form, use of blue notes, call and response, bends and slides between notes, and an AAB lyric pattern. Much of popular music retains some of these blueslike qualities.

- From its roots in Africa, the blues grew out of a blend of field hollers, minstrelsy, and church music.

- The first blues songs emerged around 1900 in the repertoire of itinerant black songsters. The Mississippi Delta is often cited as the birthplace of the blues, although the genre developed in other parts of the South as well.

- The first successful commercialization of the blues was W. C. Handy's publication of the "St Louis Blues" in 1914, and Mamie Smith's 1920 "Crazy Blues" was the first successful blues recording, leading to the development of race records.

- Two schools of blues recordings developed in the 1920s: classic blues, dominated by female artists such as Bessie Smith and Ma Rainey, and rural blues, dominated by men such as Blind Lemon Jefferson, Charlie Patton, Son House, and Robert Johnson. The record industry did much to shape the two styles.

- The Depression saw the demise of the classic blues and the beginnings of a new, band-oriented sound called the urban blues.

- The invention of the electric guitar and popularization of the radio in the 1930s and 1940s, along with northward African American migration, expanded the musical possibilities and fan base for blues. Artists such as Muddy Waters, T-Bone Walker, and B. B. King greatly contributed to the development of the genre. The popularity of the blues continues to rise and fall.

- Rock may be the most popular music in the world today. Its emergence coincided with the appearance of a youth culture, for which rock served as a primary voice. Rooted in African American R & B and jazz, the new hybrid grew to become more than the sum of its parts.

- The 1950s were a time of rapid cultural change in North America, reflected by the growth of white suburbia and Cold War anxiety. New technologies such as radio and television, as well as economic prosperity, supported the development of the new teen consumer class. Simultaneously, white teens were discovering new R & B music that was developing in black communities.

- R & B was a blend of African American styles: jazz, big band swing, gospel, blues, and boogie woogie. By the late 1940s, it had replaced swing as popular dance music, although only a few black musicians, such as

Louis Jordan, crossed the colour line. Small independent record labels emerged to accommodate the growing demand for black dance music, and in 1948 *Billboard* established the new category of "rhythm and blues."

- Early vocal groups such as the Ink Spots and the Mills Brothers were forebears of doo-wop, a new vocal style born in urban African American communities. The style centred on harmony singing and required no instruments. Groups such as the Coasters, the Platters, and the Drifters developed styles that white musicians embraced and that became central to 1950s rock. The style also paved the way for the following decade's girls groups and soul vocal ensemble sound.

- When the growth of R & B-oriented radio stations made black music accessible to white teenagers, a racist backlash followed. The vitality of the music was difficult to quash, however, as Little Richard, Fats Domino, and Bill Haley and other artists founded the music DJ Alan Freed baptized as "rock and roll."

LISTENING EXERCISES

1. 12-Bar Blues Characteristics

Listen to the 1928 recording of Bessie Smith singing "Empty Bed Blues." This recording includes most of the African musical aesthetics we have examined, including metaphors, call and response, blues inflections, blues scales, swing, syncopation, and improvisation. Smith also employs the classic form of the 12-bar blues. Identify the key features of the 12-bar blues form.

2. Blues Cover Versions

Listen to Robert Johnson's recording of "Cross Road Blues." This song was covered by a variety of artists, notably Eric Clapton when performing with the 1960s rock trio Cream. "Cross Road" tells Johnson's legendary story of trading his soul to the devil. Does the timbre of his high-pitched, edgy, singing style add to the drama of the lyrics? Johnson's guitar style and extensive vocabulary of blues licks have influenced rock and blues musicians for over fifty years. Next, listen to a sample of Clapton's version of the same song ("Cross-roads") recorded with Cream. How do the two performances compare?

3. Rural/Urban Blues Comparison

Listen to "I'm Your Hoochie Coochie Man" recorded in 1954 by Muddy Waters. What is the overall feel of the song? What is the instrumentation of the band? How does the amplified harmonica blend with the electric guitar? What roles do the piano and bass play? How does the use of "stop time" breaks, when the entire band stops playing momentarily, and the slow tempo contrast with the intensity of the lyrics and vocal delivery? Compare and contrast this performance style with Robert Johnson's "Cross Road Blues." How do they differ?

4. **Urban Blues Comparison**

Listen to "Call It Stormy Monday" recorded in 1947 by T-Bone Walker. This is one of the best-known blues songs ever recorded, with hundreds of versions by various artists. Notice the laid-back, introspective quality of the tune. How does it contrast with the feel of Muddy Waters's "Hoochie Coochie Man"? What is different about Walker's vocal style? Notice the different tones Walker gets from the guitar—from the low-register chords at the start to the fills and solos later in the song. How does he use *sustain*—the ability of the electric guitar to elongate a tone? Could Walker's melody lines have sounded as appropriate on a horn?

5. **Jump Blues**

"Saturday Night Fish Fry" (1947) by Louis Jordan demonstrates the artist's place as the most influential entertainer in early R & B. Jordan's use of humour and spoken-word performance style epitomized the Jump Band style that dominated 1940s Rhythm and Blues and early Rock and Roll. What is Jump Band Blues and how does this blues style compare with the Chicago blues style of Muddy Waters?

HISTORICAL STUDIES AND DISCUSSION QUESTIONS

1. The "Pure" Blues?

Is there a "pure" blues? Are there pure examples of any art form? Musicians seldom work in isolation from other musicians, musical styles are in a constant state of evolution, and all styles are in some sense hybrids. But blues scholars have argued for years about whether or not certain songs or artists represent the "real" blues, and some artists are criticized because their work does not meet an imposed standard of blues "purity." The 12-bar blues structure is often used as a benchmark, although legendary performers such as John Lee Hooker rarely followed the form. Many of the early legends of the blues actually sang a diverse repertoire of songs and styles, yet they were labelled blues artists. Why is music often categorized in such a rigid way?

2. Commodification and the Blues

Commodification takes place when a cultural phenomenon (a song, a story, a picture, even an artist) is turned into a commodity and marketed. When white record producers recorded Robert Johnson in a small hotel room in the early 1930s, he was in the initial stages of being commodified. He was paid a small fee and died shortly thereafter, but the process of commodifying him continues. Johnson's records have been issued and reissued, his image has been repeatedly invoked by white artists such as Eric Clapton, and the movie *Crossroads* was made to profit from the commodity called Robert Johnson. Is the commodification of music necessarily a bad thing?

3. The Guitar Pickup

A key element of electric guitar design was the pickup, a device made by wrapping a coil of wire around a magnet. The coil was placed under metal guitar strings, and their movement created an electric signal that was enhanced by an amplifier and heard through a speaker. With amplification, not only did volume increase, but guitarists could now sustain tones for long periods. This added to the possibilities of using the instrument as a solo voice, and as guitarists experimented further they found that they could manipulate the instrument's sound through distortion and feedback. Who were the earliest guitarists to exploit the new timbral possibilities of the electric guitar? How do the new sonic possibilities relate to the African musical aesthetics discussed in the previous chapter?

4. The African American Origins of Barbershop Quartets

The contemporary image of a barbershop quartet is a group of white men dressed in turn-of-the-century outfits. The roots of the style, however, lay in African American barbershops of the late nineteenth century. Barbering was a low-status occupation performed by European immigrants or African Americans. In the black community, barbershops often served as hubs of social and musical activities, and the close harmonies and performance styles of the barbershop quartet style developed in this milieu.

The early recording industry contributed to the racial shift from black to white barbershop quartets by recording primarily white barbershop groups. Once barbershop became popular in the 1930s, it was promoted by an organization called the SPEBSQSA (Society for the Preservation of Barbershop Quartet Singing in America). The group, like many other male fraternal organizations before the civil rights era, admitted only white members. Over time, the shift of barbershop from a black to a white art form became complete. Is this an isolated or recurring pattern in North American music?

5. Nat "King" Cole—America's First African American TV Host

Nat "King" Cole's success with white audiences opened doors previously closed to black performers. For example, he became the first African American to host his own prime-time TV variety show from 1956 to 1957. The program initially had no sponsors, because advertisers feared that white southern audiences would boycott their products. When no full-time sponsors ultimately appeared, producers took the show off the air. During the program's sixty-five-week run, however, many of the biggest stars in the music business—including Ella Fitzgerald, Tony Bennett, and Peggy Lee—appeared for far less than their normal salaries. How have colour lines changed in the entertainment business today? Are there any hip-hop artists hosting mainstream TV shows?

STUDY QUESTIONS

1. What role did minstrelsy play in the development of blues culture?

2. What are the African roots of the blues?

3. What are the musical qualities of the blues?

4. What were the two schools of early blues, and what led to their development?

5. How did the development of sound recording impact the evolution of the blues?

6. What role did technology and World War II play in the development of the blues?

7. Who were the early women of the blues, and what role did they play as musical and cultural role models?

8. How are the following artists important to the history of the blues: Ma Rainey, Bessie Smith, Robert Johnson, Muddy Waters, T-Bone Walker, and B. B. King?

9. What musical styles did the blues influence? Why did the blues affect so many popular music styles?

10. In what ways is rock an offshoot of R & B? In what ways is it something completely different?

11. Who were some shouters, criers, and honkers, and how did they contribute to the development of R & B and rock?

12. How did R & B innovators such as Louis Jordan and T-Bone Walker contribute to the development of rock?

13. What role did West Coast artists play in developing early rock and R & B?

14. What part did independent record labels, R & B radio stations, and DJs play in developing early R & B and rock?

15. What was the importance of the following regions and artists associated with them: New Orleans, Chicago, and Memphis?

NOTES

1. Eileen Southern, *The Music of Black Americans: A History,* 3rd ed. (New York: Norton, 1997), 237.

2. Cited in Robert Palmer, *Deep Blues* (New York: Viking Press, 1981), 45.

3. Blues definitions from Steven Tracy, *Write Me a Few of Your Lines: A Blues Reader* (Amherst: University of Massachusetts Press, 1999), 10–12.

4. Steven Tracy, *Write Me a Few of Your Lines: A Blues Reader* (Amherst: U of Massachusetts P, 1999), 10–12.

5. David Evans, "Folk and Popular Blues," in Tracy, *Write Me a Few of Your Lines,* 120.

6. Daphne Duval Harrison, *Black Pearls: Blues Queens of the 1920s* (Piscataway, NJ: Rutgers University Press, 1988), 34.

7. *Ibid.,* 36.

8. *Ibid.,* 53.

9. Lawrence Cohn, ed., *Nothing but the Blues* (New York: Abbeville Press, 1993), 25.

10. Liner notes, *Robert Johnson: The Complete Recordings,* Sony Legacy 1C2K64916.

11. Francis Davis, *The History of the Blues* (New York: Hyperion, 1995), 138.

12. Paul and Beth Garon, *Woman with Guitar: Memphis Minnie's Blues* (New York: Da Capo Press, 1992), 124.

13. Steve Waksman, *Instruments of Desire: The Electric Guitar and the Shaping of Musical Experience* (Cambridge, MA: Harvard University Press, 2000), 122.

14. B. B. King with D. Ritz, *Blues All around Me: The Autobiography of B. B. King* (New York: Avon Books, 1996), 77.

15. Helen Dance, *The T-Bone Walker Story* (Baton Rouge: Louisiana State University Press, 1987), 13.

16. King, *Blues All around Me,* 234.

17. *Ibid.,* 65.

18. Nelson George, *The Death of Rhythm and Blues* (New York: Penguin Books, 1998), x.

19. John Chilton, *Let the Good Times Roll: The Story of Louis Jordan and His Music* (Ann Arbor: University of Michigan Press, 1994), 122.

20. Charlie Gillett, *The Sound of the City: The Rise of Rock and Roll* (New York: Da Capo Press, 1996), 127.

21. Arnold Shaw, *Honkers and Shouters: The Golden Age of Rhythm and Blues* (New York: Macmillan, 1978), 64.

22. Gillett, *Sound of the City,* 132.

23. Shaw, *Honkers and Shouters,* 175.

24. Ibid., 161.

25. Liner notes to *A Life in the Blues: Charles Brown,* Rounder Records ROUN2074, 2003.

26. DRIFTING BLUES. CHARLES BROWN, JOHNNY MOORE and EDDIE WILLIAMS. © 1949 (Renewed) 1977 UNART MUSIC CORPORATION. Rights Assigned to EMI CATALOGUE PARTNERSHIP. All Rights Controlled and Administered by EMI UNART CATALOG INC. (Publishing) and ALFRED PUBLISHING CO., INC. (Print) and LEN FREEDMAN MUSIC INC. All Rights Reserved.

27. George, *Death of Rhythm and Blues,* 40–41.

CHAPTER 11

R & B and the Rise of Rock and Roll

No musical development in the latter half of the twentieth century changed the musical landscape more than the birth of rock. In a few short decades, the genre went from a nameless offshoot of R & B to the country's most powerful musical export, perhaps the most popular musical style in the world. A complex blend of blues, R & B, country, swing, and boogie woogie, rock offers the quintessential example of cultural hybridity. The main cultural force in the evolution of rock was African American music, and rock's development replicated a pattern of cultural appropriation of black musical styles in American popular music that had begun one hundred years earlier with minstrelsy. Rock, however, developed into something different, as critic Robert Palmer argues,

> The music *became something else*—not just the same old r&b or white approximations of it, but a broader idiom, influenced not only by black originators but by new production styles, new players, and the new context of a potentially wider and more diverse audience.[1]

The social and political climate of the 1950s greatly influenced the birth of rock. The era witnessed unprecedented economic prosperity, the growth of suburbia, and a baby boom (seventy-six million in the United States, seven million in Canada) that created a new class of consumer: the white teenager. Cars were increasingly available, and new music-listening technologies came on the scene. The 1950s were also shaped by the Cold War and the civil rights movement, which signalled a revolution in race relations.

The postwar era saw technological advances in radio, recording, and television. Radio had found its way into almost every home and car throughout the country. By the late 1950s, people widely used portable, Japanese-made transistor radios, which freed teenagers from adult supervision of programming choices. In 1948 two major record labels, RCA and Columbia, engaged in a "battle of the record speeds." Columbia championed the twelve-inch 33 1/3 rpm **LP record** for classical music and jazz, while RCA promoted its seven-inch **45 rpm record** for popular music. The 45 single took on a life of its own as manufacturers developed portable 45 rpm record players to market directly to teens.

Television also expanded exponentially. By 1955 nearly two-thirds of North American households had them. According to historian Glenn Altschuler,

"Television spread the gospel of prosperity, barely acknowledging the existence of poverty or conflict."[2] Popular music on national television during the early 1950s reflected the bland mix that prevailed on the pop charts. Musical variety shows hosted by stars of the swing era were popular, as were broader variety programs such as the "Steve Allen Show" and the "Ed Sullivan Show." R & B and rock-oriented dance-party shows for teens started to appear in the mid-1950s, including Dick Clark's "American Bandstand." Although some early rock acts filtered into national television programming in the early 1950s, not until Elvis Presley's eleven television appearances in 1956 did rock become firmly established in the medium.

By most standards, the mainstream pop music of the early-1950s was bland. As critic Robert Palmer pointedly notes, "It was somnolent and squeaky clean. . . . For the most part, fifties pop was treacle."[3] Popular white artists of the era included crooner Perry Como, ballad singer Frankie Laine, and vocalist Patti Page, whose big hit was "How Much Is That Doggie in the Window?" Beginning in 1949, *Billboard* magazine reorganized its hit-record charts to recognize three major categories of popular music: popular, country and western, and rhythm and blues. These largely separate musical worlds produced few crossovers, and the only African American artists featured on the pop chart for 1950 were mainstream-sounding crooners such as Nat "King" Cole and Billy Eckstine.

Within a few years, the situation had changed completely. By 1956 black and white R & B and rock artists such as Fats Domino, Little Richard, Chuck Berry, the Platters, the Coasters, Ivory Joe Hunter, Elvis Presley, Bill Haley and His Comets, Carl Perkins, and Johnny Cash had filled the pop charts. Presley, for example, had four top-ten singles that year. The shift to rock had begun.

In the early 1950s, white teens found themselves drawn in increasing numbers to the new, rhythmic sounds and adult—often sexual—lyrical content of R & B. As media commentator Jeff Greenfield recalls, "Brewed in the hidden corners of black American cities, its rhythms infected white Americans, seducing them. . . . Rock and roll was elemental, savage, dripping with sex; it was just as our parents feared."[4] As white teens began to frequent black clubs and to seek out R & B records at black record stores, the merchants took note and passed word on to radio DJs, who fed the growing teen interest. At WLAC in Nashville, Gene Nobles played jazz and early R & B in the early 1940s; in Los Angeles, Hunter Hancock played R & B on KFVD; and the legendary Alan Freed started out on WJW in Cleveland, subsequently moving to New York's WINS. One of the few early black DJs was Nat Williams on WDIA in Memphis. According to one young white listener, "It didn't make any difference what color they were, it just made me feel good."[5]

An influential DJ and the first rock concert promoter, Alan Freed (1922–1965) opened the door to white acceptance of black music by refusing to play white cover versions of R & B originals. He was also among the first to use the term *rock and roll* to describe R & B, although its earliest referent was sex, as singer/songwriter Roy Brown recounted, "Now, 'Good Rockin' Tonight,' you know what that means. I had my mind on this girl in the bedroom, I'm not going to lie to you. Listen, man, I wrote them kind of songs. I was a dirty cat."[6] Freed started working in radio in the early 1940s, playing records by Louis Jordan and other jump-blues artists. He began to call himself the "Moondog," and his show evolved into "The Moondog Rhythm and Blues House Party." He soon branched out into concert promotion, producing history's first rock concert, "The Moondog Coronation Ball," at a Cleveland hockey arena in 1952. The over-promoted event turned into a riot because of lack of security and overcrowding, and the resulting media coverage was memorable:

> There were some 20,000 rabid blues fans. . . . Males were wearing their hats inside a public space, guzzling liquor without restraint from pocket flasks, and, here and there, actually shooting themselves with narcotics in the midst of a crowd![7]

Freed also launched the first sold-out national rock tour in 1953 with an all-star R & B revue headlined by the Dominoes and the Drifters. According to singer/songwriter Paul Simon, "New York was a pool of sounds, but only one station was playing rock and roll, the station Alan Freed was on."[8] Freed's decline began in 1958 when violence erupted at one of his concerts and resulted in legal charges. He was also indicted and convicted for accepting **payola** (bribes to push certain records) from record companies. His contributions to early rock later became the subject of the popular 1978 film *American Hot Wax.*

Bill Haley (1925–1981) was the first white artist to successfully adapt the R & B style for a mass pop audience. With his band, the Comets, Haley fused elements of country, western swing, jump blues, and early R & B to produce some of the first rock hits. His "Crazy, Man, Crazy" (1953) was the first rock song to make the pop charts. Featured in *The Blackboard Jungle,* which was the first rock and roll movie, "Rock around the Clock" (1954) topped the pop charts and eventually sold 22.5 million copies. Rock music had never before been used as the soundtrack to a movie, and the film showcased rock as an emblem of teen rebellion. Both the song and the movie signalled the arrival of a new musical era.

Haley started out playing western swing and country music in the 1940s. He also learned a great deal from Louis Jordan, with whom he shared producer Milt Gabler at Decca Records. Gabler here describes his studio work with Haley's band:

> We'd begin with Jordan's shuffle rhythm . . . and we'd build on it. I'd sing Jordan riffs to the group that would be picked up by the electric guitars and tenor sax. They got a sound that had the drive of The Tympany Five and the color of country and western.[9]

Haley's voice was unmistakably white, but he drew his rhythm from black music. Haley's recording career began in 1951 with a cover version of Jackie Brenston's "Rocket 88." He experimented with his band's name, changing it from the Four Aces of Western Swing to the Saddlemen and finally to Bill Haley and His Comets. In 1954 he released "Rock around the Clock" as well as "Shake, Rattle, and Roll," a sanitized cover of Joe Turner's earlier R & B hit. Haley's popularity declined in the late 1950s, when younger rockers such as Little Richard and Elvis came across as both more attractive and more dangerous.

MICHAEL OCHS ARCHIVES/GETTY IMAGES

Bill Haley and His Comets in a 1957 publicity shot for the film *Don't Knock the Rock.*

Although listeners associated Haley's early music with teen rebellion, he was far from a rebel:

A lot of people blamed juvenile delinquency on us, hot rods, drinking, everything. But rock got the kids off the streets and around the jukeboxes. They said it was a bad influence. Well, we always kept our lyrics clean and we never did any protest songs.[10]

According to rock critic Chet Flippo,

Haley was as unlikely a rock 'n' roll star as you could find anywhere. He was too old and overweight, even at the start, and didn't have the right moves, but he did have the right songs at the right time. Haley was a country-and-western singer and bandleader who accidentally became a rock 'n' roll pioneer."[11]

REGIONAL R & B /ROCK AND ROLL STYLES

As R & B and rock developed, performers and producers generated distinctive hybrids reflecting regional musical styles. Three regions were particularly important: New Orleans, Chicago, and Memphis.

New Orleans

Known as the birthplace of jazz, New Orleans also influenced the evolution of R & B and rock. Although none of the major independent record labels headquartered there, the city hosted an active recording scene. The distinctive, piano-based sound of New Orleans R & B showed in the music of artists such as Fats Domino and Lloyd Price. Many influential early New Orleans rock records were recorded in a tiny studio built and staffed by a white producer named Cosimo Matassa. These recordings, which were sold to Los Angeles–based independent labels, made stars out of artists such as Fats Domino and Little Richard.

Fats Domino (1928–) was one of the most successful rock artists of the 1950s, second only to Elvis Presley. Selling more than sixty-five million records, Domino made the transition from R & B to rock with pleasant, upbeat songs and an engaging piano style. White audiences found him less frantic and threatening than many of his contemporaries, according to critics Grace Lichtenstein and Laura Dankner:

> Neither dynamic nor demented nor dangerous onstage . . . he was instead a pudgy little guy with a great smile beaming out beyond the keyboard who won his audience over with a catchy rolling bass line, not swiveling hips. . . . His songs had hooks that grabbed hold of listeners in an instant and wouldn't let them sit still.[12]

Listeners could instantly recognize Domino's sound. His piano style was classic boogie woogie, influenced by pianists such as Professor Longhair and Amos Milburn, and his voice was uniquely his own. Domino cowrote most of his hits with bandleader Dave Bartholomew, who helped produce Domino's characteristic New Orleans sound. The artist broke into the pop market in 1955 with "Ain't That a Shame." White teen idol Pat Boone quickly covered the tune and drove it to the top of the charts. Domino subsequently appeared in several early rock and roll movies and recorded such rock standards as "Blueberry Hill" (1956), "I'm in Love Again" (1956), "Blue Monday" (1957), and "I'm Walkin'" (1957). Other early rock artists—including Elvis Presley, Chuck Berry, Jerry Lee Lewis, and Little Richard—also covered many of his songs. Unlike the many black artists who were exploited by record companies, Domino had a contract that paid royalties to him as songwriter based on sales of records, rather than a single flat fee for a song. He was also one of the first black artists on national television in the 1950s, and he toured widely in Alan Freed's rock and roll package shows.

Little Richard (Richard Penniman, 1932–) was the first self-styled "King of Rock and Roll." His raucous stage performance, pounding piano, wild falsetto, high pompadour, outrageous makeup, flashy dress, and gleeful sexuality personified the wildness and danger of rock for white audiences. Richard's songs were up-tempo, all-out raves: he was one of rock's first composers with his 1956 hit "Tutti Frutti." His boisterous stage act influenced everyone from Jerry Lee Lewis and James Brown to the Beatles, Mick Jagger, and Jimi Hendrix. Richard's use of costumes and makeup, far in advance of David Bowie, Boy George, Queen, and Prince, also made him the first androgynous rock star, with his thinly veiled homosexuality predating that of other rock artists by decades. Producer Bumps Blackwell recalled his first impression of the artist: "There's this cat in this loud shirt, with hair waved up six inches above his

MICHAEL OCHS ARCHIVES/GETTY IMAGES

Little Richard and his band the Upsetters perform in the 1957 film *Mister Rock and Roll.*

head. He was talking wild, thinking up stuff just to be different, you know? I could tell he was a mega-personality."[13]

The Georgia-born artist began his career singing gospel, playing piano in church, and travelling with medicine and minstrel shows. A successful demo tape led Richard to New Orleans to record with producer Bumps Blackwell and the same band that backed Fats Domino. The first recordings sounded inhibited, but over a lunch break Richard started to play a throwaway tune called "Tutti Frutti," which turned into a hit:

> I'd been singing "Tutti Frutti" for years, but it never struck me as a song you'd *record.* . . . Sure, it used to crack the crowds up when I sang it in the clubs, with those risqué lyrics: Tutti Frutti, good booty / If it don't fit, don't force it / You can grease it, make it easy. But I never thought it would be a fit, even with the lyrics cleaned up.[14]

The tune's whooping vocals and wild piano-banging set a tone for Richard's future hits. Sold to white and black audiences—ultimately over three million copies—it had a widespread impact, quickly covered by white artists Pat Boone and Elvis Presley. Richard followed up with "Long Tall Sally" (1956), "Rip It Up" (1956), and "Ready Teddy" (1956), all of which white artists covered multiple times. Richard toured behind his hits with his fine and aptly named band, the Upsetters. When he left the group to work as a solo act, a young vocalist named James Brown replaced him, then another named Otis Redding did. Richard's hits continued into 1958 with "Lucille," "Keep a Knockin'," and "Good Golly Miss Molly," but by that time he had decided to leave secular music for the Christian ministry. Richard periodically returned to rock in the 1960s and 1970s, touring Europe with the Beatles and the Rolling Stones. Of the numerous "kings" of rock, Little Richard may have actually deserved the title.

Chicago

Extensive migration of African Americans from the deep South made Chicago a centre of important developments in jazz and blues for the first half of the twentieth century. The Chicago blues sound, especially the work of Muddy Waters, helped build the early musical vocabularies of many sixties groups such as the Rolling Stones, who took their name from a Muddy Waters tune. In addition, the city gave rise to Chuck Berry and Bo Diddley, who both recorded with the independent Chess/Checker Records, Chicago's seminal blues/R & B label.

Chess Records' founders, brothers Leonard and Phil Chess, were Polish Jews who migrated to the United States in the late 1940s and westernized their names to Chess. They founded Aristocrat Records in 1947, changing the name to Chess two years later. Chicago blues quickly became their specialty, and Muddy Waters, with his synthesis of rural and electric urban blues, became their star. Other Chess artists included Howlin' Wolf, John Lee Hooker, and Sonny Boy Williamson. By the mid-1950s, Chess had entered the world of rock with doo-wop recordings by the Moonglows and the Flamingos, but the work of Chuck Berry and Bo Diddley is what put Chicago and Chess records at the centre of rock history.

With the possible exception of Little Richard, no other artist deserved the title "architect of rock" more than Chuck Berry (1926–) did. According to historian Charlie Gillett,

> If importance in popular music were measured in terms of imaginativeness, creativeness, wit, the ability to translate a variety of experiences and feelings into musical form, and long term influence and reputation, Chuck Berry would be described as the major figure of rock 'n' roll.[15]

Berry was rock's first electric guitar hero and one of early rock's most prolific songwriters. He was also one of the first to understand that rock was music for teenagers, the new consumer class. Berry crafted songs specifically for teens, shaping them around blazing, T-Bone Walker–style guitar solos. His music also influenced a generation of rock artists including the Beatles, Bob Dylan, and the Rolling Stones. Berry's recording career began with "Maybelline" (1955), followed by "Roll over Beethoven" (1956), "School Day" (1957), "Rock and Roll Music" (1957), "Sweet Little Sixteen" (1958), and "Johnny B. Goode" (1958).

Berry's early musical influences included R & B and country styles; he greatly admired Louis Jordan, T-Bone Walker, and Charles Brown. Berry first auditioned for Chess with the country-flavoured tune "Ida Red," and after some reworking (and retitling as "Maybelline"), the tune became a hit. The artist's clear enunciation and vocal style also made his recordings sound eth- nically ambiguous—that is, he was a black performer who sounded "white." In addition, Berry used stage antics pioneered by T-Bone Walker, notably his patented duck walk, in which he slid across the stage, crouched with one leg in front of the other, with the guitar perched precariously in front of him.

By the end of the 1950s, Berry had become one of the most successful black entertainers of all time. In 1960, however, in a racially motivated pros- ecution, he was arrested and imprisoned for two years on trumped-up morals charges. The artist returned to make records in the 1960s and 1970s, including "Nadine" (1964) and "No Particular Place to Go" (1964), and he toured with the Beatles and the Rolling Stones. According to historian John Collis,

> Berry's effect on rock and roll was greater than any other individual. Whereas Elvis caused a revolutionary change in pop music with a voice and an image, Berry was the complete article, a writer and musician with the imagination to show that rock could venture into previously uncharted territory.[16]

Within a few weeks of Chuck Berry's first recording for Chess Records, Bo Diddley (1928–2008), one of early rock's most idiosyncratic performers, walked a few blocks from his house into the Chess Records studio and asked, "Man, y'all make records in here?"[17] His audition tape, "Bo Diddley," became one of the influential songs of early rock. The rhythmic foundation of the song, similar to the three-two clave of Afro-Caribbean music, became known as the "Bo Diddley beat" and was adopted by numerous rock performers. The idio- syncratic artist's unusual band included a maraca player and a female electric guitarist, both rarities in the male world of 1950s rock. Diddley also played an assortment of bizarre guitars, many of which he built himself. Subsequent hits included "I'm a Man" (1955) and "Who Do You Love" (1956).

Memphis

Memphis played a central role in the development of jazz, blues, R & B, and rock throughout the twentieth century. Situated on the Mississippi River in western Tennessee, near the border of Mississippi and Arkansas, the city strad- dled the route between New Orleans and Chicago; its location in part made it a magnet for aspiring musicians from throughout the region. Beginning in the late 1940s, Memphis also developed as a recording centre, and many influential artists of the postwar period got their start there.

Rock mythology would not be complete without the story of Memphis- based producer Sam Phillips and his Sun Records label. Best remembered as the man who "discovered" and first recorded Elvis Presley, Sam Phillips (1923–2003) also helped develop and popularize **rockabilly** music, and he was the first to record many influential blues artists. Phillips had an intu- ition for talent: In an eight-year period he recorded B. B. King, Howlin' Wolf, Ike Turner, Rufus Thomas, Elvis Presley, Johnny Cash, Jerry Lee Lewis, Carl Perkins, Charlie Rich, and Roy Orbison. Like other independent labels of the era, Sun Records pioneered rock and challenged the dominance of the major record labels. Phillips heard blues, spirituals, and country music while growing up in Depression-era Alabama. While working as a DJ in Memphis, he realized that there were few facilities to record the wealth of black talent in the area: "Beale Street convinced me that with the talent coming out of the Delta, especially, I really wanted to try to do something with that talent because I was very close to it all of my life."[18]

Phillips opened up his recording studio in 1950 with a straightforward business slogan: "We Record Anything—Anywhere—Anytime." At first he recorded local artists such as B. B. King and Howlin' Wolf and then sold or leased the masters to independent record labels. Phillips's recordings featured tape echo, distortion, and skillful use of room acoustics to create a big sound with unusually small groups of musicians. He hit the jackpot in 1951 with the number-one R & B hit "Rocket 88" by Jackie Brenston; many call it the first rock and roll record because of its booming boogie rhythm driven by distorted guitar. During the drive to Memphis for the recording session, the guitar amplifier fell off the top of the band's car, breaking the speaker cone. According to Sam Phillips, "We had no way of getting it fixed . . . so we started playing around with the damn thing. I stuffed a little paper in there and it sounded good. It sounded like a saxophone." This accident thus gave birth to fuzztone guitar. According to historian Robert Palmer, "From then on, when Phillips was recording a blues combo, he let the guitarist wail."[19]

Phillips established his own label, Sun Records, in 1952, and the next year he scored his first major R & B hits with Little Junior Parker's "Mystery Train" (later covered by Elvis Presley) and Rufus Thomas's "Bear Cat." Despite Sun's R & B hits, Phillips concluded that the demographic base for his product was too narrow. To solve this problem, he decided to branch out and record white artists. As his secretary, Marion Keisker, recalled, "Over and over, I remember Sam saying, 'If I could find a white man who had the Negro sound and the Negro feel, I could make a billion dollars.'"[20] With Elvis Presley, Phillips found that sound; after Presley, he pursued it repeatedly with a series of artists whom he tried to fit into his newfound rockabilly mold—Carl Perkins, Johnny Cash, Jerry Lee Lewis, Roy Orbison, and Charlie Rich. The "Sun sound" that Phillips achieved—"long on feel and short on contrivance"—is still a recording industry catchphrase.[21] Many of the artists he recorded established or redefined the musical genres in which they worked, and for many of them the recordings they did with Phillips may have been their best work.

Elvis Presley (1935–1977) stood as the first enduring national star of rock and roll and the biggest single attraction in the history of popular music. During his twenty-one-year career, he had sixty-seven top-twenty hits, thirty-eight top-twenty albums, and sold over a billion records worldwide. The first artist to effectively combine all the essential ingredients of rock—R & B, blues, country, and gospel—Presley became the first white performer of the 1950s to harness the passion and sexuality of R & B for a mass audience. With the swivel of his hips and the curl of his lip, Presley enhanced rock's aura of teenage rebellion. According to critic Dave Marsh, "Among the countless clichés Elvis embodied, 'living legend' is the most perfectly realized. There is no 'real' Elvis. That man,

MICHAEL OCHS ARCHIVES/GETTY IMAGES

Elvis Presley outraged fans with his swiveling hips on the Milton Berle television show in 1956. On his next television appearance, Presley was shown only from the waist up.

whoever he may have been, disappeared long ago into the mists of legend."[22]

Presley was born in Tupelo, Mississippi. His early musical influences came from church and the radio, where he heard blues, country, pop, and black gospel. Presley identified the Pentecostal church as his primary source of musical training:

> When I was four or five, all I looked forward to was Sundays, when we all could go to church. This was the only singing training I ever had. . . . Rock and roll is basically just gospel music, or gospel music mixed with rhythm and blues.[23]

In his early teens, Presley moved with his family to Memphis in 1948, where he grew long hair and sideburns, shopped for flashy clothing on Beale Street, entered talent shows, and participated in all-night gospel sings. His taste in blues and R & B had begun to sharpen: "I dug the real low-down Mississippi singers, mostly Big Bill Broonzy and Big Boy Crudup, although they would scold me at home for listening to them. 'Sinful music,' the townsfolk of Memphis said it was."[24]

In 1953 Presley stopped in at Sam Phillips's Memphis Recording Service to make a recording for his mother. When he sang a couple of ballads by the Ink Spots, he sufficiently impressed Marion Keisker, who was handling the studio that day, to make a backup tape of the performances to share later with her boss. Phillips eventually called Presley back to record, backed by guitarist Scotty Moore and bassist Bill Black, and after many false starts they stumbled on the new style that Phillips had in mind. Presley was on a break fooling around with blues singer Arthur "Big Boy" Crudup's "That's All Right" when Phillips's excited shouts from the control booth signalled that they finally had what he wanted. Phillips quickly arranged for a local DJ to play the tune on his show and it became a regional hit—once it was made clear that Presley was white.

Presley began to tour the South with his band, and he had regional hits with his follow-up Sun recordings. In 1955 he signed with manager "Colonel" Tom Parker, a former carnival barker, who had big plans for the young rocker. One of Parker's first moves was to shop around for another record company. Why Sam Phillips sold Presley's contract to RCA for $35,000—even though it was an impressive sum at the time—will always remain a mystery. At the RCA studios in Nashville, producers changed the artist's sound by adding vocal group harmonies, drums, heavily electrified guitars, and orchestral arrangements. According to historian Charlie Gillett, "Presley's voice became more theatrical and self-conscious as he sought to contrive excitement and emotion which he had seemed to achieve on his Sun records without any evident forethought."[25] Many purists argue that Presley's Sun sessions represent the height of his artistic accomplishment and that the haphazard way RCA handled his subsequent releases bore witness to his role as a commodity and little else.

Presley broke out onto the national scene in 1956—appearing on major television shows, topping the charts with "Heartbreak Hotel," and signing a three-movie deal. Follow-up hits included "Don't Be Cruel," "Hound Dog," "Love Me Tender," and "All Shook Up," and his first films, *Love Me Tender* and *Jailhouse Rock,* were also smashes. It all ended in 1958 as Presley was drafted into the U.S. Army and took a two-year enforced musical hiatus. When he returned to the civilian world in 1960, he devoted most of his energy to making movies. Although his undistinguished films (*GI Blues, Blue Hawaii, Viva Las Vegas,* and others) and their soundtrack albums made money, they reflected little of the artistic vision and excitement of his initial work with Sun Records. Under the guidance of manager Tom Parker, Presley engaged primarily in turning a profit. As researcher George Plasketes argues, "To a younger generation who did not grow up listening to Elvis or experiencing his liberating impact on American culture, he represents nothing more than a registered trademark."[26] With the arrival of the Beatles and Bob Dylan in the mid-1960s, Presley had already faded as a major force. He briefly rebounded in 1968 with a comeback television special and made some new recordings that did well on the charts, but then he moved into a new phase as a Las Vegas and arena performer, becoming a cultural cliché. Dressed in outlandish jumpsuits, oversized aviator sunglasses, bangles, and sequins, he approached self-parody. Presley's shows became overblown affairs crafted to appeal to the adulation of aging fans. According to critic Harry Sumrall, "The man who had virtually created the image of the rock and roll star also became the symbol of the flabby, out-of-control rock star burnout."[27]

Presley increasingly retreated into seclusion at Graceland, his Memphis mansion, and a lifestyle of overindulgence led to his death by heart failure in 1977. Critic Greil Marcus reflects on the role Presley still plays as a complex cultural symbol, reflecting many conflicting views:

> Elvis Presley is a supreme figure on American life, one whose presence, no matter how banal or unpredictable, brooks no real comparisons. . . . Elvis has emerged as a great artist, a great rocker, a great purveyor of schlock, a great heart throb, a great bore, a great symbol of potency, a great ham, a great nice person, and, yes, a great American.[28]

However one views Presley—as god or disappointment—his impact remains clear: His appearance forever transformed the face of American popular music.

Sam Phillips's success with Elvis Presley encouraged Phillips to replicate it with other young southerners who had comparable styles and materials. He switched almost completely from black singers to white artists, whom he tried to cast in his rockabilly mold: Carl Perkins, Johnny Cash, Jerry Lee Lewis, Roy Orbison, and Charlie Rich.

Carl Perkins (1932–1998) established rockabilly with his smash hit "Blue Suede Shoes" (1956) and launched Sun Records into national prominence. The song was the first rockabilly record to sell a million copies and one of the first three-way crossover hits (on the pop, country and western, and R & B charts). Perkins also served as one of rock's first singer-songwriters and an early rock presence on national television. After an auto accident, Perkins remained on the scene primarily as a second-tier country artist, often performing as a sideman with Johnny Cash.

Topped only by Little Richard for flamboyance, **Jerry Lee Lewis** (1935–) was one of the most outrageous figures of fifties rock. With three top-ten hits in the 1950s ("Whole Lotta Shakin' Goin' On," "Great Balls of Fire," and "Breathless"), he became the premier white piano and vocal stylist of early rock. According to one critic, "Lewis didn't sing his songs as much as he ravaged them."[29] Lewis's career took a dive in the late 1950s, when the press revealed that he had married his thirteen-year-old second cousin. Despite an erratic life, Lewis continued to tour as a country artist and enjoyed periodic country hits from the 1960s through the 1980s.

Texan Roy Orbison (1936–1988) started out as a Sun rockabilly artist but found greater fame after leaving Sun, with ballads that showcased a quavering tenor voice and twanging guitar ("Only the Lonely" [1960], "Crying" [1961], and "Oh, Pretty Woman" [1964]). Dressed in black, with sunglasses and slicked-back hair, Orbison became "the Caruso of rock and roll,"[30] according to one critic. Popular in Great Britain as well as the United States, Orbison toured with the Beatles and served as a bridge between rock's first golden age and the British invasion of the 1960s. Such rockers as Bruce Springsteen, Elvis Costello, and Bonnie Raitt later recognized Orbison as a seminal influence.

FIFTIES ROCK AFTER ELVIS

Numerous rock and R & B artists appeared between Elvis Presley's explosion on the national scene in 1956 and the end of the decade. Some added new levels of emotional complexity to rock, others were manufactured as "teen idols," and still others applied the power of black gospel music to secular pop styles, as African American crossover artists.

A second wave of rock artists appeared around 1957, bringing heightened emotional complexity to rock through well-crafted tunes, emotional lyrics, and soaring vocals. Most of them wrote much of their material, played their own instruments, and took a hand in record production. Though less explosive and bluesy than their immediate predecessors, these artists broadened the palette of rock.

Texas-born singer/songwriter Buddy Holly (1939–1959) created songs that combined country sweetness with a rock edge. Though he blended the backbeat of black R & B with country and pop material around the same time that Sam Phillips and Elvis Presley did, Holly's sound differed from the rockabilly of Sun Records. With horn-rimmed glasses and a shy demeanor, Holly contrasted with the flamboyant styles of Little Richard and Elvis Presley. His well-crafted songs stood the test of time; his band, the Crickets, established the classic rock-band instrumental lineup (lead and rhythm guitar, electric bass, and drums). Holly's major hits included "That'll Be the Day" (1957—later covered by Linda Ronstadt), "Peggy Sue" (1957), "Not Fade Away" (1957—later covered by the Rolling Stones), and "It's So Easy" (1958). Holly moved to New York in late 1958 to explore an orchestral sound, only to have his career cut short in the 1959 plane crash that also killed rockers Ritchie Valens and the Big Bopper.

The Everly Brothers (Don Everly, 1937– ; Phil Everly, 1939–) were a popular vocal duo of the 1950s whose tight country harmonies influenced a generation of rockers including the Beatles, the Hollies, the Beach Boys, the Byrds, Simon and Garfunkel, and the Eagles. From 1957 through 1962, the Everlys hit the top ten of the singles chart twelve times and sold more than thirty-five million records. Major hits included "Bye Bye Love" (1957), "Wake up Little Susie" (1957), All I Have to Do Is Dream" (1958), "'Til I Kissed You" (1959), and "Cathy's Clown" (1960). Displaced in the early 1960s by British invasion groups, many of whom they had inspired, the Everlys broke up in the 1970s but reunited in the 1980s to release "On the Wings of a Nightingale," written for them by an admiring Paul McCartney. The duo continued to tour nationally in the early 2000s, appearing as part of a Simon and Garfunkel reunion tour.

Other important second-wave rock artists peaked in the late 1950s. Ritchie Valens (1941–1959) became the first Chicano rock star. Early rockabilly vocalist/guitarist Eddie Cochran (1938–1960) performed the widely covered "Summertime Blues" (1958) and influenced a generation of British rockers prior to his 1960 death in a car crash in Britain. Gene Vincent (1935–1971) was a leather-clad, rockabilly bad boy whose "Be-Bop-a-Lula" (1956) was every bit as dangerous as Elvis, but when U.S. popularity eluded him, he withdrew to England to become a British rock icon. Ricky Nelson (1940–1985), the son of television's "Ozzie and Harriet," gained popularity in the late 1950s and early 1960s through heavy media exposure with a blend of ballads, rockabilly, and pop. He also became a country rock pioneer with his Stone Canyon Band in the 1970s, and was followed into the rock business in the 1990s by his sons who formed the group Nelson. Duane Eddy (1938–), rock's best-selling instrumentalist, put the "twang" in rock-and-roll guitar by playing the instrument's bass strings, thereby influencing genera-tions of rockers including John Fogerty, George Harrison, Bruce Springsteen, and Chris Isaak with tunes such as his 1958 hit, "Rebel Rouser."

Ronnie Hawkins (1935–), who is also known as "Rompin" Ronnie Hawkins, formed The Hawks, a rockabilly group, in Fayetteville, Arkansas, while attending college during the mid-1950s. A regular on the bar circuit in Arkansas, Oklahoma, and Missouri, Hawkins also owned and operated the Rockwood Club, where he and like-minded artists such as Jerry Lee Lewis, Carl Perkins, Roy Orbison, and Conway Twitty often performed. Following his first Canadian performance at the Brass Rail Tavern in London, Ontario, in 1958, Hawkins immigrated to Canada and made Peterborough, Ontario his permanent home. From here he built a successful career as a mainstay figure in Toronto's 1960s rock scene. His early recordings, "Forty Days," "Mary Lou," "Hey Bo Diddley," and "Who Do You Love?" disclose

Canada's first rock star, Ronnie Hawkins, performing at Toronto's High Park in 1985.

CP/TORONTO STAR

the raucous blues-inspired style that won him legions of fans in both Canada and in the United States. During the early-60s, Hawkins gradually replaced the members of the group with Canadians Robbie Robertson, Richard Manuel, Rick Danko, and Garth Hudson. The new line-up, which retained one original Arkansas-born Hawk, Levon Helm, later became Bob Dylan's formative backup group, The Band.

END OF AN ERA

The end of the 1950s brought a series of events that changed the character of rock: numerous artists were lost through death, conscription, imprisonment, ostracism, or religious conversion. According to singer/songwriter Don McLean in his 1969 song "American Pie," the 1959 plane crash that killed Buddy Holly, Ritchie Valens, and the Big Bopper signified "the day the music died." Holly and Valens were important new singer/songwriters who were taking the music in fresh new directions at the time of their deaths. In many ways, rock also lost its premier icon, Elvis Presley, at the height of his popularity when he was drafted into the U.S. Army in 1958. Presley was never the same, argues critic Robert Palmer:

> The Elvis Presley who returned from his U.S. Army tour of duty was no longer the sneering, ducktailed "hillbilly cat," decked out in Beale Street's gaudiest pimpwear. The new Elvis celebrated his return to civilian life by donning a tux and singing a television duet with . . . Frank Sinatra?[31]

Other losses to the rock world mounted: Little Richard entered the seminary in 1957, Chuck Berry was imprisoned on a morals charge in 1959, Jerry Lee Lewis was ostracized for marrying his thirteen-year-old second cousin in 1958, and promoter Alan Freed was indicted and convicted of payola.

Rock seemed under attack from many sides: Major record labels and music publishers wanted to regain their dominance, clergy and local politicians decried the music on moral grounds, and Congress began to probe payola. Tin Pan Alley business leaders saw their control over the music business being threatened, and rock served as a convenient target for their wrath. ASCAP, which had dominated prerock songwriting and publishing, was also threatened by BMI, which represented many rock, R & B, and country songwriters. Congressional hearings into payola took place in 1959 and 1960 at the urging of ASCAP, which sent stars such as Frank Sinatra in to demonize the new rock music business.

Although "cleanup" of the rock and roll business supposedly followed, the primary effect was the re-concentration of power in the hands of traditional music business centres at the expense of the independent labels and DJs. Radio stations reined in DJs and instituted program directors and playlists to homogenize what had been a freewheeling domain. This resulted in the sanitized pop-rock sound of teen idols. Some historians refer to the events of the late 1950s as the "death" of rock and roll, but that is an overstatement. Just over the horizon lay soul music, girl groups, surf music, and the British invasion, as well as new producers, songwriters, and performers. By 1960, rock was here to stay, and the power centres of the music business had moved to take control of a genre they had earlier dismissed.

CHAPTER SUMMARY

- When the growth of R & B-oriented radio stations made black music accessible to white teenagers, a racist backlash followed. The vitality of the music was difficult to quash, however, as Little Richard, Fats Domino, and Bill Haley and other artists founded the music DJ Alan Freed baptized as "rock and roll."

- Three major urban areas—New Orleans, Chicago, and Memphis—served as important spawning grounds for early rock styles. New Orleans, the birthplace of jazz, was the source of the piano-based roots rock sound of Little Richard and Fats Domino. Chicago's amplified urban blues gave birth to the music of early rockers Chuck Berry and Bo Diddley. Memphis and Sun Records produced a rockabilly hybrid of blues, gospel, and country music, as well as rock's first megastar, Elvis Presley.

- A second wave of late-1950s rock innovators included Buddy Holly, the Everly Brothers, Ritchie Valens, Roy Orbison, Jerry Lee Lewis, and Carl Perkins. The late 1950s also set the stage for the birth of sixties soul music with the work of Sam Cooke, Jackie Wilson, and Ray Charles. At the same time, Rockabilly performer, Ronnie Hawkins, became Canada's first significant performer of the new style.

- Rock and roll presented a threat to the music establishment, which responded with the introduction of white teen idols. As the 1950s came to a close, rock seemed to be imploding on its own with the deaths, jailings, and religious conversions of major players, as well as congressional investigations. But this was only the end of rock's first chapter.

LISTENING EXERCISES

1. Country Elements in Early Rock and Roll

"Rock around the Clock" (1956), composed and recorded by Bill Haley and His Comets, is a 12-bar blues. Listen carefully for the intermittent and tentatively played backbeat on the snare drum. In the early days of rock, the backbeat had not yet become the standard rhythmic device it is in dance music today. The song also features an electric guitar rather than a saxophone solo, another defining ingredient in the shift from R & B to rock and roll. Are there country influences in Haley's vocal style?

2. Rock and Roll as Revamped Rhythm and Blues

"Tutti Frutti" (1956), recorded by Little Richard, is a classic 12-bar blues. Benign nonsense lyrics replaced the original "offensive" lyrics. How does Richard's over-the-top vocal delivery energize the tune? Notice how Richard's piano-based rhythm section aggressively drives the song. Notice also the boogie woogie flavour of the piano, and how the sax solo reflects a classic R & B honking style. How does the use of rhythm breaks add energy?

3. Rock and Roll Guitar

"Roll over Beethoven" (1956), composed and recorded by Chuck Berry, is another early rock tune set to a 12-bar blues. Berry's ability to craft lyrics that spoke directly to teenagers gave his music great appeal. The T-Bone Walker–inspired guitar solo that starts the song was mimicked on numerous subsequent recordings by other artists, including the Beach Boys in "Surfin' USA." Berry also claims that Country music played an important role in his musical development. Can you identify those features?

HISTORICAL STUDIES AND DISCUSSION QUESTIONS

1. Recording Early Rock

Early rock records were generally made in small studios with primitive equipment—a far cry from today's multitrack, digital facilities. At Cosimo Matassa's studio in New Orleans, producer Dave Bartholomew had only one microphone for the whole band, and at Sam Phillips's Sun Records studio in Memphis, where Elvis Presley and many other early blues and rock artists were first recorded, he had two recorders: one console model and another mounted on a rack behind his head for the tape delay echo, or "slapback" for which Sun became famous. Do the technologically advanced records of today sound "better" than the recordings that Bartholemew and Phillips made; or is it vice versa? Why?

2. Conservative Reactions to Rock and Roll

The more attractive R & B became to white youths, the more controversy it engendered. Rock and roll shows often featured black artists and attracted racially mixed audiences, so adult fear of new forms of adolescent rebellion was coupled with none-too-subtle racism. Some white southern conservative groups painted rock as a plot by the NAACP to corrupt white youth. One city eliminated rock from municipal swimming pool jukeboxes because the beat attracted "undesirable elements" who practised "spastic gyrations" in abbreviated bathing suits. The popular music industry establishment grew alarmed not so much at the spectacle of teen rebellion as at threats to the bottom line. Established pop artists of the late 1940s and early 1950s, as well as the major record labels and ASCAP, grew defensive. By the end of the decade, the major players in the music business had begun a more careful strategy of co-optation, recognizing that rock could be a lasting musical style. Is the pattern of hostility and co-optation specific only to 1950s rock and roll, or is it a feature of change in North American culture? If the latter is true, can you identify other instances when new artistic expressions were subjected to this process?

3. Elvis, Race, and Cultural Appropriation

Presley's new black–white hybrid sound had to be marketed skillfully in a time of racial segregation. Once Presley and his band had recorded Crudup's "That's All Right," they joked nervously that such race-mixing might get them run out of town. When the "black" sound of Presley's initial recordings first hit the airwaves, confusion arose about his racial identity. Promoters quickly hustled Presley onto the air to announce that he had graduated from a white high school. Even so, white conservatives remained angered by his use of black dance, performance, and dress styles. Racial segregation was still the norm in many parts of the United States, and the appropriation of black styles by whites was seen as suspect. How have times changed? Does the appropriation of black styles by white pop artists such as Eminem or Britney Spears still cause white outrage? What about black outrage over such appropriations?

STUDY QUESTIONS

1. Identify the social and technological conditions that set the stage for the arrival of rock and roll.

2. What was Bill Haley's contribution to rock?

3. Why was Elvis Presley significant? What might have happened if he and Sam Phillips had not gotten together to develop their county-blues hybrid?

4. Who were some of the rock artists of the late 1950s who followed Elvis?

5. What happened to rock by the end of the 1950s? Why do some commentators argue that rock "died" at this point?

6. How did rockabilly shape early rock and roll culture in Canada?

NOTES

1. Robert Palmer, *Rock and Roll: An Unruly History* (New York: Harmony Books, 1995), 33.

2. Glenn C. Altschuler, *All Shook Up: How Rock 'n' Roll Changed America (Pivotal Moments in American History)* (New York: Oxford University Press, 2003), 10.

3. Palmer, *Rock and Roll*, 16.

4. Altschuler, *All Shook Up*, 8.

5. *Ibid.*, 18.

6. Palmer, *Rock and Roll*, 15.

7. Nick Talevski, *The Unofficial Encyclopedia of the Rock and Roll Hall of Fame* (Westport, CT: Greenwood Press, 1998), 10.

8. *Ibid.*, 14.

9. Arnold Shaw, *Honkers and Shouters: The Golden Age of Rhythm and Blues* (New York: Macmillan, 1978), 64.

10. Chet Flippo, *Everybody Was Kung-Fu Dancing: Chronicles of the Lionized and the Notorious* (New York: St. Martin's Press, 1991), 89.

11. *Ibid.*, 87.

12. Grace Lichtenstein and Laura Dankner, "Fats," in *Rock and Roll Is Here to Stay*, edited by W. McKeen (New York: Norton, 2000), 93.

13. Charles White, *The Life and Times of Little Richard: The Quasar of Rock* (New York: Harmony Books, 1984), 47.

14. *Ibid.*, 55.

15. Charlie Gillett, *The Sound of the City: The Rise of Rock and Roll* (New York: Da Capo Press, 1996), 80.

16. John Collis, *The Story of Chess Records* (New York: Bloomsbury, 1998), 130.

17. *Ibid.*, 115.

18. *Sam Phillips: The Sound and Legacy of Sun Records*, November 28, 2001, http://www.npr.org/ programs/morning/features/2001/nov/phillips/011128.sam.phillips.html, accessed on May 9, 2005.

19. Palmer, *Rock and Roll*, 202.

20. Peter Guralnick, *Lost Highway: Journeys and Arrivals of American Musicians* (Boston: Godine, 1979), 125.

21. Colin Escott and Martin Hawkins, *Good Rockin' Tonight: Sun Records and the Birth of Rock 'n' Roll* (New York: St. Martin's Press, 1992), ii.

22. Dave Marsh, *Elvis* (New York: Thunder's Mouth Press, 1992), xiii.

23. *Ibid.*, 9.

24. Gillett, *Sound of the City*, 28.

25. *Ibid.*, 29.

26. George M. Plasketes, "Taking Care of Business: The Commercialization of Rock Music," in *America's Musical Pulse: Popular Music in Twentieth-Century Society*, edited by K. Bindas (Westport, CT: Greenwood Press, 1992), 149.

27. Harry Sumrall, *Pioneers of Rock and Roll: 100 Artists Who Changed the Face of Rock* [Billboard Hitmakers' Series] (New York: Billboard Books, 1994), 212.

28. Greil Marcus, *Mystery Train: Images of America in Rock 'n' Roll Music*, 4th ed. (New York: Penguin Books, 1997), 120–21.

29. Sumrall, *Pioneers of Rock and Roll*, 166.

30. *Ibid.*, 197.

31. Palmer, *Rock and Roll*, 144.

CHAPTER 12

Trans-Atlantic Blues Revival

Every few years new generations rediscover the blues. One of the first blues revivals came in the late fifties and early sixties when record collectors and aficionados, such as Samuel Charters and James McKunc, inspired and shaped the growing interest in the blues among college-age students. In addition to white folk artists such as Pete Seeger and Peter, Paul and Mary, some acoustic blues performers—for example, Leadbelly, Big Bill Broonzy, and Son House—were presented to white audiences as "folk blues" artists. Such presentations could unfortunately be demeaning, and sophisticated and urbane Chicago bluesman Big Bill Broonzy was sometimes reduced to wearing overalls and shabby clothes in concert appearances to project an expected down-home ambiance.

The mid-1960s saw an electric blues revival, fueled by British interest in all forms of the blues. The 1965 Newport Folk Festival finally broke electric blues to a U.S. mass audience with the rock-infused blues of white artists such as the Paul Butterfield Blues Band. Both the blues and R & B influenced British Invasion groups such as the Beatles, Rolling Stones, Animals, and Yardbirds; late-1960s rock artists such as Cream (featuring Eric Clapton), Janis Joplin, and Jimi Hendrix were even more deeply rooted in the blues. For a time, the pop music audience was exposed to B. B. King, Muddy Waters, T-Bone Walker, Howlin' Wolf, Albert King, Bobby "Blue" Bland, and others who had laboured for decades in relative obscurity. Interest in the blues continued in the early 1970s with the popularity of southern white blues artists such as the Allman Brothers, Lynyrd Skynyrd, and Johnny and Edgar Winter.

Many U.S. folk blues musicians appeared in Canada, generally in coffee houses or at folk festivals, while the electric blues ensembles performed in bars and clubs. Among the handful of expatriate bluesmen that settled in Canada were the legendary guitarist Lonnie Johnson (1925–1970), who spent his last years in Toronto, and the Texas-born singer-guitarist and former Bobby "Blue" Bland sideman, Mel Brown (1939–), who moved to Kitchener, Ontario, and continues to enjoy a local legend status with his band The Home Wreckers. The growth in popularity among young, white Canadian performers in the 1960s coincided with the rise of blues-inspired British groups such as the Yardbirds and the Rolling Stones. Although initially derivative of their British counterparts, later performers and bands, such as Dutch Mason, Offenbach, Downchild Blues Band, Crowbar, and the Powder Blues Band,

PILUHIN/ALAMY

Downchild Blues Band guitarist and leader, Don Walsh, soloing on harmonica in 2006.

ROLF KLATT/WIREIMAGE/GETTY IMAGES

Blues guitar ace Jeff Healey shows lap style technique in 2006.

turned to the original musicians for their primary education in electrified **urban blues**.

The 1980s and 1990s saw another blues revival signalled by the release of two *Blues Brothers* films and an interest in "roots" music: two songs by Don Walsh of Downchild, "I Got Everything I Need (Almost)" and "Shotgun Blues," were recorded by Jake Blues (John Belushi) and Toronto-born Elwood Blues (Dan Ackroyd). Other white artists such as Stevie Ray Vaughan, Bonnie Raitt, Eric Clapton, Jeff Healey, and others spearheaded the new popularization, and a new generation of African American blues artists including Robert Cray and Keb' Mo' also appeared. Stevie Ray Vaughan, who drew equally from bluesmen such as Albert King and Muddy Waters and rockers such as Jimi Hendrix, released multiple gold albums with his band Double Trouble in the mid-1980s. During this time, Vaughan discovered Jeff Healey, the Toronto-born guitar virtuoso, whose 1988 "Hideaway" was nominated for a Grammy in the "Best Instrumental" category. The decade prior to his death in 2008 saw Healey turn to his life-long passion for early jazz as the trumpet-playing frontman for the Jazz Wizards; Healey also was the radio host for "My Kind of Jazz" on CBC Radio and Jazz FM91. Bonnie Raitt won a Grammy for her 1989 album, *Nick of Time,* and seasoned veterans such as singer/pianist Charles Brown and singer/guitarist John Lee Hooker were brought out of retirement to tour with her. In 1992 Clapton recorded a concert for *MTV Unplugged* that produced the biggest-selling record of his career. Performance venues for the blues expanded, and festivals promoted the style. As cities like Chicago and Memphis discovered the commercial potential of their blues heritage, "blues districts" were established. A thriving blues scene also developed in Austin, fostering performers such as the Fabulous Thunderbirds and Marcia Ball. Despite the revivals, the commercial recording scene for most black blues artists did not improve much. Although a few stars like B. B. King recorded on major labels, most were limited to smaller regional labels—Malaco, Alligator, Blind Pig, Stoney Plain, and a few others. Because renewed interest in the blues fuelled research and educational efforts, blues archives were established in Chicago, Memphis, and Mississippi.

ORIGINS OF EARLY 1960S BRITISH ROCK

The British Invasion stemmed from several decades of British interest in American roots music. In the early 1950s, a young Scottish musician named Lonnie Donegan (1931–2002) began recording American folk songs accompanied by guitar, bass, and washboard. Two of the tunes— "Rock Island Line" and "John Henry"—became hits in Britain and made the top ten in the United States in 1956. Donegan's music came to be called *skiffle*—drawn from an early African American term for rent-party music. The most consistent hitmaker in Britain from 1956 to 1959, Donegan drew indiscriminately from the entire folk heritage of the United States, particularly the repertoires of Leadbelly and Woody Guthrie. According to Charlie Gillett,

Blues and rock singer/slide guitarist Bonnie Raitt performing in 1978. Raitt redefines the role of women in contemporary blues.

> Donegan performed their songs with a quick dance beat, in a high, nasal, fake American voice. Despite being almost completely derivative in his material and style, he was much better at what he did than were any of the British contemporary rock 'n' roll singers at representing American rock 'n' roll.[1]

As Donegan's audiences discovered the original sources of his music, they began buying albums by artists such as Big Bill Broonzy, Leadbelly, and Woody Guthrie. One of Donegan's most important accomplishments was that he inspired countless British teens to take up the guitar to play skiffle. A Liverpool skiffle band called the Quarrymen became the Beatles; they cited Donegan's "Rock Island Line" (1956) as one of the most influential records of their youth. Many other British rock musicians, such as Van Morrison and Queen's guitarist Brian May, also saw Donegan as a primary influence. According to May, "He really was at the very cornerstone of English blues and rock. He really was the first guy to bring the blues to England. I think he's probably the principal reason I picked up a guitar."[2]

British interest in the blues was also fuelled by a London musician named Alexis Korner (1928–1984), who admired blues artists such as Howlin' Wolf and Muddy Waters. Korner formed a blues band that influenced numerous British 1960's rockers, so that by 1963, rhythm and blues had become the

© NEAL PRESTON/CORBIS

dominant style in London clubs. The sounds of mid-1950's U.S. rockers such as Bill Haley, Elvis Presley, Little Richard, and Buddy Holly were also well known to teen fans in the United Kingdom, many of whom styled themselves as "teddy boys" and sported black leather jackets and Elvis hairstyles.

Two distinct styles of British rock ultimately emerged: "beat" music from the Liverpool and Manchester areas, and rhythm and blues from London. *Beat music,* shortened from "Merseybeat" and named for the river that ran through Liverpool, was a pop music made by local bands in the Liverpool area, many of whom were former skiffle groups. The Beatles became by far the most successful of the beat groups, but others included Cliff Richard, the Searchers, Gerry and the Pacemakers, Herman's Hermits, Freddie and the Dreamers, and the Hollies. The Merseybeat groups exuded a cheerful, accessible pop sound and a well-scrubbed, nonthreatening "mod" look.

The rhythm and blues acts—or blues revivalists—came mostly from London and included John Mayall's Bluesbreakers, the Rolling Stones, the Yardbirds, the Animals, the Kinks, and the Who. These bands, according to Charlie Gillett, "exuded a more defiant spirit, expressed in snarling vocals, raucous guitars, and baleful glares at photographers"[3] than did the beat groups. The Beatles—particularly the sweeter, pop-oriented work of Paul McCartney—embodied the skiffle-Merseybeat strand, while the Rolling Stones exemplified the rhythm and blues strand of early 1960s British rock.

The Rolling Stones initially served as symbols of the English R & B movement, which challenged the Merseybeat sound of the Beatles in 1963. Promoters marketed the band as a kind of dark and dangerous anti-Beatles with the question "Would you want your daughter to go out with a Rolling Stone?"[4] One of the finest British interpreters of American R & B, the Stones developed into one of the most popular rock and roll bands of the 1960s and 1970s and sustained their popularity into the 2000s as the world's longest-lived rock band. Although contemporary teens may wonder at their continuing appeal, the Stones in their prime conveyed a dark, seductive edge.

In the 1960s, playing their version of Chicago electric blues and with Mick Jagger's flamboyant stage presence, the group cultivated an arrogant and dangerous image that made them one of the most identifiable British Invasion groups and the only serious competition to the Beatles. Journalist Stanley Booth described his first visual impression of the Stones' lead singer, Mick Jagger (1943–), and guitarist Keith Richards (1943–) in 1969:

> The Stones Gang: Wanted Dead or Alive, though only Mick Jagger, standing like a model, his knife-blade ass thrust to one side, was currently awaiting trial. Beside him was Keith Richards, who was even thinner and looked not like a model but an insane advertisement for a dangerous carefree Death—black ragged hair, dead-green skin, a cougar tooth hanging from his right earlobe, his lips snarled back from the marijuana cigarette between his rotting fangs, his gums blue.[5]

Jagger and Richards developed into a powerful songwriting team that produced such classic hits as "(I Can't Get No) Satisfaction" (1965), "Ruby

© HULTON-DEUTSCH COLLECTION/CORBIS

The Rolling Stones—the "bad boys" of the British Invasion (left to right): Brian Jones, Mick Jagger, Keith Richards, Charlie Watts, and Bill Wyman.

Tuesday" (1967), "Jumpin' Jack Flash" (1968), "Honky Tonk Woman" (1969), and "Brown Sugar" (1971). Guitarists Brian Jones (1942–1969) and Keith Richards provided lean, interlocking rhythm guitars, while the strong yet subtly swinging rhythm section of bassist Bill Wyman (1936–) and drummer Charlie Watts (1941–) anchored the band. Though they experimented briefly with psychedelia in the mid-1960s and disco in the 1970s, the Stones focused primarily on realizing their vision as a blues-soaked hard-rock quintet. They also often toured with their blues idols, including Howlin' Wolf and Chuck Berry.

Despite their self-conscious bad-boy posturing, the Stones demonstrated a dedication to their art—initially the blues, later the **hard-rock** mainstream. They continued to record and perform into the 2000s: Few other bands have enjoyed such a broad fan base or staying power. It is difficult to hear the groups that followed them without detecting some influence, whether musical or aesthetic. According to critic Robert Christgau,

> They lived the life of art, their art got better all the time, and as it got better, remarkably enough, it reached more people. But although their art survives, its heroic quality does not; the Stones betray all the flaws of the counterculture they half-wittingly and -willingly symbolized. Their sex was too often

sexist, their expanded consciousness too often a sordid escape; their rebellion was rooted in impulse to the exclusion of all habits of sacrifice, and their relationship to fame had little to do with the responsibilities of leadership, or allegiance.[6]

After the successes of the Beatles and the Rolling Stones in the 1960s, artists from the British Commonwealth (England, Ireland, and Australia) commonly made the U.S. pop charts. While many of these artists had a strong affinity for the blues, others displayed more eclectic influences.

Taking Robert Johnson as his mythic role model, Eric Clapton (1945–) was one of the first "guitar heroes" and a fervent British blues revivalist. Clapton had his first major gig with the Yardbirds in the early 1960s, but when they turned psychedelic, he left them to join John Mayall's Bluesbreakers. The resulting *Bluesbreakers with Eric Clapton* (1966) was one of the best British blues albums of the era. The following year he teamed up with bassist Jack Bruce and drummer Ginger Baker to form Cream, one of the first rock **power trios**—a group consisting of electric guitar, electric bass, and drums. This instrumentation was later common in heavy metal and hard rock. With hits such as "Sunshine of Your Love" (1968), "White Room" (1968), and Robert Johnson's "Crossroads" (1969), the band produced a deafening sound that laid the foundation for much subsequent blues-rock and hard rock of the 1960s and 1970s. After Cream broke up, Clapton scored two 1970 hits of his own with "After Midnight" and "Layla," as well as two subsequent hits later in the decade: "I Shot the Sheriff" (1974) and "Lay Down Sally" (1978). Clapton appeared in the early 1990s on MTV's *Unplugged*, a performance that produced a Grammy-winning album, and he remained active through the 2000s.

Another legendary British blues-rock band, the Who, featured ringing power chords and explosive beats that made them one of the most influential groups of their era. As the godfathers of punk, they established a violent, anarchic rock performance style with smashed guitars and blown-up drum sets that succeeding generations would embellish. The sight of guitarist Pete Townshend leaping into the air with his guitar and spinning his right hand in exaggerated windmills became a classic rock image. Major hits included "My Generation" (1967), "I Can See for Miles" (1967), "I'm Free" (1969), "Pinball Wizard" (1969), and "Summertime Blues" (1970). One of the group's signal achievements was its production of the first rock opera, *Tommy* (1970), written by Townshend. The opera was performed several times with orchestral backing, produced as a film in 1975, and mounted on Broadway in 1993.

Irish soul man Van Morrison (1945–) created a distinctive fusion of R & B, jazz, blues, and Celtic folk music, winning a cult audience that followed him throughout his career. Morrison started with skiffle and scored hits in 1965 with "Gloria" and "Here Comes the Night." He moved to Los Angeles in 1967 to go solo as a singer-songwriter, crafting a floating, folk/jazz/soul sound heard in hits such as "Brown-Eyed Girl" (1967), "Domino" (1971), and

"Moondance" (1977). Joe Cocker (1944–) parlayed a Ray Charles–flavoured vocal style and an eccentric stage presence into a string of hits such as "With a Little Help from My Friends" (1968), "She Came in through the Bathroom Window" (1970), "The Letter" (1970), and "You Are So Beautiful" (1975). Cocker remained in demand in the 1980s and 1990s as a vocalist for film scores, producing hits such as the ballad "Up Where You Belong" (1982) from the film *An Officer and a Gentleman*.

Rock music continued to develop over the final three decades of the twentieth century. The high-energy **acid rock** of the 1960s led to hard rock, which branched into arena rock and **heavy metal** by the end of the decade. The 1970s followed with an explosion of a large palette of rock styles: southern and country rock emerged, blending country influences with hard rock and blues roots; the singer-songwriter tradition initiated earlier by Bob Dylan and the Beatles expanded; art rock—an eclectic blend of rock, classical music, jazz, and other styles—developed; and soft rock emerged to offer an easy-listening alternative. To fill the void created by soft rock and to rebel against disco, the punk movement emerged in the late 1970s, returning rock to a harder-edged sound. The 1980s also saw the beginning of a fascination with world music. In the 1990s, rock styles that had come of age in the 1960s and 1970s blended to form many new hybrids; by the turn of the century, rock artists had hybridized genres as diverse as **punk**, heavy metal, **hip-hop**, funk, blues, psychedelic rock, and **garage rock** to produce an alternative rock sound that became the new mainstream.

ORIGINS OF CANADIAN ROCK

"The popularity of rock in the US gave rise to an extensive network of independent recording labels and radio stations; Canada, however, produced comparatively few records during the 1950s and early-1960s. Notwithstanding "Clap Your Hands" (1960) by The Beaumarks, the first foreign-produced Canadian rock record to enjoy international popularity, local recordings were primarily used to promote live engagements at dances, teen clubs, high schools, and week-long engagements in taverns and bars. Furthermore, the career paths for newcomers remained obscure because Canadian radio stations were generally unsympathetic to musical acts who had not first achieved success in the US. This pattern was broken by The Guess Who in 1969 when their hit release, "These Eyes," was first played on a major Canadian radio station, albeit the American-owned CKLW in Windsor, Ontario, before it went into rotation on radio stations in the United States."

The Guess Who started out as a local Winnipeg band formed by singer/guitarist Chad Allan in 1960. Following the early success of "Shakin' All Over" (1965), and after numerous name changes, the band began to cultivate an edgier hard-rock sound with the album *American Woman*, the title track of which became the group's only number-one hit in the United States. "American Woman" also earned The Guess Who the distinction for being the

MICHAEL OCHS ARCHIVES/GETTY IMAGES

The Guess Who performing "American Woman" in 1970.

first Canadian band to have a number one hit on the American charts. The original lineup of Randy Bachman (guitar), Burton Cummings (vocals and keyboards) Jim Kale (bass), and Garry Peterson (drums) held until differences between Bachman and band members caused his departure. After playing one final show at the Fillmore East in New York City on May 16, 1970, Bachman returned to Winnipeg and eventually formed Bachman-Turner Overdrive. The Guess Who continued to perform and issue more hit singles such as "Share The Land" and "Albert Flasher" until 1975. Cummings then went on to forge a successful solo career. Since that time, versions of the band led by Jim Kale have surfaced and resurfaced. In 2003, the band (including Bachman and Cummings) performed before an estimated audience of 450,000 at the Molson Rocks for Toronto SARS benefit concert. The show was the largest outdoor ticketed event in Canadian history.

The first British Invasion in 1964 inspired rapid growth in Canada's rock culture; in 1966, for example, there existed in Toronto an estimated 1400 bands. While many groups openly imitated the music of the Beatles, The Rolling Stones, The Animals, and other British R & B influenced acts, the Quebec rock style, known as *ye-ye*, disclosed an unique synthesis of Beatles-inspired songs and *chansonnier*, as is evidenced in the music of The Classels.

With the introduction of the CRTC's broadcast regulations in 1971 (see Chapter 19), the Canadian recording industry made rock a major focus of its activity. With increased production, coupled with the ground-breaking international popularity of the Guess Who, markets outside of Canada were now beginning to open up to the country's musicians. The introduction of rock music on FM radio also aided the development of Canadian album-oriented rock music led by Rush, Prism, Triumph, Trooper, Saga, and April Wine.

HARD ROCK BRANCHES OUT

The aggressive, high-volume rock of the late 1960s laid the groundwork for hard rock and heavy metal. Both styles subsequently diversified into an array of substyles: hard rock branched into mainstream arena rock, **southern rock**, and art rock; heavy metal morphed into **thrash metal**, **funk metal**, and **nu metal**. Two defining musical ingredients of early hard rock were the power trio ensemble and guitar-bass unison riffs. The *power trio*, originally a British concept embodied by the Jimi Hendrix Experience and Cream, stripped the rock band to its core: drums, bass, and lead guitar. The *unison-riff style* was comprised of riffs played repeatedly in unison by the bass and guitar to create a hypnotic effect. While hard rock and heavy metal share many musical traits, most fans and critics acknowledge some distinctions between the two styles.

Though identified with late-60s West Coast psychedelia, the music of Steppenwolf represents the emerging blues and pop hybrid which later became known as hard rock. Leader John Kay escaped from then-Communist East Germany to Toronto with his family in 1958. There he formed a blues-rock band, Sparrow, which eventually travelled to Los Angeles and became Steppenwolf, a name inspired by the Hermann Hesse novel. Some members had also played in the Mynah Birds, which also included Neil Young and Rick James. Their music won them a substantial following, and the debut LP yielded their first hit in 1968, "Born to Be Wild," the signature anthem which contains one of the earliest references to heavy metal. The political leanings of the group are clearly heard in the subsequent album, *Monster, The Second* (1969), which includes two 60s benchmark hits "Magic Carpet Ride" and "The Pusher." Both songs were featured in the film *Easy Rider*.

CP/REX

Hard rock originals Steppenwolf in 1969. From left to right: Nick St. Nicholas, John Kay, Jerry Edmonton, Gabriel Mekler, and Goldy McJohn.

HULTON ARCHIVE/GETTY IMAGES

Guitarist Alex Lifeson (left), bassist Geddy Lee (right), and drummer Neil Peart (obscured) in concert as progressive rock trio Rush.

Rush is certainly one of the most creative Canadian rock acts of the 1970s and 1980s, and is perhaps one the most important power trios in the history of rock. Formed in 1968, in the Willowdale neighbourhood of Toronto, Ontario, the band includes bassist, keyboardist, and lead vocalist Geddy Lee, guitarist Alex Lifeson, and drummer and lyricist Neil Peart. The longevity of Rush can be largely attributed to the independent status they have maintained since inception. Following the release of the band's self-titled debut album in March 1974, Rush has won a number of Juno Awards, and was inducted into the Canadian music Hall of Fame in 1994, and ranks seventy-eighth in U.S. album sales according to the RIAA with sales of 25 million units. Ironically, the band has not been nominated for entry into the American Rock and Roll Hall of Fame since their year of eligibility in 1998. Musically, the Rush style represents an amalgam of early period blues-inspired heavy metal, late-1970s progressive rock, and more recent forms of alternative rock; **new wave**, **reggae** and pop rock style traces are also heard in the group's sound.

Led Zeppelin is often cited as the godfather of hard rock and heavy metal. Guitarist Jimmy Page's Hendrix-influenced playing and vocalist Robert Plant's high-pitched, screamed delivery defined the British group's aggressive, high-volume style. Led Zeppelin's theatricality in live performance became a hallmark, as one fan recalled,

> They flailed around like dervishes, making so much sound the air was heavy with metal. Two hours after the lights went out, as the band sauntered offstage, the audience was a delirious, raving, parched mass crawling through the rock and roll desert thirsting for an encore.[7]

Hard-rock legends Led Zeppelin performing in the mid-1970s (left to right): Robert Plant, John Paul Jones, and Jimmy Page.

© NEAL PRESTON/CORBIS

Led Zeppelin's music reflected the electric Chicago blues, as well as Celtic folk music, mythology, and the occult. One of the band's most popular songs, "Stairway to Heaven," featured an elaborate arrangement that moved from acoustic folk instrumentation to a full-blown, heavy metal finale. Other tunes such as "Whole Lotta Love" (1970) and "Dazed and Confused" (1969) still receive frequent airplay. Led Zeppelin formed in England in 1968 and toured frequently in the United States during the early 1970s, performing in stadiums and laying the foundation for arena rock. The group's theatrics created a spectacle, generating enough musical energy to satisfy an audience of fifteen thousand—well before the invention of giant projection television screens. By 1973 they had broken the Beatles' box-office records, and by 1975 Led Zeppelin had become the most popular rock band in the world.

The late 1960s produced other influential hard rock groups, including Deep Purple. Formed in Britain in 1968, Deep Purple performed up through the 1990s. The group's sound started out as a blend of rock and classical keyboard styles, but by the early 1970s it had shifted to the hard-rock sound heard in "Smoke on the Water" (1973).

ARENA ROCK: THE EXPANSION OF ROCK PROMOTION

Promoter Bill Graham (1931–1991) was central to the commercial development of the late-1960s rock scene. His innovative approach to presenting rock in large-scale venues became an industry standard. An orphaned refugee from postwar Eastern Europe, Graham was a street-smart survivor who came to the West Coast in the late 1950s hoping to be an actor. Instead, he took a job as business manager for the San Francisco Mime Troupe, a political theatre group, where he came up with the idea of staging a benefit rock concert as a fund-raiser. The concert's enormous success put Graham on the road to producing ever larger, ever more-profitable rock events. Graham's bare-knuckled survivor instincts also cut a wide swath through the laid-back San Francisco rock scene, according to journalist Joel Selvin:

> He made a lot of lip service to things he didn't really live up to. . . . It was always in the interest of trying to catch an extra nickel for himself. . . . He studied very hard and he could bluff it, but he had no aesthetic judgment. . . . He equated the sale of tickets with the quality of the act.[8]

Graham opened San Francisco's Fillmore Auditorium (later moved to Fillmore West) in 1966, following up with a sister venue called Fillmore East in New York. For three years he controlled the two most important rock venues in the nation. In 1971, however, Graham closed down both theatres, seeing greater profit in promoting large-scale stadium rock shows. Bill Graham Presents subsequently became the world's most powerful rock concert production company. Graham also saw himself as a manager and developer of talent, and he briefly managed Jefferson Airplane and Carlos Santana. Further, he made a point of booking white rock bands with major black music innovators. One of the concerts he was most proud of was a 1971 Fillmore West show featuring Aretha Franklin, Tower of Power, King Curtis, and Ray Charles:

> [It was] one of the genuine orgasms of my life. For the first time in my life I was able to do something I've always dreamed of, to have a fifty-fifty audience, black and white, like each other for a night. And at the end of the night Ray and Aretha are hand in hand, King Curtis is playing and I look out into the audience . . . you can't buy that. That's why I'm in this business.[9]

Led Zeppelin's stadium-show success encouraged other bands with hard-rock roots to take a similar path, even though a successful arena rock concert required sales of over ten thousand tickets. The sound of arena rock was thus born, characterized by highly amplified music, songs that often made use of rock clichés and hooks, and exaggerated stage performance techniques, in order to be seen and heard in large sports arenas or venues of similar size.

One of the most successful and long-lived hard-rock bands of the era, Aerosmith formed in 1970 and remained active into the early 2000s. Fronted by Steve Tyler, a Mick Jagger lookalike, Aerosmith produced its first hit song, "Dream On" (1975); this became the model for the **power ballad**, which featured high-energy vocals and driving rhythms played at a slow tempo. They followed with "Walk This Way" (1976), went into decline, and later staged a comeback in the 1980s with the help of MTV. Their collaboration with Run-D.M.C. on "Walk This Way" (1986) was the first successful blend of rap and hard rock.

The Doobie Brothers started as a mellow Northern California bar band in 1970, ultimately becoming a soul-inflected arena-rock act. The band's best-known work occurred with Michael McDonald as lead vocalist in the mid-1970s. Major hits included "Listen to the Music" (1972), "What a Fool Believes" (1978), and "Minute by Minute" (1979). McDonald subsequently left the band for a successful solo career. In the mid-1970s, Boston found arena-rock success with one of the fastest-selling debut albums in rock history. The band was assembled by guitarist and MIT-trained mechanical engineer Tom Scholz, who produced most of their first records in an early home studio. Hits included "More Than a Feeling" (1976), "Don't Look Back" (1978), and "Amanda" (1986).

Journey was a high-profile, San Francisco–based group formed in 1973 by alumni of the Santana band. The group scored its biggest hits with the release of *Infinity* (1978) and *Escape* (1981), which included the hit single "Who's Crying Now." With their youthful good looks, the group benefited from the advent of MTV and continued to release successful albums through the 1980s. New York–based Foreigner's unique blend of keyboard-driven heavy metal with a pop-oriented sound achieved a mainstream success rarely garnered by harder-edged metal bands. Their debut album, *Foreigner* (1977), yielded the hits "Cold as Ice" and "Feels Like the First Time." They followed it with *Double Vision* (1978), which yielded the single "Hot Blooded." Another major hard-rock act, Bon Jovi, gained popularity in the 1980s. Founded by New Jersey–based guitarist John Bongiovi in 1983, the band's record company "de-eth-nicized" the artist's Italian surname to "Bon Jovi." For their second album, *Slippery When Wet* (1986), the band test-marketed potential album tracks to New York–area teens, resulting in massive sales. The album yielded hits with "You Give Love a Bad Name" and "Livin' on a Prayer," and MTV featured the band heavily.

In 1989, Alannah Myles' (1958–) self-titled debut album generated four hit songs, "Love Is," "Lover of Mine," "Still Got This Thing," and "Black Velvet," earning the Toronto-born singer-songwriter a Grammy Award for Best Female Rock Performance. During the years following the release of her acclaimed *Rockinghorse* (1992), Myles shed her hard rock diva image but continued to perform in acoustic settings throughout Canada and the United States.

Alannah Myles performing Grammy Award-winning "Black Velvet" in 1989.

JIM STEINFELDT/MICHAEL OCHS ARCHIVES/GETTY IMAGES

HEAVY METAL

With consistent ingredients and simplicity of form, heavy metal and its descendants offered one of the clearest evolutionary timelines in rock. The genre was also home to a devoted, predominantly youthful, white male fan base that developed into its own subculture over a period of thirty years. The British band Black Sabbath emerged in 1970 as the progenitor of the heavy metal style: "Mixing equal parts bone-crushing volume, catatonic tempos, and ominous pronouncements of doom and gloom delivered in [lead singer] Ozzy Osbourne's keening voice, Black Sabbath was the heavy metal king of the 70s."[10] The group's message of social decay, death, and darkness, infused with allusions to Satanism and the occult, came to typify heavy metal. As historian Robert Palmer observes, "Black Sabbath, borrowing their name from a lurid mid-1960s horror film, link the hoodoo traditions of the blues to a B-movie version of European occultism and take blues-based rock one step beyond—into heavy metal."[11] Though panned by critics and receiving almost no airplay, Sabbath's second album, *Paranoid* (1971), sold over four million copies. A darkly gothic poem printed on the band's first album, set inside an inverted crucifix, summed up what one critic called the band's "cheesy, comic-book demonology":[12]

> Still falls the rain, the veils of darkness shroud the
> blackened trees, which contorted by some unseen violence,
> shed their tired leaves, and bend their boughs toward a
> grey earth of severed bird wings. Among the grasses,
> poppies bleed before a gesticulating death, and young
> rabbits, born dead in traps, stand motionless, as though
> guarding the silence that surrounds and threatens to
> engulf all those who would listen.[13]

Numerous bands in Britain and the United States jumped on the heavy metal bandwagon in the 1970s and early 1980s, including a host of British groups that were called the "new wave" of British heavy metal: Judas Priest, Def Leppard, Iron Maiden, Motörhead, and AC/DC. In the United States, theatrical artists such as Kiss and Alice Cooper laid the groundwork for subsequent U.S. metal bands Van Halen, Mötley Crüe, and Twisted Sister to emerge out of the L.A. rock scene in the 1970s. Many of the groups came to be called "hair bands," for their long-hair styles.

By the late 1970s, when elements of punk began to enter the metal repertoire, "faster and louder" became the new mantra. One of the first metal bands to incorporate punk was the British group Motörhead. The U.S. group Metallica pushed the style further, playing a central role in creating a new subgenre called *power metal* and eventually moving into thrash metal. According to historian Ian Christe, "While power metal was heavy metal on steroids, thrash metal's repeated fluttering notes lifted effortlessly into flight. This music was in motion, an intricate flood of enormous sound."[14] Other thrash metal bands included Anthrax, Slayer, and Death Angel. From there the style hybridized in the 1990s, producing funk metal and nu metal.

Several bands emerged as heavy metal took off in the 1970s and 1980s. Van Halen was one of the most popular North American metal bands of the 1970s. Guitarist Eddie Van Halen developed several new electric guitar techniques that made innovative use of the instrument's neck and fretboard. The band emerged out of the Los Angeles club scene with a debut album, *Van Halen* (1978), which sold over six million copies. The act received significant MTV airplay in the early 1980s, and Eddie Van Halen's guitar solo on Michael Jackson's "Beat It" (1983) helped make the song a hit. Formed in Los Angeles in the mid-1980s, Mötley Crüe's live shows featured elaborate sets, fireworks, and female dancers. With its members' high-profile L.A. lifestyles, the band benefited from constant media exposure. Hit albums included the multiplatinum *Girls, Girls, Girls* (1987), *Dr. Feelgood* (1989), and *Decade of Decadence–'81–'91* (1991). Although other British metalists such as Judas Priest and Iron Maiden sold millions of albums in the 1980s, Def Leppard was the most successful British metal band of the decade. Sometimes called a "pop-metal" act because of its clean, well-produced sound, Def Leppard's good looks meshed with the explosion of 1980s metal on MTV; in the words of one magazine, the group was "the heavy metal band you can bring home to mother."[15] The group scored its first major hit with *Pyromania* (1982), followed by *Hysteria* (1987), which yielded the hits "Pour Some Sugar on Me" and "Love Bites."

Metallica, one of the most innovative and influential American metal bands of the 1980s and 1990s, formed in Los Angeles in 1981. Ignoring the look and sound of reigning hair bands, the group instead ingested the energy of punk to craft the intense, sophisticated sound that came to be called thrash metal. Metallica's work featured complex song structures and lyrics dealing with personal and political issues. The act debuted with *Kill 'em All* (1984), but not until the release of *Metallica* (1991) did they chart at number one. Their success continued into the next decade. Voivod, a heavy metal band from Jonquiere, Quebec, similarly patterned a mix of progressive rock, thrash metal, and drew equally from the New Wave of British Heavy Metal and the burgeoning 1980s hardcore punk scene. Voivod was one of the first thrash bands from Canada to gain popularity outside of the country's borders, reaching the peak of their global popularity with the 1989 release, *Nothingface*.

FUNK METAL AND NU METAL

Beginning in the mid-1980s, a cluster of new bands in the Los Angeles area began to play a musical hybrid called funk metal, which drew on the hard-driving guitar riffs of heavy metal and the intricate, popping bass lines and syncopated rhythms of funk. The style was pioneered by the Red Hot Chili Peppers beginning in 1983. The group featured L.A. punk roots, a love for funk master George Clinton, and an explosive stage show. Hits included *Mother's Milk* (1989); *Blood Sugar Sex Magik* (1991), which yielded "Give It Away" and "Under the Bridge"; and *Californication* (1999). Other groups, including Faith No More and Fishbone, also took up funk metal.

By the mid-1990s, young rock artists had gone a few steps further, to blend rap, sampling, DJs, drum machines, and other new techniques with guitar-driven metal to produce nu metal (also called *alt metal* or *rap metal*). Earlier successful fusions of rap and metal had included Run-D.M.C.'s collaboration with Aerosmith on "Walk This Way" (1986) and the Beastie Boys' *Licensed to Ill* (1986) album. Acts such as the Deftones, Korn, and Rage Against the Machine were nu metal's earliest innovators, followed by others including Incubus, Limp Bizkit, and Linkin Park. Popularization of the nu metal style came about with increased MTV exposure, and by the late 1990s nu metal had become a mainstream rock sound.

The Deftones were one of the first nu metal groups to alternate sinewy guitars, heavy metal crunch, and screamed vocals with more subdued music and eerie whispered vocals. The Sacramento-based group, which started out as a metal band, showed continuous willingness to experiment with their music.

The L.A.-based quartet Rage Against the Machine put out an innovative combination of progressive political rhetoric, hip-hop, and metal. The band's street-wise grooves and anti-establishment positions made them youth folk heroes with singles such as "Killing in the Name" (1992), "Bullet in the Head" (1992), and "Bulls on Parade" (1996). The Florida-based Limp Bizkit, one of the leading rock acts of 2000, combined metal, hip-hop breakbeats, and a humorous white-trash image. As critic Neva Chonin put it, Limp Bizkit was "Rage Against the Machine's rap-metal gone bad. The beginning of the end of the world as we know it and a return to all the dread 'M' words in the rock lexicon: macho, misogynistic, mediocre, moronic."[16] The Grammy-winning Linkin Park appeared in the early 2000s to give the nu metal hybrid a second wind, blending old-school hip-hop, classic rock, and electronic influences. Finally, Incubus rose to become one of the most popular nu metal bands of the early 2000s, setting themselves apart from the crowded field. According to critic Jim DeRogatis,

> Along with the Deftones and 311, the San Fernando Valley, California, quintet Incubus stands as one of the few shining examples of what nu-metal/rap-rock could (and should) be, in stark contrast to the likes of Limp Bizkit, Linkin Park and their ilk.[17]

CHAPTER SUMMARY

- The British Invasion, led by the Beatles and the Rolling Stones, changed rock music forever in the mid-1960s. The Beatles went on to become the most popular band in the history of rock.

- The evolution of rock from the 1970s to the early 2000s saw the creation of multiple new genres. While some genres were completely original, others at the end of the century were hybrids of styles previously developed during rock's first two decades.

- The roots of hard rock and heavy metal go back to the music of pivotal blues-inspired rock artists such as Jimi Hendrix, Cream, and Led Zeppelin.

- The growing popularity of rock led to expanded corporate control of rock promotion and the use of larger performance venues, giving birth to arena rock.

- The culture of heavy metal stemmed from the godfather of the genre, Black Sabbath. Heavy metal became one of rock's most consistent styles.

LISTENING EXERCISE

Comparative Analysis Between Hard Rock and Heavy Metal

Listen to "Born to Be Wild" (1968) by Steppenwolf and "Paranoid" (1971) by Black Sabbath. Pay attention to the instrumentation in each band. How do the musical parts interact to create the foundations of hard rock and heavy metal? How would you describe the vocal styles and guitar timbres? Do both songs adhere to the standard formulas of verse repeated chorus, solo, and hook? If not, what does that say about the commercial viability of the style?

HISTORICAL STUDIES AND DISCUSSION QUESTIONS

1. Indiscriminate Appropriation Equals a Rock Revolution

Beginning in the 1920s, British musicians appropriated numerous African American styles such as New Orleans jazz, swing, and boogie woogie. By the 1940s and 1950s, a movement developed in the United Kingdom that paralleled the U.S. folk revival and sought out "authentic" American roots artists. The late 1950s in Britain witnessed the appearance of *skiffle,* a crazy quilt of anything vaguely folksy, bluesy, or rootsy, as well as a blues revival. The Beatles led the mid-1960s assault of British rock acts on North American markets, presenting a "new" sound. In fact, as all of the British Invasion artists pointed out, they were recycling classic American styles and genres, albeit filtered through a British adolescent male lens. Why did the British Invasion acts sound "new" to the ears of North American teens, if the artists were primarily appropriating and recycling U.S. musical styles? What changes can happen during the process of cultural appropriation and reinterpretation?

2. Exploring the Culture of Heavy Metal

The culture of heavy metal is an interesting hybrid. Its musicians and fans are predominantly, though not exclusively, young, white working-class men. Over the years, heavy metal performance regalia has included long hair, tight leather clothing, makeup, and outsized jewelry. Song themes often centre on social alienation, and political and religious hypocrisy. Many researchers have argued that heavy metal symbols signify youthful alienation, in the same way that punk does. Some claim that young white working-class men have used heavy metal to express feelings of frustration. Researchers have also argued that androgynous performance images of men in tight leather pants who have long, carefully coiffed hair and makeup, as well as violent themes of darkness, death, and hostility, may signify a quest for identity. Ironically, that identity often affirms the same dominant culture values it seeks to undermine. What positive influences does this culture play in the socialization of youth?

STUDY QUESTIONS

1. What social, political, and commercial forces served as catalysts for the explosion of musical styles in the 1960s?

2. What were the building blocks of the British Invasion? How did the Invasion impact North American popular music?

3. What role did blues revivalism play in the development of Canadian Rock?

4. How did the evolution of rock in the early 1970s draw on the music of the 1960s? What were the major styles and bands to emerge in this era? Which styles and artists had the longest-lasting impact on rock?

5. Discuss the emergence and evolution of heavy metal music and culture. Who were the major players, and why did the culture of heavy metal remain so consistent and clearly defined?

6. What are the blues characteristics in recent heavy metal?

NOTES

1. Charlie Gillett, *The Sound of the City: The Rise of Rock and Roll* (New York: Da Capo Press, 1996), 259.

2. "'Skiffle King' Donegan Died," BBC News, http://news.bbc.co.uk/1/hi/entertainment/music/2400229.stm, accessed May 12, 2005.

3. Gillett, *Sound of the City*, 267.

4. Robert Palmer, *Rock and Roll: An Unruly History* (New York: Harmony Books, 1995), 118.

5. Stanley Booth, *Dance with the Devil: The Rolling Stones and Their Times* (New York: Random House, 1984), 9–10.

6. Robert Christgau, "The Rolling Stones," in *The Rolling Stone Illustrated History of Rock and Roll*, 3rd ed., edited by Anthony DeCurtis and James Henke (New York: Random House, 1992), 246–47.

7. Pamela Des Barres, "Every Inch of My Love," in *Rock and Roll Is Here to Stay: An Anthology*, edited by William McKeen (New York: Norton, 2000), 300.

8. Interview by the authors.

9. Jack McDonough, *San Francisco Rock: The Illustrated History of San Francisco Rock Music* (San Francisco: Chronicle Books, 1985), 41.

10. Patricia Romanowski and Holly George-Warren, eds., *The New Rolling Stone Encyclopedia of Rock and Roll*, 3rd ed. (New York: Fireside, 2001), 81.

11. Palmer, *Rock and Roll*, 125.

12. *Ibid.*, 126.

13. Ian Christe, *Sound of the Beast: The Complete Headbanging History of Heavy Metal* (New York: HarperCollins, 2003), 4.

14. *Ibid.*, 137.

15. Romanowski and George-Warren, *New Rolling Stone Encyclopedia,* 247.

16. Neva Chonin, "Limp Bizkit and Eminem Revel in Teen Angst at Friday's Cow Palace Show," http://www.sfgate.com, December 31, 1999; accessed May 16, 2005.

17. Jim DeRogatis, "Album Review: Incubus: *A Crown Left of the Murder,*" http://www.jimdero.com/News2004/FEB22Albums.htm, February 22, 2004; accessed May 16, 2005.

1760 - 2000

1765 Thomas Percy publishes a major collection of British folk music ♪

1776 U.S. Declaration of Independence and beginning of Revolutionary War

1861–1865 Civil War

1867 Canadian Confederation

1878 Lord Dufferin, Canada's Governor General, makes first Canadian recording with Thomas Edison's phonograph ♪

1880s Francis James Child publishes the Child ballad collections ♪

1898 Spanish American War

Early 1900s Cecil Sharp proves that British folk music exists in rural America ♪

1910 John Lomax publishes his collection of cowboy songs ♪

1914–1918 World War I

1919–1933 Prohibition

1922 First country artists recorded by Victor in New York ♪

1922 First country music broadcast on WSB in Atlanta ♪

1925 "Grand Ole Opry" first broadcast on WSM in Nashville ♪

1927 Ralph Peer records Jimmie Rodgers and Carter Family (Bristol Recordings) ♪

1929–1930s Great Depression; New Deal begins

1929 Don Messer begins his radio career on CFBO, Saint John, New Brunswick ♪

1930 "Border" radio stations begin broadcasting, and country music is heard throughout the U.S. ♪

1930 Wilf Carter conducts his first live radio broadcast on CFCN, Calgary, Alberta ♪

1932 Wilf Carter's "Miss Little Moonlight Lullabye" is the first Canadian-produced domestic hit ♪

1932 The Canadian Radio Broadcasting Commission becomes Canada's national public broadcaster ♪

1933 Tennessee Valley Authority established; electric power brought to rural areas of South

1933 Honky-tonks begin to flourish with Prohibition repeal, establishing a new country sound ♪

1935 Bob Wills makes first records, establishing western swing ♪

1935 New Brunswick native Bob Nolan (Sons of the Pioneers) scores a hit with "Tumbling Tumbleweeds" ♪

1936 Hank Snow begins recording career with RCA Victor ♪

1939 "Grand Ole Opry" carried nationwide over NBC for first time ♪

1929–1930s Great Depression; New Deal begins

1940s John Lomax promotes the career of songster Leadbelly ♪

1940 Woody Guthrie and Pete Seeger spearhead American political folk song movement ♪

1940–1945 World War II

1941 Bing Crosby has crossover pop hit with Bob Wills' "New San Antonio Rose" ♪

1944 Beginning of regular commercial recording in Nashville ♪

1945 Flatt and Scruggs join Bill Monroe, bluegrass emerges ♪

1946 Major Nashville publisher Acuff-Rose signs Hank Williams ♪

1947 Honky-tonk musician Ernest Tubb headlines at Carnegie Hall ♪

1947 Canadian Citizenship Act passed; Prime Minister Mackenzie King is the first to hold a Canadian passport

1948 Revival of Chansonnier tradition in Quebec: Leclerc, Levesque, Normand ♪

1948 Moses Asch founds Folkways Records ♪

1949 Newfoundland and Labrador join Dominion of Canada

1760   1860   1900   1940

Folk Ballad Legacies

1950–1953 Korean War

1950s Skiffle music lays the groundwork for the British "beat" sound ♪

1950 McCarthy "Red Scare" Senate hearings

1950 The Weavers score hits with "Goodnight Irene" and "On Top of Old Smoky" ♪

1950 Pop vocalist Patti Page has crossover hit with "Tennessee Waltz" ♪

1952 Kitty Wells becomes first major female C&W artist ♪

1952 Release of Harry Smith's *Anthology of American Folk Music* ♪

1954 School segregation outlawed; civil rights movement begins

1954 Canadian folk-activist group, The Travellers, make their CBC TV debut ♪

1954 Elvis Presley's first recordings for Sam Phillips's Sun Records in Memphis ♪

1956 *Billboard* magazine adopts the term Country and Western ♪

1958 Country Music Association (CMA) founded ♪

1958 The Kingston Trio moves folk into the mainstream with their hit "Tom Dooley" ♪

1958 Ronnie Hawkins performs in Canada for the first time ♪

1959 Chansonnier ensemble Les Bozos inaugurate Bôite à chansons in Montreal ♪

1960–1964 Folk music explodes on college campuses ♪

1961 First Mariposa Folk Festival in Orillia, Ontario ♪

1962 Ray Charles's country album hits number one on pop charts ♪

1962 Gordon Lightfoot releases first single, "Remember Me" ♪

1963 Civil rights march on Washington; John Kennedy assassinated

1963 Bob Dylan releases *The Freewheelin' Bob Dylan*, which includes "Blowin' in the Wind" ♪

1964–1973 Vietnam War

1964 Joni Mitchell and Buffy Sainte-Marie perform at Mariposa Folk Festival ♪

1964 U.S. Congress passes Civil Rights Bill

1965 Dylan goes electric at the Newport Folk Festival ♪

1965 The Byrds' version of "Mr. Tambourine Man" sets the standard for folk rock ♪

1965 First "acid tests" in San Francisco set the stage for the psychedelic explosion

1966 Vietnam War protests begin

1966 Sly Stone becomes first African American rocker to sign with a major label ♪

1966 Leonard Cohen and Anne Murray launch careers ♪

1966 Ronnie Hawkins' alumni form The Band and begin working with Bob Dylan ♪

1967 Urban riots in Detroit; "Summer of Love" in San Francisco

1967 Monterey Pop Festival; Hendrix records classic LPs ♪

1968 Martin Luther King and Robert Kennedy assassinated

1969 Woodstock Music Festival ♪

1969 Altamont Speedway Free Festival, Meredith Hunter killed by Hells Angels member ♪

1969 True North Records is founded by Bernie Finkelstein ♪

1969 President Nixon sworn in; largest antiwar rally in history held

1969 Johnny Cash's *At San Quentin* hits number one on pop album charts ♪

1970 Antiwar protesters killed at Kent State University in Ohio

1970 Jimi Hendrix and Janis Joplin die of drug overdoses ♪

1970 Anne Murray scores a number one hit with "Snowbird" ♪

1971 Canadian Content Regulations come into effect; first Juno Awards ♪

1976 *Wanted: The Outlaws* becomes first platinum country LP ♪

1980 *Country Music News* begins publication in Canada ♪

1983 Country Music Television (CMT) and The Nashville Network (TNN) launched ♪

1984 k.d. lang makes U.S. debut in New York City ♪

1988 Canada and U.S. Free Trade Agreement (CFTA) is passed: culture industries notwithstanding

1990s Garth Brooks breaks sales records, introducing a new generation of young country artists ♪

1995 Shania Twain's "Any Man of Mine" tops the *Billboard* country singles chart ♪

2001–2008 9/11 attacks; wars in Iraq and Afghanistan; collapse of equity markets

1950   1960   1970   1980   1990   2000

CHAPTER 13

Folk Origins and Early Influences

Country music is a unique and eclectic hybrid shaped by folk music, church music, minstrelsy, the blues, jazz, Tin Pan Alley, rock, and the historical and cultural context of the South. The genre is instantly recognizable for its regional accents; high, close harmonies; wailing steel guitars; fiddles; banjos; and straightforward rhythms. It also has numerous variants and substyles. Country music was originally a working-class music, and many artists experienced grinding rural poverty firsthand. It also reflected two contradictory cultural strands: God, country, mother, and home versus drinking, partying, and sex—both often permeated with a sense of sadness and loss. With a national and global audience, country music now accounts for 10 to 15 percent of the recorded music purchased in the United States and Canada and may well be the most popular contemporary musical genre.

The early roots of country originate in the music of Britain, France, Ireland, Wales, and Scotland. Folk music, dances, fiddle music, broadsides, ballads, and parlour songs from these cultures began to arrive in the interior eastern seaboard of North America during the sixteenth century. An important feature of country music is that it often tells a story, and Anglo-Celtic ballads contributed much to storytelling. The recurring themes of British and American parlour songs—home, hearth, mother, family, and God—also found a comfortable fit among rural folk on both sides of the border. The prevalence of rural lifestyles in a rugged terrain contributed to a sense of isolation that flavoured country's development in the southern United States, and the challenges of daily life also played a part, according to historian Bill Malone:

> The average rural dweller needed few reminders from the Bible or any other source to know that life was indeed tragic—a brief period filled with unrewarded labor, sadness and disappointment and ending in death.[1]

A unique folk culture and musical style began to take shape in the South, a region some scholars have called the "fertile crescent" of country music.[2] Because many southerners learned to sing in church, Protestant religious music greatly affected southern singing styles. In particular, church music influenced the development of vocal harmony in country music through the dissemination of the **shape note** system. The Great Revival of the nineteenth century also influenced southern music; the resulting southern church music came to

© ERIC SCHAAL/TIME LIFE PICTURES/GETTY IMAGES

The Carter Family, America's first family of country music, evoked traditional values with their folk-rooted acoustic music. In a 1941 photo, patriarch A. P. Carter (right) is flanked by group members, his sister-in-law Maybelle (on guitar), and his wife, Sara Carter (third from right). Daughter June Carter (second from left) later married singer Johnny Cash.

employ hymns, folk music from European American and African American sources, as well as early forms of gospel music. Songs were often tinged with what Bill Malone called "folk fatalism," portraying Christians as pilgrims in an unfriendly world.[3] The Holiness-Pentecostal movement of the early twentieth century introduced flexible worship formats that reinforced the folk qualities of southern religious music, and it integrated popular styles, such as blues and jazz, that many Christians had previously condemned as "the devil's music." Pentecostal singing styles were rhythmic, passionate, and uninhibited, building a new style of southern singing free from earlier restraint.

Despite slavery and subsequent segregation, many southerners experienced frequent black–white cultural interaction as a part of daily life. Cross-racial musical exchanges went back as far as the seventeenth century, and the performance styles and repertoires of many late-nineteenth- and early-twentieth-century songsters—black and white—were probably similar. African American elements that made their way into country music included blueslike singing styles, the banjo and various banjo techniques, innovative guitar and fiddling styles, ragtime, and jazz. Black music and musicians influenced many country music legends, including A. P. Carter, Bill Monroe, Jimmie Rodgers, Bob Wills, and Hank Williams. African American music also significantly influenced white gospel styles, and white and black gospel styles developed in parallel. Many hymns popular in white communities were composed by such African Americans as Thomas Dorsey.

Interactions between white and Mexican American musicians in the Southwest were also common, because much of the region was part of Mexico prior to 1848. The use of Anglo-Celtic ballads and *corridos* (Mexican ballads) was similar in the two cultures, and numerous country songs employed the ballad tradition. While heavily shaped by jazz, western swing was also influenced by mariachi music. In turn, western swing then influenced the Chicano *orquesta tejana* style. Further, the close vocal harmonies used by such groups as the Sons of the Pioneers resembled the traditional *dueto* and trio style of Mexican *ranchera* singing, and the polka rhythm, whose roots were European, entered country music via Mexico.

While life in the rural South may have been isolated, nineteenth- and early twentieth-century travelling shows exposed southern audiences to a range of musical styles that included parlour songs, Swiss yodelers, brass bands, Hawaiian string bands, and much more. Minstrel shows often featured the banjo and fiddle as principal instruments, and they introduced songs such as "Turkey in the Straw" (originally known as "Zip Coon") that became southern standards. Vaudeville brought Tin Pan Alley tunes to the South, and many of the songs then went through multiple countrified adaptations. The development of the railroad also impacted southern culture and music, making it possible for rural southerners to respond to the lure of city life. As historian Bill Malone describes,

> No one can document the number of people who have lain awake in quiet and darkened farmhouses listening to the lonesome wail of a distant freight engine or have seen it belching smoke as it thundered down the mountainside and longed for the exciting world that the iron monster seemed to symbolize.[4]

COUNTRY MUSIC CHARACTERISTICS

Musical elements that define country include songs, language, and instrumentation. Because few rural musicians could read music, early country versions of folk tunes, ballads, or parlour songs were often simplified so they could be learned by ear. Oral transmission contributed to this evolution, often creating completely new tunes from older ones. "Barbara Allen" was one such example: Originally a Scottish ballad, it dispersed throughout the original settlements in British North America, ending up in widely differing versions. The classic twang of southern speech is another distinguishing feature of country music. As contemporary country incorporated more rock and pop elements, southern accents sometimes became the primary distinguishing element of the genre.

The defining instrumentation of country music includes stringed instruments such as the fiddle, banjo, guitar, pedal steel guitar, Dobro guitar, mandolin, **dulcimer**, string bass, and autoharp. Harmonica, jaw harp, washboard, and simple percussion have also been used, and in recent years the drum set, electric bass, and piano have become commonplace.

Historically, the fiddle was probably the most popular instrument in rural North America. Fiddle styles may be broken down most conveniently by region (i.e., Quebec, Cape Breton, Ottawa Valley, and Arkansas) and, within those regions, by substyles varying according to type and degrees of embellishment. The first reference to fiddling in America occurred in the announcement of a contest in a 1736 issue of the *Virginia Gazette*. Throughout the nineteenth century, the instrument appeared at most social functions and served as the centrepiece of rural house parties. In Newfoundland there developed a tradition known as "chin music" (a style of vocalized fiddle playing) which was used when a fiddle was nowhere to be found. The flavour of country fiddling evolved out of British and Irish folk music, jigs, reels, folk songs, and minstrelsy. Because the fiddle was one of the most common instruments that slaves were allowed to play, African American fiddlers contributed much to the evolution of southern fiddle styles. In addition, string bands, minstrel shows, and early jazz and blues ensembles all used fiddles and influenced the fiddle repertoire.

The banjo is an American hybrid with African roots that has seen many changes during its two-hundred-year North American history. Unfortunately, the rich tradition of African American banjo music has been largely lost. As far back as 1754, it was described in the *Maryland Gazette* as the "banjer."[5] Early versions of the instrument had four strings with no frets. The addition of a fifth ("drone") string in the 1830s, and frets in the 1880s, made the instrument easier to play, and the drone sound of the fifth string became a signature country sound.

The steel guitar, originally from Hawaii, became popular on the U.S. mainland in the early twentieth century. The sliding sound of the instrument influenced African American Delta blues guitarists and also found its way into country music. In its acoustic form, now called the Dobro, and in its electric pedal steel versions, the steel guitar provides another signature sound of country music. Acoustic guitars did not come into wide use among rural musicians until the late nineteenth century, but by the twentieth century the instrument was widely available via mail-order catalogue, and it was soon second only to the fiddle in country string band instrumentation. The adoption of the electric guitar in country music came about with the rise of honky-tonk in the 1940s.

The mandolin, which was brought to North America by European immigrants in the early twentieth century, is another instrument commonly used in country. The instrument has four paired strings that are tuned like a violin, which makes it easy for fiddlers to learn as a second instrument. The dulcimer also found a home in country music, with a gentle melodic sound that was perfect for accompanying solo love songs and ballads. In addition, the piano and harmonica commonly appear in country music.

CHAPTER SUMMARY

- Country music has a complex history. Although the stars of country have generally been of European descent, the style's roots originate in European folk traditions, church music, African American music, and Mexican American music.

LISTENING EXERCISE

Creative Agency and Copyright

The study of the historical origins of folk tunes has been a key preoccupation for folklorists since the turn of the twentieth century. Encumbered by scant written records, researchers examine melodic correspondences between seeming unrelated folksongs in effort to establish a genealogy of versions and variants. Known as tune family analysis, the technique affords a fascinating glimpse into how folk songs circulate within oral cultural. For example, the text of the well-known hymn, "Amazing Grace," was written in 1772 by British slave trader turned minister, John Newton, and was set to the melody of "The Bailiff's Daughter," a folk ballad which enjoyed widespread use during that time. The hymn subsequently splintered off into a variety of patterns as it migrated to different regions in the British Empire; some of these patterns continue to be heard in today's music. The "Amazing Grace" melody, for instance, is clearly discernable in Bill Monroe's "Blue Moon of Kentucky' (1946), the recording which inspired Elvis Presley's version of the same song in 1954; and the hymn's signature (I-IV-V) harmonic progression can be found in countless pieces, including Thomas Moore's "Believe Me, If All those Endearing Young Charms" (1820), the African-American spiritual, "Swing Low, Sweet Chariot," "Wimoweh (a.k.a. "The Lion Sleeps Tonight") by the South African musician, Solomon Linde (1939), and "Honky Tonk Woman" (1969) by the Rolling Stones. Seen from this angle, it is conceivable that culture may share similar unifying pathways to those found in the genetic code.

The transmission of culture, however, does not occur in a vacuum. For although sharing or borrowing cultural expressions may have had little consequence in pre-market societies, the imposition of patent and copyright laws since the sixteenth century has, without a doubt, dramatically altered the way in which music circulates between individuals. While Muddy Waters did not sustain any legal repercussions for his "illegal" cover of Robert Petway's "Catfish Blues" (1941), the outcome was quite the opposite for the British rock group, The Verve, who recorded "Bitter Sweet Symphony" (1997) without having first won copyright clearance for the melodic bits they had cribbed from "The Last Time" (1965) by the Rolling Stones. Although the Verve claimed they had an informal "fair use" agreement (an argument which has no legal standing), the result was a lawsuit in which the court sided with the plaintiff. During this litigious escapade, no notice was paid to the strong resemblances the Jagger/Richards composition of "The Last Time" has to the similar titled (and styled!) 1960 recording by Roebuck Staples and the Staple Singers. Instances such as this raise interesting questions regarding private ownership and culture. Listen to "Bitter Sweet Symphony" and the two versions of "(This Will Be) The Last Time" and discuss the following: Where should public domain and private ownership begin and end with respect to creativity? Is it possible to draw a hard and fast line between the two? What are the advantages and disadvantages for doing so? Why is one individual's private property "more private" than another individual's private property?

HISTORICAL STUDIES AND DISCUSSION QUESTIONS

1. What Is Folk?

The search for a workable definition of folk, and by extension, folk music, is one of the perplexing challenges that faces both scholars and students alike. A number of publications dedicated to the subject have elected to provide multiple definitions of the term in the absence of there being a suitable all-encompassing definition. Why is this approach more advisable when studying other musical practices, such as heavy metal?

2. Traditional Folk Singing Practices

According to the American musicologist, Charles Seeger, the traditional folksinger gives no special thought to quality of sound, but sings in as "natural" a voice as that in which s/he talks. Moreover, "the lack of any preconception of what ought to be gives the quality of the traditional singer's singing a clearly recognizable character that can be instantly recognized by other carriers and connoisseurs of the tradition . . . the singer does not give special attention to platform exhibitionism".[6] Listen to Emma Dussenbury's 1936 recording of Barbara Allen (*American Anthology of Folk Song-L54*). Why is Dussenbury's singing style entirely appropriate for delivering the universal messages which lie at the heart of many traditional folk ballads.

STUDY QUESTIONS

1. What social and cultural factors coalesced in the South during the early twentieth century to contribute to the development of country music?
2. How did shape-note hymns contribute to development of country music?
3. What are the general musical and lyrical features of a traditional ballad?
4. Can you identify contemporary examples of traditional ballads?
5. How do the fiddling styles differ from each other?

NOTES

1. Bill C. Malone, *Country Music, U.S.A.*, rev. ed. (Austin: University of Texas Press, 1985), 15.
2. *Ibid.*, 2.
3. *Ibid.*, 13.
4. *Ibid.*, 8.
5. Cecelia Conway, *African Banjo Echoes in Appalachia: A Study of Folk Traditions* (Knoxville: University of Tennessee Press, 1995), 304–5.
6. Charles Seeger, "Versions and Variants of the Tunes of 'Barbara Allen'" in Studies in Musicology, 1935–1975 (Los Angeles: University of California Press, 1977), 285.

CHAPTER 14

The Emergence of Hillbilly Music

The commercial development of country music paralleled and frequently over-lapped with that of the blues and jazz. At first the commercial music industry did not know what to do with the rural southern musical genre that took shape in the 1920s. There was a vague sense that the music was old (or old-fashioned) and that it reflected southern rural culture: Brunswick Records called it "songs from Dixie," Columbia called it "old familiar tunes," and pro-ducer Ralph Peer coined the term **hillbilly** in 1925. Finally, *Billboard* magazine adopted the term *country and western* in 1949.

You can find country music just about anywhere in North America—especially in rural areas—and a diverse audience to go with it. One study from the early 1990s reported that 25 percent of the adult African American radio audience favoured country music. Although white performers have dom-inated the genre, influential African American and Mexican American country artists have also contributed to it.

During country's formative years, integrated string bands played in rural communities throughout the South; black and white fiddlers and songsters commonly performed side by side at country dances, serving up ragtime, blues, and traditional string band music. Deford Bailey (1899–1982) was the first black star of country music and one of country music's seminal harmonica stylists. He first starred on the "Grand Ole Opry" in 1928, remaining a regular on the show until 1941. Bailey's famous "Pan American Blues," a musical por-trait of a train leaving a station, was an Opry theme song for many years. Other African American artists such as singer/guitarist Leadbelly (Huddie Ledbetter), popular during the folk revival of the 1930s, also bridged the gap between hillbilly and race music.

HILLBILLY MUSIC AND RADIO

The invention of radio played a major role in the dissemination of country music. The earliest country music broadcast was heard in 1922 on Atlanta's WSB, with a lineup featuring a mountain quartet, gospel singers, and an old-time musician named Fiddlin' John Carson. Radio was ideally suited to rural America and the vast audience far outside city limits, for it could penetrate into isolated areas that lacked roads or rail access. As one Georgia farmer wrote to WSB in Atlanta, "I walked four miles and forded two streams just to hear your seven o'clock program."[1] Local or regional businesses owned many of these stations. For example, Sears Roebuck owned WLS in Chicago, and an insurance company owned WSM in Nashville, whose call letters stood for "We Shield Millions." Most country radio shows were commercially sponsored, many by the makers of patent medicines, which maintained a link between country and old-time touring medicine shows. Some of the more colourful medicinal sponsors were "Crazy Water Crystals," "Retonga Medicine," "Man-O-Ree," "Black Draught," and "Pe-Ru-Na." Other more prosaic underwriters included flour, coffee, farm machinery, snuff, and beverage companies.

The *barn dance* first appeared in 1923 as an early country radio format, and in 1925 WSM in Nashville started its own version—what became the legendary **"Grand Ole Opry."** The early Opry featured string bands, traditional singers, gospel quartets, and banjo players, supported by colourful announcers, comedians, and ad-libbing costumed musicians. Early Opry stars included banjoist "Uncle" Dave Macon; Deford Bailey ("The Harmonica Wizard"); the Delmore Brothers, a vocal blues-gospel duo; and the Pickard Family, a traditional vocal trio. By the 1930s, the Opry and other barn dance shows were well established, and in 1944 *Billboard* magazine estimated that there were six hundred country radio shows in the United States playing to an audience of 40 million people. Powerful radio stations also sprang up in northern Mexico along the U.S. border, sending country music out to much of North America.

Because radio broadcasts of black music in the South were rare prior to the 1940s, many black musicians spent their formative years listening to country music. Traces of country appeared in the work of early R & B artists such as Fats Domino, Wynonie Harris, Ivory Joe Hunter, Ester Phillips, and Etta James. According to James, "I want to show that gospel, country, blues, rhythm and blues, jazz, and rock and roll are really the same thing. Those are the American Music and that is the American Culture." The most famous R & B–country crossover recordings came from the great Ray Charles. A lifelong fan of country music, Charles released a two-record set called *Modern Sounds in Country and Western Music* in 1960, and two years later he released the country crossover hit, "I Can't Stop Loving You."

Country music was introduced to Canadian audiences by U.S. radio, principally WBAP (Fort Worth), WLS (Chicago), and WSM (Nashville). Country radio programming in Canada began in 1928 with George Wade on CFRB (Toronto) and with Don Messer on CFBO (St. John, NB) in 1929, and remained a significant performance medium for country artists until recordings took over in the mid-1950s. The live-broadcast variety show format of the "Grand Ole Opry" revolved around the announcer-singing star, and was replicated on radio programs on both sides of the border. Some important shows included W.D. 'Billy' Hassell on CJOR (Vancouver), "Saturday Night Barn Dance" on CKNX (Wingham, ON), and on "Mainstreet Jamboree" CHML (Hamilton).

Radio greatly influenced country performance styles. For example, the personality of the singer grew increasingly important as new microphone technologies permitted subtlety and dynamics. Humour also emerged as a significant element, and performers developed a closeness to their audiences that became a hallmark. Listeners often wrote letters to their favourite stars, and requests and dedications were answered on the air. Singer Bradley Kincaid sent this message out to his listeners,

> When I sing for you on the air, I always visualize you, a family group, sitting around the radio. . . . If I did not feel your presence, though you be a thousand miles away, the radio would be cold and unresponsive to me, and I in turn would sound the same way to you.[2]

By the 1950s, with the advent of television and rock, country radio started to take a battering. In response, the Country Music Association (CMA) formed in 1958. It successfully buttressed the industry, raising the number of country stations from eighty-one in 1961 to over six hundred by 1969. Similarly, the growth of country music in Canada saw the formation of the Canadian Academy of Country Music Advancement in 1975. In tandem the organizations ushered in an era of DJs, playlists, promoters, and tightly controlled formats that changed periodically with names such as "modern country," "countrypolitan," "real country," "contemporary country," and "young country." As of the early 2000s, about 19 percent of the eleven thousand U.S. radio stations played country music, and almost all had strict playlists. Contemporary country radio rarely includes classic country or **bluegrass** artists, however. Even when the old-time and bluegrass music sound track to the film *O Brother, Where Art Thou?* won a Grammy in 2000, it received scant airplay. According to Luke Wood, president of the soundtrack's label,

> We operate in country within a box and you can run up in the corners of the box, but if you get outside of it the gatekeepers don't like it. A few radio programmers said to the record labels after the Grammys: "Don't get any ideas: we are not going to start playing Allison Krauss and Nickel Creek because of this."[3]

The absence of doctrinaire attitudes regarding what is or is not country is perhaps the most striking difference between Canada and the United States. While the narrow-cast framework of Nashville dominates commercial country music in the United States, a glance at a list of the most popular Canadian country artists since the mid-1980s—a list which includes Rita MacNeil, George Fox, The Rankin Family, Shania Twain, k. d. lang, and Teri Clark—underscores a culture were heterogeneity is the rule rather than the exception.

Country music radio today thrives as a commercial vehicle, but according to critic Edward Morris,

> Country radio has become very good at giving fans steady and reliably pleasant background music. But that is a shamefully tepid legacy for a vehicle that once provided the rough edged excitement of barn dances, the polyglot programming of bluegrass, country, and gospel.[4]

RECORDING HILLBILLY MUSIC

Early country recording was a byproduct of the successful movement to record African American talent, which started with Mamie Smith's "Crazy Blues" in 1920. Although it is generally acknowledged that the first commercial "hillbilly" recording was made of Eck Robertson, a Texas fiddler, in 1922, recordings by traditional French-Canadian instrumentalists had already been issued on the Victor label in 1918. From the start, the record industry encouraged segregation by dividing southern vernacular music along racial lines: African American recordings were "race records"; white recordings were "hillbilly music." Ralph Peer (1892–1960), who had worked on the Mamie Smith recording session, pioneered country music recording. His earliest country recordings, made in 1923, included Fiddlin' John Carson, Gid Tanner and His Skillet Lickers, and Charlie Poole and the North Carolina Ramblers. A year later a classically trained vocalist named Vernon Dalhart scored some of the first country hits with "The Prisoner's Song" and "Wreck of the Old 97," two parlour songs with a simple guitar and fiddle accompaniment.

Having detected a large market for vernacular music, Peer quickly capitalized on it by setting up a legendary recording trip in 1927:

> I made a survey of various Southern cities. . . . In Bristol I appealed to the editor of a local newspaper and he ran a half column on his front page. This worked like dynamite. . . . Groups of singers who had not visited Bristol during their entire lifetime arrived by bus, horse and buggy, trains, or on foot.[5]

Among the artists he recorded in Bristol, Virginia, that year were the Carter Family, a traditional folk trio from southwestern Virginia, and Jimmie Rodgers, a bluesy singer/songwriter from Mississippi. As historian Nolan Petered has observed, "Bristol, August 1927 has come to signal the Big Bang of country music evolution, the genesis of every shape and species of Pickin'-and-Singin' down through the years."[6] The Carters and Rodgers shaped two seminal strands of country music. The Carters symbolized home, church, family, and tradition, while Rodgers personified rambling, drinking, partying, and the blues.

The Carter Family—A. P. Carter (1891–1960); his wife, Sara (1899–1979); and their sister-in-law Maybelle (1909–1978)—came from the mountains of southwestern Virginia. By the time they began recording in 1927, they had amassed a repertoire of traditional songs from Anglo-Celtic, religious, and sentimental sources. Their music featured two-part close vocal harmony led by Sara Carter, and the influential thumb-picked "Carter Scratch" guitar playing of Maybelle Carter. Sara and Maybelle Carter were the first female stars of country music in a time when women's roles were limited. It was only because A. P. Carter fronted the group that the women were able to perform at all, and advertising posters for their concerts assured people that "The Program Is Morally Good."[7] The Carters' repertoire of Anglo-American folk music (now simply called "Carter songs") was laboriously gathered across Appalachia by A. P. Carter, who was often assisted by Leslie Riddle, an African American blues singer and guitarist. Carter songs such as "Wildwood Flower," "Wabash Cannonball," "Can the Circle Be Unbroken," "Worried Man Blues," and "Keep on the Sunny Side" became standards.

Jimmie Rodgers (1897–1933), the "father" of country music, was a twentieth-century popular music original. He blended the blues, jazzy dance-band arrangements, a catchy vocal style, railroad images, yodelling, and steel guitar to shape an entire genre. The son of an itinerant railroad worker in Mississippi, he learned African American work songs and early blues styles, and he worked in medicine shows and minstrelsy. According to critic Nick Tosches, "Jimmie Rodgers made black music accessible to white audiences."[8] When Ralph Peer auditioned Rodgers in 1927, he declared, "I was elated. . . . He had his own personal and peculiar style, and I thought that his yodel alone might spell success."[9] Rodgers recalled the same encounter: "They want these old-fashioned things. Love songs and plantation melodies and the old river ballads. Well, I'm ready with 'em."[10] Rodgers headed for New York after the Bristol sessions, and from that time until his death in 1933 he played travelling shows, broadcast throughout the South and Southwest, made a short film, and did multiple recording sessions each year. Rodgers was also one of the first major white artists to record with racially mixed bands. The story of the artist's final 1933 recording session in New York is a sad one. Sick with tuberculosis, he rested between takes on a cot in a rehearsal hall. Two days after the session, he was dead. Rodgers was the first artist inducted into the Country Music Hall of Fame when the award was established in 1961.

Wilf Carter (1904–1996), a.k.a Montana Slim, was a singer, songwriter, guitarist, and yodeller, and is widely acknowledged as the father of Canadian country music. Carter recorded over forty original and compilation LP records for RCA Victor, including *Nuggets of the Golden West*, *Songs of the Rail and Range*, *Songs of Australia*, and *Wilf Carter Sings Jimmie Rogers*. Born in Port Hilford, Nova Scotia, Carter left home at the age of fifteen and moved to Calgary, Alberta, in 1923 where he augmented his cowboy earnings

Vocalist/songwriter Jimmie Rodgers pioneered a blues-drenched style that shaped country music for decades to follow. Sometimes called "The Singing Brakeman" for his youth spent on the railroads, here Rodgers projects a sophisticated look that belies hillbilly stereotypes.

© FRANK DRIGGS COLLECTION/GETTY IMAGES

Canada's first country star, Wilf Carter, in 1932.

GLENBOW ARCHIVES NA-2771-1

by performing at tourist dances and sundry social functions. His first radio broadcast was transmitted locally on CFCN in 1930, and soon after was heard nationally on the Canadian Railway Broadcasting Corporation (CRBC, which later became CBC). His first recording in 1933, "My Swiss Moonlight Lullaby" and "The Capture of Albert Johnson," was the first hit record by a Canadian country music performer. In 1935, Carter moved to New York City, where he performed on WABC radio and hosted a CBS country music radio program until 1937. Following a nine-year hiatus from performing, Carter resumed touring in 1949; in 1950, he attracted over seventy thousand people during a week at the Canadian National Exhibition bandstand in Toronto. He was inducted into the Canadian National Music Hall of Fame in 1984, performed his last tour in 1991, and died in Scottsdale, Arizona, four years after retiring from the music business.

CHAPTER SUMMARY

- The development of radio and of the recording industry played major roles in the evolution of country music, and their influence continues.
- Multiple stylistic innovations over seventy-five years served as bench-marks in the evolution of country music.
- Jimmie Rodgers and the Carter Family were seminal country acts, representing two strands of the genre: rambling, drinking, partying, and sex versus God, country, mother, and home.

LISTENING EXERCISES

1. **Characteristics of the Carter Family Style**

   Listen to "Keep on the Sunny Side," recorded by the Carter Family in 1927. What is the overall feel of the song? What is its message? Notice how the lyrical content contrasts with the overall feel of the tune. What is the arrangement? Listen to Maybelle Carter's guitar playing. Does it sound familiar? How would you describe Sara Carter's lead vocal style? What is the nature of the harmonies?

2. **Hybrid Characteristics of Jimmie Rodgers' Style**

   Listen to "Waiting for a Train," recorded by Jimmie Rodgers in 1928. Notice how the song blends complex sounds in an appealing way: steel guitar, yodelling, jazzy horns, and bluesy vocals, reflecting the life of a rambling railroad man. Why does this hybrid mix work so well? Notice the train sound at the beginning of the song. Listen to the New Orleans jazz break in the middle of the song.

HISTORICAL STUDIES AND DISCUSSION QUESTIONS

1. Is it Country or Hillbilly?

In the early days of country music, the term *hillbilly* was often used by musicians, their fans, and their detractors. The contradictory meanings of the term *hillbilly* reflect a view that both sentimentalizes and rejects the rural roots of southern culture. What other cultural or ethnic designations produce conflicting sets of interpretations?

2. Yodelling and Hybridity in Country Music

How the yodel became a staple of country music provides an example of cultural hybridity. The word *yodel* is of German origin. In the early nineteenth century, south German vocalists performed the style on European stages. The yodel became part of American minstrelsy in the mid-nineteenth century and was included on the earliest Edison cylinder recordings of the 1890s. Yodelling records were popular through 1920.

The first country record to include yodelling was made in 1924, and in 1927 Jimmie Rodgers released his first recording with his "blue yodel" style. A yodel is a wordless vocal sound created in the back of the throat that rapidly alternates between two pitches, which Rodgers blended with blue notes to create the blue yodel. What other artists can you name who adopted Rodgers' yodelling style?

STUDY QUESTIONS

1. What roles did Jimmie Rodgers and the Carter Family play in the development of country music? Discuss the two aesthetic perspectives associated with these artists.

2. How did the evolution of radio and recording technology impact the development of country in North America?

3. What caused the broad dissemination of Hillbilly music in both Canada and the United States?

NOTES

1. Country Music Foundation (CMF), *Country, the Music and the Muscians, Pickers, Slickers, Cheatin' Hearts, and Superstars* (New York: Abbeville Press, 1988), 66.

2. *Ibid.*, 87.

3. Neil Strauss, "The Country Music Country Radio Ignores," *New York Times*, March 24, 2002, Section 2, p. 12.

4. Country Music Foundation, *Country*, 107.

5. Ralph Peer, "Discovery of the First Hillbilly Great," *Billboard* 65 (No. 20, May 16, 1953): 20–21.

6. Country Music Foundation, *Country*, 17.

7. Nicholas Dawidoff, *In the Country of Country: People and Places in American Music* (New York: Pantheon Books, 1997), 60.

8. Nick Tosches, *Country: Living Legends and Dying Metaphors in America's Biggest Music* (New York: Scribner, 1985), 178.

9. Peer, "Discovery of the First Hillbilly Great," 20–21.

10. David Vinopal, Alabama Music Hall of Fame website, http://www.alamhoforg/rodgersj.htm.

CHAPTER 15

The Growth of Country and Western

THE SINGING COWBOYS

A "Western tinge" permeated country music in the 1930s and 1940s. Cowboy clothing and Western themes took country in a new direction, shaped by an oil boom in Texas and the westward economic migrations of the Depression and World War II.

Jimmie Rodgers pioneered the concept of the **singing cowboy** and western images in country music, and subsequent Texas performers—including Ernest Tubb, Lefty Frizzell, Floyd Tillman, and Bob Wills—often credited Rodgers as their inspiration. Gene Autry (1907–1998), the first full-blown singing cowboy, starred on the Chicago-based WLS "Barn Dance" radio show from 1931 to 1934 with a Rodgers-influenced style that included yodelling. Autry's hits included "Silver-Haired Daddy of Mine" and "South of the Border (Down Mexico Way)." Autry moved to Hollywood in 1934 to begin a long career as a singing cowboy, ultimately making over ninety movies.

With the popularity of the Hollywood image of the West, the term *Western music* was indiscriminately applied to all styles of southern rural music. The Western look—gaudy tailored suits, hats, and boots—prevailed, and many artists adopted Western-sounding names—the Light Crust Doughboys, the Sons of the Pioneers, Tex Ritter, and Roy Rogers among them. The Sons of the Pioneers were one of the most famous western groups of the era, known for their smooth, inventive harmonies and finely crafted songs. First organized in California in the 1930s by Roy Rogers, the trio sang every type of country song—even borrowing from Tin Pan Alley. Western hits for the group included "Cool Water" and "Tumbling Tumbleweeds."

Another successful cowboy artist, Tex Ritter (1905–1974), was a college-educated vocalist and performer from Texas. While trying to get work on Broadway, his thick Texas accent and storehouse of cowboy lore became his ticket to success. Cowboy music also spawned successful female artists and at least one artist of colour. Among them was Patsy Montana (1908–1996), who released "I Want to Be a Cowboy's Sweetheart" in 1939. The song, which included yodelling and a polka rhythm, was the first hit for a female country singer. Herb Jeffries (1911–), an African American vocalist, starred in several movie westerns in the late 1930s as "The Bronze Buckaroo,"

PICTORIAL PRESS LTD/ALAMY

Canadian Nashville star Hank Snow circa mid-1950s.

a black singing cowboy, and also worked with Duke Ellington.

Acknowledged along with Wilf Carter as one Canada's greatest contributions to country music, Hank Snow left home in Brooklyn, Nova Scotia, at the age of twelve to work as a cabin boy in the fishing industry based out of Lunenburg. With income from that job he ordered his first guitar from the Eaton's catalogue for $5.95. Inspired by the music of Jimmy Rodgers, Snow began to perform in 1930, and made his first radio broadcast in 1933 on CHNS (Halifax). In 1936, he produced his first recordings for RCA Victor, "Lonesome **Blue Yodel**" and "The Prisoned Cowboy," and eventually made forty-five LP recordings for the label. Snow went to the United States in 1946, adopted a cowboy image, and by 1950 had became a regular performer at the "Grand Ole Opry" on WSM (Nashville); his recording of the same year, "I'm Movin' On" was one of the most successful singles in the history of recorded country music. In 1954, Hank Snow persuaded his handlers to allow Elvis Presley to become his new opening act. Shortly following, Snow and Colonel Tom Parker formed a management team, Hank Snow Attractions, to oversee singer's fledgling career; however, by late-1955, the arrangement failed and Parker assumed full control over Presley's personal and professional affairs. Although Nashville was his permanent home, Snow returned frequently to Canada for concert and TV appearances.

One of the most important television shows to popularize country music in Canada was the "Tommy Hunter Show." Tommy Hunter (1937–) began his career as a singer and guitar player with the Golden Prairie Cowboys in 1953, and later, in 1956, he joined CBC (Toronto) as a rhythm guitarist on the television program, "Country Hoedown." The show was replaced by the "Tommy Hunter Show" in the mid-1960s and became one of the most popular Canadian variety shows until it was cancelled in 1992. Appearances on the show, a must for any touring country artist from both sides of the border, included Hank Snow, Wilf Carter, Anne Murray, Shania Twain, Garth Brooks, the Judds, and many others.

HONKY-TONK

Soon after the repeal of Prohibition in 1933, a brisk business arose in the honky-tonks of Texas and other parts of the West. Similar to juke joints, honky-tonks were usually built on the outskirts of town, with large dance floors, jukeboxes, and live music. Their development was fuelled in Texas by an oil boom, and in California by migrant farm workers in the 1930s and defence industry workers in the 1940s. Throughout the West, displaced rural people living on the fringes of urban areas wanted to dance, drink, and forget their problems on a Saturday night. According to critic Nick Tosches, "In country music, honky-tonk came to be associated with the loud, small-group sound that developed in the redneck bars of east Texas and oil-boom towns: amplified guitars and lyrics of sex and whiskey."[1] Honky-tonks catered to a rough crowd, as vocalist Ray Price recalled:

> Some of them would be just one square building. No paint on the outside. And you'd go in and it would have a wooden dance floor, a long bar, tables, and a small bandstand. They fought an awful lot in those days. You'd sweep up ear-lobes and eyeballs every morning.[2]

In the honky-tonks, country music evolved lyrically and stylistically, recasting the nature of the genre. Motherhood and pastoral themes gave way to the problems of people in a changing social environment, and the music became louder to be heard over rowdy crowds. The honky-tonk *sock rhythm* developed, with a strong electric bass pulse on beats one and three and heavy rhythm guitar on beats two and four. Piano, drums, electric guitar, electric bass, and pedal steel guitar joined the classic fiddle and acoustic guitar lineup. Honky-tonk singers were unashamedly emotional, using vocal breaks, hiccups, yodels, and cries; they slurred phrases, bent notes, and shed tears. Classics of the era included Ernest Tubbs's "Walking the Floor over You," Al Dexter's "Pistol Packin' Mama," and Hank Williams's "Your Cheatin' Heart." Ernest Tubb (1914–1984), a disciple of Jimmie Rodgers, was the quintessential honky-tonk artist and became a country music institution over his long career. Tubbs built on a deep baritone voice and years in Texas honky-tonks to fashion his relaxed, widely admired style. Joining the **"Grand Ole Opry"** in 1943, he was the first to bring honky-tonk to Nashville. Other great honky-tonkers included Floyd Tillman, Lefty Frizzell, Hank Thompson, Hank Williams, and Ray Price.

Singer/songwriter Hank Williams (1923–1953) was a country music icon who permanently bridged the gulf between country and pop, and was likely the most important representative of the **honky-tonk** style. Williams's life encompassed a swift rise and sudden, tragic fall, awash in alcohol and drugs. The Alabaman started playing guitar at an early age and was tutored by an African American street singer named Tee-Tot (Rufus Payne). Roy Acuff and Ernest Tubb also influenced Williams's vocal style. Though rejected in his first try to get on the "Grand Ole Opry," Williams returned to Nashville and was signed by a major publishing firm, recording "Move It on Over," "Honky Tonkin'," and several other early hits. He finally debuted on the "Grand Ole Opry" in 1949, where pandemonium erupted and he was brought back for six encores. Williams's hits included "I'm So Lonesome I Could Cry," "Your Cheatin' Heart," and "Hey Good Lookin'," along with crossover hits by others including Tony Bennett's "Cold Cold Heart" and Jo Stafford's "Jambalaya." Williams was a riveting performer. According to a fellow musician, "He had a voice that went through you like electricity, sent shivers up your spine, and made the hair rise

© UNDERWOOD AND UNDERWOOD/CORBIS

Vocalist/songwriter Hank Williams, backed by his band, the Drifting Cowboys, was one of country music's greatest songwriters and a superstar of the early 1950s.

on the back of your neck with the thrill. With a voice like that he could make you laugh or cry."[3] Williams also pioneered a rocking, lightly gyrating posture that Elvis Presley expanded on a few years later. As comedienne Minnie Pearl put it, "He had a real animal magnetism. He destroyed the women in the audience." Williams reflected on his own appeal:

> It can be explained in just one word: sincerity. When a hillbilly sings a crazy song, he feels crazy. When he sings "I Laid My Mother Away," he sees her a-laying right there in the coffin. He sings more sincere than most entertainers because the hillbilly was raised rougher than most entertainers. . . . You got to have smelt a lot of mule manure before you can sing like a hillbilly.[4]

Williams's short life ended sadly. An addiction to alcohol and pills adversely affected his career, and just as he was making a comeback in 1953, he died of a heart attack on the way to a gig. His funeral drew over twenty-five thousand people, including all the greatest stars of country.

WESTERN SWING

By the end of the 1930s, Americans were turning to a new style called **western swing**, a hybrid of southern string bands, swing, Tin Pan Alley, and the African American, Cajun, Tex-Mex, German, Bohemian, and cowboy cultures of the Southwest. Major innovators included Bob Wills, Milton Brown, and Spade Cooley. Bob Wills (1905–1975) did the most to develop and popularize western swing. Originally a fiddler, he honed his performing skills in medicine shows, in fiddle bands, and with the Light Crust Doughboys, combining the fiddle music of his rural roots with blues and jazz. He also used a violin section, a practice probably borrowed from Mexican mariachi music. Wills formed his band, the Texas Playboys, in 1933 and began to broadcast and record regularly. The group featured fiddles, drums, steel and electric guitars, brass, and reeds—with up to eighteen members. Wills's best-known hits included "Steel Guitar Rag" and "New San Antonio Rose," which became a pop crossover hit for Bing Crosby in 1941. After World War II, Wills changed instrumentation and spotlighted the electric pedal steel guitar in country music for the first time. According to one description of Wills,

> His irresistible personality dominated every performance . . . as he strutted across the stage, dressed in the attire of a rancher, chomping on a cigar, and pointing toward musicians as they took their instrumental breaks. . . . His shouts and hollers . . . punctuated the performance of virtually every song: "Ahh haa," "Take it away, Leon," "Aw, come in, Tommy," and on and on.[5]

Wills provided an important link between jazz, blues, multiple country styles, and the rockabilly of the 1950s, influencing rock pioneer Bill Haley, who originally named his band "Bill Haley and the Four Aces of Western Swing." He also had his followers in Canada during the 1940s in the music of Sid Plamondor, Vic Seibert, and Jim McGill. Rock variants of the genre were also created during the 1970s with Prairie Oyster, an award-winning Western Swing-inspired group from Toronto, Ontario. Formed in 1974, the band's first album for RCA, *Different Kind of Fire* (1990), was released in Canada and in the United States, and won Prairie Oyster Juno Award for Country Group or Duo of the Year in 1991.

BLUEGRASS AND OLD-TIME MUSIC

Bluegrass developed as a new style in the 1940s, although it gave the impression of being an older style because it employed **old-time music**, or early Appalachian folk music. The style took its name from the Blue Grass Boys, a band led by mandolin player Bill Monroe, who is often called the father of bluegrass. Bluegrass instrumentation combines fiddle, banjo, mandolin, guitar, Dobro, and acoustic bass. Singing is often done in the **high lonesome style**, which originated in the clear, dry, high-pitched tone of Bill Monroe's singing voice. Bluegrass vocal harmonies contain two, three, or four parts rooted in the gospel quartet styles of southern church music, and many bluegrass song lyrics are religious.

Bluegrass was shaped by the performance styles of two of its founding artists, Bill Monroe and Earl Scruggs. Monroe's aggressive single-note mandolin solo style and backbeat rhythm accompaniment, together with Earl Scruggs's three-finger picking on the five-string banjo, set the tone for the genre. Bluegrass is performed faster than other country styles; musicologist Alan Lomax once called it "folk music in overdrive." It integrates driving, syncopated

Singer/mandolinist Bill Monroe, the "father of bluegrass," toured with his band, the Blue Grass Boys, and appeared on the "Grand Ole Opry" beginning in the 1940s.

© FRANK DRIGGS COLLECTION

banjo picking with a steady four-beat feel; guitar and bass emphasize beats one and three while the mandolin and banjo answer on the back-beat. Bluegrass is also sometimes referred to as "country jazz," because of its frequent focus on improvised solos.

Kentuckian Bill Monroe (1911–1996) took up the mandolin as part of a family band. Arnold Schultz, an African American guitarist and fiddler, taught him blues licks and syncopated styles. According to Monroe, "People can tell my music is from Kentucky. . . . You see, there's feeling for Kentucky in it, the Methodists and Baptists, the old blues, the old fiddle and guitar."[6] Monroe appeared at barn dances and on the radio, first performing on the "Grand Ole Opry" in 1939. When his band's upbeat, syncopated sound started to coalesce around 1945, other musicians began to take note. Lester Flatt (1914–1979) and Earl Scruggs (1924–), two of the most inno-vative members of Monroe's band, left to form their own group called the Foggy Mountain Boys in 1948. Early compositions included "Foggy Mountain Breakdown," later made famous in the movie *Bonnie and Clyde,* and "Roll in My Sweet Baby's Arms." Flatt and Scruggs were known for flawless performance choreography and virtuoso playing, which maintained their long-term popularity. A third seminal bluegrass act, the Stanley Brothers, began in the late 1940s. Co-led by Ralph (1927–) and Carter Stanley (1925–1966), the group drew on traditional old-time mountain music. Ralph Stanley emerged as an elder statesman of bluegrass in the early 2000s, after his perfor-mance on the soundtrack of the film *O Brother, Where Art Thou?*

By the early 1950s, bluegrass was firmly established in the country music marketplace. However, even though side "B" of Presley's first single was a supercharged version of Bill Monroe's "Blue Moon of Kentucky," for example, the rock revolution presented a new challenge. The country music industry responded by shifting to the smoother Nashville studio sound, and bluegrass fell on hard times. The urban folk revival movement of the late 1950s and early 1960s, though, gave the style new life. Spurred by the popularity of such artists as Woody Guthrie, the Weavers, and Pete Seeger, the revival focused on acoustic music and traditional styles, rejecting mainstream pop and rock. Bluegrass was soon heard in urban areas and on college campuses, and blue-grass scenes developed in several northern cities. Earl Scruggs and the Stanley brothers performed at the first Newport Folk Festival in 1959.

Bluegrass periodically resurfaced in the public eye in succeeding decades. In the early 1960s, the Osborne Brothers had a crossover hit with "Rocky Top," and Flatt and Scruggs succeeded with "The Ballad of Jed Clampett," the theme from "The Beverly Hillbillies." The soundtrack to the 1967 film *Bonnie and Clyde* also featured a Flatt and Scruggs bluegrass tune, and the 1972 film *Deliverance* showcased "Dueling Banjos." Further, in the 1960s Bluegrass established a presence in Canada as an adjunct to the urban folk revival in the music of The Good Brothers and The Humber River Valley Boys. Since that time, Bluegrass substyles have been created – much to chagrin of Bluegrass purists – from interactions with prevailing rock styles; a recent example of this can be heard in the alt-rock style of Manitoba's D Rangers. Bluegrass also found new support in outdoor festivals, and today over five hundred such events take place around North America every year, including Carlisle and Waterford, Ontario.

In the 1980s and 1990s, mandolinist David Grisman became known for his progressive fusion of bluegrass and jazz, and he collaborated with a variety of artists on a series of popular recordings. Banjoist Béla Fleck went in a novel direction in the 1990s, playing a popular amalgam called "spacegrass" or "supergrass"—blending jazz, pop, and world music. Legendary guitarist Doc Watson kept traditional styles alive, and eclectic fiddler Mark O'Connor experimented with new bluegrass hybrids. Bluegrass and old-time music received another lease on life in the early 2000s with the success of the soundtrack from the film *O Brother, Where Art Thou?* Performers on the album included bluegrass legend Ralph Stanley, as well as contemporary artists Gillian Welch and Alison Krauss. Producer T-Bone Burnett reflected on the record's success: "We have machines today that can crank out perfect music all day long. This was real people playing and singing around real microphones."[7]

Fiddler, bandleader, and vocalist Alison Krauss (1971–) was already well known in bluegrass prior to *O Brother*. The Grammy-winning artist played on the *Grand Ole Opry* beginning in 1993 and toured widely with her band Union Station; she was also a respected studio musician and producer. Krauss and Gillian Welch were part of a community of contemporary female artists who broke through male-dominated traditions in bluegrass and old-time music. Rounder Records supported this trend with the 2001 release of *O Sister! The Women's Bluegrass Collection*.

CHAPTER SUMMARY

- The appearance of the singing cowboy in the 1930s completed the fusion of country with Western themes.

- The blending of jazz elements with string band styles in the 1930s by artists such as Bob Wills led to the development of western swing.

- Honky-tonk became the dominant sound of country in the 1940s and reached its zenith in the work of country legend Hank Williams in the early 1950s.

- Bill Monroe's aggressive mandolin style combined with Earl Scruggs's finger-picking banjo technique to create the bluegrass style in the 1940s.

LISTENING EXERCISES

1. The Development of Western Swing

Listen to "New San Antonio Rose," recorded by Bob Wills and the Texas Playboys in 1940. Notice how the song starts with a horn-based swing introduction. How does Wills use vocal interjections to encourage the musicians? How does the entrance of the vocalist establish a country and western flavour? After the vocal part ends, notice the Mexican mariachi flavour of the first horn break followed by a woodwind swing passage. How many genres are blended in one song? How does "New San Antonio Rose" reflect cultural hybridity?

2. The Honky-Tonk Style of Hank Williams

Listen to "Your Cheatin' Heart," recorded by Hank Williams in 1948. Focus on the lyrics. Notice their simplicity, straightforwardness, and honesty. What is the emotional feel of the song? What is the instrumentation? How does the simplicity of the arrangement "stay out of the way" of the lyrics? How would you describe the quality of Williams' voice? Why did Williams connect so powerfully to so many people?

3. The Sound of Bluegrass

Listen to "It's Mighty Dark to Travel," recorded by Bill Monroe and the Blue Grass Boys in 1947. The musicians include Earl Scruggs on banjo, Lester Flatt on guitar and vocals, Chubby Wise on fiddle, and Howard Watts on string bass. Monroe's distinctive chop-chord mandolin style and Scruggs's syncopated three-finger banjo picking, as well as improvised solos, rhythmic drive, and "high lonesome" duet singing, exemplify the fundamentals of bluegrass style. This classic recording provided a model for succeeding generations of artists who have built an almost cult-like institution dedicated to the preservation of the style. What other music practices can you identify where this behaviour is prevalent?

HISTORICAL STUDIES AND DISCUSSION QUESTION

When Does an Innovation Become a Recognized Style?

Rarely do individual musicians generate an entire style as Bill Monroe did. Historians often date the origin of the term *bluegrass* to the emergence of the Stanley Brothers, who clearly emulated Monroe's style. Although the term first appeared in the 1940s, writers and critics did not commonly use it for another ten years, and even then many musicians avoided it. What bluegrass is depends on whom you ask. Although a classic repertoire exists, many artists venture far from the traditional Monroe model by including waltzes, old-time styles, Tin Pan Alley songs, rock, and pop tunes. Does labelling a style clarify or blur our understanding of music?

STUDY QUESTIONS

1. How did the emergence of the singing cowboy and the West affect country music?

2. What was western swing and what were its connections to other styles?

3. What was honky-tonk? Discuss important American and Canadian contributors to its development.

5. What distinguished bluegrass from other styles of country music? Who contributed to its development?

6. Who were Canada's first country music stars?

NOTES

1. Nick Tosches, *Country: Living Legends and Dying Metaphors in America's Biggest Music* (New York: Scribner, 1985), 27.

2. Robert K. Oermann, *A Century of Country: An Illustrated History of Country Music* (New York: TV Books, 1999), 98.

3. Bill C. Malone and Judith McCulloh, eds., *Stars of Country Music: Uncle Dave Macon to Johnny Rodriguez* (Urbana: University of Illinois Press, 1975), 245, 246.

4. Oermann, *Century of Country*, 104.

5. Malone, *Country Music*, 174.

6. Nicholas Dawidoff, *In the Country of Country: People and Places in American Music* (New York: Pantheon Books, 1997), 108.

7. *O Brother, Where Art Thou?* website, http://www.obrothermusic.com/soundtrack.html.

CHAPTER 16

Regional Sounds and City Styles

THE RISE OF NASHVILLE

By the 1940s, Nashville had become the acknowledged centre of country music. Country's commercial appeal exploded during World War II as southern soldiers came in contact with troops from other regions, leading country singer Roy Acuff to top crooner Frank Sinatra in one poll of GIs. The demand continued after the war: According to *Newsweek,* "Hillbilly music is now such a vogue that it is just about pushing popular tunes, jazz, swing, bebop and everything else right out of the picture. . . . The demand for it has multiplied fivefold since the war."[1]

The growth of radio station WSM's "Grand Ole Opry" had much to do with the rise of Nashville. Prominent artists such as Roy Acuff, Bill Monroe, and Minnie Pearl joined the show just before the onset of World War II, and after the war the Opry began an aggressive talent drive that netted Ernest Tubb, Eddy Arnold, Hank Snow, and Hank Williams. When NBC picked up the Opry for weekly national broadcast in 1943, Nashville had truly arrived. The RCA and Decca labels also began recording in Nashville in the 1940s, and other labels followed suit, benefiting from the presence of great studio musicians such as guitarist Chet Atkins. Most major labels still maintain a presence in Nashville.

Roy Acuff (1903–1992), a traditional mountain singer and fiddler from east Tennessee, shaped the performance style and content of the Opry. His singing shifted the largely instrumental Opry to feature more vocal performances, with a repertoire emphasizing sacred and traditional songs that he delivered emotionally, sometimes weeping openly. Acuff's hits included "The Great Speckled Bird" and "The Wabash Cannonball." He also co-founded Acuff-Rose, the most successful Nashville music publishing house, in 1942. Established in part because of the fight between ASCAP and the nation's broadcasters over music licensing rights, Acuff-Rose affiliated with the new BMI and supplied new country songs to the broadcast and recording industries. Other prominent Nashville-based music publishers included Peer-Southern (co-owned by Ralph Peer), Tree, and Cedarwood.

The growth of the music industry in Nashville attracted songwriters, recreating the climate of Tin Pan Alley with a country twang. Great songwriters such as Willie Nelson, Harlan Howard, Roger Miller, and Tom T. Hall often hung out at a bar near the Opry, hoping to catch the ear of stars. As one of their number recalled, "We would sit around at the old Tootsie's Orchid Lounge, and pick each other's brains about songs. There were dozens of hit songs that I heard for the first time in there."[2] The rise of Nashville paralleled the rise of legendary producers who crafted the signature Nashville sound. Most Nashville producers initially took their stylistic cues from the "Grand Ole Opry": Fiddle and steel guitar were prominent; drums, mistrusted. The producers generally preferred the city's pool of studio musicians for recording, but the resulting sound, though consistent and professional, could be formulaic.

Elvis Presley's rockabilly explosion in 1954 presented a new challenge to Nashville. **Rockabilly** was a blend of country and black music that first emerged in the early 1950s. Developed at Sam Phillips's Sun Records Studios in Memphis by artists such as Elvis Presley, Carl Perkins, and Jerry Lee Lewis, the style took off quickly around 1954 and grew in popularity with contributions from the East (Everly Brothers, Gene Vincent), the Southwest (Buddy Holly, Wanda Jackson), and the West (Eddie Cochran). Nashville responded by playing an active role in the development of rockabilly and early rock. RCA opened a Nashville operation after signing Elvis Presley, where he recorded "Heartbreak Hotel" in 1956. The song was unlike any previous country record, and its worldwide success led to a redefinition of what could be done in Nashville. During the next few years, Gene Vincent, the Everly Brothers, Patsy Cline, Brenda Lee, Marty Robbins, and Johnny Cash were among the many singers who made records in Nashville that crossed over to mainstream pop. Among the other country artists popular in the late 1950s and early 1960s were George Jones, Don Gibson, Jim Reeves, Floyd Cramer, and Ray Charles.

Producers Chet Atkins (1924–2001) and Owen Bradley (1915–1998) are often credited with developing the **Nashville sound** that beat back the rockabilly challenge. Atkins was a respected guitarist and songwriter who headed RCA's office in Nashville for over two decades. He introduced electric instruments and polished arrangements, targeting an adult audience to broaden country's appeal. The Nashville sound also employed strings, horns, choral backgrounds, smooth tempos, reverb (echo), and innovative microphone techniques. When asked to describe the Nashville sound, Atkins jingled some coins in his pocket:

> People were in it to make a living. The Nashville Sound is just a sales tag. If there is a Nashville Sound, it's the Southern accent. You speak with it, maybe you play with it, too. . . . We took the twang out of it, Owen Bradley and I. What we did was try to make hit records. We wanted to keep our job.[3]

In addition to a skilled producer, Atkins was a sought-after session guitarist with a signature finger-picking style. He made more than a hundred recordings in his own name and hundreds more as a studio player, winning multiple Grammys. Although he belonged to the Nashville establishment, Atkins supported maverick artists later in his career, including Dolly Parton, Waylon Jennings, and Charley Pride.

Throughout the 1960s and 1970s, the success of country music paralleled the growth of country radio. Country artists popular in the 1960s included Ray Price, Roger Miller, Kenny Rogers, Glenn Campbell, Johnny Cash, Dolly Parton, and George Jones. The 1970s also saw the expansion of Nashville's record labels, with such stars as Loretta Lynn, Tammy Wynette, Charlie Daniels, Buck Owens, Charley Pride, Merle Haggard, Freddie Fender, and Crystal Gayle. Crossover hits also produced unprecedented sales, including "King of the Road" by Roger Miller, "A Boy Named Sue" by Johnny Cash, "Harper Valley P.T.A." by Jeannie C. Riley, and "Help Me Make It through the Night" and "Me and Bobby McGee" by Kris Kristofferson. Well-publicized Nashville recording sessions by Bob Dylan and Joan Baez further enhanced country's appeal.

Johnny Cash (1932–2003) was an international country celebrity who became an American icon. "The Man in Black" emerged as a star in the mid-1950s with a distinctive bass-baritone voice and an insistent rhythm guitar sound. The Arkansan got his first break in Memphis and caught the ear of Sam Phillips at Sun Records to produce such early hits as "Folsom Prison Blues" and "I Walk the Line." Cash next joined the "Grand Ole Opry" and scored more hits while touring extensively throughout the 1960s. Although touring and drug use took their toll, Cash made a comeback in the late 1960s with his classic *Live At Folsom Prison* album, a television show, and an appearance on Bob Dylan's *Nashville Skyline* album. During the 1980s he collaborated with many other classic country and rock artists, and in the 1990s he signed with an independent record label to release Grammy-winning work with *American Recordings* and *Unchained*. Cash reflected on his obsessive love of the road:

> Home life's nice and quiet. But I love the road because I get to do that show every night. I like my bus. A daily fleeting anonymous existence. I go into a city. I see the city out the hotel window. I stay in the nicest hotel they've got. Then I'm gone."[4]

Although country originated as a male-dominated genre, groundbreaking female artists periodically emerged to make significant contributions to the music. After Sara Carter retired in the 1940s, country music saw almost no women recording artists for close to ten years. Loretta Lynn recalled that when she was growing up in Kentucky in the 1940s, "You didn't hear any women. I never thought anything about it. Men came first. Men dominated."[5] This changed in 1952 with Kitty Wells' (1918–) release of "It Wasn't God Who Made Honky-Tonk Angels." The song, which voiced a woman's perspective on everyday life for the first time, was intended as a response to Hank Thompson's hit, "The Wild Side of Life." According to Wells,

> I sang "It Wasn't God Who Made Honky-Tonk Angels," but it had nothing to do with my life at all. I was looking for a hit just like everybody else. I think one of the reasons it was a hit was that it was telling the menfolk [off].[6]

Wells became the first major female star of commercial country music, and throughout the 1950s and early 1960s her songs constantly appeared

Vocalist Patsy Cline was known in the early 1950s for her passionate, earthy vocal work, which exemplified the Nashville sound. One author called her the first "down-home torch singer."

in the top ten on the country charts. In 1991, she became the first woman in country music history to receive a Lifetime Achievement Grammy Award.

Patsy Cline (1932–1963) was the first "bad-girl" superstar of country music. Cline's performing skills, however, belied her tough exterior. She was a consummate performer who, in the words of historian Nicholas Dawidoff, "brought a mannered sophistication to country music. Patsy Cline was the first down-home torch singer."[7] She skillfully embellished her full-voiced vocal tone with bent notes, sighs, and sensual growls that enabled her to cross over from country to pop, though she was ambivalent about doing so. Cline recorded her first major crossover hit, "I Fall to Pieces," in 1960, followed by Willie Nelson's "Crazy." Before Cline died in a plane crash in 1963, she had pushed country beyond its traditional borders to attract a new audience and build an enduring mystique.

Loretta Lynn (1935–) was a protégé and close friend of Patsy Cline, and her rise filled the void left by Cline's death. Lynn's prolific forty-year career, chronicled in her 1980 film autobiography, *Coal Miner's Daughter,* offered a compelling story. Born into abject poverty in the Kentucky coal country and married at age thirteen, she recorded her first single, "Honky Tonk Girl," for a small label in 1960 and then barnstormed the country with her husband to promote the record. Lynn signed with Decca in 1961 and recorded a string of hits throughout the 1960s. Like Kitty Wells and Patsy Cline, she offered a female perspective on issues of everyday life with songs during the late 1960s such as "Don't Come Home Drinkin' (With Lovin' on Your Mind)," "Coal Miner's Daughter," and "The Pill." Though she had long ceased to make the charts by the end of the century, her career rebounded in 2005 with the Grammy-winning album *Van Lear Rose,* collaboration with rocker Jack White of the White Stripes.

Like Loretta Lynn, Dolly Parton (1946–) overcame a background of rural poverty to establish a successful career as a singer, songwriter, and star of film and television. Over a forty-year career, Parton enjoyed both country and pop hits and wrote over three thousand compositions. Parton's first country hit, "Dumb Blonde" (1967), punctured stereotypes and made her a regular on the "Porter Wagoner Show." Her success continued in the 1970s and 1980s with hits including "Coat of Many Colors" and the title song from the film *9 to 5,* as well as collaborations with artists such as Kenny Rogers, Linda Ronstadt, Emmylou Harris, Tammy Wynette, and Loretta Lynn. Parton's writing talents were showcased by her song, "I Will Always Love You," which Whitney Houston covered in the 1990s. In the early 2000s, as Parton found herself left out of the mix by the youth-oriented climate of the country record industry, she returned to her Appalachian roots and released respected new work featuring all-acoustic old-time and bluegrass music.

Country music's only African American superstar was the Grammy-winning Charley Pride (1938–). With his warm baritone voice and relaxed style, Pride scored twenty-nine number-one singles and multiple Grammys between 1966 and 1986. The Mississippi-born Pride listened to the "Grand Ole Opry" as a child and was influenced by Ernest Tubb, Hank Williams, and Roy Acuff. His musical talents blossomed in the early 1960s when he moved to Nashville and was signed by Chet Atkins at RCA. Billed as "Country Charley Pride," he saw his first single released in 1966 without a picture of him on the record jacket, to downplay his race. In performances, Pride often opened with an icebreaker: "Ladies and gentlemen, I realize it's a little unique for me coming out here on a country show wearing this permanent tan."[8] Pride's rise coincided with the civil rights movement of the mid-1960s, and he found himself caught between an emerging black identity and the white country music world. As his popularity grew, Pride stopped apologizing for his "tan" and built a successful career.

Vocalist/songwriter Dolly Parton, who was a superstar in the 1970s and 1980s, returned to her mountain music roots in the early 2000s. Here she plays the five-string banjo at Lincoln Center in 1987.

Canada's contribution to country music also rests on the significant achievements of Anne Murray, whose career tangentially orbited the Nashville star-making machine. Born in Springhill, Nova Scotia in 1941, Murray was the first Canadian female solo singer to reach number one on the U.S. charts, and the first to earn a gold record for one of her career songs, "Snowbird" (1970). She is also the first woman and the first Canadian to win "Album of the Year" at the Country Music Association Awards for her 1984 album *A Little Good News*. Murray began her professional singing career in 1967 on CBC Television's "Singalong Jubilee." Her first album, *What About Me* (1968) marked the beginning of her solo career, but her second album, *This Way Is My Way*, featured the single, "Snowbird," which became a hit in both Canada and the United States. After the success of "Snowbird", Murray scored a number of subsequent hit singles on both the pop and on the country charts. Following her last hit, "Now and Forever" (1986), Murray released a series of "retrospective" recordings such as *Wonderful World, Country Croonin', I'll Be Seeing You*, and *Anne Murray*

CP

Anne Murray performing in 1971 shortly following her hit release "Snowbird."

Duets: Friends & Legends, and continues to perform mainly on television specials.

BAKERSFIELD, AUSTIN, AND THE BORDERLINE

Bakersfield, California, emerged as a new centre of country music in the 1950s and 1960s. This came about as a result of the great "Okie" migration of the late 1930s, in which hundreds of thousands of poor rural workers and families from Oklahoma, Texas, and Arkansas migrated to California in search of a better life, spurred by the lingering effects of the Depression and a multiyear drought that had turned their farmland into a "dust bowl." Many of the migrants brought with them their love of country music, so that by the 1950s Bakersfield stood at the heart of a burgeoning country scene. Surrounded by oil wells and agriculture, honky-tonks provided entertainment with a fresh Bakersfield style that launched the careers of Buck Owens and Merle Haggard.

Guitarist/songwriter Buck Owens (1929–) originated the Bakersfield sound, which was a blend of blues, rock, and country. Owens launched his recording career in the late 1950s with his band, the Buckaroos, and achieved nineteen number-one hits by the end of the 1960s. Owens's style featured his passionate tenor voice, high harmony singing, rockabilly guitar, and pedal steel guitar. Hits included "Excuse Me (I Think I've Got a Heartache)" and "Act Naturally," the latter of which the Beatles covered.

For over forty years, Merle Haggard (1937–) had one of the most influential careers in country music, with a rich baritone voice steeped in the influences of Jimmie Rodgers, Bob Wills, Lefty Frizzell, and dust-bowl ballads. Haggard recorded almost forty number-one songs, and artists as diverse as Elvis Costello, the Grateful Dead, Dean Martin, Dolly Parton, and Dwight Yoakam performed his compositions. Haggard's family participated in the great migration of the 1930s, and an early life of petty crime landed him in San Quentin prison. After his release, he embarked on a music career, eventually scoring hits with "Mama Tried," "Branded Man," and "Hungry Eyes." During the late 1960s, Haggard became a superstar and target of controversy with songs that had conservative blue-collar themes, such as "Okie from Muskogee" and "The Fightin' Side of Me." He scored again in the 1970s with "Movin' On," and he stayed active into the 2000s, recording tribute albums for Jimmie Rodgers and Bob Wills.

Although Mexican and Chicano musical styles have had a symbiotic relationship with country music, only a few Chicano performers made it into the mainstream of country. One such performer, Freddie Fender (Baldemar G. Huerta, 1937–), began his career in the late 1950s playing rock in Spanish, but in 1960 he changed his name to Freddie Fender and began recording in English. Fender had his first big country hit in 1974, the bilingual "Before the Next Teardrop Falls." According to the artist,

> My roots are in Chicano music, mariachi music, black music, and a lot of that old rock & roll. But I had the good fortune of recording a country song and all of a sudden I'm a country entertainer.[9]

Fender continued a string of hits into the late 1970s, performing bilingual songs in a variety of styles including country, rock, and Tex-Mex. In the 1990s, he teamed up with Flaco Jimenez, Doug Sahm, and Augie Meyer to form the Texas Tornados, an eclectic group playing everything from *conjunto* to country. Johnny Rodriguez (1951–) was a Mexican-Irish Texan who had a string of country hits in the 1970s. More of a straight country singer than Fender, Rodriguez's performance style combined influences of Merle Haggard with Tex-Mex styles. His first hit, "Pass Me By," was followed by eleven number-one tunes, many of which were bilingual.

In the late 1960s and early 1970s, a new musical counterculture began in Austin, Texas. The college town already hosted a thriving folk scene when a large nightclub called the Armadillo World Headquarters became the centre of a new Austin scene, with a program of country and rock that bound cowboys and hippies together in a Texas mystique of beer, longhorns, and armadillos. The scene grew, and by the early 2000s Austin hosted "South by Southwest," an influential annual national showcase for new rock acts.

In the 1970s, a group of country artists including Willie Nelson, Waylon Jennings, Kris Kristofferson, Johnny Cash, Jessi Colter, and Tompall Glaser grew tired of the formulaic Nashville sound and formed a loose network called the Outlaws. They wanted to control their own work, record with their own bands rather than studio musicians, and choose their own material, performance styles, and wardrobes. The term **Outlaw** originated with Waylon Jennings's 1972 album, *Ladies Love Outlaws,* and by the time RCA issued *Wanted! The Outlaws,* a compilation of reissues by Nelson, Jennings, Colter, and Glaser, the Outlaws (as the loose network of musicians playing this sound had also come to be called) had taken centre stage in country music. The record was the first country album to sell over one million copies. Musically the Outlaws represented a return to the "hillbilly" roots of the music, as they termed it. Arrangements were relaxed and simple, to counter the production-heavy flavour of the Nashville sound, and many of the performers favoured a tough, dressed-down appearance. By the end of the 1970s, the Outlaws were the new mainstream, and Nelson and Jennings had become superstars.

One of Nashville's finest songwriters of the 1960s, country music icon Willie Nelson (1933–) wrote hits such as Patsy Cline's "Crazy" and Ray

Price's "Night Life." He had a modest early performing career but never fit into the Nashville scene. Originally a Texan, Nelson relocated to Austin in 1972 when the new scene there was in full swing. He grew a beard and long hair, sported a headband and earring, and sponsored large outdoor festivals that placed him at the centre of the new Texas counterculture. According to Bill Malone,

> The swirling dust, unrelenting heat, boogieing fans, uninhibited youth in scanty or no clothing, marijuana fumes, and the proliferation of non-country performers such as Leon Russell combined to give these events the aura of country Woodstocks.[10]

The late 1970s were successful years for Nelson that included a duet album with Waylon Jennings and the release of the hit song "Mamas, Don't Let Your Babies Grow up to Be Cowboys." Nelson followed up with the multi-platinum "Stardust," which featured sparse, country-jazz interpretations of Tin Pan Alley standards such as Irving Berlin's "Blue Skies" and Hoagy Carmichael's "Georgia on My Mind" and "Stardust." Nelson's vocal timbre and relaxed rhythmic phrasing made him one of country's most identifiable voices, and his sparse band arrangements and acoustic guitar gave his music an appealing intimacy.

Texas-born Waylon Jennings (1937–2002) was the definitive Outlaw. With one of the most resonant voices in country music, he performed with a distinctive blend of honky-tonk, rocka-billy, rock, and blues. In his view, "Blues, rock 'n' roll and country are just about a beat apart."[11] Jennings started his career in the late 1950s as a rocker and bassist for Buddy Holly. He moved to Nashville in the 1960s but eventually grew frustrated with the town's formulaic sound. He began to insist on producing his own recordings and using his road band to record, moves that placed him at the vanguard of the Outlaws. Jennings made his first independent recording without strings, background vocals, or "studio sweetening"; grew long hair and a beard; and took on a tough "good ole boy" persona in the early 1970s. In 1976 he released *Wanted: The Outlaws* with Willie Nelson and won a Grammy for "Mamas, Don't Let Your Babies Grow up to Be Cowboys." Jennings summed up his country music experience in a song: "Come to Nashville, write some good songs, cut some hit records, make money, take all the drugs you can and drink all you can, become a wild man and all of a sudden you die."[12]

MICHAEL OCHS ARCHIVES/GETTY IMAGES

Waylon Jennings and Willie Nelson at the peak of their "Outlaw" period in 1977.

CHAPTER SUMMARY

- The establishment of Nashville as the centre of the country music industry was followed by the emergence of the smooth Nashville sound of the 1950s and 1960s.

- Beginning in the 1950s, the music of Kitty Wells, Patsy Cline, Loretta Lynn, and Dolly Parton surfaced women's perspectives in country music.

- A West Coast honky-tonk tradition led by Merle Haggard and Buck Owens developed in Bakersfield in the 1950s and 1960s.

- The Outlaws, led by Willie Nelson and Waylon Jennings, emerged out of Austin in the 1970s in response to the formulaic Nashville sound.

LISTENING EXERCISE

The Popularization of Patsy Cline

Listen to Patsy Cline singing Willie Nelson's "Crazy," recorded in 1961. The song exemplifies the Nashville sound, with the instrumental sweetening of strings and background vocals. How does Cline's clear voice mesh with the studio arrangement? Why was the song a major hit for Cline?

HISTORICAL STUDIES AND DISCUSSION QUESTION

Country Music and Race

When Charley Pride first recorded, many listeners had no idea that he was black; similarly, when Elvis Presley first came on the radio, many people could not tell if he was white or black. According to producer Sam Phillips, the fact that Presley was "a white artist who sounded black" played a major role in his success. Jazz musicians, too, often comment that players sound white or black, and some Latin jazz players insist that they can tell if musicians grew up in Cuba or Puerto Rico by the way they play. Fans sometimes say that Ray Charles's country music sounded black because he made use of soulful vocal inflections. How much do race and ethnicity contribute to an artist's sound?

STUDY QUESTIONS

1. How did the emergence of the Nashville scene change country music? Who was Chet Atkins? What role does Nashville play today in the country music industry?

2. What was the significance of Patsy Cline and Anne Murray to country music?

3. Who were the Outlaws and how did they affect the evolution of country music in the 1970s?

NOTES

1. Robert K. Oermann, *A Century of Country: An Illustrated History of Country Music* (New York: TV Books, 1999), 96.

2. *Ibid.*, 176.

3. Nicholas Dawidoff, *In the Country of Country: People and Places in American Music* (New York: Pantheon Books, 1997), 50.

4. *Ibid.*, 178.

5. Dawidoff, *In the Country of Country,* 63.

6. Country Music Foundation (CMF), *Country: The Music and the Musicians, Pickers, Slickers, Cheatin' Hearts and Superstars* (New York: Abbeville Press, 1988), 66.

7. *Ibid.*, 70–71.

8. Liner notes for *From Where I Stand: The Black Experience in Country Music,* p. 44, Warner Brothers Records, 9-46428-2, 1998.

9. Liner notes for *The Best of Freddie Fender,* MCA CD 0881701902, 1996.

10. Bill C. Malone and Judith McCulloh, eds., *Stars of Country Music: Uncle Dave Macon to Johnny Rodriquez* (Urbana: University of Illinois Press, 1975), 397.

11. Jon Pareles, "Waylon Jennings, Singer, Songwriter and Outlaw of Country Music, Dies at 64," *New York Times,* February 14, 2002, p. C17.

12. *Ibid.*

CHAPTER 17

Country Music in the Era of Rock

SOUTHERN ROCK

Southern rock—and its close cousin, **country rock**—appeared in the late 1960s and early 1970s. Southern rock was bluesy and aggressive, while country rock projected a more relaxed feel. Both styles contributed to the contemporary country music of the 1990s. Southern rock blended blues, R & B, country, and gospel with the aggressive feel of hard rock, drawing from the blues-rock of the late 1960s as well as honky-tonk and the Bakersfield sound to create a distinctive fusion. During the early 1970s, southern rock stood at the cutting edge of American hard rock.

Pivotal to the emergence of southern rock, the Allman Brothers elaborated on the improvisational tendencies and loudness of Cream and the Grateful Dead, while staying closer to rock's blues and country roots. The group coalesced with a self-titled album in 1969, featuring intricately harmonized, dueling lead guitar work and two drummers. They broke through nationally with their third recording, *Live at the Fillmore East* (1971), and later scored with "Ramblin' Man" (1973) off the popular *Brothers and Sisters* album (1973). The band's original songwriting style and infectious jam-based approach served later as a model for the **jam bands** of the 1990s and early 2000s.

Other southern-rock bands emerged as well. The Charlie Daniels band began in the 1970s as a rock group but maintained a loyal following for over thirty years as it shifted from rock to country. Modelled on the Allman Brothers, the group's biggest hit was "The Devil Went down to Georgia," off the album *Million Mile Reflections* (1979). The hardest-rocking band to follow in the tradition of the Allman Brothers was Lynyrd Skynyrd, who tried to "one-up" the Allmans by using a three-lead-guitar lineup. Formed in Florida in the late 1960s, the group produced "Freebird" (1973) and the southern-rock anthem "Sweet Home Alabama" (1974). Texas-based ZZ Top's first blues-based, boogie recordings appeared in the early 1970s, but not until the early 1980s did the band's unique look of foot-long beards, snap-brim hats, and Ray-Bans make them camp icons on MTV.

FRANK DRIGGS COLLECTION/ARCHIVE PHOTOS/GETTY IMAGES

Southern-rock innovators the Allman Brothers Band in an early publicity photo.

COUNTRY ROCK

By the late 1960s and early 1970s, rock groups had begun to experiment with country instrumentation and harmonies, producing a hybrid called country rock. Acts such as the Byrds, the Band, Poco, the Nitty Gritty Dirt Band, and Buffalo Springfield all incorporated country elements; established rock acts such as Bob Dylan, Neil Young, and Linda Ronstadt also released country-flavoured efforts. In addition, a new genre called southern rock was being developed by the Allman Brothers, Lynyrd Skynyrd, the Charlie Daniels Band, and the Marshall Tucker Band.

Gram Parsons (1946–1973) was one of the first to bridge the boundary between rock and country with the albums he made in California in the late 1960s. As historian Patrick Carr put it,

> In some ways Parsons was another Jimmie Rodgers—a new creative bridge between urban-rural and folk-pop musical forms, an edge dweller. . . . But in the crucial area of image he had none of Rodgers's skills or resources. He had long hair, and he wore marijuana leaves emblazoned on his suit.[1]

Parsons's fusion of country music and rock began with his work on the Byrds' *Sweetheart of the Rodeo* album in 1968. He subsequently formed the prototype country-rock band, the Flying Burrito Brothers, to produce such tunes as "Sin City" and "Wheels." Parsons's pioneering sound was picked up in the 1970s by Los Angeles–based bands such as the Eagles, whose "Hotel California" was one of the best-selling rock records of all time. A final musical contribution Parsons made to country rock was his discovery of singer Emmylou Harris

(1947–), who was a young folk artist when he introduced her to country. Harris succeeded where others failed in uniting country and rock fans, and she invigorated country music by exploring its roots, providing exposure for new songwriters and introducing new artists. Harris was a touchstone for a generation of subsequent female artists, and she supported the rise of the neotraditionalist movement of the 1980s as well as the **alt-country** movement of the 1990s.

Another milestone of country rock in the 1970s was the release of *Will the Circle Be Unbroken,* a classic album that bridged a generation gap and preserved in a respectful way the work of traditional country artists such as Mother Maybelle Carter, Earl Scruggs, and Roy Acuff. Organized by the members of the Nitty Gritty Dirt Band, a country rock act emphasizing roots music, the album also stunned the country music industry by selling a million copies, chiefly to young rock fans.

Featuring a relaxed blend of country vocal harmonies, pedal steel guitar, and Dobro with rock guitar, country rock emerged out of the L.A. rock scene to dominate mainstream rock briefly in the 1970s, and exerted a strong influence on rock culture in Canada in the music of The Stampeders, The Cowboy Junkies, Blue Rodeo. The roots of the style lay in late-1960s folk-rock acts such as Buffalo Springfield and the Byrds, as well as Bob Dylan's country-infused work on *Nashville Skyline.* The Byrds' release of *Sweetheart of the Rodeo* (1968), done with Gram Parsons of the Flying Burrito Brothers, anticipated the country-rock sound. Artists such as the Eagles, Poco, and Linda Ronstadt came to define the style.

Gram Parsons and his band, the Flying Burrito Brothers, were the late-1960s godfathers of country rock. The Georgia-born Parsons had the radical notion of blending the then-conservative flavour of country with the laid-back, long-haired L.A. rock sound. Other group members of the Burritos included Chris Hillman and Michael Clarke of the Byrds, and future Eagles member Bernie Leadon. Poco, formed in 1968, was another early, L.A.-based country-rock group. Founding members included Richie Furay and Jim Messina of Buffalo Springfield and future Eagle Randy Meisner.

The Eagles stood as the unchallenged superstars of country rock, ultimately producing two of the best-selling domestic rock records of all time. When the group first joined forces in 1971, as Linda Ronstadt's studio band, they developed a successful musical formula, performing a well-defined blend of simple melodies, rich country harmonies, and laid-back rhythms. After signing as the Eagles, they produced a string of hits including "Take It Easy" (1972), "Peaceful Easy Feeling" (1972), "Desperado" (1973), "Life in the Fast Lane" (1976), and "Hotel California" (1976). *The Eagles' Greatest Hits* album surpassed Michael Jackson's *Thriller* in the early 2000s to become the biggest-selling pop record in the United States.

The Stampeders, one of Canada's earliest exponents of the country-rock style, formed in Calgary, Alberta in 1964 as The Rebounds. In 1966 they relocated to Toronto, Ontario, and scored a hit with "Sweet City Woman" (1971), which won Best Single at the Juno Awards and reached number eight in the

CP/TORONTO STAR/DAVE COOPER

Blue Rodeo performing at the Toronto Dominion Centre in 2007.

United States. In 1976 they had another U.S. hit with "Hit the Road Jack," featuring legendary rock and roll DJ, Wolfman Jack. The group continues to perform across Canada at fairs, festivals, casinos, and theatres.

Formed in 1984, Blue Rodeo is one of the most successful and well-known contemporary Canadian bands. Their studio albums have sold over three million copies and have earned the band seven Juno Awards. Original members Jim Cuddy, Greg Keelor, and Bazil Donovan have all released solo albums, and Blue Rodeo members have collaborated extensively with other notable Canadian artists, including Sarah McLachlan, The Tragically Hip, The Sadies, and the Cowboy Junkies.

COUNTRY ROCK AND NEOTRADITIONALIST INFLUENCES

The retrenchment of the mid-1980s led to the rise of a new generation of stars who had grown up on rock and were easier to package for new media outlets—especially video. The development of MTV, TNN (the Nashville Network), and CMT (Country Music Television) accelerated the pace of promoting artists, and country, like other styles, became as much a visual as an auditory medium. Popular female acts during the lean years of the 1980s included Barbara Mandrell, Tanya Tucker, Crystal Gayle, the Judds, and Reba McEntire. Male acts included Alabama, the Oak Ridge Boys, Ricky Skaggs, George Strait, and Dwight Yoakam. Country also took on a strong seventies rock flavour as its "twang" faded a bit. When the group Alabama pioneered the use of a rock band format, previously rare in country, they brought many young listeners reared on rock over to country. The group marketed an easy blend of pop and country influenced by artists like the Eagles, the Allman Brothers, and Charlie Daniels. Alabama parlayed flawless vocal harmonies, AOR (album-oriented rock), and showmanship into twenty-one consecutive number-one records, including "Mountain Music" and "Tennessee River."

Another new strand of country artists of the mid-1980s were the neotraditionalists, whose music represented a return to the various roots of country music—bluegrass, honky-tonk, classic country, and rockabilly. Vocalist and multi-instrumentalist Ricky Skaggs (1954–) combined a country purist aesthetic, born-again religious convictions, and a contemporary bluegrass sensibility. Skaggs first appeared with Bill Monroe at nine and later began a decade-long run on the charts in the 1980s with tunes such as "Don't Get above Your Raising" and Bill Monroe's "Crying My Heart Out over You." The Judds—Naomi Judd (1946–) and her daughter Wynonna (1964–)—combined a hard-rocking edge with traditional roots. Wynonna's soulful vocals and Naomi's harmonies brought a new youth audience to country music by producing hits such as "Mama He's Crazy" and "Grandpa (Tell Me 'bout the Good Old Days)." Reba McEntire's (1954–) work chronicled the lives of contemporary women and raised issues such as spousal abuse and the need for personal fulfillment. Major albums included *My Kind of Country* and the Grammy-winning *Whoever's in New England*. She also worked in films, Broadway, and television. George Strait (1952–) was a low-key Texan from a straight-ahead honky-tonk and western swing background. His minimalist sound and clean-cut look of pressed shirts, jeans, and crisp Stetson influenced an entire new generation of young male artists with hits such as "Does Fort Worth Ever Cross Your Mind" and "All My Ex's Live in Texas." Kentucky-born Dwight Yoakam (1956–) brought an edgy and ironic California honky-tonk attitude to hits such as "Guitars, Cadillacs," "Honky-Tonk Man," and "Ain't That Lonely Yet." Among his influences were Buck Owens, with whom he performed and recorded a tribute record; he also enjoyed a successful film career.

NEW COUNTRY AND ALT-COUNTRY

Country music experienced an upswing in the 1990s and early 2000s with a new generation of good-looking men in cowboy hats and tight jeans—sometimes called "hat acts"—and women with fashion-model looks. Nashville record sales soared, and artists' profits from touring and endorsements dwarfed prior country efforts. One reason for the music's increased success came in 1991 when *Billboard* magazine changed the way it tallied weekly record sales. Instead of relying on phone calls from record store retailers, it moved to a computer-based reporting system called Soundscan. Accurate record keeping revealed that the country music market was larger than previously reported, and the commercial scale of country music took

New country star Shania Twain in concert in 1999.

a quantum leap. Popular male acts included Garth Brooks, Tim McGraw, Alan Jackson, Brooks and Dunn, Clint Black, Toby Keith, and Kenny Chesney. Female acts included Shania Twain, Faith Hill, Trisha Yearwood, the Dixie Chicks, LeAnn Rimes, Martina McBride, and LeeAnn Womack.

Garth Brooks (1962–), one of the biggest country acts of the 1990s, built a huge new mass audience for country by blending the honky-tonk flavour of George Strait, the arena-rock sounds of 1970s rock artists like the Eagles and Journey, and sentimental elements of singer/ songwriters like James Taylor and Billy Joel. As a marketing graduate, he understood how image and publicity translated into album sales. In performance he played guitar, wore a cowboy hat and jeans, and conveyed small-town humility. But he was also a charismatic performer whose concerts were packed with stadium rock effects such as light shows and complex stage sets; for example, he would fly from the rafters on cables with a headset mike strapped across his face. Brooks' hits ranged from the barroom honky-tonk of "Friends in Low Places," to the seventies rock of "The Thunder Rolls," to sentimental ballads such as "The River" and "The Dance."

Shania Twain (1965–) is a vocalist who projects high-energy, hook-laden, rock-flavoured country music. Born in 1965 as Eileen Regina Edwards in Windsor, Ontario, Twain spent her childhood in Timmins, Ontario, singing in local clubs and bars from a very young age to support her family. At 13, her career began to gain momentum after she was invited to perform on CBC television's Tommy Hunter Show. In 1993, she met Nashville producer, songwriter and future husband, Mutt Lange, and recorded *The Woman in Me*, which produced the hit single, "Any Man of Mine." The album topped the country charts for months, crossed over and enjoyed extensive mainstream radio airplay, and won the Grammy Award for Best Country Album as well as the Academy of Country Music award for Album of the Year. Her follow-up album, *Come on Over*, is one of the best-selling albums in the history of country music. Shania Twain has achieved both critical and financial success, having sold over 65 million albums worldwide. In 1998, her first world concert tour, the *Come on Over Tour*, was enthusiastically received by both fans and critics alike.

Faith Hill (1967–) and Tim McGraw (1967–) were "Mr. and Mrs. Country Music" of the late 1990s. Hill's two biggest-selling albums, *Faith* and *Breathe,* established her as one of the new Nashville divas of the 1990s by exploiting her pop-rock sound and fashion-model looks. McGraw emerged in the mid-1990s to challenge the dominance of Garth Brooks. Although his voice was not particularly strong, his appeal lay in his everyman earthiness; he conveyed a directness and emotion—sometimes anger—that had commercial potential. His first hit was "Indian Outlaw," a dance-oriented novelty filled with offensive stereotypes.

The Dixie Chicks, a successful female trio that blended traditional bluegrass sounds with a post-punk visual look, represented a new direction for young country. Although the group's roots lay in the alt-country movement, they broke out as mainstream stars with major albums in the late 1990s and early 2000s. The group appealed to a young audience while reflecting traditional roots. They also had some of the flavour of the earlier generation of Outlaws by playing their own instruments on recordings instead of relying on session musicians, controlling the production of their recordings, and challenging Nashville record companies over economic issues.

Another trend of the 1990s and early 2000s involved the crystallization of an alternative country movement known as *alt-country*, "Americana," "No Depression," or "roots revival," which developed in reaction to mainstream country's pursuit of pop styles and the youth market. The artists associated with the movement represented an eclectic mix of traditional country and post-punk that fell well outside Nashville parameters. Among them were country legends too old for contemporary country radio, established cult-figure singer/songwriters, bluegrass and old-time artists, and new alt-country artists. Performers associated with the movement included Lyle Lovett, Jimmie Dale Gilmore, Steve Earle, k. d. lang, Lucinda Williams, The Mavericks, Gillian Welch, Iris DeMent, Uncle Tupelo, Son Volt, Wilco, and Nickel Creek. As one record label executive put it,

> Alternative country is more of a rootsy kind of country. And artistically speaking, it's a better kind of country music. . . . And it's the kind of country that if we could ever get it on the radio, the people would absolutely love.[2]

THE FUTURE OF COUNTRY: COMMERCE VERSUS TRADITION

Country music is a flexible music built of complex cultural hybrids. Unfortunately, broadcast radio and video have forced the style into a single-format category. Whereas rock and R & B make use of multiple formats—classic rock, modern rock, **alternative rock**, classic soul, hip-hop, and **smooth jazz**/R & B—country and its multiple strands do not have such a range available. This places classic and alternative country artists at a disadvantage, as the mainstream country music industry pursues multiplatinum sales. One of the most difficult issues country music faces is the contradiction between profit and connection to roots and classic artists. As Chet Atkins, the architect of the Nashville sound, put it:

> We almost do lose our identity sometimes. We get so pop that fans turn away. . . . To young folks right now, country music just means some guy with a tight ass and a white hat. . . . Right now we're in a curve with everything sounding alike, but somebody'll come along and get us back where we need to be.[3]

In the latter half of the 1960s, the United States saw war, assassinations, protests, drugs, and the birth of a counterculture that dreamed of a revolution of peace and love. Music reflected the values and struggles of the period and remains a vivid soundtrack of the era. Much of the music that the performers of the 1960s gave us has stood the test of time to become "classic rock." The kaleidoscope of musical innovations that swirled out of the period included folk-rock, the British Invasion, and psychedelic rock.

CHAPTER SUMMARY

- The development of country rock and southern rock in the 1970s subsequently influenced commercial country music of the 1980s and beyond. *The Eagles' Greatest Hits 1971–1975* is still the largest-selling pop record in the United States.

- The development of radio and of the recording industry played major roles in the evolution of country music, and their influence continues.

- Music television and corporate control of country radio shaped a new breed of young, visually appealing country performers at the end of the twentieth century.

- An unresolved tension between commerce and tradition continued into the 2000s with the appeal of alt-country, old-time music, and bluegrass.

LISTENING EXERCISE

"The Devil's Right Hand" and the Rise of New Country

Since the 1930s, Country music migrated with its practitioners and fans to urban centres where it became increasingly subject to the commodification processes of mass media. While retaining some of its traditional style elements, country music eventually broadened its fan base by morphing into a species of popular music which became known as New Country. However, the results were not met with universal approval by members within the community. How are these differences expressed in Steve Earle's *The Hard Way* (1990) and Garth Brooks' *Ropin' the Wind* (1991)?

HISTORICAL STUDIES AND DISCUSSION QUESTION

Is Country Music Political?

The lyrics of country music traditionally focus on personal issues. Some country songs, though, have talked about politics. Sexual politics were addressed in Kitty Wells' "God Didn't Make Honky-Tonk Angels," and Loretta Lynn, Dolly Parton, and Reba McEntire have all explored female perspectives on personal relationships.

The most evident form of political expression in country lyrics has centred on conservatism, insularity, and patriotism. During the Vietnam War in the late 1960s, some country artists expressed their opposition to war protest: Merle Haggard in "The Fighting Side of Me" and "Okie from Muskogee" and Barry Sadler in "Ballad of the Green Berets." Hank Williams, Jr., later expressed anger and insularity in "A Country Boy Can Survive," and Tim McGraw used racial stereotypes in his 1994 hit, "Indian Outlaw."

The events of 9/11 generated contradictory political effects in country. Toby Keith produced the best-selling "Courtesy of the Red White and Blue (The Angry American)," whose video contained images of combat assault helicopters and confrontational lyrics; on the other hand, many country stations blacklisted the Dixie Chicks for openly stating their opposition to the U.S. invasion of Iraq. What other examples of politics can you identify in country music or other genres?

STUDY QUESTIONS

1. How did the development of music television impact country? What new trends have developed at the end of the twentieth century?

2. Why were Garth Brooks and Shania Twain the perfect artists to champion New Country during the 1990s?

3. How does New Country differ from the previous styles of country music? What motivated the industry to move in this direction?

NOTES

1. Country Music Foundation (CMF), *Country: The Music and the Musicians, Pickers, Slickers, Cheatin' Hearts, and Superstars* (New York: Abbeville Press, 1988), 509–11.

2. Robert K. Oermann, *A Century of Country: An Illustrated History of Country Music* (New York: TV Books, 1999), 311.

3. Nicholas Dawidoff, *In the Country of Country: People and Places in American Music* (New York: Pantheon Books, 1997), 50.

CHAPTER 18

The Folk Music Revival and the Birth of Folk-Rock

ROOTS OF NORTH AMERICAN FOLK MUSIC

In the late 1950s and early 1960s, a significant contribution to the evolution of rock emanated from an unlikely source—folk music. The period was marked by a **folk revival** that reflected a growing interest in European folk music, rural blues, spirituals and gospel, mountain and country music, cowboy music, and other vernacular styles from around the world. Historian Norm Cohen characterized the revival as "the 'discovery' by sophisticated, culture-conscious urban artists, of traditional, generally American folk music, and its presentation by those artists to audiences of similar social background."[1]

At the root of the folk music movement was the practice of **song collecting**, which actually originated in eighteenth-century England with British poet Thomas Percy (1729–1811). Percy claimed to have discovered a collection of old song manuscripts that had been discarded, and when he published his own extensively edited version of the collection in 1765, he initiated a continuing debate among successive generations of folk music aficionados over conceptions of purity and authenticity. A century later, Francis James Child (1825–1896) and Cecil Sharp (1859–1924) codified their versions of British and American folk music. Child's five-volume work, *The English and Scottish Popular Ballads*, became the definitive source of early folk balladry. He argued that no European folk ballad tradition had survived in the United States, though he was later proven wrong by twentieth-century song collectors who found many of the ballads in the Child collection still being performed in the vernacular and folk repertoire of American musicians in New England, Appalachia, and rural areas of the Southeast. Moreover, studies of Canada's rich and diverse folk culture by scholarly collectors such as W. Roy MacKenzie and Helen Creighton (Nova Scotia), Marius Barbeau (Quebec), Edith Fowke (Ontario), and Margaret McLeod (Manitoba) have all observed varied and attenuated versions of Old World practices in every region of the country.

One of the significant popularizers of Canadian folk music, particularly music from the Maritimes, was fiddler, band leader, and composer, Don Messer (1909–1973). Born in Fredericton, New Brunswick, Messer formed Don Messer and His Islanders in 1939 for CFCY radio in Charlottetown, Prince Edward Island. From 1944–1969, "Don Messer's Jubilee" was heard and seen

CP

Don Messer's Islanders onstage in 1948: Don Messer (fiddle), Warren MacRae (drums), Julius Nielsen (bass), Marg Osburne (vocalist), unknown (trumpet), Charlie Chamberlain (guitar), Ray Simmons (clarinet), and Jackie Doyle (piano).

nationally on CBC radio and television, and became one of the most popular musical variety shows in Canada. The half-hour program, which was structured around traditional ballads, hornpipes, reels, and original compositions, was, according to Messer, "not Western or Cowboy music. . . They're folk tunes passed from generation to generation."[2]

Later, folk revivalists of the 1960s such as Joan Baez, Judy Collins, and John Allen Cameron have recorded ballads from the influential Child collection, and Simon and Garfunkel had a hit with a variant of a Child ballad called "Scarborough Fair" (1968).

Cecil Sharp was a British composer and teacher who collected hundreds of folk songs in the Appalachian mountains to produce *English Folk Songs from the Southern Appalachians* (1917). He believed that U.S. mountain people lived in the sort of isolated conditions that constituted a kind of cultural purity linked to an idealized time in Britain's past. This generated a fantasy of folk purity that many folk revivalists of the 1950s and 1960s would replicate. The work of Child and Sharp resulted in the canonization of British, Scottish, Irish, and other music of European origins as the "true" American folk music. According to historian Benjamin Filene, "The most significant effect of the myth of the white ballad singer was to help block African American folk music from gaining a central place in the canon of America's musical heritage."[3]

John Lomax (1867–1948) and his son Alan (1915–2003) were two of the twentieth century's most important song collectors and advocates for vernacular musics. A Harvard-educated Texan, John Lomax started collecting cowboy and western songs in the early twentieth century, and his *Cowboy Songs and Other Frontier Ballads* (1910), which introduced such tunes as "Home on the Range," contributed greatly to the American folk canon. The first commercial recordings of country, African American, and Mexican American musical styles in the 1920s also expanded the conception of American folk music beyond the Child/Sharp model, encouraging the Lomaxes and other collectors to seek out additional folk music. The father-and-son team worked tirelessly throughout the 1930s to collect and promote the music and performers they found, in the process furthering the myth of the "true" folk singer. The Lomaxes also produced a landmark collection of American folk music entitled *American Ballads and Folksongs*. Alan Lomax subsequently worked for the Library of Congress as head of the Archive of American Song, collaborating with such legendary folk, jazz, and blues musicians as Woody Guthrie, Pete Seeger, Leadbelly, Jelly Roll Morton, and Muddy Waters. He later collected folk music of all styles from many parts of the world and produced an influential television series on American folk culture entitled *American Patchwork,* as well as an award-winning book, *The Land where Blues Began,* in the 1990s.

Leadbelly (Huddie Ledbetter, 1889–1949) was a twentieth-century version of an African American songster. He performed folk songs, blues, cowboy and country music, popular songs, and dance tunes. His songs "Goodnight Irene" and "Rock Island Line" became twentieth-century folk music standards. The Lomaxes, who first encountered Leadbelly in the Louisiana State Penitentiary serving a life sentence for murder, viewed him as an ideal figure to challenge the Child/Sharp canon. After the Lomaxes secured his release from prison, Leadbelly spent the rest of his career working for the Lomaxes—sometimes as a performer, other times as their chauffeur. The Lomaxes packaged Leadbelly as an authentic folk hero untainted by commercialism, encouraging him to perform in prison garb or farmer's overalls to convey authenticity. A resulting *New York Herald Tribune* headline for one of the artist's appearances proclaimed, "Sweet Singer of the Swamplands Here to Do a Few Songs Between Homicides."[4] Leadbelly's work ultimately became a staple of the folk revival. He was also honoured in a 1990 tribute album, *A Shared Vision: A Tribute to Woody Guthrie and Leadbelly,* which featured his songs performed by Little Richard, Brian Wilson, and Willie Nelson, and in 1993 Kurt Cobain and Nirvana performed a Leadbelly tune for an *MTV Unplugged* album.

REVIVAL ORIGINALS: WOODY GUTHRIE AND PETE SEEGER

The two most prominent white American folk musicians of the twentieth century were Woody Guthrie and Pete Seeger. The two came from contrasting class backgrounds: Guthrie grew up in a working-class family in

Oklahoma, where his father played guitar and banjo in cowboy bands and his mother sang British ballads and folk songs; Seeger's father was a respected musicologist and experimental classical composer, and his mother was a classical violinist.

Woody Guthrie (1912–1967) was one of the most colourful figures in twentieth-century American music, best known for composing the folk anthem "This Land Is Your Land." According to author John Steinbeck,

> He sings the songs of a people, and I suspect that he is, in a way, the people. Harsh voiced and nasal, his guitar hanging like a tire iron on a rusty rim, there is nothing sweet about Woody, and there is nothing sweet about the songs he sings. But there is something more important for those who will listen. There is the will of the people to endure and fight against oppression. I think we call this the American spirit.[5]

Guthrie's early years were a real-life version of Steinbeck's Depression-era tale, *The Grapes of Wrath*. Family tragedies left Guthrie on his own at age sixteen. The infamous dust storms of 1935 forced him, along with thousands of other dust bowl refugees known as "Okies," to head west to California. When he arrived there and experienced antimigrant discrimination firsthand, Guthrie developed a lifelong commitment to social justice. This period of his life inspired some of the artist's most famous compositions, later recorded as the *Dust Bowl Ballads*.

When the artist moved to New York in 1939, he connected with a small community of progressive urban folk revivalists that included Alan Lomax, Pete Seeger, and Leadbelly. Lomax saw Guthrie as a white, working-class troubadour, and he recorded a series of interviews and performances with him for the Library of Congress. Guthrie lived a vagabond lifestyle, travelling to

MICHAEL OCHS ARCHIVES/GETTY IMAGES

The Almanac Singers popularized the folk-song sing-along or "hootenanny." Left to right, front row: Woody Guthrie, Bess Lomax (Alan's sister), and Pete Seeger.

Oregon, where he composed "Roll on Columbia." In the early 1950s he began to suffer from degenerative health problems, which plagued him until his death in 1967. His legacy was kept alive by Pete Seeger, Guthrie's son Arlo, Bob Dylan, Bruce Springsteen, Ani DeFranco, and many others.

Pete Seeger's (1919–) repertoire of folk songs in large part comprises the contemporary canon of American folk music, and his compositions, such as "The Hammer Song" and "Where Have All the Flowers Gone," are folk standards. Seeger became fascinated with folk music as a young man when his parents were working with Alan and John Lomax. He briefly attended Harvard but dropped out to work as Alan Lomax's assistant at the Archive of American Folk Song in the Library of Congress, where he also took up the five-string banjo and learned many of the songs being archived. When Seeger met Woody Guthrie in 1940 at a migrant worker benefit concert, the two began a series of musical collaborations. Alan Lomax once described this meeting as the beginning of modern American folk music. In 1940 Seeger was a founding member of the Almanac Singers, a short-lived, New York–based political folk song ensemble. The group popularized the term **hootenanny** to describe large gatherings of folk musicians, broke new ground by using traditional folk tunes to address contemporary social topics, performed on easy-to-play instruments, and employed simple arrangements and harmonies that could be sung by untrained singers. In 1946, after returning from wartime military duty, Seeger cowrote "The Hammer Song" ("If I Had a Hammer"), one of the most popular songs in the American folk repertoire.

In 1948 Seeger joined forces with Lee Hays, Ronnie Gilbert, and Fred Hillerman to form the Weavers, a group that performed a broad range of American and international folk songs. The group had major hits in 1950 with Leadbelly's "Goodnight Irene" and an Israeli folk song, "Tzena Tzena." Though the record industry did not know how to classify the Weavers, they scored again the following year with "On Top of Old Smoky" and "Across the Wide Missouri." Because of their progressive politics, the Weavers fell victim to the Red Scare of the early 1950s, and by 1953 they had disbanded. The group later performed at periodic reunions, and a 1980 documentary called *Wasn't That a Time?* presented their history.

Pete Seeger also paid regular visits to Camp Naivelt (New World), a Jewish socialist vacation community that was operated by the United Jewish People's Order, north of Brampton, Ontario. Moved by his words of encouragement, an activist folk singing group, The Travellers, was formed in the summer of 1953 and started singing outside the camp at strikes and protests. The group continued to perform at labour rallies and political events into the 1980s, and in all produced sixteen albums of protest songs, folk songs, children's songs, international tunes, and songs about Canadian historical events. Their performance at the first Mariposa Folk Festival in 1961 ushered in a period when the group enjoyed its greatest popularity.

The Mariposa Folk Festival took its name from the fictional community in Canadian author Stephen Leacock's *Sunshine Sketches of a Little Town.* The three-day outdoor festival, which was first held in Leackcock's hometown, Orillia, Ontario, was relocated to Toronto's Maple Leaf Stadium in 1965, and later to the city's Centre Island. The initial festival presented doyens of traditional Canadian folk music, including O. J. Abbott and Jacques Leabreque, as well as newcomers, Ian and Sylvia Tyson.

Victoria, British Columbia-born Ian Tyson (1933–) started playing clubs and coffeehouses shortly after his arrival in Toronto in the early-1950s. While performing music as a full-time occupation, he met Sylvia Fricker (1940–), who became his musical partner and future wife. By 1962, the couple were living in New York City and released their first recorded compilation of traditional songs. The second album was similar to the first, with the exception of the inclusion of an early Dylan composition, "Tomorrow is a Long Time," and the title song "Four Strong Winds," which was eventually covered and made famous by Neil Young. Their third album, *Northern Journey* (1964) included their signature "You Were On My Mind," a song that was later recast as a hit single by the We Five.

Throughout the 1960s and 1970s, Mariposa was one of Canada's signature music festivals, attracting name performers from both Canada and the United States. Some artists who graced Mariposa's stages and workshops included Gordon Lightfoot, Joni Mitchell, James Taylor, Mississippi John Hurt, Bruce Cockburn, Buffy Sainte-Marie, The Staple Singers, Pete Seeger, and Jay McShann. After a tumultuous twenty-year period that began with the festival shutting down for two years in 1979 and 1980, Mariposa returned to its place of origin, Orillia, in 2000, and continues to play a significant role in the crowded calendar of summer festivals.

CP/TORONTO STAR

Folk revivalists Sylvia and Ian Tyson in 1967.

Renowned Quebec nationalist chansonnier Felix Léclerc.

The growth of Quebec nationalism in the mid-1950s found a voice in the music of the *chansonnier* (song maker). Performing in fifty to one hundred seat rooms, known as **bôites à chanson**, at the periphery of Quebec's mainstream entertainment industry, chansonniers such as Raymond Lévesque and Gilles Vigneault presented traditional French Canadian folk songs (*chanson*) with added political commentary on current events. Perhaps the greatest chansonnier of the period was **singer-songwriter**, poet, novelist, playwright and actor, Felix Léclerc (1914–1988).

Born in La Toque, Quebec, Léclerc was forced to quit his studies at the University of Ottawa due to the Great Depression. He began working as a radio announcer in the late-1930s, and was soon writing dramatic scripts and performing his songs on Radio Canada in Montreal. Léclerc released his first recording on the Polydor label after relocating to Paris in 1950. He won the top award for his second French release, and is credited for reviving the *chanson* tradition in France. Felix Léclerc returned to Canada in 1953 as Quebec's most eminent chansonnier and in 1971 was awarded the Order of Canada. His influence can be heard in the music of a host of successors that includes Paul Piché and Marie Clair-Séguin.

THE FOLK REVIVAL GETS UNDER WAY

New folk music strands and new performers began to enter the spotlight in the mid-1950s as the folk revival got under way. Harry Belafonte, a New York actor and folk singer with Caribbean roots, saw major success with a series of albums featuring **calypso**, a lively, syncopated song style with roots in

Trinidad and Jamaica. His recordings of the "Banana Boat Song" and "Jamaica Farewell" sold millions. Although Elvis swept away many U.S. teens in 1956, a growing folk scene on college campuses offered an alternative to rock. To capitalize on the trend, three clean-cut business majors in California started a singing group in 1957 called the Kingston Trio. They began their career with a series of successful folk club engagements, which resulted in a record contract and their first hit, "Tom Dooley" (1958). According to historian Norm Cohen,

> They were business administration students from elite colleges who sported neat crew cuts and button-down Ivy League sport shirts. They demonstrated overnight that one need not be a political leftist or a counterculture rebel to sing folk songs.[6]

The door thus opened for new pop-style folk singers to record commercial, polished versions of traditional folk songs. One popular folk revival group called the New Lost City Ramblers introduced old-time country and string band music of the 1920s and 1930s to the folk revival, reanimating a connection of folk styles with traditional country and bluegrass music.

Inspired by recorded anthologies like Harry Smith's benchmark Anthology *of American Folk Music* (1952), the new interest in folk music caused numerous colleges to mount folk festivals, which soon became the centre of the folk music world. At the festivals, the "old guard" of political folk song—Pete Seeger, Alan Lomax, and others—would mix with roots-music legends such as the Carter Family, Bill Monroe, and Sonny Terry and Brownie McGee, as well as younger folk performers such as Arlo Guthrie, Joan Baez, and Bob Dylan. Because the renewed political activism of the civil rights movement in the early 1960s coincided with the progressive sentiments of many folk artists, folk-based protest music became a central component at marches and rallies. Traditional folk songs such as "We Shall Not Be Moved" and American labour movement songs such as "Which Side Are You On" were recast as civil rights songs and often performed with one of the original anthems of the civil rights movement, "We Shall Overcome."

DYLAN AND HIS DISCIPLES

Few figures in the history of rock or folk music have been as influential, controversial, or enigmatic as Bob Dylan (Robert Zimmerman, 1941–). During the course of his forty-year career, people have alternately adored and despised Dylan, who all the while continued to deeply influence two generations of musicians. In 1961, twenty-year-old Robert Zimmerman moved from his home in Minnesota to New York with a guitar, a bag full of original folk songs, a new name (Bob Dylan—after poet Dylan Thomas), and a fictionalized life story. Like most teenagers of his era, Zimmerman had been a huge fan of 1950s rock, but while in college he became fascinated with Woody Guthrie. According to historian James Miller,

Bob Dylan performs at the Concert for Bangladesh in 1971 (George Harrison to Dylan's left).

Dylan almost obsessively identified with Guthrie. He would listen to Guthrie's famous Dust Bowl Ballads endlessly, mastering his Oklahoma twang, mimicking his artless, almost deadpan vocal style, admitting to one Minneapolis friend that he was "building a character."[7]

Once in New York, Dylan visited Woody Guthrie and began to perform in Greenwich Village folk clubs. Producer John Hammond signed Dylan to his first recording contract, and the artist's second album, *The Freewheelin' Bob Dylan* (1963), set his career on fire with such tunes as "Masters of War," "A Hard Rain's A-Gonna Fall," "Don't Think Twice, It's Alright," and "Blowin' in the Wind."

In 1963 the civil rights movement and the folk revival reached their peak. In the folk world, Dylan was being anointed as a new troubadour; the annual Newport Folk Festival, a central event of the folk world, ended its 1963 session with Pete Seeger joining hands with Dylan; Peter, Paul and Mary; Joan Baez; and the African American gospel group the Freedom Singers to sing "We Shall Overcome."

Dylan's songs enabled the trio of Peter, Paul and Mary to become one of the most popular folk groups of the 1960s. The group had a hit with Dylan's "Blowin' in the Wind" and "Don't Think Twice, It's Alright." Other hits for the group included Pete Seeger's "If I Had a Hammer" and a children's song called "Puff, the Magic Dragon."

Joan Baez (1941–) became one of the most promising young stars of the folk world after her initial appearance at Newport in 1959. Baez had an appealing combination of talent, passion for folk music, and commitment to social causes.

She also became a regular companion of Dylan, and from 1963 to 1965, she toured and performed with Dylan and recorded his songs. Baez generated many successful albums during the folk revival, and her ringing voice came to be closely associated with numerous protest and folk anthems.

By 1964 Dylan had begun a personal and musical transformation, using complex imagery and moving away from themes of social protest toward introspection. Many view the 1965 Newport Folk Festival as the beginning of the end of the folk revival, with Dylan as the one who put the first nail in the coffin. The most anticipated performer at the festival, the artist took the stage with an electric band and performed a truncated set of two amplified songs, leading the band with electric guitar in hand. As the audience booed loudly, folk godfathers Pete Seeger and Alan Lomax had to be physically restrained from pulling the plug backstage. Dylan abruptly left the stage, and only after much pleading did he return to do one final acoustic number, "It's All Over Now Baby Blue." For the next few years, folk fans who viewed his move to rock as a sellout treated Dylan as a pariah. Nonetheless, the cultural explosion created by the arrival of the Beatles continued to rekindle Dylan's early interest in rock. The artist's next two recordings, *Highway 61 Revisited* (1965) and *Blonde on Blonde* (1966), served as rock milestones. "Like a Rolling Stone" pushed the envelope of rock songwriting to a new level. Dylan also began to use a new group of backup rock musicians, soon known as the Band.

His interest in both rock and folk thus opened the door to a new genre, *folk-rock*. Once described by David Crosby as "folk changes with a rock and roll beat,"[8] folk-rock was characterized by folk-style vocal performances backed by amplified acoustic guitars, electric bass, and drums.

While Dylan was recuperating from a sobering 1966 motorcycle accident in Woodstock, New York, he spent several months jamming with future members of The Band, making home recordings, and exploring his folk, blues, rock, and country roots. The results were later released as the *Basement Tapes*. He also began to take a mellower musical direction on his *John Wesley Harding* album (1969). During this time, The Band also released their own seminal rock albums: *Music from Big Pink* (1968) and *The Band* (1969), becoming one of rock's most respected roots-oriented acts of the late 1960s and early 1970s.

Toward the end of the 1960s, Dylan began a confusing musical odyssey. His first stop was Nashville, where he recorded the country-flavoured *Nashville Skyline* (1969), which scored hits with "Lay, Lady, Lay" and "Girl from the North Country," a duet with Johnny Cash. He ended the 1970s with the announcement that he had become a born-again Christian, and a 1979 song reflecting his new faith called "Gotta Serve Somebody" garnered him his first Grammy. In 1992 Columbia Records held a concert honouring the thirtieth anniversary of Dylan's first record release, and he followed up with the release of his first folk-oriented record in thirty years, the Grammy-winning *World Gone Wrong* (1994). Although Dylan's musical choices and changing personas often perplexed the public, he stood out as one of North America's greatest songwriters and innovators who pioneered multiple genres and influenced myriad artists.

FRANK DRIGGS COLLECTION/GETTY IMAGES

The Band in the early-1970s. From left to right: Levon Helm, Garth Hudson, Robbie Robertson, Rick Danko, and Richard Manuel.

Deeply influenced by Dylan's blend of folk and rock, the L.A.-based Byrds in turn shaped the sound of subsequent artists such as the Eagles, Tom Petty, R.E.M., and Fleetwood Mac. Formed in 1964, the Byrds were hailed by some as Los Angeles's answer to the British Invasion. Bandleader/guitarist Roger McGuinn worked with vocalist David Crosby to craft the band's close har monies and jangly twelve-string guitar sound. At Dylan's suggestion, they recorded his "Mr. Tambourine Man" (1965), a hit that solidified the folk-rock style, and they scored again with "Turn, Turn, Turn" (1966), a melody by Pete Seeger set to lyrics from the Bible. The group subsequently went psychedelic with "Eight Miles High" (1966), a song influenced by LSD and jazz saxophonist John Coltrane. By 1968 many group members had moved on to other projects, but the remaining Byrds, joined by country devotee Gram Parsons, recorded one last influential album called *Sweetheart of the Rodeo* (1968). The work's country rock hybrid laid the groundwork for the sounds of the Eagles as well as contemporary country music of the 1990s and 2000s.

CHAPTER SUMMARY

- A folk revival got under way in the 1950s, advanced by urban intellectuals and embodied by the music of Woody Guthrie, Pete Seeger, the Weavers, the Travellers, Leadbelly, and the thousands of songs collected by John and Alan Lomax.

- By the mid-1960s, folk-rock emerged, led by Bob Dylan, who was influenced by Woody Guthrie. Other folk-rock innovators included the Byrds and Simon and Garfunkel.

LISTENING EXERCISES

1. Politics and the Folk Revival

What are the political issues expressed in Woody Guthrie's "Talking Dust Bowl Blues," The Weaver's "This Land is Your Land," and Bob Dylan's "Oxford Town"?

2. Bob Dylan's Contributions

Listen to Bob Dylan's "Blowin' in the Wind" (1963). The piece is one of the most well known folk songs of the twentieth century and a defining example of Dylan's early folk style. Listen carefully to the lyrics. Why did some folk musicians of the early sixties view Dylan as their new "messiah"? Since the early 1960s, he has served as one of the most influential artists in rock and folk. How did he alter the course of popular music in the 1960s?

HISTORICAL STUDIES AND DISCUSSION QUESTION

What Is Folk Music?

During the revival, folk music was also defined as acoustic music performed in the style of folk songs that dated back fifty years or more. In addition, many folk adherents promoted images of folk music as rural, simple, honest, pure, and admirable; pop music, on the other hand, was often characterized as urban, crass, dishonest, and polluted. What issues do such distinctions raise?

STUDY QUESTIONS

1. Who was Don Messer and what role did he play in disseminating Canada's folk culture?
2. What were the origins of the folk revival in Quebec and English Canada?
3. What social, political, and commercial forces served as catalysts for the explosion of musical styles in the 1960s?
4. How did American folk music evolve in the twentieth century, and what were the sociopolitical implications of its codification? What precipitated the folk revival of the early 1960s, and who were some key innovators?
5. Which artists most influenced the emergence of folk-rock music? Discuss Bob Dylan's importance as a songwriter and lyricist.

6. How did the singer-songwriter tradition evolve over three decades from its inception in the 1970s? Discuss dominant figures and their musical contributions.

NOTES

1. Norm Cohen, *Folk Song America: A 20th Century Revival* (Washington, DC: Smithsonian Institution Press, 1991), 4.

2. Richard Green, "Don Messer and His Islanders," in *Encyclopedia of Music in Canada*, edited by Helmut Kaplan, Gilles Petain, and Kenneth Winters (Toronto: University of Toronto Press, 1981), 619.

3. Benjamin Filene, *Romancing the Folk: Public Memory and American Roots Music* (Chapel Hill: University of North Carolina Press, 2000), 27.

4. Filene, *Romancing the Folk,* 62.

5. John Steinbeck, quoted in Joe Klein, *Woody Guthrie: A Life* (New York: Knopf, 1980), 160.

6. Cohen, *Folk Song America,* 46.

7. James Miller, *Flowers in the Dustbin: The Rise of Rock and Roll, 1947–1977* (New York: Simon & Schuster, 1999), 220.

CHAPTER 19

The Counterculture and Psychedelic Rock

The United States and Canada, to a lesser degree, went through a difficult period of social turmoil in the mid-1960s. The left-leaning, non-violent social activism of the early-folk revival gave way to a charged radicalism which openly confronted (often physically) the governing authorities on issues arising from the war in Vietnam, women's rights, environmentalism, and nationalist movements within Quebec and within the urban Black communities in the U.S. The political environment of the 1960s inspired many young people to dream of a "revolution" that would enshrine social equality and personal freedom in a new transformed political system: this message became intertwined with the music of the era. To add to the mix, the Beatles imported new styles of long hair and outrageous clothing from London, an uninhibited attitude toward sexuality began to develop, and in some parts of the United States and Canada a back-to-the-earth movement took shape as young people opted out of "the system." This amorphous composite of alternative ideologies and lifestyles was known at the time as the **counterculture**.

A particularly flamboyant strand of the 1960s counterculture developed in San Francisco, flavoured by a new style of psychedelic rock music and the hippie countercultural movement. **Psychedelic music**, or acid rock, drew its inspiration from the experience of taking mind-altering drugs, with characteristic features including modal melodies, lengthy instrumental solos, esoteric lyrics, and special electronic effects. Though the same social unrest experienced by the rest of the country fueled the counterculture, it took on a different flavour when a new mind-altering hallucinogenic drug called LSD (lysergic acid diethylamide), or acid, was added to the mix. The drug was said to create heightened awareness, make time stand still, bring the world alive with new colours and images, and imbue the simplest things with profound meaning; the term *psychedelic* came into use to describe the experience. However, with **LSD** the desired euphoria could turn into a lengthy nightmare, and impure doses could lead to psychosis. Nonetheless, LSD and marijuana became the movement's drugs of choice, and one of the results of the massive chemical experiment was the development of psychedelic music.

In 1965, author Ken Kesey teamed up in San Francisco with a band of friends known as the "Merry Pranksters" to stage LSD happenings called "acid tests." The music for these events was supplied by a ragged, R & B-inspired band called the Grateful Dead. For the price of a dollar, one could receive a dose of acid and admission to a house decorated and wired for a psychedelic multimedia experience. The Grateful Dead provided the music, and the events lasted the length of a typical acid trip—eight to twelve hours. According to Ken Kesey,

> Americans invented the blues: This is what we have got to be proud of. It ain't the nuclear stuff, it's not putting the man on the moon, it's the blues. And when the blues ran up against psychedelics, rock and roll really took off.[1]

With music as its central feature, the psychedelic scene expanded in San Francisco over the next few years. Hundreds of new rock bands formed, including the Grateful Dead, Jefferson Airplane, Janis Joplin with Big Brother and the Holding Company, Santana, Country Joe and the Fish, and Sly and the Family Stone. Huge dance parties took place at venues such as the Avalon Ballroom and the Fillmore Auditorium, and audiences flocked to the experimental, psychedelic sounds. The music was illuminated by light shows that transformed performance spaces, removing the barrier between performer and audience. Accompanying the music was a crazy Day-Glo world of posters, art, clothing, and underground comics.

The psychedelic scene burst into the national spotlight in 1967 when a massive "Human Be-In" took place in San Francisco's Golden Gate Park. The hippie gathering featured music, poetry, and food. The national media blanketed the event, broadcasting images of willowy flower children and hirsute, blissed-out revolutionaries. By the time of the "Summer of Love" that year, young people from throughout the country, drawn by Scott McKenzie's song, "San Francisco (Be Sure to Wear Flowers in Your Hair)," had flocked to San Francisco's Haight/Ashbury neighbourhood to "tune in, turn on, and drop out." Within a year, however, the myth had devolved into a dead end, and the Haight was overrun with homeless, unemployed, often drug-addicted youth living on the streets.

In late 1967, L.A. rock producer Lou Adler and his partner John Phillips of the Mamas and the Papas vocal group staged their own commercialized version of a San Francisco hippie gathering in the picturesque coastal town of Monterey. The three-day Monterey Pop Festival brought together an eclectic group of artists: Indian sitar virtuoso Ravi Shankar, soul singer Otis Redding, South African trumpeter Hugh Masakela, the Byrds, the Who, Simon and Garfunkel, Buffalo Springfield, the Mamas and the Papas, Jefferson Airplane, Janis Joplin, the Grateful Dead, the Paul Butterfield Blues Band, and Jimi Hendrix. This watershed event attracted fifty thousand participants, as well as top record industry executives anxious to cash in on the new music. According to critic Joel Selvin,

> The performers came to make their statements, not their careers. Nevertheless, many powerful people in the music industry experienced the new music for

the first time in Monterey. . . . The festival managed to simultaneously sum up and accelerate the dramatic changes sweeping through pop music. . . . Never again would rock music be the charmingly uncorrupted force it was at Monterey.[2]

THE SAN FRANCISCO PSYCHEDELIC ERA

The Grateful Dead served as the standard-bearers for psychedelic music for more than thirty years. According to guitarist Jerry Garcia,

> For some people, taking LSD and going to a Dead show functions like a rite of passage. Each person deals with the experience individually. . . . But when people come together, this singular experience is ritualized. I think the Grateful Dead serves a desire for a meaningful ritual, but it's a ritual without dogma.[3]

The Dead were a mix of trained and amateur musicians. Although their earliest acid test performances were ragged, they soon developed an improvisational style that fit the psychedelic mindset. The band lived communally in San Francisco's Haight/Ashbury, performing free outdoor concerts regularly, and their music remained much the same for three decades—a mix of country, folk, and rock with extended, rock-based improvisations. The Dead built their reputation on live performance, and by the early 1970s their mammoth, custom P.A. systems set the standard for high-quality rock amplification. Though they found only limited commercial success with recordings, their legions of fans, known as Deadheads, travelled thousands of miles to hear the band perform for entire tours of twenty or thirty shows. As critic Blair Jackson once observed,

> Deadheads flock to Grateful Dead concerts like cripples to Lourdes. . . . A Dead concert is a symbiosis on a grand scale. . . . Together, the Dead and their fans form a peculiarly amorphous organism that is completely unlike anything that lives or breathes in this world.[4]

But there was another view of the Dead, as historian Jack McDonough reports: "In the face of all this homage let it be acknowledged that there are plenty of people who think the Dead the most consummately boring band in the world."[5] The band's seminal albums were *Working Man's Dead* (1971), *American Beauty* (1971), and *Live Dead* (1970), featuring songs such as "Uncle John's Band," "Casey Jones," "Truckin'," "Ripple," and "Dark Star." The group appeared at the Monterey Pop Festival in 1967, Woodstock in 1969, and the Watkins Glen Festival in 1973 before a crowd of over six hundred thousand.

No one represented the passion, fantasy, and tragedy of the psychedelic era better than Janis Joplin (1943–1970), the first female superstar of rock. Joplin's meteoric rise and tragic, drug-induced death typified the ecstasy and overindulgence of rock stardom. She was a white blues singer with a harsh, emotionally intense vocal style so raw that it actually damaged her vocal cords. The Texas-born Joplin left home at age seventeen and moved to San Francisco, where she hooked up with Big Brother and the Holding Company, quickly becoming the popular band's main attraction. At the Monterey Pop Festival, Joplin put on the show of her life with an incendiary performance that thrust her and the band into the national spotlight. A subsequent hit album, *Cheap Thrills* (1968), presented searing Joplin renditions of "Summertime," "Piece of My Heart," and "Ball and Chain." Within a year, Joplin left Big Brother, toured extensively, and appeared on national television. As her popularity grew, so did her drug use. Her work on the album *Pearl* (1971) appeared promising, but she died of a drug overdose shortly before its completion. The posthumously released album produced a number-one hit with "Me and Bobby McGee."

Formed in 1965, Jefferson Airplane became the first San Francisco band to achieve national visibility, as well as popularity on the psychedelic dance scene with songs of drugs, politics, and love. The band's sound reflected an eclectic mix of rock, folk, and blues performed in an improvisational style that generally struck a fine balance between song structure and psychedelic

© AP/WIDE WORLD PHOTOS

Jefferson Airplane from the cover of the album *Surrealistic Pillow*.

flexibility. Originally formed by vocalist Marty Balin (1942–) and guitarist Paul Kanter (1942–), the Airplane's biggest impact on the rock world came with their second album, *Surrealistic Pillow* (1967), which featured singer Grace Slick (1939–) on "White Rabbit" and "Somebody to Love." Slick was a powerful vocalist whose voice blended well with Balin's, and their dual vocal style defined the band's sound. Over the next few years, the Airplane's material became increasingly controversial, culminating with *Volunteers* (1969), which reflected the increasingly radical sentiments of the counterculture in the chorus of the song, "We Can Be Together": "Up against the wall, motherfucker." By 1970 the band had begun a series of seemingly unending personnel shifts and name changes (Jefferson Starship), though a brief reunion produced "Miracles" (1975), one of their biggest hits. Over the years the band moved away from politically infused psychedelia to a middle-of-the-road pop sound, exemplified by their mid-1980s hit, "We Built This City."

San Francisco Bay Area–based Creedence Clearwater Revival dominated top-forty radio for two years during the late 1960s while remaining popular with the counterculture—no easy feat. At its peak, the group produced rock standards such as "Proud Mary" (1969), "Bad Moon Rising" (1969), and "Born on the Bayou" (1969), all written and sung by bandleader John Fogerty (1945–). Creedence was not a psychedelic band; instead, they featured a distinctive rockabilly hard-rock sound flavoured by vocalist Fogerty's southern drawl. After Fogerty left the group in 1972, he released several solo recordings.

Jimi Hendrix (1942–1970), likely the greatest guitarist in the history of rock, became one of the genre's dominant icons. Hendrix revolutionized the electric guitar in rock, and many components of his style are virtually required repertoire for rock guitarists. His dynamic stage performances also served as prototypes for the pop extravaganzas standard in the music industry today. Although the artist's entire output of studio recordings included only three releases over a two-year period—*Are You Experienced?* (1967), *Axis: Bold as Love* (1968), and *Electric Ladyland* (1968)—much of his work still sounds fresh. According to critic David Fricke,

> The combination of that creative drive with his stunning technique, sonic imagination, and ingenious, painterly exploitation of effects like **wah-wah**, feedback, distortion and sheer earthquaking volume transformed rock and roll—and its primary instrument, the electric guitar—forever. Hendrix left an indelible, fiercely individual mark on popular music, accelerating rock's already dynamic rate of change in the late Sixties with his revolutionary synthesis of guitar violence, improvisational nerve, spacey melodic reveries and a confessional intensity born of the blues.[6]

Hendrix was steeped in the guitar traditions of two generations of African American performers. He grew up in Seattle listening to Robert Johnson, Muddy Waters, T-Bone Walker, Charlie Christian, B. B. King, and Chuck Berry. Unlike most of his less-experienced psychedelic contemporaries, the artist honed his

Jimi Hendrix at the Woodstock Rock Festival.

© ALLAN KOSS/THE IMAGE WORKS

guitar skills through extensive work on the R & B circuit as a sideman with artists such as Jackie Wilson, Sam Cooke, Wilson Pickett, Little Richard, and the Isley Brothers.

Hendrix was performing in New York in 1966 when a member of the Animals heard him and convinced him to move to London, where the artist assembled his prototype power trio. He broke the mould for British fans who expected an African American musician to fit stereotypes of electric Chicago blues or classic soul; instead, they found themselves confronted with a completely original psychedelic style. The Beatles, the Rolling Stones, the Who, and Eric Clapton were some of the artist's most avid fans; Clapton wrote his classic "Sunshine of Your Love" as a tribute to Hendrix after hearing a live show.

Hendrix burst onto the U.S. rock scene in 1967 with an incendiary performance at the Monterey Pop Festival, where once again he confounded white expectations by appearing dressed in modish ruffles and splashy colours and by playing psychedelic music at an outrageous volume with a British band. Hendrix let out all the stops: He played the guitar behind his back and with his teeth like T-Bone Walker; he thrust the instrument provocatively between his legs like Chuck Berry, while playing intricate lead and rhythm guitar simultaneously like Robert Johnson; and he drenched the audience in the psychedelic effects of the wah-wah pedal, controlled distortion, and screeching **feedback**. As the set reached its climax, Hendrix burned his legacy into the annals of live performance when he knelt before his guitar, doused it with lighter fluid, lit it on fire, and fanned the flames like a possessed snake charmer. As the guitar burned, Hendrix picked it up by the neck and smashed it to pieces while feedback still issued from the instrument.

Within days Hendrix was a sensation. His first album, *Are You Experienced?* was released in the United States, and songs such as "Purple Haze" and "Foxey Lady" received wide airplay. He rapidly became one of rock's most popular acts, touring and recording at a blistering pace. In summer 1969, Hendrix appeared at Woodstock and delivered a riveting psychedelic performance of "The Star Spangled Banner" that became etched in the memory of a generation. He next assembled an African American rock/funk trio, the Band of Gypsys; recorded a live album at the Fillmore East on New Year's Eve, 1969; and branched out to jam with jazz musicians such as Miles Davis. However, just when Hendrix's music seemed to be entering a new creative phase, he died of an apparent drug overdose in 1970. Hendrix had created a

© BETTMANN/CORBIS

Racially integrated innovators of early funk, Sly and the Family Stone, in 1968. (Sly is standing second from the left.)

repertoire that ranged from sensitive ballads to blistering rock—all infused with the blues and a transcendent psychedelic quality. According to critic Greil Marcus: "Every hard-rock and heavy-metal band from Anthrax to ZZ Top owes great debts of inspiration and often direct influence to the Jimi Hendrix experience."[7]

Sly Stone (Sylvester Stewart, 1944–) developed a soul-rock synthesis in the late 1960s that, together with James Brown's innovations, formed the basis of funk. By harnessing many of the disparate musical and social trends of the late 1960s, Stone created a hybrid of soul, rock, R & B, and psychedelia that broke down musical and cultural boundaries. Rock critic Greil Marcus describes the appeal of Sly and his band, the Family Stone:

> There was an enormous freedom to the band's sound. It was complex, because freedom is complex; wild and anarchic. . . . And it was all celebration, all affirmation, a music of endless humor and delight, like a fantasy of freedom.[8]

Stone dominated pop music from 1968 to 1970, appeared at Woodstock, and offered a new direction for soul and rock after the death of Otis Redding and the growing disillusions of the white counterculture when it became evident that there was a downside to flower power. The San Francisco–based band was rock's first fully integrated group—black and white, male and female—and its sound stemmed from the black music of Stax and James Brown as well as the open spirit of acid rock. Before Stone, few black groups had delved into political and social commentary; after him, it became a tradition. The band's sound combined Stone's gospel-tinged vocals and organ, jazzy horns, and soul-rock guitar, as well as bassist Larry Graham's innovative slap-style bass lines, which hypnotized dancers and inspired an entire generation of bass players. According to historian Rickey Vincent,

> For mainstream America the ambassador of funk was . . . Sly Stone. His out-landish appearance, infectious smile, throaty soul-singing voice, and hyperactive rock music turned America on at a time when the nation was searching for identity.[9]

Originally a DJ and record producer, Stone recruited a six-piece band in 1966 that could play the latest rock with the energy of soul and gospel singers. The band signed with Columbia in 1966, making Stone the first black rock star packaged by a major corporate label. The 1968 album *Dance to the Music* was a major success, with a crossover hit single of the same name. The next album, *Stand!* (1969), produced hits such as "I Wanna Take You Higher" and "Stand!" More hits followed: "Hot Fun in the Summertime" (1969) and "Thank You (Falettin Me Be Mice Elf Agin)" (1970), seen by some as the first funk masterpiece. By late 1970, Stone was performing erratically and went into seclusion, but he returned in 1971 with a challenging, politicized album, *There's a Riot Going On,* which confounded fans who were expecting more party music. The album's one hit, "Family Affair," pioneered the use of the electronic drum machine in pop music.

Sly Stone had a wide impact on black music. His innovative funk led to new arrangements for Motown's Temptations and the Jackson 5. Jazz pianist Herbie Hancock began to play Sly-influenced funk on his *Headhunters* album. Finally, other funk bands appeared in the early 1970s following Stone's dance funk formula—Kool and the Gang; Earth, Wind, and Fire; War; K. C. and the Sunshine Band; the Commodores; and the Ohio Players. Rickey Vincent summarizes Stone's influence as follows:

> He was the catalyst for a culture of musical and social unity not known before or since. . . . The Godfather broke the door open, but Sly let everyone in. The standard by which togetherness is measured is Sylvester Stewart's richest gift to music.[10]

A unique Latin rock sound emerged from the multicultural setting of San Francisco's Latino/bohemian Mission district in the late 1960s, when integration and cultural acceptance were the norm. Latino, African American, white, and Asian American musicians merged to build San Francisco Latin rock. Carlos Santana (1947–) was the most influential rock musician of Latino origin in the United States. His appealing fusion of Afro-Caribbean percussion, the blues, and a signature crying electric guitar spanned five decades and outlasted numerous musical trends. Over the course of his career, Santana garnered many Grammys as well as a 1998 induction into the Rock 'n' Roll Hall of Fame. Born in Jalisco, Mexico, as the son of a mariachi violinist, Santana first played in his father's mariachi group. He discovered American rock and blues when the family moved to Tijuana. In the 1960s, when flower power and a new rock scene were blossoming, he migrated to San Francisco. One night in 1967 when he sat in on a **jam session** at the Fillmore Auditorium, Santana's playing so impressed rock impresario Bill Graham that he quickly booked Santana's band as the opening act for the Who. Graham also took over management of the Santana group and got them a slot at the Woodstock festival in 1969, where a searing performance of "Soul Sacrifice" provided one of the festival's highlights. Success at Woodstock led to other hits such as "Evil Ways," "Jingo," "Black Magic Woman," and Tito Puente's *Oye Como Va.* Santana's sound was not distinctly Mexican. According to critic Rubén Guevara, "The muse that Carlos followed was the blues—all that note-bending on guitar plus the wave of percussion he took from *salsa.*"[11] Although the artist was a major force in rock throughout the 1970s, by the 1990s he had no record contract. Then he signed with Arista Records and released the multiple Grammy-winning *Supernatural* (2001), featuring younger stars such as Lauryn Hill, Rob Thomas, Everlast, and Wyclef Jean. According to rock critic James Sullivan, "Santana, the guitarist with the parabolic **sustain**, might well be the only classic rocker from his era to translate for the new millennium."[12]

In the wake of Santana's success, record labels descended on the San Francisco Bay Area. Hordes of multicultural barrio garage bands got a chance to record—many of them with large horn sections influenced by soul, jazz, Latin big bands, and horn groups such as Chicago and Blood, Sweat and Tears. One of the first Latin rock groups to follow Santana was Malo, formed in 1971. The band introduced horns to Latin rock and had a hit with *"Suavecito,"* which is still a staple of Chicano popular culture. The band's first album cover featured a memorable image of an Aztec warrior holding his sleeping princess. The most creative

Latin rock legend Carlos Santana in the late 1960s.

MICHAEL OCHS ARCHIVES/GETTY IMAGES

of the San Francisco Latin rock bands, Azteca, produced a powerhouse of musical talent, including musicians who later worked with Journey, Chick Corea, and Herbie Hancock. One of the band's most popular tunes was "Whatcha Gonna Do." Group cofounder Pete Escovedo went on to a successful career in Latin jazz as a percussionist and bandleader.

THE L.A. ROCK SCENE

Around the same time that the psychedelic rock scene was developing in San Francisco in the late 1960s, Los Angeles was witnessing a new, eclectic pop scene in the aftermath of surf music. The styles that emerged ranged from Beatles imitators, to middle-of-the-road pop, to innovative hybrids of folk, rock, and country.

Several Beatle-esque, L.A.-based rock groups sprang up: Gary Lewis and the Playboys (1965–1966), a band led by the son of comedian Jerry Lewis, which had hits such as "This Diamond Ring," "Count Me In," and "She's Just My Style"; Paul Revere and the Raiders (1966–1969), who sported American colonial costumes and mimicked British Invasion groups with hits such as "It's Just Like Me," "Kicks," and "Hungry"; and the Monkees (1966–1968), a corporate construction who starred on their own wholesome television show and produced a series of chart-topping pop hits such as "I'm a Believer," "Last Train to Clarksville," and "Pleasant Valley Sunday."

Sonny and Cher were a middle-of-the-road pop duo with modest folk-rock roots. Sonny Bono (1935–1998) was an apprentice to producer Phil Spector when he met the teenage, big-voiced Cher (Cherilyn Sarkisian, 1946–). The pair signed with Atlantic records and had a series of hits from 1965 to 1967 that included the Dylan-penned "All I Really Want to Do," "I Got You Babe," and "The Beat Goes On." They starred in a hit television show in the early 1970s, and Cher later pursued a solo career which produced sporadic dance pop hits.

Another L.A. group, the Mamas and the Papas, plied the folk-rock genre. The vocal quartet featured the lustrous vocal harmonies of Cass Elliot, Michelle and John Phillips, and Halifax-born Denny Doherty backed up by some of the finest studio musicians in Los Angeles. Their first album, *If You Can Believe Your Eyes and Ears* (1966), topped the American charts in a rare challenge to the Beatles with hits such as "California Dreamin'" and "Monday, Monday." Bandleader John Phillips also coproduced the Monterey Pop Festival and wrote "San Francisco (Be Sure to Wear Some Flowers in Your Hair)," the song that drew thousands of young Americans to San Francisco in the 1967 "Summer of Love."

Buffalo Springfield was a short-lived but highly influential band which, together with the Byrds, pioneered folk-rock in Los Angeles from 1966 to 1968. The group combined electric instrumentation and drums with incisive songwriting and intricate vocal harmonies, at times expanding beyond their folk-rock base into hard rock and psychedelia. Buffalo Springfield featured three excellent singer-songwriter-guitarists—Neil Young (1945–), Steven Stills (1945–), and Richie Furay (1944–). Major hits included "For What It's Worth," "Rock and Roll Woman," and "Broken Arrow." Interpersonal tensions and creative battles caused Young to leave for a solo career, though he would later reunite periodically with Stephen Stills. Other band members went on to form high-profile groups such as Little Feat, and Loggins and Messina.

Crosby, Stills, and Nash (and sometimes Young) stood as the quintessential close-harmony, acoustic, singer-songwriter supergroup of the late 1960s. Formed from the Byrds (David Crosby, 1941–), Buffalo Springfield (Stephen Stills, 1945–), and the Hollies (Graham Nash, 1942–), the band was periodically joined by Neil Young (1945–), who contributed a harder-edged rock flavour. For years, other groups would emulate the artists' unmistakable sound. The band performed at Woodstock, and they were among the first rock artists to adopt political and environmental causes. Their debut album, *Crosby, Stills, and Nash* (1969), featured tunes such as "Marrakesh Express," "Suite: Judy Blue Eyes," "Helplessly Hoping," and "Wooden Ships." After Neil Young joined, they produced *Déjà Vu* (1970), which featured songs such as "Woodstock," "Teach Your Children," and "Our House." The band split in 1970 but released a final live album that included "Cowgirl in the Sand," "Southern Man," "Ohio," and "Love the One You're With."

A different sort of L.A. band, the Doors, showed little connection to the warmth of folk-rock. Their approach was anchored in the nihilism, surreal poetry, and sexuality of lead singer Jim Morrison (1943–1971), as well as the jazz-influenced keyboard work of Ray Manzarek. Over their brief career from 1967 to 1971, the Doors explored the dark side of life, years before heavy metal or punk. The band's debut album, *Light My Fire* (1967), became a massive hit that blended blues, classical music, Eastern music, and pop into dark but beguiling melodies. The album was also one of the first popularized through the new alternative medium of FM radio, and it stayed on the charts for two years. Other memorable songs produced by the group included "People Are Strange," "Hello I Love You," "Riders on the Storm," and "L.A. Woman."

TORONTO AND THE YORKVILLE SCENE

Through the 1960s, lively musical scenes began to flourish in the coffeehouses on Canadian university and college campuses. At the same time, the performance venues in bohemian enclaves of Vancouver's Kitsilano district and Toronto's Yorkville area provided modest financial opportunities for countless musical and spoken-word artists, where on any given week one could hear a broad cross section of North American music by artists such as Sonny Terry and Brownie McGee, Doc Watson, Buddy Guy, Lenny Breau, Buffy Sainte-Marie, and Neil Young. Perhaps the most important contribution of the coffeehouse

TORONTO STAR/FRANK LENNON

Yorkville street jam circa 1969.

in English Canada and the *bôite à chansons* in Quebec was role they played in nurturing the artistic development of Canada's early singer-songwriters and chansonniers.

Toronto's teeming musical life centered on a string of Yonge Street bars and taverns, and also on a cluster of coffeehouses in the city's Yorkville district. Founded in 1830, Yorkville is roughly situated a short distance from the intersection of Bloor Street and Yonge Street, and was home to The Bohemian Embassy, The Penny Farthing, The Pornographic Onion, and The Riverboat. Though the artistic activities of Yorkville revolved around music, a number of Canada's most noted literary figures, including Margaret Atwood and cyberpunk writer William Gibson, also contributed to the vitality of the scene. The creative spirit of Yorkville included nearby Rochdale College at the University of Toronto, which opened in 1968 as an experiment in counterculture education. It was the largest of more than three hundred tuition-free universities in North America, and offered no structured courses, curriculum, exams, degrees, or traditional teaching faculty. It became a hot bed of free thought and radical idealism; however, the communal and educational ideals of Rochdale were eventually overtaken by a rapacious drug culture which forced the college to close its doors in 1975.

Bernie Fiedler's Riverboat was unquestionably the flagship coffeehouse in Yorkville. Seating about one hundred in a narrow basement, the Riverboat opened in 1964 and played host to scores of established and beginning performers until it went out of business in 1978. Two of Fiedler's significant acts where the singer-songwriters Bruce Cockburn and Murray McLauchlan.

Ottawa-born Cockburn (1945–) made his first solo appearance at the Mariposa Folk Festival in 1967 and was the headliner when Neil Young cancelled in order to appear at Woodstock in 1969. In 1970 he released his first, self-titled, solo album. Though Cockburn's songwriting and performing skills have made him tremendously popular in Canada, he did not gain any notoriety in the United States until his 1979 release of *Dancing in the Dragon's Jaws*. His unique and engaging solo guitar style, which also won him many admirers, is responsible for inspiring a culture of virtuoso folk-oriented guitarists, including Rick Whitelaw, Stephen Fearing, David

JIM STEINFELDT/MICHAEL OCHS ARCHIVES/GETTY IMAGES

Bruce Cockburn in concert during the 1990s.

Essig, Eve Golberg, and Don Ross. Murray McLauchlan (1948–) emigrated from Paisley, Scotland to Canada with his family, where as a teenager he began playing at coffeehouses in Toronto's Yorkville area. Though he is best known in Canada for his "The Farmer's Song" and "Down by the Henry Moore," McLauchlan has also achieved a degree of success in other pop-related formats.

One of the more innovative bands on the scene was Lighthouse. Formed in Toronto in 1969, the band reflected the current rock-jazz-rhythm and blues fusion experiments of Miles Davis, Sly Stone, Larry Coryell, Chicago, and Blood, Sweat and Tears. The thirteen member lineup of the original Lighthouse included Skipp Prokop on drums, Ralph Cole on guitar, Paul Hoffert on keyboards, and future Oscar Award-winning film composer Howard Shore on saxophone. The group performed at the Monterey Jazz Festival, the Newport Jazz Festival, and received four Juno Awards from 1971 to 1973. Two of their releases, "Hats Off to the Stranger" and "Pretty Lady," were successful on both Canadian and U.S. charts.

Yorkville's frenetic cultural life belied the almost insurmountable financial difficulties many musicians experienced from performing their music. According to David-Clayton Thomas, the lead singer for the Bossmen, a Toronto-based blues band, and who later sang with Blood, Sweat and Tears,

> I worked for ten years in Toronto, and I had hit records – five of them. But I didn't make any money, and I wasn't able to make any sort of living. I was lucky to pull in $123 dollar a week, and that doesn't give you much incentive.

TORONTO STAR/PETER POWER

Lighthouse mid-1990s reunion concert at BCE Place in downtown Toronto.

Scuffling around the country like starving rats, begging agents for an extra fifty bucks a week so that we could get some new strings for the bass guitar, or a new drum skin.[13]

Furthermore, in the 1970s, redevelopment put the commercial feasibility of the coffeehouses into jeopardy; and as the clubs began to fold so too did the scene.

EARLY CANADIAN SINGER-SONGWRITERS

By early-1970s, the worldwide music business was worth roughly 4 billion dollars, making it the leading industry in the overall entertainment business. The industry's growth was largely driven by university-age baby boomers whose voracious appetite for "concept" 33 1/3 rpm LPs was easily matched by ready access to a significant pool of disposable income. It is also at this time that the industry raised the price of individual LPs to what the market would bear (from ten to fifteen to twenty dollars per unit). LPs were now the gold standard until the arrival of CDs in the 1980s. It is against this backdrop that the developments in the English Canadian music industry were articulated.

Prior to 1970, Canada offered limited opportunities for career advancement to its musicians. Accordingly, with a few notable exceptions, many artists elected to move to the United States, including Hank Snow, Wilf Carter, Joni Mitchell, and Neil Young. At the same time, the Canadian recording industry consisted of a number of niche-oriented record labels, and three foreign-owned subsidiary companies: Quality (MGM), Musicana (EMI), and Phonodisc (Motown). The three majors subsidiaries showed little inclination to sign and support Canadian artists, but enthusiastically set up pressing plants in order to escape the 17 percent import tax that was levied on all imported goods to Canada—instead of paying the Canadian government 17 percent tariff on every album entering the country, the parent major record companies merely paid the 17 percent on the imported master tape(s) of big-name U.S. and British artists, the contents which when released in Canada were worth millions of dollars.

In 1971, the Canadian government moved to protect and enhance a perceived demand for home-spun music by mandating the Canadian, Radio and Telecommunications Commission (CRTC) to institute the first Canadian Content (CanCon) regulations for radio: FM radio was required to play 20 percent Canadian music, while AM was required to play 30 percent. The designation for Canadian content, MAPL (Music, Artist, Production, and Lyrics), stipulates that two or more MAPL functions have to be performed by Canadians.

In an effort to meet the licensing requirements set out by the CRTC, three radio broadcasters, Moffat, Standard, and CHUM, organized FACTOR (Foundation to Assist Canadian Talent on Record) in 1981 in order to disperse loans to new Canadian musicians in order to help them defray the costs of making professional demo-recordings. In 1985, the Canadian government instituted the SRDP (Sound Recording Development Programme) to funnel five million dollars into the construction of recording facilities. In the end, the combination of private and public policy initiatives spurred the growth of an industry which ultimately boosted the financial fortunes of many Canadian singer-songwriters such as Leonard Cohen, Gordon Lightfoot, and later, Bryan Adams, Shania Twain, and Alanis Morissette.

Since the 1980s, however, the recording industry in Canada has faced numerous threats to its survival. For example, in 1988, Canada signed the Free Trade Agreement with the United States in which the Canadian negotiators argued successfully for the exclusion of cultural products (i.e. music) from the agreement. However, no sooner had the ink dried on the CFTA when the U.S. government began to lobby the Canadian government to overturn the cultural exemption, arguing that Canadian artists had gained under the agreement an unfair advantage over American artists in the Canadian market—an ironic position given that US-based companies have a virtual stranglehold on the world market for recorded music.

More recently, the combination of peer-to-peer digital **file sharing**, and the dwindling appetite of baby boomers to spend money on new artists, has negatively impacted the industry. In the face of these challenges, enterprising individuals like Terry McBride, manager of Canada's Barenaked Ladies, have found unique solutions to the growing antagonisms between the digital world and the music industry; for example, McBride allows fans to download and freely mix the studio files created by those artists he represents.

GETTY IMAGES

Gordon Lightfoot on TV in the 1970s.

Gordon Lightfoot's (1938–) music career has spanned more than forty years, producing more than two hundred recordings. He helped define the folk-pop sound of the 1960s and 1970s, influencing artists such as Bob Dylan, Jimmy Buffett, and Jim Croce. Born in Orillia, Ontario, Lightfoot learned to sing under the direction of choirmaster Ray Williams, in the city's St. Paul's United Church. He moved to California in 1958 where he studied jazz composition and orchestration for two years at Hollywood's Westlake College of Music. To support himself, he sang on demonstration records and wrote, arranged, and produced commercial jingles. Upon his return to Canada, Lightfoot performed with The Swinging Eight, a group featured on CBC TV's "Country Hoedown." Encouraged by Pete Seeger to switch to guitar from piano, his principal instrument, he soon became known in the Toronto coffee houses promoting folk music.

Lightfoot's success as a live performer continued to grow throughout the late 1960s. He embarked on his first Canadian tour in 1967, was signed to Warner Bros./Reprise in 1970, and recorded over the next seven years a series of successful albums which confirmed his reputation as one of North America's premier singer-songwriters. While maintaining his permanent residence in Toronto, Lightfoot wrote several major hits, including "The Wreck of the Edmund Fitzgerald," the iconic ballad which was inspired by the actual sinking of the ship on November 10, 1975. Though his popularity peaked in the mid-1970s with a number-one gold LP and single, both entitled *Sundown*, Lightfoot continues to perform and record new songs.

Joni Mitchell demonstrating her open-string guitar tunings in the early 1970s.

Joni Mitchell (1943–), an adventurous and respected singer-songwriter, first entered the New York scene in 1968 as a confessional folksinger, producing work that ultimately covered a range of styles, and came to influence artists as diverse as Prince, Madonna, Herbie Hancock, Robert Plant, Donna Summer, Tori Amos, and Courtney Love. According to vocalist/composer Elvis Costello,

> The people that have been overtly influenced by her, with the possible exception of Prince, are nowhere near as good as she is. Her range is much greater. . . . It's not just that she has no rivals among female singer-songwriters. She has very few peers among any songwriters.[14]

The artist scored her first hits as a songwriter in the late 1960s when Judy Collins recorded "Both Sides Now" and Tom Rush released "The Circle Game." Mitchell's first platinum album, *Ladies of the Canyon* (1970), produced a hit with "Big Yellow Taxi," which Janet Jackson sampled thirty years later. Although critics considered Mitchell's autobiographical *Blue* (1971) one of her finest albums, her first experiments with fusing folk, rock, and jazz on the album *Court and Spark* (1974) are what pushed her into the popular mainstream with the hit song "Help Me." Mitchell also became known for collaborations with prominent jazz musicians in the 1970s, and her 1994 album *Turbulent Indigo* was both a critical success and a Grammy winner. Mitchell has, through photography or painting, created the artwork for each of her albums. Although she stopped recording over the last several years to focus on her visual art, in 2008

Neil Young on stage with his fabled Les Paul guitar in 1976.

Mitchell returned to Calgary to premiere a new ballet titled *Dancing Joni*.

Singer-songwriter Neil Young's (1945–) quavering tenor voice flavoured an eclectic repertoire of acoustic folk ballads, mellow country rock, high-energy garage rock, and horn-based R & B. In the 1990s, some post-punk musicians even proclaimed him the godfather of grunge. As critic Don McCleese observes, "Young has served as an inspiration for his contemporaries and younger musicians alike . . . to blast away without diminishing one's artistry, to grow old without growing soft."[15] The Canadian-born artist had his first major gig with the late-1960s folk-rock act Buffalo Springfield, and he subsequently joined Crosby, Stills, Nash, and Young, contributing the hit song "Helpless" (1970). At the same time, he established his own long-running group called Crazy Horse, with whom he recorded *After the Gold Rush* (1970) and *Harvest* (1972), as well as his biggest hit, the country rock–flavoured "Heart of Gold." His work is characterized by deeply personal lyrics, distinctive guitar work, and an instantly recognizable singing voice. Young has directed a number of films, including *Journey Through the Past* (1973), *Rust Never Sleeps* (1979), *Human Highway* (1982), and *Greendale* (2003). He is an advocate for environmental issues and co-founded the benefit concert Farm Aid.

Leonard Cohen (1934–) was a noted Montreal poet and novelist before turning to music in the 1960s. His songs have been widely covered by Judy Collins ("Suzanne," "Famous Blue Raincoat"), Aaron Neville ("Bird on a Wire") and Jeff Buckley ("Hallelujah"), among others. Cohen studied English literature at Montreal's McGill University and later at Columbia University in New York. His first poetry book, *Let Us Compare Mythologies* (1956), was published while Cohen was still an undergrad. *The Spice-Box of Earth* (1961) made him well known in poetry circles in both Canada and in Europe. Recurring themes in Cohen's work include love and sex, religion, psychological depression, and music itself. Cohen's background as a novelist and poet enabled him to bring a darker, deeper edge to these themes. In 1967, Cohen relocated to the United States to pursue a career as a folk singer-songwriter. His signature song, Suzanne," was culled from his 1966 collection of poems, entitled *Parasites of Heaven*. After performing at a few folk festivals, he came to the attention of Columbia Records representative John H. Hammond (who signed

IAN COOK/TIME LIFE PICTURES/GETTY IMAGES

Leonard Cohen in the recording studio in the early 1970s.

artists such as Bessie Smith, Billie Holiday, Bob Dylan, Bruce Springsteen, and Stevie Ray Vaughan). *Death of a Ladies' Man* (1977) was produced by Phil Spector (see Wall of Sound), whose penchant for Wagnerian grandeur clashed with Cohen's preferences for austere instrumental accompaniments. In 1979, he returned to more traditional settings in *Recent Songs,* and subsequently released the often-covered "Hallelujuh" in *Various Postions* (1984). His hallmark recording, *The Future* (1992), in which he explores the healing power of redemption and hope in the face of betrayal and failure, preceded the artist's retreat for five years to the Mount Baldy Zen Centre near Los Angeles. In 2008, Cohen staged a series of remarkable retrospective concerts in cities across North America and in Europe.

Guitarist/vocalist/songwriter Robbie Robertson (1944–) was one of the premier songwriters of the rock era of the late 1960s and early 1970s. Born in Toronto, Canada, the son of a Jewish father and Mohawk mother, Robertson listened to Native and country music as a child. At age fifteen he joined the backup band for rockabilly star Ronnie Hawkins. Robertson and the Hawks stayed with Hawkins until 1963, when they came to the attention of Bob Dylan. Dylan hired them as the supporting band for his 1965–1966 world tour, when he shocked the music world by going electric. Robertson and his bandmates renamed themselves "The Band" and became one of rock's seminal acts. They made a series of influential records, including *Music from Big Pink* (1968) and *The Band* (1969), which featured songs written by Robertson that examined American mythology and lore. After the breakup of The Band, Robertson pursued a successful career in the 1980s writing film scores. In

Native rights activist and singer-songwriter Buffy Sainte-Marie in 1971.

1994 he returned to his roots, teaming up with a coalition of contemporary Native American artists called the Red Road Ensemble to produce *Music for the Native Americans*, an album for a television documentary series. The album brought contemporary Native music to a mass audience for the first time.

Born on a Cree **First Nations** reservation in Canada, singer/songwriter Buffy Sainte-Marie (1941–) conveyed a strong sense of her heritage in her music. Sainte-Marie's earliest albums appeared at the height of the 1960s folk music boom, and over the next several decades artists such as Janis Joplin, Barbra Streisand, Elvis Presley, Neil Diamond, and Tracy Chapman recorded her work. One of her most popular songs, "Up where We Belong," was used as the theme of the film *Top Gun* in the 1980s. Sainte-Marie, who continues to perform, is an officer of the Order of Canada and has received a number of lifetime achievement distinctions, including joining the Western Canadian Music Awards hall of fame in 2007. Her song, "Universal Soldier" was inducted into the Canadian Songwriters Hall of Fame in 2005.

WOODSTOCK, ALTAMONT, AND THE END OF AN ERA

The decade of the 1960s did not go "quietly into the night." As the volatile period came to a close, the Woodstock and Altamont music festivals of 1969 symbolized the contradictions of the age. Woodstock, which could have been a disaster, signified much that was good about the 1960s; Altamont revealed a darker side.

The Woodstock rock festival was a three-day rock marathon, held in summer 1969, which featured most of the great bands of the decade. Promoted as "three days of music and peace," the event was modelled on the Monterey Pop Festival. A ticket for the whole weekend cost eighteen dollars, and promoters sold fifty thousand tickets in advance. When close to four hundred thousand people showed up, the organizers abandoned ticket sales and announced that the concert was free. Supplies of food and water ran short, portable toilets overflowed, rain created a giant mud pit, and hundreds were treated for bad reactions to LSD—but the music played on. For three days, the youth counterculture had somehow actualized its philosophy of peace and love. For many, Woodstock represented the musical and social culmination of the counterculture, and a popular film of the event cemented its mythic status.

A second free concert in 1969 held at Altamont Speedway in California provided a different story. Hastily organized by the Rolling Stones' management to serve as the backdrop for a concert film, the event started out on the wrong foot when the Hells Angels motorcycle gang was hired to do security for the concert and they were paid in beer. Like Woodstock, the event was overcrowded with rowdy concert-goers, though in this case they were enclosed in a much smaller space. When the Angels assaulted concertgoers with pool cues in a misguided attempt at crowd control, they injured hundreds of people; one person, Meredith Hunter, was stabbed to death, possibly by the Angels. Jefferson Airplane refused to play after lead singer Marty Balin was knocked out. By the time the Stones came on to perform, the situation was uncontrollable. The film of the event, *Gimme Shelter,* offered a grim reminder that the myth of peace and love of the 1960s could sometimes be little more than naïve hype.

As the 1960s came to a close, it seemed to many young people who had bought into the counterculture myth that things were falling apart: the Beatles were on the verge of breaking up, rock was being usurped by reassertion of corporate control, the Vietnam War was escalating, Richard Nixon was president, and the ideals of the civil rights movement and the youth counterculture also seemed to have been co-opted.

CHAPTER SUMMARY

- The origins of psychedelic rock are traced to the San Francisco counterculture and the use of LSD to generate the new music of the Grateful Dead, Jefferson Airplane, Janis Joplin, Jimi Hendrix, and Sly and the Family Stone.

- A similar scene in the coffee houses of Toronto's Yorkville district provided a context from which Neil Young, Joni Mitchell, and David Clayton-Thomas would launch their careers.

- The Canadian government passed legislation in 1971 which forced commercial radio to play a minimum percentage of Canadian recordings in a broadcast day.

- In the late 1960s, Los Angeles saw the emergence of the folk-rock sounds of Buffalo Springfield and Crosby, Stills, and Nash (and Young), as well as the darker, apocalyptic visions of Jim Morrison and the Doors.

- Some saw the Woodstock festival in 1969 as the musical and social culmination of the counterculture era. Others viewed it as the tipping point in the commercialization of rock.

LISTENING EXERCISE

Funk Origins

Listen to Sly and the Family Stone's recording of "Thank You (Falettin Me Be Mice Elf Agin)" (1970). The song was number one on both the pop and R & B charts at the same time, and many critics have identified it as the first funk tune. Listen to the popping bass, funky rhythm guitar, syncopated drumming, and unison ensemble vocals—all key funk ingredients. What made this a popular dance tune?

HISTORICAL STUDIES AND DISCUSSION QUESTIONS

1. Canadian Identity and Music

The issue of Canadian identity has been hotly debated since Europeans first arrived on the East Coast shores of Canada in the seventeenth century. Frequently, Canadians have defined themselves by who they are not: Colonial Canadians, particularly French Canadians, defined themselves as "not British"; contemporary Canadians define themselves at "not American"; and First Nations peoples often define themselves as "none of the above." The search for "Canadianisms" in popular music is likewise fraught with difficulties. First, and perhaps foremost, is the fact that popular music is largely driven by business imperatives that are openly hostile to musical practices which express local, regional, and national idiosyncrasies. Secondly, the preferred market status of the United States exerts tremendous pressure on a smaller country like Canada to bring its resource, industrial, financial and cultural industries in line with the U.S. economy. Moreover, the enormous effort required to survive the rough and tumble world of the music business necessitates that pop musicians of all stripes adopt the aesthetic standards of the preferred market, and therefore diminishes the likelihood that one will hear about the plight of Canada's fishing industry on *American Idol*. Thirdly, the passage of Canadian content legislation in 1971 crested the same wave of nationalistic fervour (which included Expo '67, a new Canadian flag, and the installation of "O Canada" as the national anthem) that brought the federal government's initiatives to stem the growing separatist movement in Quebec. Consequently, musicians with Canadian passports had an opportunity to record songs with Canadian images and themes, hear the recordings played on Canadian radio, and ultimately contribute to the government sponsored construction of a universal Canadian identity. Seen from this vantage point, Canadian identity is a result of public policy initiatives.

Undaunted, the search for the elusive Canadian identity continues in earnest. Is there such a thing as an intrinsic identity that is shared by all Canadians? Is it expressed in popular music? If so, by whom?

2. Drugs and Music

Throughout history, drugs and music have had a symbiotic relationship: For example, both have played essential roles in the religious rituals of many cultures. In U.S. pop music before the 1960s, many legendary musicians were associated with drug use, though few credited drugs as the source of their creativity. Alto saxophonist Charlie Parker, for example, was addicted to heroin, but no one suggested that it contributed to his genius.

On the other hand, many artists consciously identified LSD as a source of creativity during the psychedelic era. Psychedelic rock innovators spoke of the sense of timelessness that the drug created. Many of the textures still used in contemporary rock—feedback, fuzztone, and wah-wah—stem from the LSD-inspired sounds of the late 1960s.

Discuss acid rock characteristics in the music of the Jefferson Airplane (*Volunteers)* and Jimi Hendrix *(Electric Ladyland).*

STUDY QUESTIONS

1. What was acid rock? What were its roots and how did it become a central style of rock and roll? Who were the prominent groups of the genre, and what later styles of music did they influence?

2. What innovations in popular music occurred in Los Angeles in the late 1960s?

3. What is the relationship between the counter-cultural politics if the 1960s (i.e., peace movement, environmental movement) and use of drugs such as LSD?

4. Which rock musicians from the 1960s do you think are the most important? What music from the 1960s still appeals to you? Why?

5. Why did the Canadian government impose content legislation on the broadcasting industry in Canada? Who did and who did not benefit from the new policy?

NOTES

1. Robert Palmer, *Rock and Roll: An Unruly History* (New York: Harmony Books, 1995), 157.
2. Joel Selvin, *Monterey Pop* (San Francisco: Chronicle Books, 1992), 5.
3. Palmer, *Rock and Roll*, 161.
4. Jack McDonough, *San Francisco Rock: The Illustrated History of San Francisco Rock Music* (San Francisco: Chronicle Books, 1985), 135.
5. *Ibid.*
6. David Fricke, *Rolling Stone*, No. 623, February 6, 1992, p. 45.

7. *Ibid.,* 46.

8. Greil Marcus, *Mystery Train: Images of America in Rock 'n' Roll Music,* 4th ed. (New York: Penguin Books, 1997), 70.

9. Rickey Vincent, *Funk: The Music, the People, and the Rhythm of the One* (New York: St. Martin's Press, 1996), 89.

10. *Ibid.,* 99.

11. Rubén Guevara, "The View from the Sixth Street Bridge: The History of Chicano Rock," in *The First Rock and Roll Confidential Report,* edited by David Marsh et. al. (New York: Pantheon, 1985), 123.

12. James Sullivan, "Santana's Glorious Rebirth," *San Francisco Chronicle,* May 6, 2003, p. D3.

13. Ritchie Yorke, *Axes, Chops and Hot Licks: The Canadian Rock Music Scene* (Edmonton: Mel Hurtig Ltd, 1971), 115.

14. Bill Flanagan, "Lady of the Canyon," *Vanity Fair,* June 1997, p. 38.

15. Don McCleese, "Neil Young," in *Trouble Girls: The Rolling Stone Book of Women in Rock,* edited by Anthony DeCurtis and James Henke (New York: Random House, 1992), 331.

1906 Telharmonium inventor, Thaddeus Cahill, demonstrates first electric sound generating machine ♪

1914 Luigi Russolo presents first concert of electrically generated sound ♪

1920 Theremin is invented, and is later used in science fiction movie soundtracks and Beach Boys' "Good Vibrations" ♪

1920s First compositions to use turntables (*turntabilism*) as a creative tool ♪

1923 First electronic organ ♪

1940s Use of magnetic tape in compositional process (*Musique Concrète*) ♪

1951 First electronic sound sequencer/synthesizer ♪

1954 First live/electronic performance (*Deserts:* Edgard Varèse, 1883–1965) ♪

1954 First computer-program-assisted composition (Hiller/Isaacson: *Illiac Suite*) ♪

1964 Moog synthesizer (first MiniMoog issued in 1970) ♪

1966 Beach Boys release Pet Sounds ♪

1967 Beatles release *Sgt. Pepper's Lonely Hearts Club Band* ♪

1968 *Switched-On Bach* (Wendy Carlos)

1970s The synthesizer takes on a greater role in almost all forms of music-making ♪

1971 Deaths of Jim Morrison (The Doors) and Duane Allman (Allman Brothers Band) ♪

1973 Pink Floyd releases *Dark Side of the Moon*, which stays in the top 200 albums for 14 years ♪

1974 President Nixon resigns over Watergate

1974 Punk emerges; the Ramones become house band at CBGB's in New York; Patti Smith releases first record ♪

1974 Joni Mitchell goes electric with *Court and Spark* ♪

1975 Kraftwerk introduces electronica with the release of "Autobahn" ♪

1975 Bruce Springsteen hits the charts with "Born to Run" ♪

1976 Elton John has three number-one hits in one year ♪

1976 The Eagles' first greatest hits album becomes the biggest-selling domestic album in history ♪

1977 Fleetwood Mac releases Rumours ♪

1977 Sex Pistols release *Never Mind the Bollocks, Here's the Sex Pistols* ♪

1977 Elvis Presley dies ♪

1977 The Clash releases self-titled first album ♪

1979 Sony Walkman introduces age of personal listening devices ♪

1979 Sugar Hill Gang's single "Rapper's Delight" becomes the first rap record on a major label ♪

1980s Rock splinters into new genres—new wave, post punk, and synth-pop ♪

1980s Emergence of House Music (Chicago) and Techno (Detroit) ♪

1980 Emergence of digital technology (MIDI: Musical Instrument Digital Interface) ♪

1981 AIDS epidemic first recognized

1981 Creation of MTV ♪

1982 Compact disc is invented, and recorded music goes digital ♪

1983 David Bowie's "Let's Dance" hits number one with Stevie Ray Vaughan on guitar ♪

1983 Run-D.M.C.'s first hit; rap goes mainstream ♪

1984 Bruce Springsteen releases *Born in the USA* ♪

1984 Creation of MuchMusic ♪

1986 First annual inductions into the Rock and Roll Hall of Fame ♪

1987 Paul Simon releases *Graceland* recorded with South African musicians ♪

1987 U2 hits number one with *The Joshua Tree*; the album is the first of many Brian Eno and Daniel Lanois co-produced recordings ♪

1987 Public Enemy's *Fear of a Black Planet* sets the standard for political hip-hop ♪

1988 NWA releases *Straight Outta Compton* ♪

1989 Berlin Wall falls; Cold War fades

1989 TV begins to program rap regularly with "Yo! MTV Raps" ♪

1989 "Let Your Backbone Slide" by Maestro Fresh Wes is the first hit single in Canadian hip-hop ♪

1900   1920   1940   1960   1980

Art Rock, Punk, Electronica, and Hip-Hop

1990s Alternative styles blend punk, metal, singer-songwriter, funk, and rap into new hybrids ♪

1990s The Internet age and digital online file sharing grow steadily into the early 2000s

1990s Queen Latifah signals the emergence of female rappers ♪

1991 First Persian Gulf War

1991 Grunge sound breaks through with Nirvana's *Nevermind* ♪

1992 Los Angeles riots following Rodney King trial

1992 Second-generation singer-songwriters Annie Lennox and Tori Amos release their first albums ♪

1992 Seattle becomes ground zero for grunge ♪

1994 Nirvana's Kurt Cobain dies; Green Day and Weezer debut ♪

1995 Alanis Morissette's *Jagged Little Pill* breaks sales records for a solo artist ♪

1996 Creation of Urban Music Association of Canada ♪

1996 Creation of MusiquePlus ♪

1995 Rapper Tupac Shakur hits the charts, dies within a year ♪

1996 Internet and MP3 transform music commerce ♪

1999 Juno Awards install hip-hop as a key musical category ♪

2000s Classic rock 1960s bands mount repeated reunion tours ♪

2001 FLOW 93.5 (FM), Canada's first urban music station ♪

2008 Barack Obama elected first African-American U.S. President ♪

1990   2000

CHAPTER 20

Art Rock, Punk, and Their Descendents

ART ROCK

The term **art rock** (also called *progressive or album-oriented rock*) began to appear in the 1970s to describe artists who drew on a wide range of musical styles, including rock, classical, folk, electronic, and jazz. Many historians point to the influence of the Beatles' *Sgt. Pepper* album (1967), with its complex layers of multiple musical styles, as being pivotal to the development of art rock. Although considered by some to be "bombastic and pretentious,"[1] the Moody Blues were one of the earliest pop groups to attempt a classical-rock fusion. The group started out as an R & B act, but by 1967 they were recording and performing with a full symphony orchestra. The string-infused "Nights in White Satin" (1967) became their biggest success, followed by *Days of Future Passed* (1968). However, the achievements of the Moody Blues and their contemporaries pale when measured against the standard that was set by the Beatles.

The Beatles (John Lennon, 1940–1980; Paul McCartney, 1942– ; George Harrison, 1943–2001; Ringo Starr, 1940–) were the most important rock group in history. From their arrival on U.S. shores in early 1964 until their breakup in 1970, the group took rock in important new directions. According to critic Greil Marcus,

> The Beatles combined the harmonic range and implicit equality of the Fifties vocal group (the Dell-Vikings, say) with the flash of a rockabilly band (the Crickets or Gene Vincent's Blue Caps) with the aggressive and unique personalities of the classic rock stars (Elvis, Little Richard) with the homey this-could-be-you manner of later rock stars (Everly Brothers, Buddy Holly, Eddie Cochrane) with the endlessly inventive songwriting touch of the Brill Building, and delivered it all with the grace of the Miracles, the physicality of "Louie Louie," and the absurd enthusiasm of Gary "U.S." Bonds.[2]

The story of the Beatles began in 1957 when John Lennon, who was playing with a rock-skiffle group, met Paul McCartney in Liverpool. They began to write songs together and appeared as a duo until in 1958 they added fifteen-year-old guitarist George Harrison. They named themselves "the Beatles," with a spelling that emphasized the word *beat*—as in Merseybeat. From 1960 to 1961, the band played in the seaport dives of Hamburg and Liverpool, honing their style.

By 1962 they had settled on Ringo Starr on drums and hooked up with manager Brian Epstein, who wangled them a record contract. Once in the studio, the group began a long-term association with producer George Martin, a classically trained oboist and composer later known as the "fifth Beatle," who was won over by their originality. Early Beatles albums featured combinations of originals with covers of U.S. R & B hits such as "Twist and Shout" (Isley Brothers), "Roll over Beethoven" (Chuck Berry), "Baby It's You" (the Shirelles), "You've Really Got a Hold on Me" and "Money" (Smokey Robinson and the Miracles), "Long Tall Sally" (Little Richard), and "Please Mister Postman" (the Marvelettes).

The Beatles' 1963 release "Please Please Me" hit number one in Britain, followed by "Twist and Shout," the band's showstopper that featured Lennon literally screaming at the top of his lungs. This began the growth of a pop explosion known as "Beatlemania." Late in 1963, the band released "She Loves You," the best-selling British record of the 1960s, and they captivated a growing audience by shaking their mop-tops and crying "wooo" in a self-conscious imitation of Little Richard. Teen hysteria mushroomed as teens mobbed the group's hotel and followed their limousine in packs. At first the Beatles did not catch on in the United States, but within a year Beatlemania hit the country full force. Following the release of their first U.S. smash, "I Want to Hold Your Hand," the Beatles came to the United States in 1964, not long after Kennedy's assassination. Capitol Records mounted a crash publicity campaign, and the group's historic performance on the "Ed Sullivan Show" became a national cultural event seen by seventy-three million people, then the largest audience in the history of television.

A seemingly unending series of releases poured out of the Beatles from 1964 to 1966, as did two movies—*A Hard Day's Night* and *Help!* During one week in 1964, they had the top five records in the country, and in 1965 they achieved six number-one LPs. The band improved rapidly as musicians Lennon and McCartney grew as songwriters. In 1966 they released the breakthrough *Rubber Soul* album. Inspired by Bob Dylan and the folk-rock sound blossoming in the United States, the musical texture of the Beatles' sound in *Rubber Soul* differed greatly from their previous work. Tunes ranged from acoustic pieces such as "Yesterday" and "You've Got to Hide Your Love Away," to the sitar of "Norwegian Wood," to the fuzztone guitar of "Think for Yourself," to the French cabaret style of "Michelle," to the yearning introspection of "In My Life." According to Paul McCartney, when he saw Bob Dylan after the release of *Rubber Soul,* Dylan said, "Oh, I get it. You don't want to be cute anymore."[3]

The Beatles performing on the "Ed Sullivan Show" in 1964.

The Beatles went on their last tour and ended public performances in 1966, arguing that their most recent music had become almost impossible to reproduce on stage and that they were seldom heard over screaming crowds. Spurred by the new psychedelic sounds of their pop competitors Bob Dylan *(Blonde on Blonde)*, the Beach Boys *(Pet Sounds)*, and the Byrds *(Fifth Dimension)*, the Beatles went back into the studio and produced *Sgt. Pepper's Lonely Hearts Club Band* (1967). It featured experimental recording techniques, diverse song styles, and hallucinogenic images. The album's release was a monumental event, and its sound blanketed the world. As critic Langdon Winner recalled,

> I happened to be driving across the country on Interstate 80. In each city where I stopped for gas or food—Laramie, Ogallala, Moline, South Bend— the melodies wafted in from some far-off transistor radio or portable hi-fi. It was the most amazing thing I've ever heard. For a brief while the irreparably fragmented consciousness of the West was unified, at least in the minds of the young.[4]

Shortly after the release of *Sgt. Pepper,* the Beatles' manager Brian Epstein died, and the group began a slow slide to their 1970 breakup. They briefly dallied with an Indian guru and put out a poorly received film called *Magical Mystery Tour.* They also took control of their own recordings and business affairs by forming AppleCorps, and in 1968 they released a two-disc *White Album* (actually entitled *The Beatles*), which featured solo vocals and divergent musical visions from the band's two lead songwriters—harder rock tunes for Lennon and softer melodies for McCartney. The Beatles released the well-regarded *Abbey Road* in 1969, but by 1970 the breakup was a fait accompli. Lennon explained his rationale for leaving the band: "My life with the Beatles had become a trap. A tape loop. . . . I started the band. I disbanded it. It's as simple as that."[5]

Genesis, formed in 1966, also contributed greatly to art rock. The group's first vocalist, Peter Gabriel, performed in a theatrical style with elaborate costumes, and the band practised a kind of early performance art that built a cult following. When Genesis replaced Gabriel with drummer/vocalist Phil Collins in 1974, the group took on a more mainstream pop flavour, and both the band and vocalist Collins, who had his own successful career as a producer and solo artist, became two of rock's most popular acts in the mid-1980s. After his departure from Genesis in 1974, Peter Gabriel (1950–) performed as a successful solo act for three decades. His biggest commercial success came with *So* (1986), which included the funky hit "Sledgehammer."

Pink Floyd was probably the most prominent art-rock band. Formed in 1965, the group performed a psychedelic blend of rock, blues, electronic effects, folk, country, and classical. They also experimented with extended compositional forms and were one of the first British acts to incorporate light shows into live performances. With *Dark Side of the Moon* (1973), Pink Floyd hit its commercial stride, producing an album that remained on the *Billboard* Top 200 for more than fourteen years, longer than any other album in history. "The

© HULTON-DEUTSCH COLLECTION/CORBIS

Art-rock legends Pink Floyd (left to right): Roger Waters, Nick Mason, Syd Barret, and Richard Wright.

themes were unremittingly bleak—alienation, paranoia, schizophrenia—and the music was at once sterile and doomy."[6] *The Wall* (1979), another dark and apocalyptic work, cemented Pink Floyd's position as a pop legend and yielded the number-one hit, "Another Brick in the Wall." This dark perspective resonated with succeeding generations of alienated youth for almost four decades. On *Dark Side of the Moon,* songs were joined together by means of foreboding bits of taped dialogue, and the surprise hit, "Money," made use of a tape loop of cash register drawers opening and closing.

David Bowie (1947–) constructed a forty-year career that featured a bewildering array of changes in persona and musical style. According to critic Jon Pareles,

> One of rock's most astute conceptualists since the 1960's, he has toyed with the possibilities of his star persona, turned concerts into theater and fashion spectacles, and periodically recharged his songs with punk, electronics and dance rhythms.[7]

The British artist began his career in 1966 as a singer-songwriter, but by 1970 he had begun his transformation into a performance artist with the release of "Space Oddity." Influenced by New York pop artist Andy Warhol and the music of the Velvet Underground, Bowie created his theatrical alter ego, Ziggy Stardust, in 1972 by adorning himself with futuristic clothing and theatrical makeup. Bowie embraced several more stylistic shifts, including Philly soul, post-punk, and dance pop.

PUNK

In response to the excesses of disco, arena rock, and art rock, punk rock developed in the 1970s. It was rebellious and intentionally outrageous in its cacophonous musical assault on the senses, lyrics of outrage, and extremes of appearance. Punk was calculated to challenge cultural orthodoxies by celebrating individual uniqueness and by practicing social and musical equalitarianism. Punk music returned rock to its basics—three chords and a simple melody—but it did so by being louder, faster, and more abrasive than prior rock styles. Punk challenged the exclusionary pretensions of 1970s pop and rock by suggesting that anybody could get up on a stage and play loud, distorted, angry rock and roll. Punk also manifested distinct national and regional sounds in locations across North America, Europe, as well as South Africa and the Middle East. With each national/regional sound there grew a unique punk "ideology" and mindset that may or may not have had a connection to neighbouring punk communities. Subsequent styles spawned by the genre included new wave (though it is important to note that in the 1970s punk was also referred to as "new wave," and only in retrospect is there a distinction), **post-punk**, and the alternative-rock movements of the 1990s and early 2000s.

PUNK ORIGINS

The earliest **proto-punk** groups or punk precursors were raw-sounding mid-1960s garage bands such as the Kingsmen, the Standells, and Question Mark and the Mysterians, the Monkees, and the Peruvian group, Los Saicos. As one artist put it, "Garage music means just that—garage—as in inept, crummy, loose, primitive fun."[8] They were followed by the more artistically ambitious Doors, Velvet Underground, Iggy and the Stooges, and MC5. When these latter groups hit the spotlight, according to historian Robert Palmer, many listeners found them "decadent, crude, dark, negative, abrasive, nihilistic, and incompetent; 'The only thing this will replace,' predicted Cher when the Velvets first visited Los Angeles, 'is suicide."[9] Still, The Doors' music played a significant role in the development of the later L.A. punk scene: Jim Morrison is often cited as 'the first punk', and Doors keyboardist Ray Manzarek went on to produce punk bands with Electra Records.

Although never commercially successful, the Velvet Underground had an extraordinary influence on punk. The group's raw sound and singer Lou Reed's (1942–) lyrics contributed a level of poetic sophistication and social realism to rock. According to one punk artist, "I think it started with the Velvets, the whole thing, in about 1965. No one was writing about real experiences—the Velvets did."[10] In the midst of the flower power movement of the 1960s, the Velvet Underground were deliberately subversive; dressed in black, they sang about sadomasochism and drugs, and they made painful use of feedback and amplifier noise. When the band toured the United States, they inspired the Doors in Los Angeles, Iggy Pop and the Stooges and MC5 in Detroit, The Screamers in L.A., and the The Polkaholics in Toronto. Major releases included *The Velvet Underground and Nico* (1967), which contained "I'm Waiting for the Man"; *White Light/White Heat* (1967); and *Loaded* (1970), which contained "Sweet Jane," one of vocalist Reed's best-known songs. Reed subsequently pursued a solo career, and in one of his best-known works, "Walk on the Wild Side," he saluted the misfits, male hustlers, and transvestites of New York.

Iggy Pop (1947–) and his band the Stooges played sexually charged and aggressive music. Pop formed the band in 1967 in the Detroit area, inspired by Lou Reed and the Doors' Jim Morrison. According to the artist,

> What our band did was basically make a big noise and create some movement with that noise. . . . A lot of it was based on the attitude of juvenile delinquency and general mental grievance that I'd gotten from these dropouts I was hanging around with, mixed in with the sort of music that I like: hard r&b, hard rock and roll, and the exciting elements of jazz, 'cause I was starting to listen to John Coltrane. . . . And then an added element was . . . like the drill presses at the Ford plant. . . . I thought, "Those are sounds that even we could master."[11]

One of rock's most exciting performers, Pop worked himself into such a frenzy by stage diving that he was often bleeding by the end of the night. Major releases included *Iggy and the Stooges* (1969), *Funhouse* (1970), and *Raw Power* (1973).

The New York Dolls, whose members sometimes were said to resemble a cross-dressing street gang, contributed to a new form of hard rock that presaged both punk rock and heavy metal. Building on the sound of the Rolling Stones, the androgyny of Mick Jagger, girl-group pop, glam rock, and the anarchic noise of Iggy and the Stooges, the Dolls influenced a generation of musicians in New York and London. Although the Dolls self-destructed quickly, the group's two albums, *The New York Dolls* (1973) and *Too Much Too Soon* (1974), numbered among the most popular cult records in rock history.

Punk began to take hold in New York in 1974. At that time, a group called Television inaugurated a bar in the Bowery as an underground rock venue. Called CBGB & OMFUG, it was a dive with great acoustics and sound system. Most important, however, was owner Hilly Crystal's willingness to hire raw, unsigned bands. Heavily influenced by Velvet Underground, Television was a guitar-based band featuring challenging lyrics and sonic excursions that explored the ringing harmonics of the electric guitar. The early work of Television on their first album, *Marquee Moon* (1977), clearly forecast the jangly guitar sounds of 1980s post-punk bands such as U2 and R.E.M. The group may also have inaugurated the punk look, as Robert Palmer describes it: "Spiky, cropped hair, torn T-shirts and jeans that might well be held together with safety pins, and a glazed, 'pretty vacant' mien that spelled either 'youth apocalypse' or 'heroin.'"[12]

Rarely found in the limelight of commercial success, punk innovator Patti Smith (1946–) was seen by many as one of rock's finest poets—in the same mould as Bob Dylan. A regular at CBGB's, she was one of the first of the artists who played there to land a record deal. Her first recording, the 1974 single "Hey Joe," backed with "Piss Factory," is often cited as the first punk record. Although Smith only recorded sporadically, her rebellious poetry made her an icon in the punk and post-punk scene. Smith's most popular album, *Easter* (1978), had a modest hit with the Springsteen-penned "Because the Night."

The Ramones shaped the sound of punk in New York and inspired Canadian groups, such as The Action (Ottawa), The Demics and The Sinners (London), Simply Saucer (Hamilton), and The Battered Wives (Toronto). Dressed in torn blue jeans and leather jackets in homage to 1950s rockers, the Ramones turned the conventions of 1970s rock inside out. Vocalist Joey Ramone described the band's sound as "sick bubblegum music."[13] Songs by the Ramones were short, simple, and fast—often with dark lyrics and depressing titles, blending early rock, girl-group pop, and surf rock. The Ramones toured constantly beginning in 1976, and when they played in London they jumpstarted the British punk movement. According to Johnny Ramone, "Everywhere we went, we met kids that said they were starting a band that week, and some of them turned out to be the Damned, the Clash."[14]

Poet and performer, Patti Smith, in concert in 1976.

CHUCK KRALL/MICHAEL OCHS ARCHIVES/GETTY IMAGES

Blondie was the most commercially successful group to emerge out of the New York punk movement. With a passion for the Brill Building/girl-group sound, and fronted by a striking blonde singer named Debbie Harry (1945–), the band combined punk with a clean, sparse, and catchy sound featuring synthesizers and electronic keyboards that anticipated new wave. Harry's voice had a detached flavour, exemplified in the disco-inflected "Heart of Glass" (1978). Other tunes such as "The Tide Is High" explored reggae, later influencing the work of bands such as No Doubt.

Talking Heads drew on funk, African music, and *minimalism* (an artistic aesthetic stressing simplicity) to craft original and danceable music. Formed by a quartet of art school graduates and fronted by quirky vocalist/songwriter David Byrne (1952–), the band first played at CBGB's in 1975. Well-known tunes included "Psycho Killer" (1978), Al Green's "Take Me to the River" (1978), and "Burning Down the House" (1983). Multiple albums and individual members' projects followed, with *Speaking in Tongues* (1983) becoming their most popular album. A well-regarded film called *Stop Making Sense* documented one of their tours, and the film's soundtrack album spent two years on the pop charts.

BRITISH PUNK

British punk was born in 1976. Far from cohesive, punk in Great Britain grew out of a generation of unemployed youths and disaffected middle-class adolescents who formed the base of the subculture that ran its own clubs, formed its own record labels, and designed its own clothes, giving birth to punk's "do it yourself" (D.I.Y.) ethic. From this arose a wide range of aesthetic viewpoints, political orientations, and musical styles, which include The Exploited, CRASS, SubHumans, and GBH.

Tours by the Ramones got things started, and former New York Dolls manager Malcolm McLaren pushed the movement along by forming the Sex Pistols. Though their career was short-lived, the Sex Pistols revolutionized the idea of what rock could be. For a short time, some saw the band's disturbing image, lyrical violence, and anti-establishment attitude as an actual threat to the British government and monarchy. The Sex Pistols' cacophonous wall of sound and front man Johnny Rotten's disrespect for authority galvanized a legion of disenfranchised working-class British youth. Historian Robert Palmer describes the artist: "There stood Johnny Rotten in his 'I Hate Pink Floyd' T-shirt, with

© BETTMANN/CORBIS

Punk icons Sid Vicious and Johnny Rotten of the Sex Pistols performing during their 1978 U.S. debut.

a sneer that was a dental disaster, eclectic musical tastes, zero musical experience, and a 'singing' voice that would make Bob Dylan sound mellifluous."[15] The publicity generated by the band's caustic first single, "Anarchy in the U.K." (1976), caused their record label to drop them, and their next record, "God Save the Queen" (1976), further outraged public sensibilities. The band toured the United States in 1978 but self-destructed after fourteen days. As Rotten asked the audience at the Sex Pistols' final show in San Francisco, "Ever get the feeling you've been cheated?"[16]

The Clash took the anger of the Sex Pistols and other British punk rockers and fashioned it into a more lasting political and aesthetic agenda. The musically adventurous band also branched out to encompass reggae, funk, and rap. The Clash performed their first concert in 1976 on the same bill with the Sex Pistols. Early albums such as *The Clash* (1977), featuring the hit "White Riot," and *Give 'em Enough Rope* (1978) did well in Britain. Not until the release of their double album, *London Calling* (1979), did they do well in the United States. Subsequent albums included the three-disc *Sandinista!* (1980) and *Combat Rock* (1982), which garnered a U.S. hit with "Rock the Casbah."

Not long after it appeared on the public's radar screen, punk splintered into three general genres in the 1980s: new wave, a term used by the media to indicate a pop oriented punk style; post-punk, which was more experimental and artier than punk; and alternative rock, which maintained the initial punk aesthetic. Included in the mix is the myriad of substyles which collectively evolved into what became known as **electronica** in the 1990s, and which flowed in interdependent streams alongside Punk's tributaries.

NEW WAVE

While retaining the vigour and irreverence of punk, new wave added a fascination with electronics, style, and art, and its emergence coincided with the development of MTV and MuchMusic. The early 1980s brought the dawning age of the synthesizer in rock. Synth pop, a spare, synthesizer-based dance pop sound, was its first embodiment. At the start of the decade, several groups, including Berlin, Gary Numan, Depeche Mode, Human League, and the Eurythmics, began to adapt the electronic innovations of the influential German band Kraftwerk to make music with a sterile, vaguely menacing, almost disembodied sound. As the style continued to evolve, it was reshaped by the bleach-blond MTV darlings Duran Duran, who grafted synthesized hooks onto a dance beat and produced appealing videos set in tropical landscapes.

At the confluence of punk, new wave and disco, new Canadian independent labels and artists increasingly took advantage of the promotional opportunities afforded by the new CRTC content regulations. The result was a revitalized music scene in country's bars and clubs during the late-1970s and early-1980s. In step with world wide trends, punk rock/new wave artists, such as D.O.A, Teenage Head, Rough Trade, Spoons, Men Without Hats, populated Canada's

GETTY IMAGES

Singer-songwriter and producer, Daniel Lanois, in concert in 2006.

musical landscape. The period also saw marked improvements in the sound quality of new releases, improvements which can be attributed to presence of gifted sound engineers like Daniel Lanois.

Daniel Lanois (1951–) was born in Hull, Quebec, spent his formative years in Ancaster, Ontario, and later in Hamilton, Ontario, where he operated his legendary Grant Avenue Studio. Lanois' early work as a producer centred around a diverse circle of individuals and bands who were connected to Canada's Punk/ New Wave scene, including The Parchute Club, Martha and the Muffins, and Nash the Slash. As a singer-songwriter, Lanois released a number of albums of his own work, *Acadie* (1989) and *Shine* (2003), and since the late-1980s, he has mainly worked collaboratively on projects with Brian Eno (his mentor), U2, Bob Dylan, Peter Gabriel, The Neville Brothers, and Robbie Robertson. While Canada has certainly generated its share of significant producers, Jack Richardson (Guess Who) and David Foster (Céline Dion) being two noteworthy examples, Lanois' trademark Eno-inspired ambient minimalism is immediately recognizeable, emotionally evocative, and is artistically superior to the work of most of his peers. In 1996, Lanois won a Grammy for his work with Emmylou Harris, *Wrecking Ball* (1995), and has been inducted into Canada's Walk of Fame in 2005.

Elvis Costello (1954–) emerged from London's pub-rock scene in the mid-1970s with a sound that could not have differed more from the prevailing punk sounds of the era, featuring retro-flavoured rock and ballads rooted in R & B, soul, old-time rock and roll, and even lounge music. With literate and complex lyrics, Costello's songwriting was always his greatest asset. Beginning with his first album, *My Aim Is True* (1977), Costello blended rock, country, Tin Pan Alley, reggae, and other genres. Costello released a series of well-regarded albums that yielded "From a Whisper to a Scream" (1981), "Everyday I Write the Book" (1983), "Veronica" (1989), and "The Other Side of Summer" (1991).

Formed in the late 1970s, the Pretenders and singer/songwriter Chrissie Hynde (1951–) bridged the gaps between punk, new wave, and top forty. Hynde was an appealing singer with a clear, intelligent sound, as well as a fine songwriter who refashioned the traditionally male lead singer role. The Pretenders featured a jangly guitar sound and a tight rhythmic feel. Their chart-topping, self-titled debut album in 1980 put them on the map, and over the years they had hits with "Brass in Pocket" (1980), "Message of Love" (1981), and "My Baby" (1987). As rock critic Neva Chonin says, "The Pretenders might have had their heyday in the '80s, but their music, so imbued with rock tradition, transcends eras."[17]

The reggae-influenced minimalist pop sound of the British trio the Police made them one of the most popular groups of the late 1970s and early 1980s. The trio had become global superstars by the time they disbanded in the mid-1980s. They crafted music with a rhythmic elasticity that could be hypnotic (as in "Tea in the Sahara," 1983), methodical (as in "Every Breath You Take," 1983), or driving (as in "Message in a Bottle," 1979). Bassist Sting subsequently parlayed his experience with the Police into a successful solo career, serving up a smooth, multicultural blend of jazz-inflected light rock to adult contemporary audiences. Critic Joel Selvin describes the artist's later work: "His musical integrity is unimpeachable, even if he tends toward the pedantic, and he cloaks his earnest entreaties in agreeably exotic musical atmospheres."[18]

POST-PUNK

A style called post-punk developed in the 1980s. While still adhering to the D.I.Y. punk ethic, post-punk artists often showed an artistic orientation that was at odds with the pop aesthetics of new wave groups such as Duran Duran and the Police. The post-punk sound of the mid-1980s took varying forms: avant-garde noise, jangling guitars, anthemic stadium rock, or roots rock.

Formed in 1979, the Minneapolis-based Hüsker Dü wrapped angst, abandon, and well-crafted pop songs into a furious guitar squall, contributing to the template for **indie rock** and grunge. Critics viewed the group's 1984 double album *Zen Arcade* as a classic, and 1985's *New Day Rising* was equally well regarded, as were *Candy Apple Grey (1986)* and *Warehouse: Songs and Stories (1987)*. Rock critic David Fricke once described Hüsker Dü as

> a breathtaking canvas of rainbow slam pop and lyric liberation that eclipses nearly everything else in Eighties post punk rock, here or abroad, and an embarrassment to superstar acts that strut down from the mountaintop with their stone tablets every two or three years.[19]

Other groups would follow. Formed in New York City in 1981, Sonic Youth had its roots in the experimental music of Avant-Garde composer Glen Branca, and in the performance art of Laurie Anderson.

According to critic Dave Thompson,

> A battered combination of punk, hardcore, no wave, pure noise, and feedback, Sonic Youth built their career by pushing every musical boundary beyond its breaking point to a place where new sound erupted, widening the definition of what alternative sound could become.[20]

Bad Moon Rising was the group's first album to secure a widespread release in both the United States and Britain, featuring "I'm Insane" and "Death Valley '69." In 1990 Sonic Youth signed with Geffen Records, building their reputation as godfathers of alternative rock with *Goo, Dirty,* and *A Thousand Leaves.* Group members also played a key role in the subsequent signing of Nirvana to Geffen Records, and they were pivotal to the formation of Courtney Love's band, Hole. Sonic Youth toured with Nirvana in 1991 and later with Neil Young.

Godspeed You! Black Emperor (a.k.a. GYBE) is a Montreal-based ensemble which was formed in 1994 and took its name from the title of a 1974 Japanese documentary about a biker gang, the Black Emperors. The dystopian soundscapes of GYBE, as evidenced in the album *F#A#~,* shows progressive rock, punk, classical music and avant-garde influences. The band, which can be as large as twenty and as small as nine, affirms anarchist values (i.e., the group remains leaderless), and is collectively hostile to the mainstream music industry, corporate-controlled media, and to the militarism of contemporary political culture. Like the iconoclastic American group, The Residents, GYBE members (with the exception of Efrim Menuck) do not give interviews, preferring instead to remain anonymous. Their performances are multimedia events which employ film loops, rock and orchestral instruments, and often include samples of an evangelical street preacher, a gas station attendant, children singing in French, and sundry recorded excerpts. In keeping with their anarchist principles, the band allows audience members to record and release live performances in advance of "officially made" releases.

Combining ringing guitar hooks with mumbled, cryptic lyrics and a D.I.Y. aesthetic, R.E.M. marked the point when post-punk turned into alternative rock. Their first single, "Radio Free Europe" (1981), brought guitar-based rock back into the mainstream. Formed in Georgia in 1980, R.E.M. achieved a growing cult status for their folksy, "jangle-pop" sound. According to historian Robert Palmer, "Together with Tom Petty and the Heartbreakers, the Athens, Georgia–based R.E.M. revived the jangly 12-string guitar textures and folksy finger picking of the mid-sixties Byrds for audiences too young to remember the original."[21] By the early 1990s, R.E.M. was popular worldwide, acknowledged as a forerunner of the thriving alternative-rock movement; by the end of the decade, it was an institution. Important singles included "Orange Crush" (1988), "Losing My Religion" (1991), and "What's the Frequency, Kenneth?" (1994).

Through a combination of zealous righteousness and post-punk experimentalism, the Irish rock band U2 became one of the most popular groups of the 1980s. Known for a sweeping sound and grandiose statements about politics and religion, U2 were rock crusaders in an era of synthesized pop and heavy metal. As lead singer Bono puts it, "It would be wrong for me to say, 'Yes, we can change the world with a song.' But every time I try writing, that's where I'm at. I'm not stupid. I'm aware of the futility of rock & roll music, but I'm also aware of its power."[22] U2's ever-shifting sound featured everything from jangly post-punk to country, techno, and hip-hop. Guitarist Dave "The Edge" Evans contributed to the group's signature sonic landscapes with his ringing, heavily processed guitar work, and lead vocalist Bono had a knack for grand gestures that played well in large arenas. By 1987 U2 had attained superstardom with the release of *The Joshua Tree*. Important singles included "Sunday Bloody Sunday" (1983), "I Still Haven't Found What I'm Looking For" (1987), "With or Without You" (1987), "Discotheque" (1997), and "Beautiful Day" (2000).

Fronted by guitarist/vocalist Mark Knopfler (1949–), the British act Dire Straits played with a laid-back, blues-rock style laced with country, jazz, and progressive rock. Although the group appeared in the post-punk era, they owed little to punk; rather, the roots revivalism of British pub rock fuelled the band. Dire Straits' rootsy music was offset by Knopfler's introspective lyrics and Dylanesque delivery. The band's sixth album, *Brothers in Arms*, became an international blockbuster. Major hits included "Sultans of Swing" (1979), "Money for Nothing" (1985), and "So Far Away" (1985).

The mid-1980s also saw brief stirrings of a social conscience on the part of rock artists. Numerous benefit recordings, as well as charity events from large-scale rock megaconcerts to small punk festivals were organized, as major pop stars realized that they could use their power for social good. The godfather of charity rock was actually Beatle George Harrison, who sponsored and hosted his "Concert for Bangladesh" in 1971 to help raise money to fight famine in Bangladesh. A series of benefit concerts including "Band Aid," "U.S.A. for Africa," "Live Aid," and "Farm Aid" were held in the mid-1980s, each serving a different worthy cause. Benefit recordings were also produced, the most famous being "We Are the World" (1985). The 1980s also saw charities run by punk communities, such as the BYO (Better Youth Organization), and recordings released by bands for specific social causes.

ALTERNATIVE ROCK

From the 1990s through the early 2000s, a new generation of artists created collages of punk, metal, hip-hop, funk, and singer-songwriter styles, crafting a new, guitar-driven, post-punk derivative called alternative rock. For most of the 1980s, the style was heard mainly on college campuses, in small clubs, and on small independent labels—and so it was also called *indie rock*. Alternative rock intertwined multiple prior strands of pop music for a young audience who had little concern for prior genre boundaries. If rock in the 1980s was a duel of guitar versus synthesizer, then by the 1990s the guitar—the louder and more distorted the better—had clearly won.

The alternative sound had its roots in punk and post-punk. A subgenre of alternative rock that developed in the late 1980s was called **industrial rock**, but the true hallmark of alternative rock was the **punk-metal** hybrid, which framed walls of raw noise into tight pop song structures, cementing the blueprint for alternative rock. One of the era's biggest bands was Seattle-based Nirvana, who embodied the **grunge** blend of punk, metal, and singer-songwriter styles. The Seattle area also saw the emergence of the feminist punk **riot grrrl** sound. Other acts, many from California, developed a **nu-metal** hybrid of metal and hip-hop, while others pumped out a related **funk-metal** hybrid. Still others were associated with **lo-fi**, an artsy amalgam that fluctuated from simple pop and rock songs to free-form song structures to pure noise and arty experimentalism. Britain also continued as an active source of innovation with the Beatles/Stones-influenced sound of **Britpop**, and a punk-pop sound retained an active underground scene in many parts of the country. Jam bands, a folksy, blues-based style featuring extended jams, also developed, and a style called *emo* emerged as well, combining the thoughtfulness of folk with the D.I.Y. ethic of punk. Emo (or "emocore") refers to a style of 1980s hardcore music, such as Rites of Spring or Dag Nasty, and also to less aggressive offshoot bands like Sunny Day Real Estate; it refers to a fashion style of tight jeans and sweaters, large-framed glasses, Converse high-tops, black hair, and a demeanor that is shy, overly emotional, and sensitive.

Despite the diversity of subgenres and approaches of rock in the 1980s and leading up to the 1990s, the music industry employed the imperfect blanket designation of "alternative" to describe them for over a decade. Radio stations scrambled to develop new formats, floating terms such as *rock of the nineties* or *modern rock* to package the music for a younger audience, and the influential annual Lollapalooza and the Vans Warped rock tours offered a new generation of teens their own mini-Woodstock. The new sound presumably served as an alternative—but to what? In part it was an alternative to the existing mainstream of top-forty radio and MTV—the 1980s-flavoured playlists that did not speak to the next teen generation. It also presented an alternative to the macho posturing of mainstream rock culture. Some critics argued that the alternative rock of the 1990s offered nothing new—that it simply recycled prior genres. Nonetheless, the era gave birth to a series of genre-bending hybrids of styles that had been previously thought of as discrete. Art takes its own path in each generation, and rock at the turn of the twenty-first century was a hybridized field of rich reinvention.

One precursor of alternative rock was industrial rock. Pioneered by Cleveland's Nine Inch Nails, the industrial sound was characterized by a tinny guitar roar and white noise. Fronted by vocalist Trent Reznor, the act scored with *Pretty Hate Machine* (1989) and *The Downward Spiral* (1994). Some likened Reznor's self-absorbed, dark sexuality in performance to that of the Doors' Jim Morrison.

In a similar vein is Skinny Puppy, an industrial band which formed in Vancouver, B.C., in 1982. Self-releasing their first cassette in 1984, Skinny Puppy soon signed to Vancouver label Nettwork, and developed an influential sound that showed a fusion of noise, new wave, electro, and rock music. Over the course of several years, the band became known for theatrical, horror-themed live performances and videos, drawing attention to issues such as animal testing and chemical warfare.

The most influential sound in alternative rock was punk-metal, embodied in the work of bands such as Jane's Addiction or the Pixies. Jane's Addiction's debut album, *Nothing's Shocking* (1988), blended metal, punk, folk, and jazz rhythms into a fresh, challenging sound, and *Ritual De Lo Habitual* (1990), the band's breakthrough, produced the singles "Been Caught Stealing," "Stop," and

"Three Days." The group's lead singer, Perry Farrell, also founded Lollapalooza, the alternative-rock extravaganza, in 1991. Lollapalooza proved that eclectic and daring lineups could succeed commercially, promoted alternative culture, and made indie music mainstream in the 1990s. According to critic Jim DeRogatis,

> At its best in the early '90s, Lollapalooza represented a generation celebrating its individuality. However illusory, for one day, the outcasts took over. Musically, politically and socially, the traveling daylong alternative music festival was like the revenge of the nerds.[23]

Barenaked Ladies (a.k.a. BNL) is a Canadian skiffle-inspired band composed of Jim Creeggan, Kevin Hearn, Steven Page, Ed Robertson, Tyler Stewart, and formerly Andy Creeggan. Formed in 1988 in Scarborough, Ontario, they are best known for their hit singles, "One Week," Pinch Me," "If I Had A Million Dollars" and "Brian Wilson." Their first release was the 1991 *Yellow Tape*, a demo tape which was originally created for the band's performance at the South by Southwest Festival in Austin, Texas. The band's first full album, *Gordon* (1992) was a big success in Canada, and included some of the aforementioned songs. In 1996, Jason Priestly, a BNL friend and fellow Canadian, negotiated for the band to make a guest appearance on *Beverly Hills 90210*. At the same time, the release of *Rock Spectacle* scored a modest radio hit in the United States with one of the songs, "Brian Wilson." It became the band's first gold record in the United States, and earned BNL the distinction of being one the few Canadian bands to have an established market on both sides of the forty-ninth parallel.

Barenaked Ladies in 1998, from left to right: Jim Hearn, Jim Creeggan, Ed Robertson, Tyler Stewart, and Steven Page.

CP/PAUL CHIASSON

Tragically Hip's Gord Downie (foreground) and guitarist Paul Langlois (background) open for the Rolling Stones in 2005.

The Tragically Hip, on the other hand, enjoy widespread popularity in Canada but not so in the United States, a result which is perhaps owing to the Canadian-centric content of their songs. This situation is perhaps owing to the content of their music, which often touches on Canadian historical and cultural themes. Formed in 1983 in Kingston, Ontario, Gord Downie (lead vocals), Paul Langlois (guitar), Rob Baker (guitar), Gord Sinclair (bass) and Johnny Fay (drums) took their name from a skit in Michael Nesmith's video, *Elephant Parts*, and did not achieve success until the release of 1989's *Up To Here*. In 1993, they created the Another Roadside Attraction festival to promote Canadian bands. Their energetic and improvisational performance style has won them a die-hard fan base and numerous awards. In 2005 the band was inducted into the Canadian Music Hall of Fame.

By marrying punk to the power of metal and the emotional possibilities of the singer-songwriter style, **grunge** artists of the 1990s took the underground into the mainstream. Centred predominantly in the Seattle area, the first wave of grunge bands—Green River, Mudhoney, Soundgarden, and The Gits—were heavier than the second wave, which started with Nirvana. Though artists derived the guitar sound of grunge from early-1970s metal, the music's aesthetic and lyrical content proved more complex, and Nirvana was more melodic than their predecessors. After Nirvana crossed over to the mainstream, grunge lost many of its independent and punk connections and became the dominant hard-rock style of the 1990s. Similar bands included Pearl Jam, Alice in Chains, Smashing Pumpkins, and Creed.

During its brief existence, Nirvana turned youth culture inside out and dragged alternative rock onto centre stage. Lead singer-songwriter Kurt Cobain (1967–1994) and his band mates could play hard and croon softly, tempering aggression with vulnerability. Nirvana's sound appealed to a broad-ranging youth audience with songs such as the hallmark "Smells Like Teen Spirit." The group's breakthrough second album, *Nevermind* (1991), reshaped the rock world, knocked Michael Jackson from the top of the charts, and signaled an end to the 1980s. By the time its follow-up, *In Utero,* appeared in September 1993, Nirvana's look and sound defined its generation.

Still, attempts to move grunge towards the mainstream were met with mixed results. For example, the Halifax-based grunge rock group, Sloan, released their first album, *Smeared* on Geffen Records (who also recorded Nirvana) in 1992. Although the recording did modestly well in both Canada and in the U.S., Geffen nevertheless elected not to promote the second album, *Twice Removed,* and thus blocked any possibility for the group to build a larger fan base in the U.S. Following the collapse of the relationship with Geffen, Sloan returned to Los

Nickelback on "The Tonight Show" in 2001, left to right: Ryan Peake, Daniel Adair, Chad Kroeger, and Mike Kroeger.

KEVIN WINTER/GETTY IMAGES

Angeles to record *Action Pact* in 2003, a radio-friendly release that failed to make an impact in the U.S. market. Sloan nonetheless continues to play an active role in the independent music scene on Canada's east coast.

Through the last decades of the twentieth Century, a number of Canadian cities both big and small played host to a thriving independent music culture. One such scene flourished in Guelph, Ontario, and gave rise to King Cobb Steelie, Royal City, and the Constantines. Certainly the most successful band to emerge from Canada's late-1990s independent rock scene is the Hanna, Alberta-based group, Nickelback. Now relocated in Vancouver, Nickelback released their initial album, *Curb*, in 1996. The second recording, *The State* (2000), was distributed on EMI, and achieved gold status in both Canada and the United States. The third album, *Silver Side Up* (2001), generated a number of radio-friendly hit singles, such as "How You Remind Me," "Too Bad," and "Never Again," which helped propel grunge-inspired rock towards the mainstream centre stage.

Riot grrrl was a feminist punk movement that developed out of early-1990s indie rock in the music of L7, The Go Team, Frightwig, and Bikini Kill. The genre blended personal expression with political activism, presenting lyrics that addressed gender-related issues and were framed by punk-styled blasts of noise. This predominantly, though not exclusively, female culture advocated women finding their voice through alternative music, in a "do-it-yourself" fashion. Artists opposed alternative rock's corporate crossover success; the label that released many records in the style was called "Kill Rock Stars." The leading band of the riot grrrl movement was Bikini Kill, and the trio Sleater-Kinney emerged from the scene to become well-known indie stars, featuring songs with consummate instrumental skill and appealing hooks. Rebecca

Sevrin, who originally played with Saskatchewan's No Policy, went on to play with the influential Frightwig in California.

During the late 1980s and early 1990s, lo fidelity—lo-fi—became a distinct genre, fluctuating from simple pop and rock songs, to free-form song structures, to electronica, pure noise, and arty experimentalism. By 1992, groups such as Pavement had become popular cult acts with willfully noisy, chaotic recordings. According to critic Joe Hagan,

> Ironic references were de rigueur and the half-hearted try was the badge of the so-called slacker generation. . . . An amalgam of garage rock, smart-alecky lyrics and haunting pop melodies, Pavement's music at its best was about transcending the banalities of suburbia through art. The band was a graduate school version of Nirvana.[24]

One of the most inventive and eclectic lo-fi figures was Grammy award-winner, Beck. The artist offered a host of contrasts, from the funk of *Midnite Vultures* (1999), to the skewed, abstract humour of *Mellow Gold* (1994) and *Odelay* (1996), to the ruminative acoustics of *Mutations* (1998) and *Sea Change* (2002). Beginning with his 1994 hit "Loser," many journalists saw Beck as the voice of the 1990s "slacker" generation. But there was more to his music, as critic Gerald Marzorati suggests:

> Beck's approach to music evinces a comprehension of bricolage and the impossibility of esthetic originality in a post-modern moment of information overload. . . . He's figured out that it's OK to be sincere and ironic about something worth caring about.[25]

Ever since the Beatles, a long-running British tradition of tuneful, guitar-driven pop bands had continued. The term Britpop refers to a generation of 1990s British bands who embraced the melodic pop-rock tradition more than ever before.

Oasis broke out in 1994 by adopting the street-tough image of the Stones, blending it with Beatlesque melodies and hooks, song structures like those of the Kinks, and the guitar roar and sneer of punk. Oasis had several successful records—*Definitely Maybe* (1994), *(What's the Story) Morning Glory?* (1996), and *Be Here Now* (1997)—before their popularity began to subside. The group Blur was another early leader of Britpop, revitalizing guitar pop in Britain. The group reinvented themselves in the late 1990s by incorporating indie rock and lo-fi influences to achieve American success. Influential releases included *Parklife* (1994), *The Great Escape* (1995), and *Blur* (1999). Rounding out the first wave of Britpop, Radiohead was a 1990s success story influenced by Pink Floyd and U2. They first came to prominence with the single "Creep" (1993), which featured a pounding three-guitar **arena rock** attack and piercing feedback. With the Grammy-winning *OK Computer* (1997), according to critic Gerald Marzorati,

> Radiohead confronted the looming end of album-based, guitar-saturated, lyric-dense rock by counterintuitively releasing "OK Computer," a 70's-redolent **concept album** stuffed with grandly contoured melodies, rigorous guitar patternings, odd time signatures, melancholy minor chords and atonal changes. . . . [A] painstakingly wrought . . . beautiful concept album.[26]

The second-wave Britpop quartet Coldplay found the middle ground between accessibility and complex musicianship. In doing so, they produced the Grammy-winning debut album *Parachutes* (2000) and hit single "Yellow." They followed with a second Grammy winner, *A Rush of Blood to the Head* (2002).

Punk-pop (or pop-punk) was a post-grunge strand of alternative rock that combined pop melodies and chord changes with speedy punk tempos and loud guitars. Green Day and Weezer were the first bands to popularize the sound in the early 1990s, and many followed their stylistic blueprint. The style **emo** (short for *emotive,* also called *emocore*) was an arty outgrowth of hard-core punk with lyrics that were often intimate confessionals. It played an important role in underground rock by the late 1990s. Important emo figures included Fugazi, Jimmy Eat World, and Dashboard Confessional. With snappy, three-chord songs powered by driving rhythms and straight-ahead vocals, Green Day set the standard for punk-pop and resurrected the catchy, three-minute pop song. Based in Berkeley, California, the band moved from an active local punk scene to national prominence, bringing the sound of late-1970s punk to a new generation with *Dookie,* their 1994 major-label debut. Green Day's Grammy-winning rock opera *American Idiot* (2004) renewed their status as a leader.

L.A.-based quartet Weezer straddled the territory between pop-punk and emo. Fronted by songwriter Rivers Cuomo, who cultivated an ironic, nerdish cartoon image, the band's debut album, *Weezer* (*Blue Album,* 1994), sold

© KIM KULISH/CORBIS

Green Day poses to promote their 2004 release "American Idiot" (left to right): Mike Dirnt, Billy Joe Armstrong, and Tre Cool.

1.5 million copies in the United States. Subsequent albums *Pinkerton* (1996) and *Maladroit* (2002) did as well. As critic Stephen Dalton puts it, "The band . . . proved itself effortlessly adept at inspiring euphoric stage-diving hysteria with its anthemic, highly melodic bubblegum grunge."[27]

During the 1990s, punk-pop took direct aim at adolescent females. Two principal performers in this arena were Canadian singer-songwriters Alanis Morissette and Avril Lavigne. Morissette (1974–) became a major star in the mid-1990s with her angst-ridden alternative rock. *Her Grammy-winning Jagged Little Pill* (1995) was the largest-selling album by a solo female artist in history, yielding "You Oughta Know," "Ironic," and "Hand in My Pocket." Morissette won further Grammys for "Uninvited" (1998).

Belleville, Ontario-born (1984–), Avril Lavigne began her musical career after moving to Napanee, Ontario in 1989. In 1998, she appeared in concert alongside Shania Twain, and completed her first album, *Let Go,* which produced four hit singles: "Complicated," "Sk8er Boi," "I'm With You," and "Losing Grip" in 2002. Her career firmly established, Lavigne's niche as a pop-punk diva soon won her Best New Artist at the 2002 MTV Video Music Awards, and four Juno Awards in 2003.

The jam band style appeared in the early 1990s, influenced by the aesthetics of the Grateful Dead and the Allman Brothers. This folksy, blues-based style was characterized by extended jams that borrowed a variety of elements—everything from classic rock and bluegrass to soul jazz and world beat. The earliest jam bands such as Blues Traveler, Hootie and the Blowfish, and the Spin Doctors were primarily rock-oriented, but as the decade progressed, the more eclectic approaches of Phish and the Dave Matthews Band appeared.

Phish stood out among other jam bands for their musical eclecticism, technical abilities, and popularity, though they have never signed to a major record label. Like the Grateful Dead, they sold more tickets than records. As critic Jon Pareles observes,

> The whole Phish template—making every performance different, allowing audiences to make and trade concert recordings, archiving and tabulating its collective works, letting every fan feel like an initiate rather than a consumer, never acting like rock stars—came from the Dead, as did a significant part of its musical approach.[28]

Alanis Morissette performing her hit "You Oughta Know" in 1996.

© DAVID BERGMAN/CORBIS

Avril Lavigne in concert in 2003.

The Dave Matthews Band, formed by South African vocalist/guitarist Dave Matthews in Virginia in the early 1990s, presented a pop-oriented version of the Grateful Dead crossed with the world beat explorations of Paul Simon and Sting. As critic Neva Chonin describes the group: "An introspective, frequently dark singer-songwriter matched with a crack team of musicians, he and his group have gained a reputation for being the jam world's version of a fraternity house band."[29]

A new generation of garage-rock revival bands appeared in the early 2000s, emphasizing three-minute songs and retro influences from the blues and 1960s rock. Artists playing in the style included the Vines, the Hives, the Strokes, the White Stripes, and the Yeah Yeah Yeahs.

Influenced by the proto-punk sound of Iggy Pop and the Stooges and the Velvet Underground, the Strokes were a New York–based quintet that produced aggressively simple, well-crafted pop songs about love and partying. With the look of studiously dishevelled fashion models, the band took MTV and the charts by storm in the early 2000s with *Is This It* (2001) and *Room on Fire* (2003). The White Stripes were a Detroit-based, minimalist blues-rock duo formed in 1997. Singer/songwriter/guitarist Jack White morphed between the folk blues of Blind Willie McTell, the 1960s garage pop of the Kinks, and the show tunes of Cole Porter to produce hits such as *The White Stripes* (1999) and the Grammy-winning *Elephant* (2003). White also collaborated with country legend Loretta Lynn to produce her Grammy-winning comeback album, *Van Lear Rose* (2005).

CHAPTER SUMMARY

- The Beatles become the most popular band in the history of rock.
- Art rock, which began in the mid-1960s with the release of *Pet Sounds* (1966) by the Beach Boys and *Sgt. Pepper's Lonely Hearts Club Band* (1967) by the Beatles, blended rock with classical music and other musical influences.
- The emergence of punk in the 1970s laid the groundwork for many of rock's most important innovations over the next three decades. Early punk innovators, including the Ramones, the Sex Pistols, and the Clash, returned to the raw roots of rock with simple arrangements, short songs, hard-edged sounds, and a message of rebellion.
- The new wave sound of the late 1970s and early 1980s mixed punk aspirations with pop sensibilities to create a marketable pop sound.
- Electronically driven synchs-pop of the 1980s spawned by the German group Kraftwerk was embodied in the synth-based music of artists such as Gary Numan, Depeche Mode, Human League, and the Eurythmics.
- In the 1990s, numerous hybrid alternative styles of rock appeared that blended punk, metal, rap, funk, classic rock, garage, and other styles. The new hybrid styles, which came to dominate mainstream rock, included grunge, riot grrrl, funk metal, nu metal, lo-fi, Britpop, punk-pop, emo, jam bands, and garage rock.

LISTENING EXERCISES

1. Politics and Music

Listen to "White Riot" (1977) by The Clash. This is a classic example of late-1970s British punk, flavoured with political undertones. The high-energy, up-tempo, guitar-driven song lasts only two minutes, and the simple politicized lyrics work well with the catchy groove: "White riot— I wanna riot/White riot—a riot of my own / White riot—I wanna riot/ White riot—a riot of my own." What were the social and political forces which animated British Punk of the mid-1970s?

2. Noise Aesthetics

Listen to an excerpt from "Teenage Riot" (1988) by Sonic Youth, a seminal post-punk/alternative rock group of the 1980s and 1990s. This recording demonstrates more of a melodic style than earlier work by the band, which often focused on white noise. What musical elements do you hear that may have influenced alternative rock bands of the early 2000s?

HISTORICAL STUDIES AND DISCUSSION QUESTIONS

1. Art as Commerce, Commerce as Art

It has often been observed that the commercial music industry is perhaps more concerned with the look or an attitude of an artist than it is with the quality of the music itself. In today's industry, sex appeal, intensity, and strange or dangerous appearances are exploited for their cross-promotional opportunities. Does the music sell the beer or does the beer sell the music?

2. "Holidays in the Sun": Defining Punk

Rock historians have observed four key values which form the basis of the punk aesthetic. First, punk relies almost exclusively on live shows to establish an identity and build a community base; second, the sound ideal refuses the perfection afforded by the amplified "voice"; third, punk eschews the confidentiality of the romantically laden forms of popular music in favour of a declamatory address which projects and affirms individual difference; and fourth, minimalism is celebrated in virtually all aspects of musical training and production. Listen to the Sex Pistols' "Holiday in the Sun" (1976) and discuss the merits of the above points.

3. Censorship and Commerce

In 1985, the Parent's Music Resource Centre (PMRC) was formed to combat the perceived harmful effects that some forms of popular music were having on America's youth. In their published report, *Rock Music Report*, the PMRC condemned what they claimed to be the five major themes in the music: rebellion, substance abuse, sexual promiscuity and perversion, violence-nihilism, and the occult. The organization subsequently argued for and won a ratings system similar to the one used in the film industry. Although many of the PMRC's claims were laughed off during the Congressional Hearings into the alleged anti-social effects of rock, a ratings system was nonetheless implemented and continues to be used. While some artists benefited from having the Parental Advisory Warning label on their album covers, many others suffered financial loses because key distributors like Walmart refused to shelve stickered releases. The only option, then, was to acquiesce to the demands of the distributors. How did record companies and artists meet this new challenge? Is there a place in a democratic society for any kind of censorship?

STUDY QUESTIONS

1. Is it justifiable to call The Beatles the greatest rock band of all time?

2. How does the art rock aesthetic compare with the nineteenth-century notion of "art for art's sake"?

3. How does art rock differ in form and style from the previous forms of rock and roll?

4. How does the D.I.Y. punk aesthetic affirm the anarchistic values of the avant-garde movement(s) that flourished in the second decade of the twentieth century?

NOTES

1. Patricia Romanowski and Holly George-Warren, eds., *The New Rolling Stone Encyclopedia of Rock and Roll* (New York: Fireside, 2001), 665.

2. Greil Marcus, "The Beatles," in *The Rolling Stone Illustrated History of Rock and Roll*, 3rd ed., edited by Anthony DeCurtis and James Henke (New York: Random House, 1992), 217.

3. James Miller, *Flowers in the Dustbin, The Rise of Rock and Roll, 1947–1977* (New York: Simon and Schuster, 1999), 231.

4. Greil Marcus, "The Beatles," in *The Rolling Stone Illustrated History of Rock and Roll*, 3rd ed., edited by Anthony DeCurtis and James Henke (New York: Random House, 1992), 216–17.

5. John Lennon, "The Ballad of John and Yoko," in *Rock and Roll Is Here to Stay,* edited by William McKeen (New York: Norton, 2000), 314–15.

6. Romanowski and George-Warren, *The New Rolling Stone Encyclopedia*, 761.

7. Jon Pareles, "David Bowie, 21st Century Entrepreneur," *New York Times*, June 9, 2002, sec. 2, p. 1.

8. Robot Hull, "The Original Punks: The Greatest Garage Recordings of the Twentieth Century," in *Rolling Stone's Alt-Rock-a-Rama*, edited by Scott Schinder et al. (New York: Delta, 1996), 62.

9. Robert Palmer, *Rock and Roll: An Unruly History* (New York: Harmony Books, 1995), 177.

10. Legs McNeill, in *Punk: The Definitive Record of a Revolution,* edited by Stephen Colegrave and Chris Sullivan (New York: Thunder's Mouth Press, 2001), 32.

11. Palmer, *Rock and Roll,* 176.

12. Palmer, *Rock and Roll,* 272.

13. *Ibid.,* 271.

14. *Ibid.,* 273–74.

15. *Ibid.,* 273.

16. *Ibid.,* 278.

17. Neva Chonin, "Pretenders Are Still the Real Thing: Hynde's Band Stirs Sold-Out Warfield with Tough, Timeless Rock," http://www.sfgate.com, March 3, 2003; accessed May 16, 2005.

18. Joel Selvin, "Sting, Where Is Thy Sting: Pretty Boy Can't Cut Loose," http://www.sfgate.com, February 20, 2004; accessed May 16, 2005.

19. David Fricke, "CD Review: *Warehouse: Songs and Stories,*" http://www.rollingstone.com/reviews/, March 26, 1987; accessed May 16, 2005.

20. Dave Thompson, *Alternative Rock* (San Francisco: Miller Freeman, 2000), 643.

21. Palmer, *Rock and Roll,* 285–86.

22. *Rolling Stone's Alt-Rock-a-Rama,* edited by Scott Schinder et al. (New York: Delta, 1996), 138.

23. Jim DeRogatis, "Alternative Fest: Frats Outnumber Freaks," http://www.jimdero.com/News2003/July14Lolla.htm, July 14, 2003; accessed May 16, 2005.

24. Joe Hagan, "A Thinking Slacker's Rock Hero, Slightly Aged," *New York Times,* March 25, 2001, Arts, p. 33.

25. Gerald Marzorati, "Beck's Fugue," *New York Times Magazine,* March 23, 1997, p. 32.

26. Gerald Marzorati, "The Post-Rock Band," *New York Times Magazine,* October 1, 2000, p. 44.

27. Stephen Dalton, "The Glory That Is Geek," *Times of London,* August 24, 1996, p. 17.

28. Jon Pareles, "True to Form, Phish Disbands on Its Own Maverick Terms," *New York Times,* May 27, 2004, sec. E, p. 1.

29. Neva Chonin, "Matthews' Mellow Set Punctuated by Must-Boogies," *San Francisco Chronicle,* August 4, 2003, p. D1.

CHAPTER 21

Electronica and Hip-Hop

ELECTRONICA

Beginning in the 1980s, dance music became the musical home for a host of electronically generated musical styles now referred to as electronica. Many critics suggest that the German group Kraftwerk initiated the electronica movement, which subsequently evolved into such subgenres as house, techno, trance, jungle, drum 'n' bass, trip-hop, breakbeat, and newer hybrids including acid house and ambient house.

Kraftwerk was the best-known group in the electronica genre, as well as the band most often cited as its progenitor. According to historian Simon Reynolds,

> Kraftwerk invented the pristine, posthuman pop phuture we now inhabit. The story of techno begins not in the early 80s Detroit, as is so often claimed, but in the early 70s Düsseldorf, where Kraftwerk built their Klingklang sound factory and churned out pioneering synth-and-drum-machine tracks like "Autobahn," "Trans-Europe Express," and "The Man-Machine."[1]

The group first appeared in 1970 with a minimalist, rhythmic, electronically generated sound that subsequently became a worldwide model for electronica. The group's first hit was the title song from the album *Autobahn* (1975), featuring the distinctive sound of the early Moog synthesizer. The group followed up with a string of albums that included *Trans-Europe Express* (1977), *The Man Machine* (1978), and *Computer World* (1981). Kraftwerk also developed a following in the African American hip-hop community, and Afrika Bambaataa borrowed directly from two Kraftwerk songs—"Trans-Europe Express" and "The Numbers"—for his 1982 hit, "Planet Rock." Derrick May, one of the founders of techno, also credited Kraftwerk as a direct influence. Kraftwerk toured and recorded into the early 2000s, performing on a bare stage with laptop computers, while a computer-controlled light show was projected behind them.

Early electronica first became popular in the disco and postdisco club scenes of Great Britain and Western Europe before migrating to North America. Electronica further evolved in the late 1980s and 1990s in Britain as the sound-track for **raves**—all-night parties held in fields, farms, or warehouses. DJs played acid house, trance, and other styles of electronica including techno until dawn, and a new drug called Ecstasy often fuelled the dancing. The rave culture spread to the United States and Canada in the 1990s, but it never achieved the same degree of popularity as it had in Europe. Multiple genres of electronica developed over two decades, and codification of the principal styles of electronica saw continuous flux, subjecting it to a variety of interpretations.

House music emerged in Chicago in the early 1980s as a postdisco underground dance style that was initially popular in black and gay clubs. The term house came from "The Warehouse"—the name of the club where the style originated. The disco-influenced style was propelled by an insistent 4/4 beat and deep bass, overlaid with Latin soul, synth-pop, reggae, rap, or jazz. Early hits included "On and On" by Jesse Saunders, "Jack Your Body" by Steve "Silk" Hurley, and "Move Your Body—The House Music Anthem" by Marshall Jefferson. By the late 1980s, the style had spread to Detroit, New York, and London, and it appeared in the work of popular artists such as Madonna. As the house style spread, an offshoot called acid house became the first popular music of the rave scene. "Where's Your Child" by Bam Bam exemplified acid house. In the United States, the popularity of house peaked in the 1990s, but it remained popular in Europe into the early 2000s.

Techno emerged from the Detroit house music scene of the mid-1980s. Techno innovator Derrick May credited Kraftwerk's influence, describing the style as "Sounding like George Clinton and Kraftwerk stuck in an elevator with only a sequencer to keep them company."[2] A completely electronic style,

MICHAEL BUCKNER/GETTY IMAGES

Windsor native and Detroit techno DJ Richie Hawtin mixing recording in 2007.

techno remained primarily an underground phenomenon until the early 1990s. "The Bells" by Jeff Mills, "Innovator" by Derrick May, and "Faces and Phases" by Kevin Saunderson embodied the style. Later, British-born Windsor native Richie Hawtin (1970–) (a.k.a Plastikman) participated in Detroit's second-wave techno scene in the early 1990s, and became one of the important DJs in the substyle known as Intelligent Techno. Hawtin collaborated with choreographer Enzo Cosimi to create a composition called *9.20* (an oblique reference to John Cage's *4'33"*) for the 2006 Winter Olymics opening ceremony.

Richard Hall (a.k.a. Moby) was one of the few individual artists in the field of electronica to achieve major commercial success. His ability to mix techno-style grooves into a song-oriented format made his music accessible. The artist's self-titled album included his first major hit, "Go" (1992), and it was credited with bringing rave music into the commercial mainstream. Moby briefly moved away from electronica toward alternative rock in the mid-1990s, but he redeemed himself in the eyes of techno fans with the release of *Play* (1999). The album provided an eclectic mix of sounds crafted into a collage of seductive new dance grooves and melodies that sold over ten million copies.

C FLANIGAN/GETTY IMAGES

Moby spinning records in 2008.

Trance music focused on brief, repeated synthesizer lines looped (repeated) over and over with minimal variations and occasional "ear candy"—synthesized musical effects—layered on top of a trance-inducing basic rhythm track. In the late 1990s and early 2000s, trance became one of the most popular electronic dance styles worldwide. Recorded examples of trance included "An Accident in Paradise" by Sven Vath and "Sandstorm" by Darude.

The terms **breakbeat** and **trip-hop** first appeared in the English press in the early 1990s to describe a new style of electronica that emulated jazz, funk, and soul-inflected, hip-hop grooves. With rhythmic roots in funk, breakbeat emphasized syncopation and clearly defined percussion, with a heavy backbeat on beats two and four. Rhythmic breaks also occurred, in which all musical elements were suddenly suspended, creating a kind of "musical hiccup." "Take California" by the Propeller Heads was an example of breakbeat. Trip-hop was usually wordless, and it reflected a more ambient, psychedelic quality than did traditional hip-hop. One of the first styles of electronica to reach the musical mainstream, trip-hop remained popular into the early 2000s. Examples of trip-hop could be found on the albums Nine Deadly Venoms by Depth Charge and *Massive Attack* by Blue Lines.

Drum 'n' bass and *jungle* were closely related styles that critics often compared to American hip-hop. Both styles relied on electronic drums and deep bass played at frenetic tempos to create high-energy music. **Drum 'n' bass** was also blended with jazz, reggae, **dub**, calypso, and trip-hop to create new sounds. Montreal-based Brazilian musician Amon Tobin (1972–) is best known for his creative use of sampling, delays, sound effects, and odd-metered rhythms to transform what was once familiar into its opposite. Forerunners of this technique can be heard in *musique concrète* compositions, such as *Collage#1: Blue Suede* by former York University professor/composer James Tenney (1934–2006). Similarly, Winnipeg-based artist, Aaron Funk (a.k.a Venetian Snares) electronically alters received sounds to create self-described "surrealistic" environments. **Jungle** was an electronica style with British origins that featured the use of a deep resonant bass for the melody. Examples of drum 'n' bass include "Warhead" by DJ Krust and "Inner-City Life" by Goldie.

One of the most experimental components of electronica, ambient music had a formlessness that sometimes caused people to call it "space music." The lack of steady tempo and definable melody made limitless variations possible. Almost any sound could be mixed with another to create ambient music, and most electronica styles incorporated some ambient-infused derivatives. Brian Eno became one of the best-known proponents of the style.

HIP-HOP

During the last three decades of the twentieth century, North American pop music became dominant around the globe. In R & B, soul faded, but a modernized, smoother R & B style developed. A style called funk also emerged, whose rhythm tracks and bass lines were sampled heavily in the 1980s to build hip-hop, the most significant development in American popular music in the late twentieth century. Hip-hop, in turn, yielded scratching and turntablism in the 1990s and 2000s. In the mid-1970s, dance music exploded with the advent of disco, which influenced electronica in the 1990s and 2000s. By the 1980s and 1990s, new technologies of music production and distribution—including digitization, sampling, portable music devices, music videos, and the Internet—had revolutionized modalities of music production and dissemination, and record companies consolidated into a small number of media conglomerates.

The invention of the polyphonic analog synthesizer in the 1970s, followed by the digital synthesizer with its sound sampling capabilities in the 1980s, influenced music almost as much as the musicians themselves did. Sampling technology enabled artists to digitally copy almost any sound and seamlessly blend it into their music. The advent of smaller music playback hardware—the Walkman cassette player in the 1970s and 1980s, portable CD player in the 1980s and 1990s, and **MP3** player in the 2000s—increased the availability of music. Low-priced digital recording and editing hardware and software further revolutionized popular music in the 1990s, so that almost anyone could produce a recording with a modest investment. The growth of the Internet in the 1990s created another vital access point for music. Online file sharing and digital music files gained momentum from the creation of the MP3 electronic file format, which decreased the memory required to store and transmit musical files. Music industry profits plummeted, so that in the early 2000s, the online distribution of music was a mixture of record industry lawsuits and promising commercial distribution efforts.

HIP-HOP ORIGINS

The appearance of hip-hop, especially its subgenre rap, was the single most important development in late-twentieth-century North American popular music. According to historian Tricia Rose, at its most basic, "rap music is a form of rhymed storytelling accompanied by highly rhythmic, electronically based music. . . . Rap music is a black cultural expression that prioritizes black voices from the margins of urban America."[3] At its start, rap represented a new musical genre, although it had direct African and African American musical roots. Many critics argue that it has now taken its place as one of four major black musical forms: the blues, jazz, rhythm and blues, and rap. Equally importantly, rap and its accompanying hip-hop culture expressed a voice of rebellion, something that had been absent from most popular music for decades. Through the new genre, people in the poorest urban communities crafted a new cultural product that came to pervade popular music and popular culture—from clothing styles to music to language.

Rap and hip-hop reflected African and African American cultural traditions interacting with contemporary technologies and social conditions. As we have seen, traditional African societies highly valued oral traditions, saw oration as a sophisticated form of expression, and treated the griot as a respected member of society. The capacity to command oral language—seen in ministers, politicians, poets, and other artists—remains an important dimension of African American culture. Other black oral traditions such as call and response, use of double meanings, jive talk developed by jazz hipsters such as Cab Calloway, Louis Jordan's early spoken-word R & B hits, and "playing the dozens" (competitive word games) all became sources for the language of rap and hip-hop.

Predecessors to rap came in the 1960s and 1970s in the work of the Last Poets, whose performance pieces, such as "Niggers Are Scared of Revolution" and "White Man's Got a God Complex," were chanted over African percussion. Poet-singer Gil Scott Heron's (1949–) work also influenced rap and bridged the gap between African American oral and musical traditions. His classic "The Revolution Will Not Be Televised" combined poetry, song, social commentary, and the everyday language of black communities. Rap also owed much to the funk of James Brown and George Clinton, as well as the earthy raps of singer Millie Jackson.

Immigration patterns from the Caribbean to New York added many things to the rap mix: the massive sound systems of Jamaican music, the toasting of Jamaican DJs, the recitations of Jamaican dub poets, and the macho boasting and social criticism of Trinidadian calypsonians. Afro-Cuban music also contributed a focus on breaks—the rhythmic breakdowns common in salsa—as well as break dancing. According to rap innovator Afrika Bambaataa,

> Break music is that certain part of the record that you just be waiting for to come up and when that certain part comes, that percussion part with all those drums, congas, it makes you dance real wild. . . . That break is so short in the record, you get mad, because the break was not long enough for you to really get down to do your thing.[4]

The term **turntablism** came about to describe a new style of music making developed by hip-hop DJs. It was coined to distinguish DJ techniques such as scratching and beat juggling from simple mixing. According to San Francisco–based DJ Pone, **scratching** "comes from the simple motion of moving a record back and forth to cue the record. Scratching has two primary components: moving a record back and forth, and turning the sound of the turntable off and on."[5]

Beat juggling occurs when DJs bounce back and forth between two grooves. A turntablist is a DJ who has mastered the live performance art of creating new sounds and grooves using two or more turntables. The blended recordings create a new composition that often leaves the original source of the music unrecognizable.

Because turntablism and scratching were closely tied to the development of hip-hop, rap, and acid-jazz, DJs became part of the standard instrumentation of many hip-hop and rock acts. One of the first recorded works of turntablism was Grandmaster Flash's "The Adventures of Grandmaster Flash on the Wheels of Steel" (1981). DJ Grandmixer DST's scratching on Herbie Hancock's hit fusion tune "Rockit" (1983) provides another early example. DJ Jazzy Jeff's turntablist work with Will Smith, when the latter was known as the Fresh Prince, on *He's the DJ, I'm the Rapper* (1987) also exemplified the early development of the style. Turntablism gained respect in the mid-1990s as scratch DJs moved from beat juggling and live remixing to the composition of original music via turntables. DJ Q-Bert's recording of "Razor Blade Alcohol Slide" from the album *Wave Twisters* (1996) stood as a strong example of pure turntablism.

OLD-SCHOOL HIP-HOP

The earliest manifestations of hip-hop culture—which included rap music, break dancing, graffiti, and street fashions—appeared in the mid-1970s in the work of two influential DJs: DJ Hollywood and DJ Cool Herc. These artists attracted the attention of black and Latino youths who were unmoved by disco. Rather than being generated through commercial studio recordings, early hip-hop was a live art form performed by New York City DJs for dancers and audiences in parks and clubs. The absence of recordings precluded radio airplay, although taped mixes of hip-hop performances began to make the rounds, sold on street corners and played on boom boxes.

DJ Hollywood (1954–) stood at the top of the rap hierarchy in the Bronx of the late 1970s. According to entrepreneur Russell Simmons, "In the days before hip-hop records were being made, Hollywood expanded the market in New York for MC-ing and break beats. . . . Of all the party rockers, Hollywood was the best entertainer."[6]

Another rap innovator, Jamaican immigrant Kool Herc (1955–), brought the Jamaican toasting and sound system culture to New York, spinning short sections of records and talking over them. He also played records on two turntables at the same time; with the aid of a sound mixer he faded in and out between records, sometimes mixing passages from one song into another. The artist often set up his massive speakers (called "Herculords") and turntables outside a housing project or a park. According to historian Robert Palmer,

> His dances attracted homegrown aspirants who begged for a chance to "get
> on the mike" and "rock the house," and an athletic new breed of "break"
> dancers who cut jerky, robot-like movements in with more fluid steps, then
> flipped over and stood on their heads, spinning and whiplashing to the
> rhythms.[7]

A third pivotal force in the early days of rap was former gang member and DJ Africa Bambaataa (1960–), who organized Universal Zulu Nation (an international hip-hop awareness group) to channel the anger of African American and Puerto Rican youths into music, dance, and graffiti art.

Grandmaster Flash (1958–), an electronics student by day, was early rap's technical genius who paved the way for record sampling:

> I was in the experimentation phase of trying to lock the beat together. I had
> to be able to hear the other turntable before I mixed it over. . . . I'm saying to

myself, wow, how can I take these records and blend them on time, keep this music going without missing a beat.[8]

The wiring of twin turntables to a mixer allowed a performer to "scratch" the sound of two different records while rapping into a mike. Following Flash's invention of sampling, DJs began to tap into huge catalogues of records and other sounds. Sampling became hip-hop's link with history and tradition, according to Africa Bambaataa,

> Myself, I used to play the weirdest stuff at a party. . . . I'd throw on the Pink Panther theme for everybody who thought they was cool, and then I would play "Honky Tonk Woman" by the Stones and just keep that beat going. I'd play something from metal rock records like Grand Funk Railroad. . . . I'd throw on "Sergeant Pepper's Lonely Hearts Club Band"—just the drum part. . . . I'd throw on the Monkees.[9]

A consistent nomenclature developed. Hip-hop described the urban youth culture of music, dance, dress, speech, and art that was associated with—and included—rap music. Two distinct performance functions also emerged: the MC and the DJ. The **MC** worked the crowd at the front of the stage, performing raps and rhymes, mixing elements of slang, personal experience, and humour. MCs had to be authoritative, and "dissing" the competition became a cornerstone of early rap. The DJ (sometimes two DJs) worked the turntables to create musical collages and percussive scratching effects. They also employed techniques created by Grandmaster Flash such as *cutting* (moving between tracks exactly on the beat), *back-spinning* (manually turning records to repeat brief samples of sound), and *phasing* (manipulating turntable speeds).

At first, rap and hip-hop did not offer much competition to established performers and recording artists, but in 1979 one of disco's last hits, Chic's "Good Times," was sampled for its rhythm track to make rap's first commercial hit—"Rapper's Delight" (1979) by the Sugar Hill Gang. The song featured staccato wordplay and verbal dexterity layered over funk rhythms.

Grandmaster Flash and the Furious Five quickly followed with their own "Superrappin'" (1979), establishing a group sound in which different rappers alternated, taking a verse and infusing it with their own style. Flash next released "The Message" (1982), a piece demonstrating that hip-hop could be a vehicle of social commentary as well as dissing and boasting. Kurtis Blow (1959–) was one of rap's first solo performers on a major white-owned label (Mercury). Blow was managed by Russell Simmons, who soon became an entrepreneurial magnate of hip-hop music and culture. Blow struck a macho posture, in both lyrical content and attire, featuring a bare chest and heavy gold chains. Not to be upstaged, Africa Bambaataa released his first major commercial record, "Planet Rock," in 1982. Sampling from German techno-rock group Kraftwerk and using a drum machine, Bambaataa gave birth to a sound he called electro-funk—combining the synthesized beats of disco and the sound-system bass of early Jamaican dancehall styles. Bambaataa also incorporated the new industrial sound that was influencing rock and heavy metal. "Planet Rock" paved the way for the introduction of funk, techno, and drum synthesizers into rap.

Although predominantly an African American style, rap has had many other influences. As the genre expanded, Latino artists made contributions, as did white artists. Global developments in rap included French rapper MC Solaar as well as hybrids blending rap and Indian bhangra music. Rap and hip-hop culture came to reach around the globe, from Poland to Peru, Jamaica to Japan.

Latino artists made Spanish bilingual rap records as early as 1981, and U.S. Latino rap acts included Kid Frost, Cypress Hill, Mellow Man Ace, and Gerardo. The L.A.-based Kid Frost expanded rap's vocabulary by celebrating his Chicano heritage. His debut album, *Hispanic Causing Panic*, and his single "La Raza" (1990) became an anthem for Chicano hip-hop fans. In 1995 he shortened his name to Frost and recorded several more albums with a G-funk-influenced L.A. gangsta sound. L.A.-based Chicano rappers Cypress Hill were the first Latino hip-hop superstars. The group's slow, rolling bass-and-drum loops mirrored G-funk. The group's self-titled debut album in 1992 scored with "How I Could Just Kill a Man" and "The Phuncky Feel One," and *Black Sunday* (1993) produced the crossover hit "Insane in the Brain." Subsequent albums integrated rock, reggae, and rap.

White rappers also made names for themselves—some respected, some not. Major white rappers included the Beastie Boys, Vanilla Ice, Eminem, Kid Rock, and Everlast. The Beastie Boys were the first white artists to make hip-hop their main focus. By the time they recorded their 1984 single, "Rock Hard," they were deeply into rap, and their first album, *Licensed to Ill* (1986), mixed metal and rap. Their second album, *Paul's Boutique* (1989), prefigured much of the genre-bending eclecticism that would follow in 1990s rock, and they refined their approach with 1992's *Check Your Head*. Major singles included "(You Gotta) Fight for Your Right (to Party!)" (1987), "Hey Ladies" (1987), "Get It Together" (1994), and "Intergalactic" (1998). As critic Neva Chonin observes, "No other hip-hop crew or rock band combines politics and surreal goofing so seamlessly."[10]

As hip-hop developed, approaches to describing and differentiating the sounds of the genre also evolved. By the early 2000s, musicologists were devising aesthetic systems to classify the sounds of rap.

EAST COAST HIP-HOP

East Coast rap dominated much of the genre's first decade. The East Coast style gravitated toward aggressive beats and sample collages, and MCs prided themselves on their dexterity in crafting complex lyrics. By the late 1980s, East Coast rap had become a music intended as much for listening as for dancing, and the style started to gain respect as an art form. Although West Coast rap and southern rap became major forces in the 1990s, the East Coast continued as an important influence.

© LYNN GOLDSMITH/CORBIS

Rap legends Run-D.M.C. in 1988 (left to right): Run, Jam Master Jay, and D.M.C.

Rap's first superstars, Run-D.M.C., catapulted the genre into the crossover mainstream. With spare beats and excursions into heavy metal, the trio were tougher and more menacing than their predecessors. Emerging from a middle-class section of Queens, Run-D.M.C. performed in street clothes such as black fedoras, unlaced Adidas sneakers, sweat suits, and warm-up jackets. The artists released their first single, "It's Like That"/"Sucker M.C.'s," in 1983, a hit that sounded like no other rap at the time—stripped down and sparse, with hard beats, powerful vocals, and two MCs overlapping to finish each other's lines. Follow-up hits included "Hard Times"/"Jam Master Jay" (1983) and "Rock Box" (1984). Run-D.M.C.'s career peaked in 1986 with the album *Raising Hell*, which scored hip-hop's first MTV hit, "Walk This Way," performed with aging hard-rockers Aerosmith. When *Raising Hell* became rap's first platinum album, it elicited the first widespread coverage of hip-hop culture by the mainstream media. The group's use of the power of hard rock also pioneered the subsequent metal-rap hybrids that flavoured much of the mainstream rock of the 1990s and early 2000s.

L. L. Cool J (James Todd Smith, 1968–) began his career with "I Can't Live without My Radio" (1986), which embodied the importance of music to African American youth. L. L. also developed an alternate "lover's rap" style epitomized by "I Need Love" (1987). His follow-up 1989 album, *Walking with a Panther*, featured an image of the artist with three black women, a bottle of champagne, a cell phone, and a panther on a thick gold chain. When criticized by more politicized rappers, L. L. responded with the Grammy-winning "Mama Said Knock You Out" (1990).

By the late 1980s, some were accusing popular rappers such as Run-D.M.C. and L. L. Cool J of having lost touch with the streets, and new groups such as Public Enemy, KRS-One, and XCLAN, which had political messages, stepped in. Public Enemy, the brainchild of a college student named Chuck D (Carlton Ridenhour, 1960–), became the most influential and controversial rap group of the late 1980s and, for many, the definitive rap group of all time. From their 1987 release, *Yo! Bum Rush the Show*, to their 1994 recording, *Muse Sick-N Our Mess Age*, Public Enemy set the standard for political—or "conscious"—rap. According to Chuck D,

> Everybody in rap at that time was talking about gold chains and being stupid, and . . . I wanted to find a new direction. . . . What always gave rap a leg up on other music was the anger in it, but the anger was always directed at other rappers. . . . When we came along, we decided to direct our anger at something real.[11]

As hip-hop's leading public intellectual, Chuck D pointed to the spiritual and physical maladies of urban America. In a much-quoted statement, he called rap "the black CNN."

Musically, Public Enemy was just as revolutionary. Their production team, called the Bomb Squad, crafted a dense sound with unrecognizable samples, piercing sirens, and relentless beats. The group's second album, *It Takes a Nation of Millions to Hold Us Back* (1988), served as their most influential and innovative work. Major singles included "Bring the Noise" (1988), "Fight the Power" (1989—done for Spike Lee's film *Do the Right Thing*), and "911 Is a Joke" (1990). Other socially conscious rappers included A Tribe Called Quest and De La Soul in the early 1990s, followed by Mos Def in the mid-1990s.

The most successful hip-hop entrepreneur and producer of the mid-1990s, Sean Combs (Puff Daddy or P. Diddy, 1970–) crafted appealing, groove-based party jams that often relied on rhythm tracks of familiar tunes. The Howard University graduate started his career producing hits for Mary J. Blige and Heavy D and the Boyz, and by 1993 he had his own firm, signing Craig Mack and multiplatinum artist Notorious B.I.G. Both soon found success—Mack with "Flava in Ya Ear" (1994) and B.I.G. with "Big Poppa" (1995). Combs also signed R & B vocalist Faith Evans, and he produced numerous artists for other labels. Acting out a mythical battle between East Coast and West Coast rap, Combs soon became embroiled in a set of tragic events. After he and B.I.G. began feuding with rapper 2Pac and Suge Knight, the head of L.A.'s Death Row Records, 2Pac was shot in 1996, and B.I.G. was shot in 1997. Combs subsequently issued his first solo album, the Grammy-winning *No Way Out* (1997), featuring a B.I.G. tribute called "I'll Be Missing You," as well as other songs of sorrow and anger. Subsequent misadventures diminished the artist's output in the late 1990s, but by the early 2000s he was starring in a Broadway revival of the classic African American drama by Lorraine Hansberry, *Raisin in the Sun*.

Although rap began as a male-dominated genre, some major female artists emerged, notably Salt-N-Pepa, MC Lyte, Queen Latifah, Lil' Kim, Foxy Brown, Eve, and Missy Elliott. Queen Latifah (Dana Owens, 1970–) was the first female rapper to become a major star. While in college, the New Jersey–born artist became influenced by the Afrocentric hip-hop philosophy of Afrika Bambaataa. Her first album, *All Hail the Queen* (1989), which contained the influential single "Ladies First," offered a mix of conscious hip-hop, reggae, and R & B. According to critic Gerri Hirshey, "The Queen has said that she is not so much about pan-feminism as about 'getting mine.' . . . 'Ladies First' . . . is the ultimate answer to James Brown's 'It's a Man's Man's Man's World,'"[12] Latifah was also the first female rapper to branch out into other media, appearing in numerous films.

Missy "Misdemeanor" Elliott (Melissa Elliott, 1971–) was the reigning female rapper of the early 2000s. Before breaking into rap, she worked as a

writer, arranger, and producer in the 1990s, contributing to over twenty hit songs for divas such as Aaliyah, Whitney Houston, and Mariah Carey. Elliott established herself with her debut album, *Supa Dupa Fly*, in 1997, and she also became known for her stylish and eccentric videos. Hits included "She's a Bitch" (1999), the Grammy-winning "Get Ur Freak On" (1999), and "Work It" (2002).

Jay-Z (Shawn Carter, 1970–) dominated the New York rap scene in the late 1990s and early 2000s. Though catchy enough to become pop hits, his songs were sufficiently witty and detailed to maintain his hip-hop reputation. According to journalist Harry Allen, "Jay Z has great density. He writes very compact code. His lyrics do more per word than most artists'."[13] The artist's debut album, *Reasonable Doubt* (1996), showcased a hard-core gangsta flavour, but subsequent albums, such as *In My Lifetime* (1997), shifted to a more accessible pop-rap style. By the release of *Blueprint* (2001), the artist had secured his position at the top of the heap in New York rap. Hits included "Ain't No Nigga/Dead Presidents" (1996), "Big Pimpin" (2000), and "'03 Bonnie and Clyde" (2003). Jay-Z also experimented with interesting hybrids, including rapping over the Beatles' *White Album* and rapping over an Indian bhangra record.

Hip-hop superstar and industry mogul Jay-Z in concert in 2007.

WEST COAST HIP-HOP

The West Coast—mainly Los Angeles and Oakland—dominated hip-hop for much of the 1990s with **gangsta rap**, a toughened sound with gritty, street-level subject matter that reclaimed rap's primary function as party music. N.W.A., the L.A.-based group that introduced gangsta rap, also introduced important artists such as Ice Cube and Dr. Dre. Dre drove the West Coast sound of the 1990s, discovering Snoop Dogg; developing a slow, rolling signature sound called G-funk; and shaping the sound of Death Row Records. Other important L.A. artists in the gangsta style were Ice-T, 2Pac, and Coolio; northward in Oakland, rapper Too Short produced a variant that extolled the pimp life. Additional artists active in the West included Oakland's pop rapper MC Hammer and funk-flavoured Digital Underground, as well as Los Angeles' alternative jazz-rappers Pharycyde, Latino rappers Cypress Hill and Kid Frost, and Seattle's Sir Mix-A-Lot.

N.W.A. (Niggaz With Attitude) first appeared in Los Angeles in the late 1980s, capitalizing on the sonic breakthroughs of Public Enemy, while largely ignoring their social message. During its brief life, the group celebrated the violence and hedonism of the thug life in blunt language. The group's most influential record, *Straight Outta Compton* (1988), established gangsta rap and the West Coast sound with harsh raps written by MC Ice Cube (1969–) and innovative production by Dr. Dre (1965–). *Straight Outta Compton* gained a national audience with neither radio nor MTV support. The group also caught the attention of the FBI, who issued the group's record label a warning regarding the single "Fuck tha Police." N.W.A. did not last long. Ice Cube was the first to leave in 1989, to score several successful solo albums as well as a lucrative film career. Dre went on to form Death Row Records with the unsavoury Suge Knight. There, Dre produced his first solo album, *The Chronic* (1992), which established him as hip-hop's premier producer of the mid-1990s. His signature *G-funk* sound involved George Clinton–influenced synthesized bass, deep, rolling grooves, with whiny treble synthesizers on top. Together with Snoop Dogg and 2Pac, Dre made Death Row the dominant hip-hop label of the early 1990s. Dre subsequently left Death Row, formed his own label, and did strong production work with Snoop Dogg, Eminem (whom he discovered), and the vocal group Blackstreet.

Eminem (Marshall Mathers, 1972–) became one of the top rappers of the early 2000s. A protégé of Dr. Dre, the artist emerged in 1999 with biting verbal skills, venting his displeasure on myriad topics. Originally from Detroit, Eminem worked to win over underground hip-hop audiences by battling other MCs in hard-core rap clubs. A tape of his music came to the attention of influential producer Dr. Dre, who was surprised to learn that Eminem was white, and Dre began to work with him. Major albums included *Slim Shady* LP (1999), Marshall Mathers LP (2000), and *The Eminem Show* (2002). Hit singles included "My Name Is" (1999), "The Real Slim Shady" (2000), and "The Way I Am" (2000). Eminem also helped discover and produce influential hard-core East Coast rapper 50 Cent, who topped the charts in the early 2000s.

Ice-T (Tracy Morrow, 1959–) contributed to the founding of the L.A. gangsta rap sound. The New Jersey–born artist grew up in South Central Los Angeles and gained a national audience with *Rhyme Pays* (1987) and *O.G.: Original Gangster* (1991). He was criticized in the media—and gained career-enhancing exposure—for his 1992 song, "Cop Killer" (1992). Ice-T was also active in films and television.

Snoop Dogg (Calvin Broadus, 1972–) embodied 1990s gangsta rap. Discovered by Dr. Dre, Snoop grew famous for his slow, drawled rhyming. Dre's singles "Nuthin' but a 'G' Thang" and "Dre Day" prominently featured Snoop, and they became crossover hits in 1993. Snoop's hit solo album, *Doggystyle* (1993) yielded the hits "What's My Name" and "Gin and Juice." He subsequently scored several high-profile movie roles, and by the turn of the century, Snoop's albums were secondary to his clownish yet subversive media personality.

2Pac (Tupac Shakur, 1971–1996) was a definitive rapper of the 1990s, a compelling film presence, and an iconic hip-hop martyr with a taste for the thug life. The New York–born artist followed his successful debut album, *2Pacalypse Now* (1992), with a strong acting performance in the film *Juice*. His 1995 album, *Me Against the World*, entered the charts at number one, followed by *All Eyez on Me* (1996), which produced "California Love." 2Pac enjoyed further successful acting roles, but the real gangsta world soon intervened, as his feud with rival Notorious B.I.G. ended with 2Pac's death in a drive-by shooting in 1996. Major hits by 2Pac included "Brenda's Got a Baby" (1992), "Keep Ya Head Up" (1994), and "Dear Mama/Old School" (1995).

SOUTHERN HIP-HOP

Southern rap, centred in Atlanta, Miami, and New Orleans, emerged in the 1990s as a fertile scene distinct from the East Coast and West Coast styles. Its earliest example appeared in the late 1980s with the work of Miami-based 2 Live Crew; Atlanta–produced artists such as Arrested Development, OutKast, Goodie Mob, and Ludacris; and New Orleans–produced Master P and his No Limit posse and Mystikal.

2 Live Crew popularized the booming, hard-driving sound of Miami bass music and a dance-oriented rap style with explicit chants and up-tempo grooves known as "booty rap." Group leader Luther Campbell and his crew ignited controversy with the graphic sexual content of their 1989 album, *As Nasty as They Wanna Be*. The album's hit single, "Me So Horny," climbed into the top forty despite nonexistent airplay.

OutKast—Andre Benjamin (Andre 3000, 1975–) and Antwan Patton (Big Boi, 1975–)—brought to rap an understanding of the roots of funk and soul, a command of rap flow and rhyme, and solid musical production skills. Starting out as rivals, the eclectic rappers teamed up and released their first hit single, "Player's Ball," in 1994, followed by their debut album, *Southernplayalisticadillacmuzik*. With its easy funk groove, lyrics that reflected everyday life, and sample-free production, the record went platinum. OutKast's subsequent hit albums included *ATLiens* (1996) in which they imagined themselves as comic-book extraterrestrials; *Aquemini* (1998), featuring the single "Rosa Parks"; and *Stankonia* (2000), which included the hits "Ms. Jackson" and "So Fresh, So Clean." The stage was set for the 2003 release of the Grammy-winning *Speakerboxxx/The Love Below*, which produced multiple hits including "Hey Ya," "The Way You Move" (a collaboration with Earth, Wind, and Fire), and "Roses."

Ludacris (Chris Bridges, 1978–), who started out as a DJ in Atlanta, released the hit single, "What's Your Fantasy" (2000), followed by the album *Incognegro*. Supported by producers such as Timbaland and the Neptunes, the artist's *Word of Mouf* (2001) album yielded the hits "Area Codes" and "Saturday Ooh Ooh." Ludacris's rapid flow and comedic wit took centre stage on his 2003 album, *Chicken-N-Beer*, which featured the hit "Stand Up." According to critic Touré, "Ludacris is one of the most liquid MCs in the game today. He varies his flows with such dexterity and has so much musicality in his tones that his mouth truly seems like an instrument."[14]

© GARY HERSHORN/REUTERS/CORBIS

Andre 3000 singing "Hey Ya!" at 2004 Grammy Awards ceremony.

CANADIAN HIP-HOP

The emergence of American hip-hop in the early-1980s quickly took root in all of Canada's major cities. Although robust scenes were most observed in the large cities with sizeable black communities, such as Toronto and Montreal, hip-hop, nonetheless, also flourished in enclaves where the opposite was also true. Stylistically, American hip-hop has and continues to exert a profound influence on the Canadian scene. The black community in Canada is largely populated by people from the Caribbean, and more recently, by people from West and East Africa. Accordingly, Canadian artists tend to show influences which are not commonly heard in the mainstream American forms of the genre. For example, English Canadian hip-hop leans towards Jamaican, Trinidadian, and Somalian influences (Dream Wariors, Kardinal Offishall, and K'naan), while Haitian influences are evidenced in the Montreal hip-hop style of Dubmatique, the first French language hip-hop group to break through to Canada's Francophone pop charts. The willingness to incorporate virtually any sound can be heard in the country, rock, folk, and blues mash-ups of Canada's East Coast artists (Buck 65); and more recently, the Electronica/U.K. grime-inspired style of Edmonton's Cadence Weapon shows innovation in expanding the music's textural palette.

Like their rock counterparts during the 1960s, Canadian hip-hop artists where unable to get their music into the hands of the record-buying public because of lacklustre radio play and the attendant absence of commercial incentives to support the culture. However, a sequence of events, which included the formation of the Urban Music Association of Canada (1996), the creation of Canada's largest hip-hop website publication, *HipHopCanada.com* in 2000, and most importantly, the arrival of Canada's urban music radio station in 2001 (CFXJ Flow 93.5), and the subsequent proliferation of similar stations across the country, served to usher in a watershed period in the culture's history.

The first Canadian hip-hop artist to gain mainstream exposure was Toronto's Maestro. Known as the "godfather of Canadian hip-hop", Maestro (a.k.a. Wesley Williams, b. 1968–), was the first to have a Top-40 hit, "Let Your Backbone Slide" (1989). The release remains the best-selling Canadian hip-hop single of all time, and likewise, his debut album, *Symphony Effect* (1989). Following his second album, *The Black Tie Affair* (1991), and after an unsuccessful attempt to

TORONTO STAR/PETER POWER

The "Godfather of Canadian Hip-Hop" Maestro on the Scarborough Walk of Fame in 2006.

Vancouver's Rascalz, shown here in 1998, set to raise the profile of Canada's hip-hop scene.

crack the U.S. market, Maestro released two hit singles, "Stick to Your Vision" and "416/905 (T.O. Party Anthem)." He is the recipient of two Juno Awards and has been inducted into the Scarborough Walk of Fame.

On the heels of Maestro's success, Rascalz, a group from Vancouver, played an important role in the artistic and commercial development of Canadian hip-hop. Formed in 1989, the group released four very successful recordings: *Really Livin'* (1992), *Global Cash Crop* (1997), *Warming* (1999), and *Reloaded* (2002). Although Rascalz won a 1998 Juno for *Cash Crop*, the group declined to accept the award – the first artists to ever do so – on the grounds that their award was to be given off-camera in an also-run category. Their actions prompted the Juno Awards to install rap in the main ceremony, and in 1999, Rascalz became the first Juno recipients in the new category for their iconic single "Northern Touch."

Toronto musician Kevin Brereton (1972–) (a.k.a. k-os, meaning *Knowledge of Self* or *Kheaven's Original Sound*) incorporates a wide variety of music genres, and often focuses on promoting a "positive message" vis-à-vis mainstream hip-hop culture's obsession with money, fame, and glorification of violence. As a university student, k-os released his first single "Musical Essence" in 1993. His debut album *Exit* (2002) incorporates a blend of hip-hop, soul, rock, R & B, folk, and reggae. Two singles from the release, "Heaven Only Knows" and "Superstarr Pt. Zero," earned him critical acclaim in both Canada and the United States. The second album *Joyful Rebellion* (2004) generated the award-winning single "Crabbuckit."

CHAPTER SUMMARY

- Technological changes dominated the development of North American popular music in the last three decades of the twentieth century. Major innovations included synthesizers, personal computers, personal listening devices, CDs, music television, digital recording/editing hardware and software, and Internet file sharing in the MP3 format.

- The release of "Rappers Delight" in 1979 signalled the beginning of the hip-hop era. Rap and the hip-hop culture that surrounded it evolved into a variety of styles and subcultures including East Coast, West Coast, Southern, and Canadian. Hip-hop also influenced a variety of other styles including rock, electronica, and R & B:

- Over two decades, hip-hop became the most influential American popular music style.

- It served as the basis for a new global-youth cultural identity.

- Rich African and African American cultural and musical traditions provided its source.

- It evolved from the country's poorest communities to produce a valued and profitable art form.

- It served as a new voice of rebellion against cultural domination.

- The use of sampling became popularized through hip-hop.

- Interest in poetry and spoken-word expression and dance increased because of hip-hop.

- The subgenre of turntablism came from it.

- Electronica developed from disco-era music styles and the invention of the synthesizer. Subsequently, electronically generated music played a dominant role in dance music for three decades. This led to the evolution of the role of the DJ from record spinner to musician and composer, an evolution that also resulted from the development of scratching and turntablism.

LISTENING EXERCISES

1. **Rap and Rhythmic Flow**

   Listen to an excerpt from "Rapper's Delight" (1979) by the Sugar Hill Gang. Heard through a contemporary ear, the rapping in "Rapper's Delight" sounds simplistic in its verbal flow, rhyme schemes, and rhythms. Notice how each spoken line is divided into predictable rhythms that fit within the 4/4 metre of the tune. Contemporary MCs now rap across bar lines in less predictable ways by playing with the beat and sometimes ignoring the metre of the tune, creating complex spoken-word styles. Has the lyric content of rap changed as well?

2. Gangsta Rap

Listen to L.A.-based Chicano rap group Cypress Hill's 1993 hit "Insane in the Brain." Cypress Hill helped move gangsta rap performance beyond the confines of the African American community. The "in your face" style of gangsta rap dominated rap music in the 1990s. What is the musical appeal of this recording? Does their use of harsh language have the same shock value today that it might have had in the early 1990s?

3. Turntablism

Listen to "Razor Blade Alcohol Slide" by DJ Q-Bert. Turntablism turned the art of scratching into a new form of electronic composing. DJ Q-Bert created an entirely new musical composition that might be described as a sound collage. How does Q-Bert's work compare with that of a traditional DJ? Do you think that turntablism will ever make it into the top forty?

HISTORICAL STUDIES AND DISCUSSION QUESTIONS

1. The Evolution of the Music Industry

The advent of Internet file sharing in the late 1990s initiated an important debate over the equitable dissemination of popular music. Record labels claimed that the illegal downloading of music files represented the biggest threat the music industry had ever faced. In fact, the entire history of popular music has seen an evolving series of technological innovations that periodically raise issues of ownership and control, beginning with the first sheet music. Music formats have shifted numerous times over one hundred and fifty years of North American popular music, with each shift causing a significant disruption in the business model of the previous era. First, map out the key periods in technological change (see Timelines) and locate the musical styles that emerged around those times of change. Would you say that the public's appetite for recorded music has increased or diminished during times of change? What does this tell us about recent predictions of the industry's imminent collapse?

2. Gangsta Rap, Violence, and Responsibility

The lyrics of gangsta rap engendered controversy from the style's inception. While some criticized the style for its misogyny and glorification of violence, others defended it as a reflection of inner-city life. Because record industry executives were usually more concerned with the bottom line than with social and political implications, the criticism directed at gangsta rap actually created the opportunity for multilevel marketing by media conglomerates. Further, because the parent companies of media giants such as AOL/Time Warner also owned most major record companies, a *Time* magazine cover story on the evils of gangsta rap could enrage one population segment while encouraging the sale of millions of records to another. Was gangsta rap a source of cultural empowerment for inner-city African Americans, an expression of violence and misogyny, a form of corporate manipulation, or some of each? Explain.

STUDY QUESTIONS

1. What are the roots of rap? Trace the evolution of contemporary rap from old-school styles to the early 2000s. Who were the major artists and how did the music evolve?

2. What is electronica? What were its primary styles, and how did it impact dance pop music during the last two decades of the twentieth century? What is turntablism?

3. How does independent (or alternative) culture differ from mainstream culture?

4. What factors promoted the development of Canada's hip-hop scene?

NOTES

1. Simon Reynolds, *Generation Ecstasy: Into the World of Techno and Rave Culture* (New York: Little, Brown, 1999), 15

2. *Ibid.*, 14

3. Tricia Rose, *Black Noise: Rap Music and Black Culture in Contemporary America* (Hanover, NH: Wesleyan University Press, 1994), 2.

4. Robert Farris Thompson, "Hip-Hop 101," in *Droppin' Science: Critical Essays on Rap Music and Hip-Hop Culture*, edited by William Eric Perkins (Philadelphia: Temple University Press, 1996), 215.

5. Interview with the authors.

6. Russell Simmons with Nelson George, *Life and Def: Sex, Drugs, Money, and God* (New York: Crown, 2001), 36–37.

7. Robert Palmer, *Rock and Roll: An Unruly History* (New York: Harmony Books, 1995), 281.

8. William Eric Perkins, ed., *Droppin' Science: Critical Essays on Rap Music and Hip-Hop Culture* (Philadelphia: Temple University Press, 1996), 7.

9. *Ibid.*, 8.

10. Neva Chonin, "Beasties Keep Rocking the Mike at BFD," June 14, 2004, http://sfgate. com/cgi-bin/article.cgi?file=/chronicle/archive/2004/06/14/DDGBF74FLE1.DTL, accessed May 14, 2005.

11. Perkins, ed., *Droppin' Science: Critical Essays on Rap Music and Hip-Hop Culture*, 21.

12. Gerri Hirshey, *We Gotta Get Out of This Place: The True, Tough Story of Women in Rock* (New York: Atlantic Monthly Press, 2001), 148.

13. Quoted in Touré, "Superstardom Is Boring: Jay-Z Quits (Again)," New York Times, November 16, 2003, p. 23.

14. Touré, "Ludacris CD Review," http://www.rollingstone.com/reviews/cd/review. asp?aid=2047638&cf=78466, accessed May 14, 2005.

acid house Style of electronica that was an offshoot of house music and was the first popular music of the rave scene.

acid rock Music inspired by the experience of mind-altering drugs and characterized by modal melodies, lengthy instrumental solos, esoteric lyrics, and special electronic effects. Synonymous with *psychedelic music*.

aerophones Wind instruments that produce sound by the vibration of air.

alt-country Country movement that developed in reaction to mainstream country's pursuit of pop styles and that represented an eclectic mix of traditional country, post-punk, and other influences.

alternative rock Guitar-driven style that developed in the 1990s, with roots in punk and post-punk and characterized by hybrids of punk, metal, hip-hop, funk, and singer-songwriter styles. Mainly produced by small, independent record companies. Synonymous with *indie rock*.

ambient house Experimental, atmospheric electronica style designed to relax the listener with soothing sounds sampled from the environment or electronically generated, with no steady tempo and no definable melody.

arena rock Rock concert taking place in front of a crowd of ten thousand or more; characterized by highly applied music, songs that often make use of rock clichés and hooks, and exaggerated stage performance techniques, in order to be seen and heard in large sports arenas or venues of similar size.

arranger One who writes individual parts for the instruments in a given ensemble, transforming often simple compositions into dramatic ensemble statements.

art rock Also called *progressive rock*, an eclectic blend of rock, classical music, jazz, and other styles that first developed in the late 1960s.

ASCAP The American Society of Composers, Authors and Publishers, founded in 1914, to help ensure copyright protection for musical compositions.

backbeat A sharp attack on beats two and four of a 4/4 measure.

ballad opera A form of musical theatre popular in the eighteenth century that used spoken English dialogue and songs and lampooned society; one precursor of musical comedy.

beat The underlying pulse of a rhythm.

beat juggling DJ technique of bouncing back and forth between two grooves.

bel canto ("beautiful singing") An Italian style of operatic singing that originated in eighteenth-century opera and that emphasizes mastery of vocal technique to produce a beautiful, clear sound throughout the vocal range. The style was also used in parlour songs and boleros.

bhangra Traditional form of Punjabi (North Indian) music, featuring the heavy, resounding beat of the *dhol*, accompanied by smaller *tumbi* drums and Punjabi lyrics; hybridized in hip-hop, electronica, and dance club music in the early 2000s.

big band A large jazz ensemble that developed in the 1930s and featured three to five trumpets, two to five trombones, three to five saxophones, and a standard rhythm section.

blackface A makeup style associated with minstrelsy in which the face is darkened with burnt cork and exaggerated facial features such as large lips and big eyes are drawn.

blaxploitation movies Black-themed action films of the early 1970s that capitalized on a mass public fascination with African American inner-city stereotypes and style.

blue notes Flatted third, fifth, and seventh notes of a major scale.

blue yodel A yodelling style blended with blue notes that was developed by Jimmie Rodgers in the 1920s. A *yodel* is a wordless vocal sound created in the back of the throat that rapidly alternates between two pitches.

bluegrass Acoustic country music style that combines fiddle, banjo, mandolin, guitar, Dobro, and acoustic bass and vocally often involves either a high lonesome style or gospel-inspired harmonizations integrated with driving, syncopated banjo picking and a steady four-beat feel.

blues scale An African American creation, closely related to the minor pentatonic scale, that uses six notes (including the flatted third, flatted fifth, and flatted seventh of a major scale) to reach an octave; also called a hexatonic (six-tone) scale.

bôites à chanson Performance venue for *chansonniers* (akin to a coffee house).

bongo drums Two small hand drums attached together with a piece of wood, one drum usually slightly larger than the other and pitched lower, played with the fingers and hands.

boogie woogies An influential post-stride piano style that flourished in the 1930s and 1940s and became a central component of R & B and early rock and roll.

borderland The transitional space between cultures where people do not belong fully to one culture or another, or where they identify with multiple cultures; borderlands are often the source of important cultural innovations.

brass band A wind band with brass and percussion instruments only.

breakbeat Style of electronica emulating jazz, funk, and soul-inflected hip-hop grooves and emphasizing syncopation and clearly defined percussion, with a heavy backbeat on beats two and four.

bridge A transitional passage that connects two musical passages of greater importance.

Brill Building Located at 1619 Broadway in New York City, the place where the music industry briefly dominated rock in the early 1960s by returning to the traditional Tin Pan Alley songwriting model.

British Invasion U.S. rock revolution beginning in 1964 with the arrival of the Beatles and followed by other British bands.

Britpop Music played by a generation of 1990s–2000s British bands who embraced the melodic pop-rock tradition of the Beatles and the Rolling Stones.

broadside ballad Eighteenth-century British style of music with witty, often ribald, topical verses that uses everyday vocabulary.

burlesque Theatre style, related to vaudeville, that contains a unifying thematic element, comedy with sexual themes, and female dancers.

call and response A musical statement by a singer or instrumentalist followed by a response from other vocalists or instruments.

calypso Trinidadian music style stemming from Creole songs, neo-African styles, British ballads, and *calinda;* today performed to a syncopated rhythm with a two-beat feel and lyrical content peppered with sexual innuendo and humour.

camp meeting A large, multiday, outdoor religious celebration attended by both blacks and whites; part of the Second Awakening, an evangelical movement of the early nineteenth century.

canon The body of knowledge that is said to be central to a discipline.

chansonniers Politically inspired Quebecois singer-songwriters during the 1950s and 1960s.

chord A combination of three or more notes sounded or played simultaneously.

chordophones Instruments that produce sound by means of a vibrating string.

chorus A lyric statement following the verse that is often repeated periodically throughout the song, usually containing the same lyrics and melody.

classic blues Early style of blues, primarily associated with female vocalists, that had a sophisticated, urban flavour and jazz accompaniment.

clave A group of syncopated rhythmic patterns that functions as an underlying unifier, connecting the polyrhythms of Afro-Cuban music.

claves Latin percussion instrument: a pair of wooden sticks played by resting one stick on the fingertips of a cupped hand that acts as a resonator, while tapping with the other stick.

commodification Process by which noncommercial goods or services such as a song, a story, a picture, or an artist are turned into marketable commodities.

concept albums Recorded works with a unifying artistic theme.

concept musical A type of musical, pioneered by Stephen Sondheim, that focuses on a single theme, often without a linear narrative or definitive resolution, and uses small casts with minimal sets.

Congo Square Established in 1817, an outdoor gathering place in New Orleans that served as an active centre of African music and dance until the late nineteenth century.

coon song Popular style in the late nineteenth century that featured offensive racial stereotypes, strong rhythms, syncopation, and quick tempos that demanded a robust delivery.

counterculture A cultural group whose values differ from those of the dominant culture. The term is most commonly used to refer to the rebellious youth culture of the 1960s.

counterpoint The combination of two or more independent melodies into a single harmonic texture in which each melody retains its linear character.

country rock A hybrid of country and rock music that features a relaxed rhythmic feel and country-style vocal harmonies, blending country instrumentation (often including pedal steel guitar or Dobro) with hard-rock-style electric guitar and a rock rhythm section.

crier Early R & B vocalist who projected the image of being overcome by emotion.

crooning A smooth personal vocal style enabled by the invention of the microphone.

crossover Occurs when a song or musician associated with one style achieves popularity in two or more genres.

cultural appropriation Process by which members of one cultural group take cultural elements from another cultural group, reshape them, and claim them as their own.

culture The changing pattern of human knowledge, belief, and behaviour learned and transmitted through generations.

cutting contest A competition in which rival musicians challenge one another's prowess.

delta or rural blues Form of the blues originating with northwestern Mississippi sharecroppers; influenced by church hymns and field hollers and characterized by an AAB lyric structure and flexible rhythm structures; often performed solo with guitar accompaniment.

diaspora The scattering of people far from their homelands, which leads to transmission of cultural and economic resources among countries when immigrants stay connected to their homelands.

disco A formulaic, R & B–based commercial sound accompanied by a hedonistic party scene, popular in the mid 1970s and early 1980s.

distortion The electronic alteration of a musical tone to produce an intentionally unclear or fuzzy timbre.

DJ A person who plays recorded music on the radio and for social functions; also, a performer who works the turntables to create musical collages and percussive scratching effects.

Dobro An acoustic steel guitar.

dominant culture A culture that is more powerful than others within a society.

doo-wop Group vocal harmony grounded in black gospel and barbershop harmony; a hallmark sound of the 1950s.

drum 'n' bass Style of electronica characterized by electronic drums and deep bass played at frenetic tempos to create high-energy music blended with jazz, reggae, dub, calypso, and trip-hop.

dub Mixed-down versions of tunes stripped to their instrumental basics to allow Jamaican DJs to toast (speak) over them in dancehall settings.

dulcimer Stringed instrument with a gentle melodic sound.

electric blues Form of the blues using amplified, sometimes distorted instrumental sounds of the guitar and harmonica in an ensemble setting.

electronica Describing several electronically generated musical styles that developed in the 1980s from dance music.

emo Short for *emotive* (also called *emocore*), an arty outgrowth of punk in the early 2000s with lyrics that were often intimate confessionals.

Ethiopian delineators Performers in minstrel shows who speak and sing in poor imitations of Black English dialect.

Ethiopian dialect A stereotyped imitation of African American speech used in minstrel shows.

ethnic musical Musical that takes place in a cultural setting exotic to the U.S. cultural mainstream.

Eurocentrism The dominant view of Western culture that privileges European-derived cultural forms and generally reflects white, upper-middle-class, heterosexual male perspectives.

falsetto A method of voice production used by male singers to sing notes higher than their normal range.

feedback A squealing electronic effect achieved by placing a microphone or guitar pickup directly in front of the speaker through which it is being amplified.

field holler African-derived music sung or chanted by individual workers in rhythm with their work.

file sharing The act of making files on one computer accessible to others in a network; sharing music in this way became prevalent in the 1990s because of the evolution of the Internet and the MP3 audio file format.

First Nations The indigenous cultures of North America; term that replaces the erroneous term *Indian* used by Columbus.

folk music Vernacular music that originates with the ordinary people of a given culture. Folk music is usually acoustic music that survives without the reinforcement of commercial media.

folk revival In the 1950s and 1960s, U.S. interest in European folk music, rural blues, spirituals and gospel, mountain and country music, cowboy music, and other vernacular styles from around the world.

folk-rock A blend of rock and folk music characterized by folk-style vocal performances backed by amplified acoustic guitars, electric bass, and drums.

form The organizational structure of a musical composition.

45 rpm record Seven-inch-diameter record format primarily used for recording pop, R & B, rock, and country singles, first promoted in 1948 by RCA.

funk A highly syncopated style of pop music.

funk metal Musical hybrid that draws on the hard-driving guitar riffs of heavy metal and the intricate, popping bass lines and syncopated rhythms of funk.

fusion See *jazz-rock fusion*.

fuzz-tone An electric guitar effect that sounds exactly as the name implies (see *distortion*).

gangsta rap A tough rap sound with gritty, street-level subject matter.

garage rock Rock genre of the early 2000s emphasizing three-minute songs and retro influences such as the blues and 1960s rock; also referring to a simple, raw form of rock and roll created by several North American bands in the mid-1960s.

girl groups Groups of female performers producing a sweet and melodramatic sound that mixes hooks and doo-wop harmonies. Girl groups of the 1960s were usually trios or quartets fronted by a lead singer.

gospel music African American religious genre characterized by instrumentation of soloist, choir, piano, organ, rhythm section, horns, and guitar; lyrics covering a wide rang of spiritual topics; rhythmic intensity; structure akin to popular music; bent tones; and improvisation.

gramophone A device invented in 1887 that recorded sounds on a disc etched by the vibrations of a stylus.

"Grand Ole Opry" Country music's most famous performance venue in Nashville and for many years a radio program that featured string bands, traditional singers, gospel quartets, and banjo players, supported by colourful announcers, comedians, and ad-libbing costumed musicians.

griot A West African tribal storyteller, tribal historian, and entertainer.

groove An African-derived rhythmic feature constructed by playing several highly rhythmic parts simultaneously, creating a momentary feeling of resolution when multiple parts arrive on the same beat.

groove-based tune Music that relies on repeated, open-ended structures and rhythmic themes rather than on a chorus/verse form.

grunge A 1990s blend of punk, metal, and singer-songwriter styles.

guiro A serrated cylinder made of gourds, metal, wood, or fiberglass that is scraped and struck with a stick in a variety of rhythmic patterns.

hard rock Rock style rooted in the power trio ensemble and guitar-bass unison riffs. Hard rock evolved into a diverse range of additional musical styles that included complex song forms with varying degrees of harmonic sophistication, a wide assortment of lead vocal styles, diverse instrumentation, and a broad range of song subjects.

harmony (1) Two or more musical notes produced or sounded at the same time, (2) the underlying chord structure of a song or piece of music, or (3) the study of the overall musical structure within a composition, genre, or style.

head arrangements Riff-based tunes that can be played by ensembles of all sizes without sheet music and that serve as the musical structure for improvisation.

heavy metal Rock style characterized by lead vocal styles rooted in high-pitched, aggressive singing/shouting; limited harmonic choices; heavy reliance on blues roots; and dark song subjects.

high lonesome style Vocal bluegrass style characterized by a clear, dry, high-pitched tone.

hillbilly Early term for country and western music, now considered offensive.

hip-hop The urban youth culture of music, dance, dress, speech, and art that is associated with—and includes—rap music.

homophonic Describing a harmonic texture created by a melody performed with simple harmonic accompaniment.

honker Early R & B performer who played a screaming, honking tenor saxophone.

honky-tonk (1) A loud, earthy, country music style, flavoured with pedal steel guitar and lyrics about love (both lost and found) and partying, that developed in the late 1940s. (2) Depression-era bar in the South, usually built on the outskirts of town, with a large dance floor, jukebox, and live music.

hook A catchy melody, rhythm, or lyric in a song that stays with the listener.

hootenanny Large gathering of folk musicians.

house music Disco-influenced style of electronica that emerged in Chicago in the early 1980s and was propelled by an insistent 4/4 beat and deep bass, overlaid with Latin soul, synth-pop, reggae, rap, or jazz.

hybridity The blending of different cultures or cultural forms such as music, language, or art.

idiophones Percussion instruments made of materials such as wood, ceramic, or metal that have their own unique sound.

improvisation The spontaneous creation of musical ideas; music that is composed on the spot.

indie rock See *alternative rock*.

industrial rock Precursor of alternative rock, characterized by a tinny guitar roar and white noise.

instrumentation The group of instruments used in a performance.

interval The relationship or distance between two musical pitches or notes.

jam band A folksy, blues-based rock style featuring extended jams, which appeared in the early 1990s and was influenced by the aesthetics of the Grateful Dead and the Allman Brothers.

jam session Gathering of musicians to play together and match skills with one another.

jazz-rock fusion The blending of jazz with various components of rock, funk, and electronic amplification.

Jim Crow Minstrel character: a disabled African American stable hand who moves with a shuffle.

juke joint A rudimentary nightclub or bar, usually located in an old building outside of town.

jump blues Aggressive rhythmic R & B style, evolving out of black big bands of the 1930s and 1940s, that featured simple riffs, blues-based tunes, explosive improvised solos, and spontaneity.

jungle Style of electronica, originally from Britain, featuring the use of a deep resonant bass for the melody.

keyed bugle Invented in 1810, instrument that fostered the formation of all-brass ensembles that could play outdoors or in other settings inhospitable to chamber music.

lining out A traditional Scottish music instruction technique in which a leader sings one line at a time to the congregation, who repeat the newly learned material in a call and response format.

lo-fi An artsy amalgam from the 1990s that fluctuated from simple pop and rock songs to free-form song structures to pure noise and arty experimentalism.

LP record The 12-inch 33 1/3 rpm record format first promoted in 1948 by Columbia Records that enabled the recording of up to 45 minutes of music on two sides of a vinyl disc and offered the possibility of grouping songs thematically; initially used for classical and jazz recordings, it became used for pop recordings in the late 1950s and early 1960s.

LSD A mind-altering hallucinogenic drug (lysergic acid diethylamide), also known as *acid*.

lyrics The words or vocal sounds included in a musical composition.

mandolin A small guitar-shaped instrument, played like a guitar, with a fretted neck and four paired strings that are tuned like a violin, which makes it easy for fiddlers to learn as a second instrument.

marimba A wooden xylophone with resonating tubes below each wooden bar.

MC Performer who works the crowd at the front of the stage and performs raps and rhymes, mixing elements of slang, personal experience, and humour.

measure A consistent grouping of beats in time.

melismas Vocal turns and embellishments, originating in gospel music and spreading to R & B and other genres.

melody A song or tune; a succession of musical notes or pitches that seem to have a relation to one another and that express a musical thought.

membranophones Drums.

metre The way beats are grouped, or number of beats per measure.

microtone A note that falls between two notes on the Western chromatic twelve-note scale.

minstrelsy The first indigenous American theatrical and popular music genre, popular in the 1800s; a variety show based on crude stereotypes of African Americans.

monophonic Describing a musical texture created by a single unaccompanied melody.

motor rhythm A constant beat played at a consistent tempo.

MP3 Electronic file format developed in the 1990s that decreased the memory required to store and transmit musical files.

musicianer An African American slave who played music professionally.

Nashville sound Country music style that evolved in the fifties involving electric instruments and polished arrangements, targeting an adult audience, and employing strings, horns, choral backgrounds, smooth tempos, and reverb (echo).

neo-soul R & B substyle that emerged in the late 1990s, characterized by a sweet, retro tone as well as a social conscience.

New Jack Swing A highly rhythmic, rap-infused R & B style of the 1980s that employed snippets of rap, synthesized drum and bass lines, and multipart doo-wop harmony.

new wave Punk subgenre of the 1980s centred on pop and featuring a fascination with synthesizers, electronics, style, and art.

novelty song A humorous song, often with a nonsense theme, sometimes employing special sound effects.

nu metal Hybrid of rap, sampling, DJs, drum machines, and other new techniques with guitar-driven heavy metal; popularized in the late 1990s.

off-Broadway A theatrical venue for the production of low-budget, small scale, or experimental works.

old-time music Early Appalachian folk music, which formed the basis of bluegrass.

opera Words set to music in a dramatic presentation involving characters and plot.

operetta European style of musical theatre blending plot, music, lyrics, dance, and an integrated story line.

Outlaw Country music sound originating in a loose network of musicians in the 1970s who favoured a return to relaxed and simple arrangements, to counter the production-heavy flavour of the Nashville sound.

parlour songs Sentimental ballads that speak of life, home, hearth, and family; prevalent in nineteenth-century North American popular music.

patting juba African American–derived body drumming—striking the knees, shoulders, or other body parts with the hands to produce a rhythmic sound.

payola Bribes given by record companies to radio stations to promote certain records.

pentatonic scale Five-note scale.

Philadelphia soul Smooth R & B style of the early 1970s, orchestrated with strings and horns. Supported by a relaxed, steady groove, it shaped the sound of disco. Also known as *Philly soul*.

phonograph Invented by Thomas Edison in 1877, the first device capable of reproducing sound.

plantation songs Nineteenth-century songs that portrayed nostalgia for the preindustrial tranquility of plantation life. In some cases, African Americans were portrayed in a sympathetic and humanistic light.

player piano The first mechanism for recording and reproducing music with good fidelity; operated by means of small holes, punched onto a roll of paper, that trigger a pneumatic lifter to strike the appropriate key on a specially manufactured piano.

pleasure gardens Private parks, originating in England, featuring arbours, fruit trees, mineral springs, tea gardens, fireworks, and music; inspired nineteenth-century composers to write love songs that formed the basis of parlour songs.

polyphonic Describing a musical texture that contains different melodies and rhythms that interlock.

popular culture The mass cultural forms of everyday life.

post-punk Style that developed in the 1980s, in part as a reaction to the nihilism of punk, that took the form of avant-garde noise, jangling guitars, anthemic stadium rock, or roots rock.

power ballad Rock song featuring high-energy vocals and driving rhythms played at a slow tempo.

power trio A group consisting of electric guitar, electric bass, and drums. This instrumentation is common in heavy metal and hard rock.

progressive rock See *art rock.*

proto-punk Describing raw-sounding garage bands of the 1960s that served as a precursor to punk.

psychedelic music Music inspired by the experience of mind-altering drugs and characterized by modal melodies, lengthy instrumental solos, esoteric lyrics, and special electronic effects. Synonymous with *acid rock.*

punk-metal The most influential sound in alternative rock, a hybrid form that developed in the late 1980s and that frames walls of raw noise into tight pop song structures.

punk-pop A post-grunge strand of alternative rock that combines pop melodies and chord changes with speedy punk tempos and loud guitars.

punk rock Genre that developed in the 1970s, characterized by a cacophonous sound, lyrics of outrage, and extremes of appearance. At the time, it returned rock to its basics—three chords and a simple melody—but in a way that was louder, faster, and more abrasive than prior rock styles.

quadruple metre (4/4) A rhythmic pattern composed of recurring groups of four evenly spaced beats.

ragtime A piano-based music mixing complex syncopated rhythms with traditional European musical forms.

rap The influential African American musical genre that first emerged in the late 1970s, in which rhyming, spoken-word lyrics are chanted to rhythmic accompaniment often made up of sampled sounds or scratched records.

raves All-night parties held in fields, farms, or warehouses and featuring electronica.

reggae Jamaican music combining the old-time shuffle feel of mento, the beat of rock steady, an electric guitar playing a steady off-beat rhythm, and a heavy bass underpinning; often has religious or political themes.

revue Broadway show similar to burlesque that includes music, comedy, dance, simple plots, and female dancers.

rhythm The arrangement of time in music, consisting of beat, tempo, measure, and metre.

rhythm section The chord-playing, bass, and percussion instruments of popular music, with standard instrumentation usually consisting of drum set, acoustic or electric bass, guitar, and piano or keyboard.

riff A short musical phrase, often repeated throughout a popular music composition.

ring shout An African-derived shuffling circular dance of chanting and hand clapping that often transports participants into an ecstatic trance.

riot grrrl A feminist punk movement that developed out of early-1990s indie rock; the genre is a blend of personal expression and political activism, with lyrics that address gender-related issues and are framed by punk-styled blasts of noise.

ritard To slow down gradually in a piece of music.

rockabilly A blend of country and R & B that first emerged in the early 1950s.

rubato To play music in a relaxed rhythm.

rural blues See *Delta* or *rural blues.*

sacred Having a religious or spiritual function or connection.

sampling The art of digitally reproducing sounds and blending them into music.

scratching The rapid movement of a vinyl record back and forth while it is playing on a turntable, creating a distinctive grating sound that is characteristic of hip-hop (including rap).

secular Not connected to religious concerns; worldly.

shape note Early American music notation system that gives each note in the scale a different shape—triangles, squares, circles, or diamonds—enabling nonliterate singers to perform complex multipart choral arrangements.

shouter Early R & B performer in a jump-style band who produced high-energy, blues-based vocals that were very nearly shouted.

singer-songwriter Singer who writes and performs his or her own songs.

singing cowboy Concept pioneered by Jimmie Rodgers that began the association of western images with country music.

skiffle Music pioneered by British musician Lonnie Donnegan in the 1950s that was an indiscriminate blend of American folk and blues styles. Most British Invasion artists were influenced by skiffle.

smooth jazz A groove-based, jazz, funk, and R & B–based instrumental style of jazz with a lighter sound than fusion.

SOCAN Society of Composers, Authors and Publishers of Canada (formerly CAPAC and PROCAN) collects royalties in Canada.

soft rock Smooth, melodic style popular from the 1960s through the 1980s that consists of slow-tempo, melodic songs with vocal harmonies, performed over simple rhythmic grooves.

song collecting Practice of gathering music manuscripts and samples of songs, particularly of folk music, begun by British poet Thomas Percy in the nineteenth century.

song plugger A person hired by Tin Pan Alley publishers to put sheet music into the hands of successful vaudeville performers in the early twentieth century.

songster An itinerant black musician of the nineteenth and twentieth centuries who played music with European and African sources that included comic songs, social songs, ballads, minstrel songs, and the blues.

sonority The overall tonal texture of a musical composition or performance.

soul music An African American musical style of the 1960s with roots in gospel, R & B, and blues; themes of civil rights, love, and passion; vocals delivered with emotional power; and groove-based rhythms.

sound system A portable disco, originating in Jamaica and consisting of up to thirty speakers, a turntable, and a DJ; essential to the early development of rap in New York in the late 1970s.

southern groove Soul music with a harder edge, more gospel influences, and fewer formal arrangements than the Motown sound.

southern rock A blending of blues, R & B, country, and gospel with the aggressive feel of hard rock, drawing from the blues-rock of the late 1960s as well as honky-tonk and the Bakersfield sound to create a distinctive fusion.

spiritual Nineteenth-century African American religious vocal genre focusing on Biblical events and figures and blending traditional African melodic concepts with European hymn melodies; used to construct community, provide hope for a better life, offer metaphors of liberation, and preserve African cultural memory.

steel guitar Stringed instrument with a sliding sound that originated in Hawaii and became popular on the U.S. mainland in the early twentieth century.

stride piano Style of piano playing in which the left hand plays a bass note on the first and third of every four beats and a basic chord on the second and fourth beats and the right hand plays melody.

subordinate culture A culture that lacks access to power and is therefore less powerful than the dominant culture in a multicultural society.

surf music Genre from the early 1960s that features twangy, trebly guitars; Chuck Berry–style guitar licks; falsetto male vocal harmonies; throbbing tom toms; and topical lyrics of car and surf culture.

sustain The extension of the duration of a musical tone, often created through electronic amplification.

swing (1) African-derived triplet-based rhythmic feel often encountered in jazz, blues, and R & B. A typical swing rhythm can be approximated by taking a series of even beats, then lengthening the first and shortening the second beat to create a sequence of pairs of long and short notes. (2) A period in jazz history, usually dated from the early 1930s through 1945, dominated by big bands playing in the swing style.

syncopation Accenting the weak or unexpected part of the beat.

synth pop A spare, synthesizer-based dance pop sound of the 1980s.

techno Style of completely electronic music that emerged in Detroit in the mid-1980s.

teen idol Attractive young performer, largely the product of record companies, sculpted to appeal to perceived youth taste and used to promote record sales.

tempo The speed of the beat in a piece of music.

texture The overall timbre created by a variety of instruments or voices producing musical sounds in a performance.

32-bar form A musical form consisting of two melodically identical eight-measure verses, followed by an eight-measure bridge, followed by a final eight-measure verse that may contain new lyrics or a restatement of an earlier verse, common in Tin Pan Alley–era songs and jazz.

thrash metal Late 1970s heavy metal subgenre with elements of punk; basis for funk metal and nu metal.

Tin Pan Alley Centre of the music publishing industry in New York City from the beginning of the twentieth century through about 1950.

TOBA Theatre Owners Booking Association; owned by whites, a performing circuit of the 1920s in which many African Americans performed blues and vaudeville under difficult working conditions.

tone A quality of music that has four main components: pitch, timbre, duration, and dynamics.

trance Style of electronica with brief, repeated synthesizer lines looped over and over.

trap drum set A set of percussion instruments including the bass drum, tom tom, snare drum, and cymbals.

trip-hop Style of electronica, usually wordless, emulating jazz, funk, and soul-inflected hip-hop grooves and emphasizing a more ambient, psychedelic quality than traditional hip-hop.

triple metre (3/4) A rhythmic pattern composed of recurring groups of three evenly spaced beats.

turntablism A technique in which DJs use multiple turntables and various audio effects to blend snippets of sound from existing vinyl records to create new music.

12-bar blues A musical form written in three phrases of four measures each; the form can be repeated many times without the use of a chorus.

urban blues Form of the blues that developed in the 1930s, characterized by the coordinated use of guitar, piano, and sometimes a full rhythm section in an ensemble setting, playing a consistent, often up-tempo rhythm.

vaudeville An outgrowth of minstrelsy, a variety show featuring songs, dances, and comedy sketches with minimal plots.

vernacular music Folk or traditional music played in communities as a part of everyday life.

verse A lyric statement that tells a story, with each verse of a song presenting new information to the listener while following a similar melodic structure.

vibrato Light and rapid variations in pitch.

VJ Video DJ.

vocables Lyrics made up of syllables that have no clear linguistic meaning but are often considered sacred; characteristic of Native American music.

vocalese A jazz singing technique that uses recorded instrumental solos as the basis for vocal melodies, which often are then harmonized.

wah-wah An electronic effects pedal used with an electric guitar, keyboard, or other amplified instruments that modulates the timbre of an amplified tone to create a "wah"-like sound.

wall of sound Production technique, developed by Phil Spector in the early 1960s, achieved by packing the studio with musicians, running prior recordings through the studio sound system to fill out the sound, and using echo chambers.

waltz A musical style written in triple metre; popular at the end of the nineteenth century.

wax cylinder Medium on which sound recordings were made at the end of the nineteenth century.

western swing A 1930s hybrid of southern string bands, swing, Tin Pan Alley, and the African American, Cajun, Tex-Mex, German, Bohemian, and cowboy cultures of the Southwest, exemplified by the music of Bob Wills and the Texas Playboys.

wind band An ensemble with instrumentation usually consisting of brass, woodwind, and percussion instruments.

work song African-derived music sung by workers in rhythm with their work; often a call and response in which a lead singer acting as foreman sings a lyric to direct the work, then workers answer and perform the required task.

Zip Coon Minstrel character: an African American "city slicker" who makes imperfect attempts to imitate white city folk.

A